H. H. Asquith

H. H. Asquith

Last of the Romans

V. Markham Lester

LEXINGTON BOOKS
Lanham • Boulder • New York • London

Published by Lexington Books
An imprint of The Rowman & Littlefield Publishing Group, Inc.
4501 Forbes Boulevard, Suite 200, Lanham, Maryland 20706
www.rowman.com

6 Tinworth Street, London SE11 5AL, United Kingdom

Copyright © 2019 The Rowman & Littlefield Publishing Group, Inc.

All rights reserved. No part of this book may be reproduced in any form or by any electronic or mechanical means, including information storage and retrieval systems, without written permission from the publisher, except by a reviewer who may quote passages in a review.

British Library Cataloguing in Publication Information Available

Library of Congress Cataloging-in-Publication Data

Names: Lester, V. Markham, author.
Title: H. H. Asquith : Last of the Romans / V. Markham Lester.
Description: Lanham, Maryland : Lexington Books, 2019. | Includes bibliographical references and index.
Identifiers: LCCN 2019019003 (print) | LCCN 2019020227 (ebook) | ISBN 9781498591041 (electronic) | ISBN 9781498591034 (cloth) | ISBN 9781498591058 (pbk)
Subjects: LCSH: Asquith, H. H. (Herbert Henry), 1852–1928. | Prime ministers—Great Britain—Biography. | Great Britain—Politics and government—1837–1901. | Great Britain—Politics and government—1901–1936.
Classification: LCC DA566.9.O7 (ebook) | LCC DA566.9.O7 L47 2019 (print) | DDC 941.083092 [B] —dc23
LC record available at https://lccn.loc.gov/2019019003

For my wife, Jeanne,
and my best friend, Clark Malcolm

Contents

Acknowledgments	ix
List of Abbreviations	xi
Introduction	1
1 Family, Youth, and Education (1852–1874)	9
2 Early Legal Career and Election to Parliament (1875–1892)	29
3 Home Secretary (1892–1895)	51
4 Waiting in the Wings (1896–1905)	81
5 Chancellor of the Exchequer (1905–1908)	117
6 Prime Minister (1908–1914)	141
7 Family Troubles and the Road to War (1905–1914)	189
8 Leading a Liberal Government at War (August 1914–May 1915)	219
9 Leading a Coalition Government at War (May 1915–December 1916)	253
10 Last of the Romans (December 1916–October 1927)	311
Conclusion	341
Bibliography	347
Index	357
About the Author	369

Acknowledgments

In writing this book, I have incurred debts to many people whom I would like to thank for their generosity, time, and help. They include my colleagues in the Birmingham-Southern College Department of History, Dr. William Huswit, Dr. Randall David Law, Dr. Matthew Levey, Dr. Victoria Ott, and Dr. Mark S. Schantz; members of the Southern Conference on British Studies who offered helpful comments to earlier drafts of parts of the book presented at the annual conferences; Dr. Michael Leslie and the British Studies at Oxford program that allowed me the opportunity to carry out research in the Bodleian Library, University of Oxford; Reverend Brian Mountford, and his wife, Annette, together with His Honour Judge Philip Head and his wife, Erica, for their generous hospitality when I visited England; Dr. Guy Ward Hubbs for his support throughout my sabbatical year, particularly his editorial comments; my office assistant Debbie Smith for her support; Amy Silberman for her assistance with photography permissions; Dr. William Anthony Hay for his helpful comments and suggestions; my colleague Dr. David W. Ullrich for his special friendship and constant encouragement of my scholarship; Michael Hughes of the Bodleian Library for his assistance; and especially my editor at Lexington Books, Eric Kuntzman, and his assistant, Ellen McDaniel, as well as my production editor, Lisa Dammeyer.

In addition, I wish to thank Virginia Brand, copyright holder The Bonham-Carter Trustees, and the Bodleian Library for permission to quote from the Asquith Papers; the British Library for permission to quote from letters of William Gladstone, Sir Henry Campbell-Bannerman, and Arthur Balfour; the Parliamentary Archives for permission to quote from the Bonar Law Papers; the National Archives of the United Kingdom for assistance with Crown copyright material; Oxford University Press for permission to purchase the right to quote from letters of Venetia Stanley in Michael and Eleanor Brock, eds., *H. H. Asquith: Letters to Venetia Stanley* (1982); the Bodleian Library and Warden and Fellows of New College for permission to quote from a letter of Alfred Milner, Viscount Milner; the Bodleian Library and The Bonham Carter Trustees for permission to quote from letters to Asquith from Bonar Law, Sir Henry Campbell-Bannerman, Sir Edward Grey, R. B. Haldane, and Robert Crewe-Milnes, 1st Marquess of Crewe; Lady Kenya Tatton Brown for permission to quote from letters of the 1st Earl Kitchener; the 4th Earl Lloyd-George of Dwyfor for permission to quote letters of David Lloyd George; the 7th Earl of Roseberry to quote from letters of the 5th Earl of Rosebery; and Lord Ponsonby of Shulbrede for permission to quote from the letters of Arthur Ponsonby.

My friend for more than half a century, Dr. Clark Malcolm, deserves special recognition. He painstakingly spent untold hours using his professional eye to edit several drafts of my manuscript. More importantly, this book gives me the special opportunity to thank him publicly for his devoted friendship over all these many years. His friendship has been one of my life's great treasures.

Most of all, I want to thank my wife Jeanne Jackson. Years ago, she was the first person I told that I wanted to write this book. With patience, devotion, assistance, and unlimited love, she has been with me every step of the way until the book's completion.

V. Markham Lester
February 15, 2019

Abbreviations

BL	British Library
HHA	Herbert Henry Asquith
MA	Margot Asquith
MT	Margot Tennant
NA	National Archives
VS	Venetia Stanley
WEG	William Ewart Gladstone

Introduction

If Herbert Henry Asquith had died in the summer of 1914, there is little question he would have been considered one of the greatest British parliamentarians and Prime Ministers. For until then, the trajectory of his political career had been one of almost uninterrupted success with one triumph following after another.

Born into a middle-class, Congregationalist, Yorkshire family in 1852, Asquith had a keen intelligence that produced a brilliant academic record at the City of London School, succeeded by a first in "Greats" at Oxford. With only meager financial resources, he became a struggling barrister, soon showed his talent for the law, and ultimately emerged as one of the leaders of his profession. His family had always been enthusiastic supporters of the Liberal Party, and in 1886 he was elected as a Liberal member of parliament for East Fife in Scotland. The leadership of the Liberal Party soon picked up on Asquith's potential, as over and over again he demonstrated his forensic skills both inside and outside the House of Commons. In 1892 Prime Minster Gladstone reached over the heads of many more senior Liberals MPs to select Asquith as Home Secretary. Considered one of the most effective Home Secretaries in the entire nineteenth century, Asquith was credited with numerous reforms including the Factories and Workshops Act of 1895. During the Liberals' decade of exile from power between 1895 and 1906, Asquith played a significant role in holding the party together when it dangerously split over the South African War. Although closely aligned with the pro-war imperialist wing of the Liberal Party, Asquith was the figure whom most elements of the party trusted and, more than anyone else, was responsible for avoiding a debilitating division in the Liberal ranks.

After the South African War, Conservative–Unionist Joseph Chamberlain concluded that free trade was no longer a viable option for Britain and took his case for economic protectionism to the country. Fast on Chamberlain's heels, following him from city to city throughout Britain, was Asquith, who successfully championed the cause of free trade. Largely as a result of this debate, the Liberals closed ranks and were returned to power in 1906 with Asquith becoming Chancellor of the Exchequer. Time and time again, the House of Commons witnessed the new Chancellor's ability as a great parliamentarian. When asked in 1912 who was the "biggest man" in the House, Sir Edward Grey, the Foreign Secretary and one of Asquith's closest friends, responded without hesitation, "Undoubtedly Asquith is the first man." When asked who was second, he again responded "Asquith." For to Grey and to most other Liberals, Asquith had become "by far the biggest figure" with "the most knowledge and the best judgement."[1] Even Liberal Sir Charles Dilke, one of the most experienced parliamentarians of the day and not known for his compliments, allowed that Asquith was an even greater parliamentarian than Gladstone.[2]

Asquith's brief tenure as Chancellor of the Exchequer was indeed remarkable. His 1907 budget for the first time introduced the progressive principle of differentiation between "earned" and "unearned income" income, establishing a vast new source of revenue for the government. As historian Asa Briggs has observed, in so many ways Asquith was a bridge between the old and the new—the key link between old Liberal virtues and the "new liberalism." On the one hand, he practiced the old Gladstonian Liberal virtue of economy by cutting unnecessary expenditure whenever possible, while on the other hand he actively formulated "new liberal" programs such as old age pensions.[3]

Upon the resignation of Sir Henry Campbell-Bannerman for health reasons in April 1908, Asquith assumed the leadership of the Liberal Party and became Prime Minister. During his tenure in office, Britain faced the most difficult problems and challenges since the Napoleonic Wars. The "People's Budget" of 1909 led to a constitutional crisis over the power of the House of Lords, a problem that had been brewing for decades. Before the issue could be resolved with the Parliament Act of 1911 limiting the powers of the House of Lords, Asquith had to fight two bitter general elections in 1910 and even threaten the use of the royal prerogative to create additional peers to ensure passage. The wings of the House of Lords now clipped, Home Rule for Ireland became a possibility. Asquith brilliantly shepherded the bill's passage through three sessions of Parliament. Final victory was denied only because of the outbreak of the First World War. This was not all. Numerous other national issues of monumental importance surfaced during Asquith's premiership, ranging from women's suffrage to the threat of German naval rearmament. Through all of these crises, Asquith never deviated from his nineteenth-century Liberal heritage of respect for economy, the British Constitution, and Parliament. Yet he also was a supportive midwife for a major new political departure for Britain toward a greater concern for the social welfare. He was in short, as one historian as put it, "at once a link and a new departure."[4] Considering the profound problems Britain faced when Asquith was Prime Minister and the adroitness with which he successfully handled those problems, it is not surprising that no less a figure than Winston Churchill called Asquith "probably one of the greatest peace-time Prime Ministers we have ever had."[5]

Asquith, of course, did *not* die in the summer of 1914. Rather, in that fated season he led Britain into the First World War and barely two years later found himself out of office and discredited as war leader. The war had slowly turned into a slaughter in the trenches of the Western front, and in May 1915 he was forced to form a coalition government. The final British defeat at Gallipoli, combined with the staggering casualties at the Battle of the Somme in the summer of 1916, further eroded his popularity. Over time what was perceived as Asquith's "wait and see" attitude proved more and more frustrating to those like Lloyd George, much of the press, and others who wanted to see a more vigorous prosecution of the war. In December 1916, Asquith was out-maneuvered by his opponents and replaced by Lloyd George as Prime Minister in a new coalition government.

The question of the quality of his war leadership aside, Asquith's political downfall was in some measure his own fault. He was never a self-promoter, and in an age where the press played a crucial role in forming public opinion, he deliberately ignored journalists and what they wrote about him. Even his official biographers, J. A. Spender, the well-known Liberal journalist and editor of the *Westminster Gazette*, and his youngest son, Cyril, admitted that "in war the stage needs to be set and lit for the principal figures, and Asquith's ingrained habit of self-effacement left the public without the sense of exciting and dramatic movement which it looked for in a Government at war."[6]

After the war, he clung to the leadership of what had become a dying Liberal Party. In the "Coupon" election of 1918, he suffered a humiliating defeat, losing his own seat for East Fife that he had held for more than thirty years. Many saw his refusal to make amends with Lloyd George as hastening the decline of Liberal fortunes. Even so, there were a few moments where the old spark could be seen, as during his famous by-election campaign in Paisley in 1920 where he eloquently placed classic Liberal ideals in a modern context and successfully regained a seat in Parliament. For the most part, however, his last years saw few accomplishments and many disappointments. Shortly before his death in 1928, Asquith described himself with the lines of Coleridge,

> Like a lone Arab, old and blind,
> Some caravan had left behind.[7]

After his death a few attempted to keep alive Asquith's memory and rehabilitate his reputation. Foremost among these were his second wife, Margot, and his daughter, Violet Bonham Carter. Both of these women, Margot in her memoirs and Violet in her career as a Liberal Party activist, remained true to their belief in Asquith's greatness. In 1932 Spender and Asquith published their laudatory "official" biography, which remained the standard work for decades. Predictably Spender and Asquith overly praise their subject. The book recognizes that Asquith faced hardships, but the emphasis is so much on his self-control and success that one hardly realizes the tremendously complex nature of the many adversities he overcame. As Winston Churchill commented, "The course of Asquith's life was not all so smooth and cool, so easy and unruffled as Mr. Spender's pages suggest." Asquith's picture should have been drawn with "stronger strokes, with higher lights and darker shadows."[8]

Three decades passed before another major Asquith biography appeared. With Violet Bonham Carter's permission, Roy Jenkins gained access to some of the Asquith papers and in 1964 produced *Asquith: Portrait of a Man and an Era*, a sympathetic, but still largely objective account of Asquith, and was hailed by some as one of the best political biographies to appear in England in recent years.[9] Jenkins was himself a politician, and his work benefits from his practical experience. His admiration for Asquith's brand of progressive Liberalism seems to preclude critical judgment of his hero. After the publication of Jenkins's biography, Asquith's reputation began to wane once more.

To a great extent, this fall from favor was inversely proportional to the rising reputation of his rival, David Lloyd George. More praise for Lloyd George almost invariably meant criticism of Asquith. In one form or another, this state of affairs has actually been going on since 1928 with the publication of Lord Beaverbrook's *Politicians and the War 1914–1916*.[10] As Roy Jenkins has pointed out in the preface to the 1988 edition of his Asquith biography, the "Beaverbrook school" of historians "have damned Asquith as faithfully as they have promoted Lloyd George."[11]

Stephen Koss's 1976 biography, *Asquith*, presents a fairer and more balanced life than earlier works.[12] Koss argues for two Asquiths. The first was the solid Yorkshire nonconformist in the first part of his career. Asquith's ambition, ability, and discipline are credited with the many accomplishments of his career through the 1890s and, to a certain extent, the impressive Liberal social reforms of 1906–1914. The second Asquith begins to emerge after the death of his first wife and his marriage to Margot Tenant in 1894, after which Asquith lived more freely and lavishly, enjoying the high life and the social round. He pictures Asquith slowly losing his grip on government leadership as the pressures of the First World War mount, ultimately leading to his loss of power.

More recently, Asquith received favorable treatment in George H. Cassar's *Asquith As War Leader* and Colin Mathew's entry on Asquith in the new *Oxford Dictionary of National Biography*.[13] Both of these works praise Asquith's adroitness in bringing Britain into the First World War and his early direction of the war effort.

There are a number of reasons to take a new look at one of Britain's most important Prime Ministers in the modern period. To begin with, since the last major biography of Asquith, a great deal of solid historical research has questioned older assumptions, particularly Koss's characterization of "two Asquiths," the young and the old, with the older in slow and decadent decline. Foremost has been Cassar's impressive *Asquith As War Leader*. Cassar carefully examines Asquith's war record and concludes that, in meeting the novel challenges of war on an unprecedented scale, the Prime Minister actually did quite well. While acknowledging Asquith's "serious defects" as a war leader, Cassar makes a powerful case that his accomplishments were "substantial and impressive," and "his reputation should rest safely beyond mediocracy."[14] Moreover, previous biographies have given insufficient weight to the fact that Asquith was Prime Minister during what Field Marshall Sir William Robertson, who served as Chief of the Imperial General Staff during the war, has termed "the most anxious" half of the war.[15] The first two years of the war required impressive leadership to hold the fragile British government together as it struggled to meet unprecedented challenges and lay the foundation for ultimate victory.

Previous studies of Asquith have also tended to gloss over his early years. Some biographers have even gone so far as to argue that Asquith's early development "did not contribute materially to his mature outlook" and therefore is not worth a detailed investigation.[16] *The Last of the Romans* challenges this premise. Asquith's early years, when he seemed to move effortlessly from success to success, are not only instructive but also, as Sir Charles Mallet observed in his obituary of Asquith, "There is something irresistibly attractive about the picture of these early years."[17] For one thing, previous biographers have, for the most part, skimmed over two very important events—his tenure as Home Secretary and his professional career as a barrister. Asquith has always been recognized as one of the most capable Home Secretaries, yet there has never been a detailed study of his leadership at the Home Office. This book attempts to fill in the record.

Even less has been written about Asquith's career as a barrister. Although his first love was always politics, he had to earn a living. He did so by working hard to become one of the most successful and respected barristers of the late nineteenth century, earning a good living for himself and his family. Part of the reason for the neglect of this aspect of his life is the lack of historical evidence. There are, however, records of some of the more important cases he handled and other anecdotes regarding his career in the law. Even with such limitations, much insight can be gained about the future Prime Minister by accurately and completely placing him for the first time in the broader context of the late Victorian legal profession.

Just as Asquith's early career needs further examination, so too could we benefit from a closer look at his career after leaving office in 1916 until his death twelve years later. These years have mostly been described as a rather embarrassing and sad story of an old man struggling too long to hold on to the leadership of the Liberal Party in opposition to the challenges of Lloyd George against the backdrop of the Liberal Party going though its death throes. While there is more than some truth to this description, there is much more to the story. During these years Asquith continued to do what he did best—to articulate the Liberal position with vigor and clarity at a time when such a formulation was desperately needed. If there is single theme that runs throughout Asquith's entire career, it is his devotion to liberalism and the Liberal Party. While he was still Prime Minister, an American academic writing in the *Political Science Quarterly* summed it up distinctly, "He has served his party. He has loved Liberalism."[18] His devotion to the Liberal cause did not end when he left the premiership. His victory in 1920 to represent Paisley in one of the most dramatic campaigns of the inter-war years was his last hurrah. Far from being the effort of a man trying to cling to what was left of his leadership it was a truly great campaign for the ideals of the Liberal Party, as a close examination will show.

There is another reason to visit the dimly lit periods of Asquith's life. Asquith has often been described as the "last of the Romans," a phrase believed to have been first used by Julius Caesar to describe Brutus, whom Caesar saw as the last leader with the old Roman spirit. The phrase often appears in descriptions of Asquith by contemporaries, in biographies, and even on the blue memorial plaque on the house where he lived in Sutton Courtenay. According to the plaque, Asquith was known as the "last of the Romans" because of "his noble character and ideals." Indeed, many of his contemporaries saw Asquith as the last of a breed of politicians whose careers began before the days of mass media and universal suffrage and, largely because of this, they practiced a more refined, educated, and gentlemanly brand of politics. My central argument is that the key to understanding Asquith is to understand his unshakeable belief in the classic virtues of rational thought, eloquence, and self-control. Beginning with his early mastery of Greek and Latin at the City of London School and culminating in a first in "Greats" at Oxford, these classic virtues were so instilled in him as to become part of his very nature. This is not, of course, to argue that at all times and in all places his actions reflected these virtues—far from it—but if there is a consistent thread that runs throughout his life, it was his desire to be a political leader who reflected classical ideals of virtue and character.

NOTES

1. Lord Riddell, *More Pages from My Diary* (London: Country Life, 1934), 85.
2. Asa Briggs, "The Political Scene," in Simon Nowell-Smith, *Edwardian England 1901–1914* (London: Oxford University Press, 1964), 80.
3. Ibid., 81.
4. Jospeh Grimond, "H. H. Asquith," in Herbert Van Thal, *The Prime Ministers*, 2 vols. (London: George Allen & Unwin, 1975), 2:207.
5. Winston S. Churchill, *Great Contemporaries*, rev. edn. (London: Thornton Butterworth, 1938), 150–51.
6. J. A. Spender and Cyril Asquith, *Life of Herbert Henry Asquith, Lord Oxford and Asquith,* 2 vols. (London: Hutchison, 1932), 2:230.
7. Samuel Taylor Coleridge, "Love's Apparition and Evanishment: An Allegoric Romance," quoted in Algernon Cecil, "Lord Oxford and Asquith," *Quarterly Review* 260 (January 1933): 26.
8. Churchill, *Great Contemporaries*, 146.
9. Roy Jenkins, *Asquith* (London: Collins, 1964).
10. Lord Beaverbrook, *Politicians and the War 1914–1916*, 2 vols. (London: Collins, 1928 and 1932).
11. Jenkins, *Asquith*.
12. Steven Koss, *Asquith* (New York: St. Martin: St. Martin's Press, 1976).
13. George H. Cassar, *Asquith As War Leader* (London: The Hambledon Press, 1994); H. C. G. Matthew, "Asquith, Herbert Henry, First Earl of Oxford and Asquith," *Oxford Dictionary of National Biography* (Oxford: Oxford University Press, 2004), 2:735–54.
14. Cassar, *Asquith As War Leader*, ix.
15. Field-Marshall Sir William Robertson, *Soldiers and Statesmen 1914–1918* (London: Cassell, 1926), 284.
16. Koss, *Asquith*, 3.
17. Sir Charles Edward Mallet, "Lord Oxford's 'Life,'" *Contemporary Review* CXLIII (1933): 34–35.
18. Wallace Notestein, "The Career of Mr. Asquith," *Political Science Quarterly* 31 (September 1916): 378.

Chapter One

Family, Youth, and Education (1852–1874)

Alone, a man in a thick overcoat with a traveling cap pulled down close to his eyes strode confidently across the platform at Charing Cross to catch the nine o'clock continental boat train for Paris. Newspaper boys at the station that April evening in 1908 shouted the news that after months of speculation Prime Minister Sir Henry Campbell-Bannerman had formerly offered his resignation because of a heart condition. Although many had discussed when exactly the Prime Minister might give up office, there was no doubt in anyone's mind as to his successor. Ever since the aging Campbell-Bannerman had taken office in 1905, his Chancellor of the Exchequer, H. H. Asquith, had been marked to succeed him.

The plans for the transfer of power were well laid. Weeks before, Sir Henry called Asquith to his bedside and told him of his coming resignation and of the king's intention to name Asquith as his replacement. The one complication in the plan was that King Edward VII, as was his habit, was not in England at this time of year but rather in France at the resort town of Biarritz. His Majesty had made it absolutely clear that should it become necessary for the Prime Minister to resign in the King's absence, he would not return to London. Asquith would have to travel to Biarritz to kiss hands and receive the seals of office. And so, having moved the adjournment of the House of Commons on the afternoon of April 6, Asquith went to his house in Cavendish Square, bid farewell to his wife, Margot, who was too ill to travel with him, and left for the station. Since the travel plans were secret, no crowds were on the platform, and only his secretaries and two friends saw him off on his journey.

As the train pulled away, the fifty-seven-year-old Asquith may have finally found a moment to reflect on the remarkable path that brought him to this juncture, a path that had taught him well the vagaries of life. He may have recalled with some pain the early death of his father that abruptly ended an idyllic childhood and left his family at the mercy of relatives. Or his thoughts may have turned to his unhappy early school days or perhaps his later successes at the City of London School. Then, of course, there was the brilliant "first" he earned at Oxford, always irrationally discounted in his own mind because of his failure to win the coveted top Herford or Ireland Prizes. Oxford had been followed by lean and rather boring years as a young barrister, his election to Parliament, and the happy moments with his first wife, Helen, who tragically died of typhoid fever, leaving him alone with five young children. There was the meteoric political career—his selection, by no less than William Gladstone, to be Home Secretary and the youngest member in that venerable leader's last government. After marrying the wealthy and vivacious Margot Tennant, with his Liberal Party out of power, he had gone on to spend a decade as a successful barrister and prominent proponent of imperialism. Finally, he might well have looked back with satisfaction at his many successes in the last few years as Chancellor of the Exchequer, shepherding the Liberal Party's program though the Commons.

After meeting the King's secretary in Biarritz, he checked into the Hôtel du Palais, the same hotel where the King was staying. As reported to his daughter Violet the next day, he put on a frock coat, met with the King, and in a ceremony lasting only a minute and a half, became Prime Minister. Several days later he returned to London, to be greeted by cheering throngs and to serve as Prime Minister longer than anyone else between Lord Liverpool and Margaret Thatcher and lead Britain through some of its most challenging years.

Asquith's journey began in the small Yorkshire town of Morley, where he was born on September 12, 1852. Described as nothing more than "one of the nooks or corners of Old England," Morley was within ten miles of what were then the expanding textile centers of Leeds, Huddersfield, and Bradford.[1] A visitor to Morley in the 1850s could already see that the quaint English village of old was gone. Such a visitor would have reached the town by way of the new Leeds and Manchester Railway constructed in 1845. Like most of England, Morley had experienced what might without exaggeration be called a population explosion over the previous half-century. In 1851 Morley's population of 5,000 was double what it had been only fifty years earlier and a decade later would grow to 7,000.

Despite the changes taking place in Morley as it became part of a new industrialized England, families that had been a part of the history of the village for centuries, as attested by the tombstones in the churchyards or the vestry lists, were still prominent in 1850. The Scratcherds, the Dodgshuns, and the Dixons, to name a few, often still intermarried and pretty much ran the affairs of the community. Prominent too among the list of notable Morley families were the Asquiths, sometimes spelled with a "q," sometimes with a "kw." Some have claimed to trace the Asquith ancestry as far back as mayors of York during Henry VIII's reign, but this is questionable. Although the specifics of the Asquith ancestry are difficult to trace, the family appears to have been known as enthusiastic Puritans (later Congregationalists). Records show that a Joshua Asquith participated in the "Farnley Wood Plot" in 1663. In October of that year, a group of twenty or so nonconformist, West Riding conspirators met in a place called "The Trench" in Farnley Wood three miles from Leeds. Their object was to restore the Long Parliament and avoid the payment of excise taxes. Led by Captain Thomas Oates, the conspirators printed a declaration calling for rebellion. Betrayed by spies and confronted by regular troops, the rebellion collapsed almost as soon as it started. Authorities imprisoned Joshua Asquith for a while in York castle, but he escaped the hangman's noose, some alleging he had turned informer.

The role of the Asquith family in the life of Morley becomes much clearer in the eighteenth century. The name William Askwith of Morley, a husbandman, appears in a deed dated February 10, 1685. The names Joseph, Thomas, Samuel, and William Asquith appear with regularity throughout the eighteenth and early nineteenth centuries as persons who served as "Overseers of the Poor in the Township of Morley," and a Joseph Asquith served as Churchwarden in 1725 and 1733. The Asquith name also appears in lists of those taking Poor Law apprentices as early as 1720.

Times change, and there is no guarantee that a family will maintain its prominence from generation to generation. This is especially the case when rapid social and economic change is taking place as it was in late eighteenth- and early nineteenth-century England. Some Morley families that stuck with the old way of life undoubtedly were washed away by the tide of the Industrial Revolution. Others had the intelligence, ingenuity, and foresight to make the adjustments and transitions necessitated by the challenges of a new age. One such person was Joseph Asquith, born in Morley in 1778.

Little is known of Joseph's youth or even his early cloth-making operations. Records show that in 1817 he was one of about thirty cloth manufacturers from Morley attending the Coloured Cloth Hall in Leeds. Because of the large number of Morley manufacturers in attendance, it is perhaps safe to assume that these men were relatively small producers. More significant are the steps the small manufacturers took to remain competitive. In 1834, Joseph Asquith, along with forty other cloth manufacturers, put up £3,000 to form the Gillroyd Mill Company, under the title "Asquith, Clark and Co." This new enterprise constructed a mill and began the mass production of cloth. All indications are that the enterprise proved successful, and Joseph Asquith prospered.

In 1824 Joseph married Esther Dixon, twenty years his junior and a member of another prominent Morley family. They had only one child, Joseph Dixon Asquith, born in Morley a year after their marriage. The Asquiths were sufficiently affluent to send their son to a nearby boarding school at Toadcaster and even to provide the young man with a pony and a piano while away at school. The young Joseph's apparent charm is recorded on his grave stone, which memorializes him as "the idol of his parents." A contemporary described him as "a very handsome man, very intellectual and charming in manner."[2] Like his father, he became a cloth merchant and developed business associations, not only in Morley, but also in nearby Leeds and Huddersfield. It was probably on one of his business trips to Huddersfield that Joseph Asquith had the opportunity to meet his future bride, Emily Willans.

For a young wool merchant from the small town of Morley, Emily Willans was quite a catch. Emily's father was a prominent Huddersfield wool stapler, William Willans. In 1825, the young Willans came to Huddersfield from Leeds to seek his fortune. He did well, but what marked Willans in his new hometown was not so much his success in business as his deep Congregationalist convictions. As a young man, he worked for the Leeds Juvenile Missionary Society with the future prominent Liberal newspaper editor, Edward Baines. Once in Huddersfield, Willans became one of the most active members of the Ramsden Street Chapel, which has been described as a "young man's church in a young man's town."[3] He served on the chapel building committee in the 1820s and as a deacon from 1833. Willans married Elizabeth Wrigley, and in addition to Emily (born in 1828), they had a number of children. As his family expanded, so did Willans's interest in public affairs. He held numerous civic offices and at the height of his career in 1861 became both Justice of the Peace and President of the Huddersfield Chamber of Commerce. As with most nonconformists, he was a Liberal, and he became active in local Liberal Party politics. He worked in all the general elections, particularly the 1857 campaign of free trade leader Richard Cobden, and he himself was only narrowly defeated for Parliament in 1852.

Willans's daughter Emily was not a particularly attractive woman. In photographs she looks rather plain and has the appearance of a man wearing a woman's wig. Despite her modest looks, she nevertheless had a great deal to offer. She came from a relatively wealthy family and was intelligent with a particular knack for foreign languages. Contemporaries often commented that she was well read, had a sharp wit and good sense of humour, all of which made her an excellent conversationalist.

Joseph and Emily married in 1850 and made Morley their home. The couple chose as their dwelling the substantial "Croft House," Wind Mill Hill, at the eastern edge of the town. The owner of the mill, Isaac Crowther, had originally built the two-story Georgian structure at the end of the eighteenth century as his residence. Soon after moving to Morley, the Asquith family began to grow. Their first son, William Willans, was born in 1851. A year later on September 12, 1852, the future Prime Minister, Herbert Henry, was born in Croft House. The Asquiths had three more children, all daughters, but only one, Emily Evelyn (born in 1855), survived until adulthood.

The focal point of the Asquith family was not Croft House but Rehoboth Chapel, a Congregationalist church located on the opposite side of the village. Joseph and Emily were both filled with religious fervour, and religious worship and other church activities formed the focus of the young couple's lives. They were not alone in this regard, for Morley in 1850 was a religious town.

In 1833, the congregation of Morley's "Old New Chapel" built a new house of worship renamed "Rehoboth Chapel," a substantial stone structure in the simple Greek revival style favored by Congregationalists at the time, and this is where the Asquith family chose to worship. The Rehoboth Congregationalists were part of one wing of the broader Puritan movement and later were associated with the evangelical revival that took place in England in the second half of the eighteenth and early nineteenth centuries. This new evangelicalism emphasized a personal relationship with God and Christ's atonement for the sins of the world. As was the Puritan and evangelical practice, a large part of the Asquiths' Sabbath day was spent in chapel, singing hymns, reading scripture, and listening to sermons. Even more importantly, the Asquiths also maintained a puritanical home life. Dancing, drinking, theater, and card playing were off limits, although Henry was allowed to teach his mother whist after substituting chessmen for cards.

As Congregationalists, the Asquiths were heirs to a rigorous intellectual tradition. Joseph and Emily considered the education of their children of utmost importance and were willing to make sacrifices to achieve it. Although the exact reason is not known, the Asquiths decided that their sons, William and Henry, should not attend day school at Morley but instead be educated at home by their mother and a governess. Their father also participated in the boys' education, taking great interest in their homework when they were later enrolled in school.

As young boys, Herbert and his older brother William were constant companions. One of Herbert's earliest recollections was that of his village celebrating the end of the Crimean War in 1856. The scene could have been that of almost any small town in England at the time. Citizens bedecked the buildings with flags and banners. The parade which began in early afternoon included school children proceeded by banners, with the Asquith brothers marching at the head of the children carrying two homemade banners inscribed "Peace on Earth" and "Good will towards men." At the end of the march, all gathered in Mr. Cowburn's field and sang the national anthem followed by a "grand pyrotechnic display." As evidence of the strong Puritan spirit of the Morley citizenry, a record of the event notes with pride that no money was spent on intoxicating drinks. In 1858 the family moved to Mirfield, a small village about seven miles toward Huddersfield. No explanation has ever been given for this move, and considering Joseph's close ties with Morley, it seems rather odd. Perhaps Emily Asquith wanted to be closer to her family in Huddersfield. More than likely, their sons' education had some role to play in the move, for even though the Asquiths had never enrolled their boys in a school at Morley, immediately upon arrival in Mirfield, they placed them in the Mirfield Moravian School.

Joseph did a good job supporting his family. Neither a rich man nor a particularly successful businessman, he was able to provide his family with many of the trappings of a *petit bourgeois* Victorian life. The Asquiths had sufficient funds, through either Joseph's earnings or outside family support, to have a nurse for the boys, a Mrs. Ellis, who had worked for the family for a number of years. Many years later when Asquith became Prime Minister, she still referred to him as "Master Bertie." The Asquiths also had sufficient means to have a portrait painted of their three children. This earliest known image of Henry Asquith shows him with three of his siblings—all well dressed, solidly middle-class Victorian children. Emily sits on a chair holding some flowers as her two brothers stand watchfully by in their matching outfits of white trousers and velvet smocks, all against a pastoral background. It is one of those Victorian portraits that conveys a false sense of security and serene domesticity. The Asquiths, while not tremendously wealthy, were well off enough that they could protect themselves from many of the greater difficulties of life—or so they thought.

All of this, what Asquith later called a life of "simple comfort amid semi-rural surroundings," mirrored in the portrait of the children, was jeopardized in June 1860 when Joseph died of a sudden illness.[4] This was to be the first of several abrupt turns-of-events in Henry Asquith's life. Even though Joseph Asquith had been able to provide well for his wife and children, like so many Victorian middle-class families, there was little or no reserve to call upon in an emergency like the sudden death of the principal breadwinner. Fortunately for Emily and her three children, Emily's father, the well-to-do William Willans, had the means to support the young family. Nevertheless, the stable, idyllic days Asquith had known up to this point in his life were over.

Willans moved his daughter and grandchildren to Huddersfield and established them in a house near his own. The boys were enrolled in Huddersfield College as day scholars, and a short time later, in August 1861, the Asquith brothers enrolled in a Moravian boarding school at Fulneck near Leeds, a school that exists to this day. One of the great attractions of Moravian schools to Emily Asquith was their strict religious education and discipline, qualities less important to young boys. After only a few days at Fulneck, Asquith sent a letter to his mother, already demonstrating his keen lawyer's ability to get to the point: "I do not like either the masters or boys and therefore I do not like the place at all."[5] Still, Asquith always acknowledged that the Moravians were excellent teachers and laid a solid foundation for his education.

After only a little over a year, Asquith's life took another one of its abrupt turns. Again it was the death of a family member, this time his grandfather, William Willans, in 1863 that precipitated change. By itself, Willans's death would not necessarily have had a tremendous impact, but two other factors came into play. Over the years Emily Asquith had developed a number of ailments and had become, for the most part an invalid. With her father's death Emily Asquith could now follow her doctors' advice to move to a warmer climate in the south of England—St. Leonard's on the Sussex coast. With her sons boarders at school, her move did not require them to change schools; however, to Emily it must have seemed a good time to change to a more prestigious school with the added advantage of being closer to her new home.

Emily's elder brother, John Willans, lived in London and was married to the daughter of Edward Baines, a friend from youth of William Willans and a prominent newspaper editor and Liberal MP from Leeds. The London Willanses had no children and graciously agreed not only to pay William and Herbert's tuition, but also to board them while they attended a new school. Emily took their offer, and the Asquith brothers were enrolled in the City of London School in January 1864. Although Asquith could not possibly have known it at the time, from then on he was, in his own words, "to all intents and purposes a Londoner."[6]

The City of London School was very much a part of the great imperial metropolis. It had opened in 1837, but the benefaction upon which it was founded dated to 1442.

Situated in a three-story Gothic-style school building, the City of London School where the Asquith brothers enrolled was in the center of London on the site of the former Honey Lane market in Milk Street, north of Cheapside. Asquith years later remarked, "we spent our days not only within the sound of Bow Bells but of the roar and traffic of Cheapside itself."[7]

What must have been a major factor in the evangelical Congregationalist Emily Asquith's decision to send William and Herbert to the City of London School was its strong and unique tradition of complete religious freedom at a time when nearly all large English schools required the teaching of Anglican theological doctrine. While the school did offer Anglican religious instruction, it was not required, and this made the school a favorite with dissenting families seeking a quality education for their children.

Another attractive feature of the City of London School was its broad curriculum. The school was constantly adding new subjects of study in a day when most public schools were still limiting their curriculum to Latin and Greek. The first chemistry lesson in an English school was given at the City of London School in 1847, and prizes were awarded for the study of Shakespeare from 1850. By the time the Asquiths arrived, many considered the school to have the best instruction in mathematics in London and perhaps in all of England. Two years after their arrival, the school became the first to make English literature and grammar compulsory subjects.

For two young boys, ages eleven and twelve, the move to London must have been both traumatic and exciting, for they had grown up in a country town and a small city and, even though accustomed to boarding at school, the move to a thriving metropolis meant a whole new way of life for them. Just the walk to school each morning was an adventure. A month after his enrollment, Asquith walked up Ludgate Hill to school only to be confronted by the famous gang called the "Five Pirates." No need to fear, however, for they were only the bodies of these brigands hung neatly in a row with white caps covering their heads. They would not be cut down until an hour after their death. Indeed Asquith made the point years later that, as he looked back, he realized how significant a contribution the daily walk through the busy London streets made to his education.

Asquith progressed steadily at his new school. Entering in the second form, he reached the sixth form only three and a half years later, ultimately receiving the William Tite Scholarship that paid £25 a year.[8] His main interests were English and classics, and a schoolmate recalled that he showed little, if any, attention to other subjects. His exercise book from 1866 includes pages of quotes and translations from Livy, Horace, and other classical writers. Many pages are written in Greek.[9] He told his mother that same year that for one examination he had to "prepare so as to be able to translate + answer any questions on 600 lines of Euripides, 250 lines of Horace, 3 speeches of Cicero against Catiline, 20 pages of Lucian."[10] In fact, he demonstrated such promise in classics, always being at the top of his form, that the school allowed him to forgo some instruction in mathematics. As one of the leading students in his form, Asquith soon caught the attention of the school's renowned headmaster, Dr. Edwin Abbott (1838–1926). Seeing Asquith had promise, he made special exceptions for the boy including taking him out of his mundane penmanship and bookkeeping class and giving him a few minutes each day of special instruction in the classics.

Asquith was undoubtedly a serious and disciplined student but not so much so that he lacked the humour and the tricks of an ordinary schoolboy. He was known for his "irreverent jests" in chemistry classes and singing ribald songs with his classmates when the mathematics master left the room. When his German class, including Asquith, was not well prepared, his fellow students could always count on Asquith to carry on a conversation (in English) with the teacher until there was no time left to speak German.

The school day lasted from nine in the morning until three in the afternoon, and the physical facilities of the school were, in Asquith's words, "contracted, gloomy, and a trifle squalid."[11] There was no eating hall as such, and students had to find food for themselves in the city at such dark cellar eateries as "Mother Sumner's Tuck-shop." One former student complained that "most of us were wearing spectacles before we left school" because "our class-rooms were illuminated by flaring and unshaded gas-jets and the height of our desks bore no relation to the height of boy sitting there."[12] Unlike other schools located in a rural environment, the City of London School had no playing fields. A dark underground corridor served as the boys' playground.

Despite these handicaps, a real esprit de corps existed at the school. The students knew they did not have the traditions or facilities of an Eton of Harrow, but they also recognized, even though perhaps some years later, that they were receiving an excellent education in one of the most unique educational environments in England.

Almost from the beginning of his time at the City of London School, Asquith showed a keen interest in and talent for public speaking, not surprising considering his background. Throughout his childhood, preachers filled Asquith's ears with the cadences of the Sunday sermon. As a result, by his teens he already had the critical capacity that could discern good voice and oratory from bad. His family, particularly the Willans, involved itself in Liberal politics and the political issues of the day. The extent to which the family discussed politics can be seen in Asquith's letters to his mother at the time. They are filled with comments on current political events, from Robert E. Lee's surrender at Appomattox to the disestablishment of the Irish church. Then too, the nineteenth century was the golden age of political oratory and debate, with the *Times* and other newspapers regularly reporting lengthy Parliamentary debates verbatim. Clashes between Parliamentary giants like Disraeli and Gladstone had the public spotlight as much as sporting events do today. With his school in the center of London, Asquith could easily hear the great politicians, lawyers, and preachers of the day. In May 1865, Asquith reported to his mother that his uncle had taken him to Parliament where he had the chance to hear Disraeli speak; however, Robert Lowe made by far the "cleverest speech."[13]

To attend Parliament was something of a special occasion, but there were other opportunities to hear talented speakers almost daily in the great metropolis. The law courts were within walking distance, and Asquith and some of his schoolmates would often spend their short break between morning and afternoon classes observing cases being tried. One former classmate whom Asquith often took with him to the Old Bailey remembered Asquith "eagerly following the speeches and watching the procedure of counsel in cross examination."[14] Asquith's letters describing these adventures show a maturity and seriousness of purpose for a boy his age. One letter to his mother described a trial at the Court of the Queen's Bench presided over by Lord Chief Justice Cockburn. What is remarkable, however, about the letter is that this thirteen-year-old boy writes that he planned to return the next day because he desperately wanted to hear the Chief Justice's summation. Already Asquith was showing great admiration for those who could concisely and cogently present their thoughts to an audience.

In addition to Parliament and the Law Courts, among Asquith's favorite haunts were the church and the chapel, where he enjoyed listening to sermons. In 1866 he reported to his mother that he had gone to hear the famous C. H. Spurgeon at the Metropolitan Tabernacle. The crowd was so large that he had to have a ticket. He noted that as soon as Spurgeon "got up to pray the effect on the assembly was wonderful," but the boy's real interest was in the famous preacher's speaking style. "The most wonderful thing about him" he reported, "is his voice" which "[w]ithout any apparent effort he quite fills the place."[15]

To Asquith's great fortune, the City of London School provided a number of opportunities for him to develop his skills as a public speaker. He acted in plays, and in one single day in 1868 he played the Bishop of Carlisle in *Richard II*, Orleans in *Henry V*, and Guillaume in *L'Avocat Palelin* (apparently in French). But it was in the Sixth Form Debating Society where Asquith repeatedly demonstrated his growing skills. The Society met often and addressed a variety of resolutions from "the execution of Mary Queen of Scots was unjustifiable" to "woman is mentally though not morally inferior to man." Both students and faculty quickly noticed his natural talent. Years later, fellow student Mortimer Angus, who became a Professor of Latin and Philology at the University College of Wales, recalled that Asquith's speeches "differed from that of the ordinary schoolboy's as that of Macaulay's history differs from 'Little Arthur's.'" Asquith's superior performance was due in large measure to his disciplined preparation, but he clearly had a natural gift. "Even then," Angus noted, "it was not fire or passion, not so much powers of persuasion or sarcasm, but fine phrasing, the elaborate periods, the ambitious rhetoric that impressed us."[16] Asquith dominated the scene. So much so that, as another fellow student recalled, "I am afraid some of us . . . were disposed to criticize him, as he was rather inclined to talk above our heads and use long words."[17]

Asquith's days at the City of London School were crowned in 1869–1870 when he was selected as Captain of the School. Looking to the future, Dr. Abbott encouraged Asquith to apply for one of the nation's top scholarships—that of Balliol College, Oxford. At that time the City of London School had much closer contacts with Cambridge University, and most of the City of London School's scholarship winners attended Cambridge colleges. Asquith's final triumph was the Balliol scholarship, the first to a student from the City of London School.

A. E. Douglas-Smith in his history of the City of London School quotes Asquith as saying, "What shall I say of the City of London School, when I owe all I have in the world to the City of London School?"[18] This may have well been an exaggeration, perhaps an applause line at a reunion of "Old Citizens," as former students were known. Yet the influence of the City of London School on Asquith has consistently been understated. He entered the school with no record of particular distinction. Seven years later he left the school a worldly, confident, well-spoken, disciplined student of proven academic distinction. He undoubtedly had an impressive native intelligence. With his years at the City of London School, he experienced first-hand the heartbeat of a great urban center, and this added immensely to his maturation and knowledge of all sorts of people. Day in and day out he watched the struggle of thousands of Londoners making their living, a vast encyclopedia filed away for future reference. He left London knowing much more of life than a school boy educated in the hothouse environment of Eton or Harrow. Decades later when Asquith became a political leader advocating the "new liberalism" of social responsibility, he had a distinct advantage over many other British leaders. They could call upon their Oxbridge classical educations, but unlike Asquith few could also bring to bear memories of Mother Sumner's Tuck-shop or the hanging of the "Five Pirates" gang.

In the autumn of 1870, Asquith went up to Oxford to begin his studies at Balliol College. The college sits on Broad Street just outside where the medieval city walls once stood and in front of the spot where the three Oxford protestant martyrs, Bishops Latimer, Ridley, and Cranmer were burned at the stake during the reign of Queen Mary. Although the college is one of Oxford's oldest, receiving its charter in 1282, when Asquith arrived, Balliol had a freshness about it, a freshness that was beginning to distinguish it and eventually transform it into one of Oxford's most famous colleges.

The new energy at Balliol would have been readily apparent, even to the casual passer-by on the Broad in 1870. Even though the college's long front course of buildings had a Gothic look about them so as to blend in with much of the medieval architecture of the university, they were in fact recently constructed neo-Gothic structures, the product of the well-known Victorian architect Alfred Waterhouse.

More important to Balliol's new look than new buildings, however, was its growing reputation for openness, as shown in the increasing diversity of its student body. In the decade or so before Asquith matriculated, Balliol like its other Oxford counterparts drew the bulk of its students from the historic English public schools. Of the almost 250 Balliol men who came into residence between 1854 and 1863, almost half came from a select few of these public schools, a quarter from Eton alone. Likewise, the public school boys captured almost all the open scholarships.

In the 1870s, things began to change. With some obvious exaggeration, C. E. Vaughn, who came up to Balliol three years after Asquith, described Balliol's students as "Japanese and Scots, Hindoos and Frenchmen, Americans and Englishmen, Brahmins and Catholics, Nonconformists and high Anglicans, Jews and Gentiles . . . sparks of nobility and artisans; a bazaar of all nations and languages, the whole world in miniature."[19] Vaughn's description is somewhat confirmed by the records. The *Oxford Undergraduate Journal* in 1871 reported that Balliol was the third largest college in Oxford and the fastest growing of all the colleges. Asquith would still have felt to be somewhat of an outsider, arriving at Balliol from what was considered an undistinguished school; nevertheless, the trend was changing. By the decade after Asquith left Oxford, the numbers of students admitted to Balliol from Eton and Harrow, for example, while still substantial, represented only half of what they had been several decades earlier. By the end of the 1870s foreign students represented 16 percent of the student body.

Balliol's growing distinction among Oxford Colleges had not come about by chance. It resulted in large measure from the leadership of one man, one of the most distinguished Victorian educators—Benjamin Jowett. By the time of his death in 1893, the words "Balliol" and "Jowett" had almost become synonymous.

Jowett's early career followed the usual path of an Oxford don. Educated at St. Paul's and Balliol itself, he gained a fellowship at Balliol in 1838 and became a distinguished classical scholar. Jowett gained notoriety in 1860 with publication of his essay "The Interpretation of Scripture" in *Essays and Reviews*, which argued for the use of reason and interpretation in examining.

Jowett became head of the college in 1870, and his view of his role was simple and yet demanding. "The Head of a College should be identified with the interests of the College," he wrote in a private memorandum in 1875. "The life of the college is his life. His money is the money of the college. He is married to the College and has a duty to support his family."[20] The mild manner conveyed by a contemporary Spy caricature of Jowett, with his cherub-like face and reading glasses perched on his nose, belies an individual with an incredible drive and singularity of purpose. Jowett's reforms transformed Balliol. He moved to abolish clerical fellowships, reduce religious observation, and remodel divinity teaching. Tutors were finally allowed to retain their fellowship after marriage. Perhaps his greatest contribution was his drive to provide a university education to as broad a deserving group as possible. "It is very important," he wrote to Earl Russell, "to provide a means of giving the best education to the best intelligences in every class of Society."[21]

As a "fresher" coming from the City of London School and with little social background, Asquith must have felt a certain degree of awkwardness as he took up residence at Balliol. Yet over time Balliol proved to be a most congenial place, and his circle of friends grew. He became identified with an outstanding group of undergraduates at the college, dubbed "the Clique," that shared a common interest in scholarship and the Oxford Union, the university debating society. Asquith became its leader, and according to T. H. Warren, a member of "the Clique" and future President of Magdalen College, Asquith was the group's "hero and centre."[22] In addition to Warren and Asquith's brother, William, the group included among others Herbert Paul, Thomas Raleigh, A. R. Cluer, Joseph Soloman, W. H. Mallock, Henry Broadbent, and Charles Gore.

The mid-Victorian world of Oxford these men inhabited was, at least in their memories, one of magic and romance. As novelist W. H. Mallock put it in his memoirs, life was filled with "the charm of certain cloistered buildings . . . and the shades of Addison's walk; with country drives in dog-carts to places like Whitney and Abingdon; with dinners there in the summer evenings . . . with supper parties during race weekends."[23] It was a world where they would gather in Asquith's rooms at the top of staircase IV, attired in their oriental-style smoking caps, to have discussions late into the evening.

One of the things that brought "the Clique" together was their mutual interest in the Oxford Union, a club-like organization that organized formal debates among its members. The debate questions were wide-ranging and included such topics as the disestablishment of the Church of England and intervention in the Franco-Prussian War. In contrast to the Liberal-leaning Asquith, the overall membership in the Union tended to be Tory or as Jowett, speaking at the Union's Jubilee banquet in 1873, described the organization, "fearfully High Church and Conservative."[24]

Asquith actively participated in the Union's activities, speaking there in the very first month he was at Oxford. The Union elected him its treasurer in 1872, and while holding this position he introduced smoking and afternoon tea. He lost his first bid to be elected President, a defeat many attributed to his Liberalism; however, the Union elected him its leader in his last year at Oxford.

Although later descriptions of Asquith's debating skills may be somewhat colored by his subsequent Parliamentary successes, no doubt he was an exceptional undergraduate debater. T. H. Warren recalled that he was "ready for any emergency," being "cool and courageous, intellectually alert, well informed, sure of himself, with a voice clear and sufficiently strong and flexible, if not especially powerful" with "a striking command of apt and incisive language."[25] The *Oxford Undergraduate Journal* reveals that Asquith seemed to avoid Union debates over local issues such as athletics and management of the university, focusing instead on national and international questions in which he almost always put forward the orthodox Liberal view. Liberal Prime Minister William Gladstone was at the height of his first government at the time, and Asquith gladly carried the party's banner in the Union. He spoke in favor of motions supporting the separation of church and state and opposed the death penalty and British intervention in the Franco-Prussian War. Not always meeting success in the predominantly Conservative Union, he did occasionally carry the day. Oddly enough for a later champion of imperialism, one of Asquith's triumphs was carrying the question "That the disintegration of the Empire is the true solution of Colonial difficulty."[26]

An acknowledged champion debater, Asquith also showed academic promise. Already he had shown a great talent for the study of Latin and Greek at the City of London School. It was only natural then that he chose *Literae Humaniores*, or as it is more commonly referred to, "Greats," as his course of study at Oxford. "Greats" had become a famous university institution, although by the time Asquith had arrived, its prestige was being overshadowed by philosophy. "Greats" was primarily a study of the history, thought, and society of ancient Greece and Rome, with the addition of some modern philosophy to link the study to more contemporary issues. Perhaps the best way to understand this course of study is to look at some of the final examination questions: "How far was the want of Poor Laws recognized and supplied by ancient states?," "Estimate the social and political effects of the absence of professions in a state," and "Specify some of our political ideas and institutions to which it is impossible or difficult to find analogue in Greece."[27]

A few of Asquith's college text books still exist, and they provide a small window into his study habits.[28] Classic Greek texts such as Thucydides's *History* were rebound with a blank page for notes alternating with text, where Asquith meticulously wrote detailed annotations. In many instances the notes are written in Greek. These books are the record of a highly disciplined mind at work. There are no erasures or strike-outs, only page upon page of detailed, well-crafted notes. Much has been written about the apparent ease with which Asquith achieved his academic success, and there is no doubt he had a quick mind, but these text books show that he also put in hours and hours of hard labor to achieve his success.

A Greats education consisted essentially of the critical analysis of a set group of ancient texts. As a result, students graduated with powerful analytical skills applicable to almost any problem. It was, however, an education in the abstract and often led Greats students to believe that the ancient texts gave them sufficient knowledge without more practical experience. After Asquith's death, historian R. B. McCallum commented on this problem with Asquith's Greats education. Acknowledging that Asquith after leaving Oxford assimilated vast amounts of factual information on modern history, law, and economics, nevertheless McCallum believes that Asquith suffered from a "characteristic vice of Greats training," that is, "a too formal and critical approach to living questions, an over-proud reliance on intellectual analysis as compared with experience." This might have "fortified him against fads and fallacies," but it also "narrowed the range of his vision and excluded important considerations from his view."[29]

Some historians downplay Oxford's influence on Asquith thinking, particularly the role of two of his most important teachers, Benjamin Jowett and T. H. Green. They argue that either Asquith had for the most part already formed many of his ideas and goals or his ability to integrate these two professors' rival views demonstrates that neither teacher had great influence.[30] Yet Asquith's later professional and political career mirrors so much of Jowett's and Green's teachings. This could hardly be coincidental.

Asquith never had Jowett as a tutor, but he did have lengthy contact with him at breakfasts and long walks, and the master's influence on his charge is readily apparent. Jowett's personal view of life and the role of education, as one of his former students observed, "represented a certain moral and mental attitude not just of Balliol but to the age in general."[31] At its core were the Victorian notions of progress and control. The possibilities of human improvement were endless, and with self-discipline one could, to some degree, direct one's destiny. Jowett's biographer, Sir Geoffrey Faber, has noted how he emphasized to his students the "power over self: power in a man to control and drive his own life, instead of drifting on the currents of fortune and self-indulgence."[32] Jowett instilled in his students the potential of the possible. He had no admiration for the ineffective, head-in-the-clouds person whose insistence on principle only leads to failure. It may well be true that Jowett's views were, to a great extent, those of the Victorian age in general; nevertheless, Jowett was an important conduit of these ideas to Asquith who adopted them wholeheartedly. Like most Liberals, Asquith saw almost unlimited possibilities for improvement. Success to Asquith came from disciplined work, and there was almost always a matter-of-fact, practical tone to Asquith's efforts.

Asquith studied directly under T. H. Green. While Jowett's influence at the university was waning, Green's was on the ascendancy, and he ultimately became one of Oxford's most famous philosophers of the nineteenth century. Influenced by German idealists, he challenged the eighteenth-century empiricists and argued a philosophical idealism combined with a mild rationalistic optimism. To Green, human action could not simply be the result of natural forces. Rather, any intelligible system must imply that a person not only knows what to do but also has the power to do it. These views transformed Green into a reformer who believed in a direct correlation between ethical potential and community service. The first Oxford don to be elected to the Oxford City Council, Green urged his students to lead lives of service, so that their fellow citizens could realize their own human potential.[33]

Those who minimize Green's influence on Asquith have put too much weight on Asquith's one statement that, although he owed "more than I can say to Green's gymnastics, both intellectual and moral," he never "worshipped at the Temple's inner shrine."[34] Asquith was referring to Green's system of philosophical idealism, and he looked sceptically at Green's more abstract ideas—or anyone else's for that matter. As Asquith wrote in lines immediately following his denial of worshiping at Green's inner shrine, "My own opinions on these high matters have never been more than those of an interested amateur."[35] Though Asquith sided much more with Jowett's realism than with Green's idealism, he owed much to Green. Harold Laski, for example, in a conversation with Asquith years later became convinced that Balliol had prepared Asquith for the social legislation he introduced while leading the Liberal Party.[36] While Asquith might not have accepted Green's philosophical idealism in its entirety, Asquith's political career shows that he fully accepted the philosopher's ethical call for civic service in response to the needs of the people.

Much in Asquith's early years worked to define his character and worldview. Although he came from a respectable middle-class family and was educated at Oxford, most of Asquith's experiences as a youth can be best described as those of an "outsider." Being slightly different was in his blood. Both his nonconformist paternal and maternal families, dating back over a century, had never minded their alienation from the established church and took pride in what might even be called unorthodox religious zealotry. It must have seemed to the young Asquith only natural to have been schooled in Moravian educational institutions and the untraditional City of London School. Closely connected to this religious nonconformity was his introduction at a very early age to a general openness in both thought and action. Whether it was the religious toleration of the City of London School or the broad admissions policy of Balliol, the institutions which molded Asquith were well ahead of their time in notions of education and inclusion. Even though Asquith made friends among his intellectual equals at Oxford, he never appears to have been accepted by his social superiors. He knew what it was like to be an outsider and, as a result, came to appreciate openness and inclusion. This translated itself into what one contemporary recalled as Asquith's unique ability to give "freshness and point to everything he discussed" and to demonstrate a "freedom from vanity and self-consciousness."[37] A minor yet telling incident illustrates this point. As President of the Oxford Union, Asquith had the power to appoint the organization's secretary. Instead of choosing one of "the Clique" or another popular student, in a surprise to everyone, he nominated an outsider, a young Canadian who had just come to Oxford for a year or two as a "non-collegiate student."[38]

We also see in Asquith's early years the beginnings of Greek and Roman stoicism that so much defined his personality as an adult. The impact of the sudden death of his father and the later death of his grandfather, events that abruptly changed his life, must have been jarring and disappointing. Despite this, there is no record of complaint, and Asquith did not leave us with personal philosophical reflections from which we might discern the origins of his stoicism. Perhaps it was the evangelical influence of seeing all events as the will of God. If so, Asquith certainly had this fatalistic notion reinforced in his reading of the Greek and Roman stoic writers while at both the City of London School and Oxford. Whatever the source, Asquith left his youth armed with a fatalistic stoicism that would become his hallmark in the years to come.

On a much more practical level, by the end of his youth Asquith had discovered and sharpened his natural talent at debate and public speaking. Almost from the very beginning of his taking part in public speaking activities, he displayed a remarkable precociousness and talent. Dr. Abbott, who had the habit of correcting papers while chairing meetings of the debating society of the City of London School, found that, as Asquith developed his speaking talents, grading papers when the young man spoke "became more and more difficult, and finally, whenever he entered the lists of orators I resigned myself to a willing attention, and was content to take my exercises away with me uncorrected."[39] Debating time and time again before the Oxford Union only sharpened his natural talent even more. By the time he left Oxford, he was an experienced and polished public speaker, and it was upon this talent that Asquith laid the foundation for both his legal and political careers.

Asquith ended his Oxford days on the top of the heap. He was one of five students and the only Balliol student to receive a "first" in Greats at the university in 1874.[40] In Asquith's mind, the only "serious disappointment" of his academic career was his failure two years in a row to receive the famed Ireland Prize in classics.[41] Even so, he was awarded the Craven Scholarship and was elected to a Balliol fellowship. With no intention of pursing an academic career, his scholarship and fellowship did provide him with enough income for relaxation. It was a quiet and delightful time. He took on a few students, began to examine Gibbon, and for a brief period was a tutor to Lord Lymington, eldest son of the Earl of Portsmouth. Residing with the Earl's family at Hourstbourne Park in Hampshire or at Eggsford Palace in north Devon, he obtained "a glimpse of a kind of life which was new to me."[42] There were also reading parties with his friends and even the opportunity to learn to play golf, a passion that remained with Asquith for the rest of his life. Describing these reading parties, his friend Herbert Warren wrote, "We consumed vast quantities of Scotch viands, especially raspberry tarts, shortbread and whisky and water. The smokers smoked, the whist players played whist, and one and all we talked as ever, interminably, on all things human and divine."[43] Asquith knew these delightful days were numbered; he had the profession of law and a passion for politics to pursue.

NOTES

1. William Smith, *Rambles About Morley with Descriptive and Historic Sketches* (London: John Russell Smith, 1866), v.
2. Frank Elias, *The Right Hon. H.H. Asquith, MP: A Biography and Appreciation* (London: James Clarke, 1909), 12.
3. Clyde Binfield, *So Down to Prayers: Studies in English Nonconformity 1780–1920* (London: J. M. Dent & Sons, 1977), 149.
4. Earl of Oxford and Asquith, *Memories and Reflections 1852–1927*, vol. 1 (Boston: Little Brown, 1926), 6.
5. Spender and Asquith, *Life of Asquith*, 1:19.
6. Asquith, *Memories*, 1:9.
7. Ibid., 1:14.
8. BL, MS. Bonham Carter 638, ff. 3–4.
9. BL, HHA exercise book, MS. Bonham Carter 639.
10. HHA to Emily Asquith, 21 Nov. 1866, BL, MS. Bonham Carter 636, ff. 50–51.
11. Asquith, *Memories*, 1:14.
12. A. E. Douglas-Smith, *The City of London School* (Oxford: Basil Blackwell, 1965), 175.
13. Spender and Asquith, *Life of Asquith*, 27.
14. Douglas-Smith, *City of London School*, 170.
15. HHA to Emily Asquith, 19 Sept. 1866, BL, MS. Bonham Carter 636, ff. 46–47.
16. Douglas-Smith, *City of London School*, 187.
17. Ibid., 185.
18. Ibid., Preface.
19. John Prest, "Balliol, For Example," in M. G. Brock and M. C. Curthoys, eds., *The Nineteenth Century*, vol. 7, part 2 of *The History of the University of Oxford* (Oxford: Clarendon Press, 2000), 163.

20. John Jones, *Balliol College: A History, 1263–1939* (Oxford: Oxford University Press, 1988), 224.

21. Prest, "Balliol, For Example," 163.

22. J. P. Alderson, *Mr. Asquith* (London: Methuen, 1905), 11.

23. W. H. Mallock, *Memoirs of Life and Literature* (London: Chapman and Hall, 1920), 51.

24. M. G. Brock, "A 'Plastic Structure,'" in Brock and Curthoys, *The Nineteenth Century*, 63.

25. Alderson, *Mr. Asquith*, 19.

26. Ibid., 21.

27. W. H. Walsh, "The Zenith of Greats," in Brock and Curthoys, *The Nineteenth Century*, 316.

28. These books are in the possession of the author.

29. R. B. McCallum, *Asquith* (London: Duckworth, 1936), 16.

30. Jenkins, *Asquith*, 11–23; Koss, *Asquith*, 6.

31. Mallock, *Memoirs*, 61.

32. Sir Geoffrey Faber, *Jowett: A Portrait with a Background* (London: Farber & Farber, 1957), 359.

33. Melvin Ricter, *The Politics of Conscience: T.H. Green and His Age* (Cambridge, MA: Harvard University Press, 1964), 134.

34. Asquith, *Memories*, 1:24.

35. Ibid.

36. Ricter, *Politics of Conscience*, 294–95.

37. Herbert Paul to Violet Asquith, 19 Feb. 1928, BL, MS. Bonham Carter 208, ff. 45–47.

38. Alderson, *Mr. Asquith*, 21.

39. Ibid., 9.

40. *Oxford University Journal*, no. 167, 18 June 1874, 141.

41. Asquith, *Memories*, 1:25.

42. Ibid., 31.

43. Alderson, *Mr. Asquith*, 29.

Chapter Two

Early Legal Career and Election to Parliament (1875–1892)

By the time Asquith completed his studies at Oxford, he had clearly fallen in love with politics. He also realized that he had to support himself financially and never considered earning a living by doing anything other than practicing law. Yet he always viewed the law as merely a convenient *occupation* to make possible the *career* he sought as a politician. The law was a common gateway into politics in the Victorian era, especially for those like Asquith who came from a comparatively humble background. Almost a fifth of all the Cabinet Ministers in the nineteenth century had been called to the Bar. If the route was clear, it was not without substantial obstacles, especially for a man with little means and few connections. Asquith knew this. Success was by no means assured, and he might just have easily opted for the less unpredictable academic career that awaited him. Yet apparently without the least hesitation and with a large dose courage and confidence he set off to practice law.

Fortunately, the young Oxford graduate had acquired a number of traits necessary for a successful law career. Edward Cox, in *The Advocate, His Training, Practice, Rights, and Duties,* published in 1852, outlined what he termed the "physical," "intellectual," and "pecuniary" qualifications for a successful law practice. A prospective barrister needed "a healthy frame, capable of enduring long-continued exertion of mind and body" ready to endure five hours of sleep and irregular meals. The judgment, the ability to reason "combined with a quality of quickness," together with imagination "to give shape to thoughts, to infuse the glow of colour into expression, and to make words pictures" were essential. He also mentioned a need for "perception," which he defined in terms of a "keenness of observation" and a "clearness and quickness of comprehension." Finally, Cox spoke of the need for a propensity for "courage, self-confidence, cautiousness, and firmness."[1] None of these requirements presented Asquith with the least difficulty. His strong constitution knew virtually no illness throughout his entire life, and hardly a sharper mind than his came out of Oxford or Cambridge in his generation. As for caution, this seems to have been thrown to the wind in his decision to practice law, all the while demonstrating a high degree of courage, self-confidence, and firmness.

The problem was money. An article entitled "The Bar and Its Prospects" in the *Oxford Undergraduate Journal* during Asquith's first term at Balliol described the hurdle. It frankly warned undergraduates that it was a mistake to enter the Bar without "independent means." Noting that only four or so out of every twenty who enter the Bar earn their own livelihood in the first fifteen years of practice, the article concluded, "Years, perhaps twenty, of disappointment, of hopes never realized, of scanty living, have told the tale on the heart of that young lawyer."[2] Edward Cox's manual confirmed this dismal prospect, claiming that only twenty in the entire history of the Bar made it without "an assured income, sufficient at the least for a maintenance, possessed by them independently of their Profession."[3]

Asquith became a student at Lincoln's Inn in November 1875 and had to pass a general examination, a requirement instituted in the year he began his studies. Apparently there is no record of Asquith's score on the examination, but in light of his outstanding academic performance at Oxford, there is little reason to believe he had any difficulty in passing.

As a further part of his preparation to be called to the Bar, toward the end of the summer of 1875 Asquith took lodgings in Mount Street with his close friends, Herbert Paul and Thomas Raleigh, and began to read law as a pupil of Charles Bowen. "Pupilage" had long been a common practice among the Bar. Students, as well as young barristers, would spend some time under the tutelage of more senior members of the Bar. The amount of time spent as a pupil varied, although two years was often recommended. The usual fee, payable in advance, was a hundred guineas a year. Soon after beginning his pupilage, Asquith wrote to his uncle, J. W. Willans, that he would remain with Bowen until the next summer when he would "be able to judge better than I can now whether any further preparation is necessary, before I begin to practice on my own account."[4] Asquith must have considered himself lucky to work with Bowen, considered to be one of the rising stars of the Bar. Originally from Gloucestershire and educated at Rugby, Bowen like Asquith was one of the superior products produced by Balliol and unlike Asquith had won the coveted Hertford and Ireland prizes. He went on to become a Lord Justice of Appeals before his untimely death at the age of only fifty-nine in 1894.

A pupil drew conveyances, prepared pleadings, and wrote opinions for the barrister. Students were warned to deal with these matters "just as if they formed a piece of work which his own client had delivered for him to do" and to spend "as much care and trouble on them as if his reputation with his own clients depended on the result."[5] Bowen could be a hard taskmaster. "There were few things more disheartening, when one was summoned to his inner room," Asquith later recalled, "than to see the 'pleading,' over which one had perhaps spent hours of industry and research, cancelled page after page and rewritten by his pen, or worse still, lying in fragments in the wastepaper basket."[6]

The "better opinion" was that a student should spend at least two years as a pupil, yet a little less than a year after beginning his pupilage, Asquith decided that he was ready to be "called to the Bar," an ancient term that appears to have come from the custom of summoning students, once they had reached a certain standing, to the bar that separated the Benchers' dais from the rest of the hall of the inn of court. To be "called to the Bar" meant that you could actually appear in court as opposed to being merely "admitted" to the Bar. Even so, in 1885 only 38 percent of those "called" to the Bar actually actively practiced in the courts.[7] During Asquith's time, "call night" was an elaborate occasion when the student's gown without sleeves was removed and replaced with that of a barrister. Wearing their wigs for the first time, the new barristers would then process single file into the hall of their Inn and sign their names in a book. As one described the occasion at Lincoln's Inn, "newly called Barristers take desert and wine with the Benchers; the senior Bencher present proposes their health and then the Benchers retire and leave those called to spend the evening together."[8]

Despite being called to the Bar in a relatively short period of time, Asquith was about to enter one of the most difficult and frustrating periods of his life. After briefly having his chambers in the Temple and Hare Court, he joined with his friends and fellow pupils of Bowen, Henry Cunynghame and Mark Napier, in sharing chambers at No. 6 Fig Tree Court. They were an interesting group. Cunynghame, after a brief military career, attended Cambridge where he received a degree before reading for the Bar. A brilliant mathematician and linguist, according to Asquith, Cunynghame never developed an extensive practice because of his "versatility of faculties and interests." Napier was also a Cambridge man and, much like Cunynghame, did not overextend himself at the practice of law. After a while he left the law and eventually became the chairman of Reuters news agency. These chambers with Cunynghame and Napier became, in Asquith's words, his "professional workshop" for the next seven years.[9]

In referring to his chambers as a "professional workshop," Asquith was for the most part exaggerating, since actually he had, as he himself admitted, little professional work during this period. "For the first five or six years at the Bar" he explained, "my practice was small, intermittent, and from a material point of view neither productive nor promising."[10] Of course, he was not alone in this regard. Sir Charles Biron, a noted barrister of the day, reflecting on his first years of practice, observed, "No one who has been though it can realize the depression of waiting day after day, young and eager for work that never come." Some said that Charles Bowen, Asquith's tutor, would never walk by the chambers where he started his practice because it brought back such sad memories.[11] Although some have suggested that Asquith's penury during this stage in his life has been exaggerated, there is no doubt that these were difficult times, and ultimate success at the Bar must have seemed far, far away.[12]

Many of Asquith's early difficulties may have been of his own making. There was an unwritten rule that, in order to survive and advance your practice, it was necessary to take whatever briefs came your way no matter how small or insignificant. As the *Punch* jingle put it,

> He fareth best who loveth best
> All fees both great and small.
> For the Bench declares that the etiquette
> Of the Bar is "Pocket All."[13]

Asquith did not follow this advice or at least did not follow it as aggressively as other young barristers, for he preferred not just any business but "good" business.[14] The critical question for him was what was the best way to attract such clients? He faced the dilemma of developing a reputation by either accepting work that he felt was beneath his talents or holding out for the better briefs. For the most part, Asquith took the risk of holding out. Such a course also meant that he would have to shy away as much as he could from going on circuit unless, of course, there was a brief for which he would be exceptionally well paid. London barristers became the well paid specialists, while those on circuit tended to become general practitioners. The best barristers stayed in London.

As expected, legal fees in the early years of practice were meagre. Thomas Blofeld, called to the Bar in 1862, reported that his total income, including supplemental income from writing for the *Solicitor's Journal*, grew from £5 in 1862 to only £116 five years later.[15] Another important barrister of the period Sir Frank Lockwood earned 120 guineas in 1872, his first year of practice, yet that figure had increased to 600 guineas by 1875.[16] Almost certainly Asquith received some support from his family, and he never claimed to have totally supported himself during his early years as a barrister. His wife had a small income, he earned money writing for various publications and from an occasional lecture, and he probably received some support from his Willans relations. It is safe to assume that the amount earned from legal work was small in these early years, based upon the experiences of so many other young barristers. In Asquith's case, the lean years did not last long. In his pocket diary for 1881 under the heading "Cash Account—Received," Asquith lists a total income for the year of just over £831. He was already earning a rather handsome sum for a barrister called to the Bar only five years earlier.[17]

What is known about Asquith's early law practice is what he himself reported in his memoirs. He had a "normal practice [that] was almost entirely on the civil side in London," and, after a short period of a "fairly regular appearance at the Leeds Assize," he discontinued his practice on the circuit. Since his practice was small in these early years, some of his hours were spent educating himself in the law. He read a great deal at the Lincoln's Inn library. For "recreation" he would spend a morning watching Sir George Jessel at the Rolls Court in Chancery, even though he did not have much of a chancery practice. He also attempted to write a treatise on Mercantile Law, which he never finished, and taught several courses on commercial law to the Incorporated Law Society.[18]

For someone with Asquith's ambition and talents, these early years were surely trying. He was a proud young man with dreams of a bright future, knowing success at the bar would not come quickly. He would have to earn his stripes. One can imagine the hurt he must have felt by an Oxford don's comment about the university system reported in *The New Review*. "The worst of our system . . . ," the don wrote "is that nobody ever hears anything of our crack men. Look at Asquith! What a career he had here, and now his name is never mentioned."[19] Years later in 1892, in one of his most revealing letters, Asquith wrote to his close friend, Lady Frances Horner, about these lean years. He described the feeling of having "the capacity for power and yet that you have no field to exercise it" and reflected that "no one who has not been through it can know the chilling, paralyzing, deadening, depression of hope dashed and energy wasted and vitality run to seed." It was a monotonous routine. "I went by the train to the Temple, and sat and worked and dreamed in my chambers, and listened with feverish expectation for a knock at the door, hoping it might be a client with a brief."[20]

A bright spot in Asquith's life during these difficult years was his marriage to Helen Kelsall Melland in 1877. Seven years before, Helen and her sister, Josephine, were visiting their Kelsall cousins at St. Leonards-on-Sea in East Sussex, when she first met Asquith, whose family happened to be friends of the Kelsalls. Helen came from a nonconformist Liberal family similar to Asquith's. Her father, Dr. Frederick Melland, a prominent physician in Manchester and Resident Surgeon at the Manchester Royal Infirmary, was a Liberal and strongly supported free trade and repeal of the Corn Laws. One of the highlights of this first meeting was the two families' amateur theatrical production of "The Cares of State," written by none other than Asquith, himself, who played the lead role of a Prime Minister during a national crisis in which the Chancellor of the Exchequer allowed everything to be stolen including the national debt.[21]

Little is known of Asquith and Helen's courtship. Asquith's letters to Helen were all destroyed at her death, most probably by Asquith himself.[22] There only remain some of Helen's letters to him. Asquith was taken by the fifteen-year-old Helen from their first meeting, and they were secretly engaged several years later during Asquith's last year at Oxford. For two years they maintained their secret. Finally in September 1876 Asquith sought Dr. Melland's approval for the marriage, an approval far from certain to Asquith who had only recently embarked on his legal career and had not yet established himself as a member of the Bar. Despite his hesitancy to approach Dr. Melland, he told his sister, "I found him very reasonable and kind, and though he would not sanction a formal engagement until we are a little better acquainted, he practically gave his consent to the whole thing." A month later Dr. Melland wrote to the young barrister telling him that he had made "certain inquiries" that had satisfied him to give his consent to the marriage of his daughter.[23]

Helen wrote Asquith letters almost daily throughout the engagement, sometimes twice a day filled with lines of affection referring to him as "my pet" and telling him how she longed "to be the wife of the noblest dearest man in the whole world." For Valentine's Day she sent him a printed check from "Lover's Banking Company" to pay on demand her entire love, signed "Cupid."[24] A letter written to Josephine well before the couple's formal engagement provides more telling evidence of Helen's sincere love. The envelope is marked to be opened upon Helen's death, and she instructs her sister in such case to send to Asquith a diamond ring, a bookcase, an edition of Thackeray's works, and £1,000 as a token of her love for him.[25]

After their wedding on August 23, 1877, held at the Mellands' Congregational Church, the young couple established themselves in London at Eaton House, a cream-colored Georgian house in Hampstead, immediately across the street from the house where the poet John Keats had once lived. The life of the Asquiths at Hamstead reflects that of an ordinary middle-class Victorian family. Helen was far from an heiress, but she did have a private income of a few hundred pounds a year, and this enabled the newlyweds to enjoy a slightly better life than they could otherwise have afforded. Fourteen months after their marriage, in November 1878 Helen gave birth to their first child, Raymond, followed with the births of Herbert ("Beb") in 1881 and Arthur ("Oc") in 1883.

Asquith has often been described as having a somewhat cold personality, rarely expressing emotion. Reminiscences of those who knew him during the years at Hampstead paint quite a different picture. As his law practice grew, of course, he became more and more preoccupied with his career, but Asquith could always compartmentalize his affairs. As his son Beb recalled, when he came home, he discarded "his black coat and with it the weight of professional cares, which he seemed to keep in a compartment of their own, the door of which he could lock and bolt and open again, when the time came to deal with them. . . ."[26] What we see is a loving father bringing home fireworks, watching cricket at Lord's, playing chess, and going with Helen and the boys to the zoo on occasion.[27] He was a voracious reader with a special interest in biography. In one letter he reported that he had waded through Samuel Smiles's *Life of George Moore* "without weariness, but it is about three times too long. . . ."[28] Asquith never really enjoyed music, rarely attending concerts, but he did relish the theater, even though there were occasional disappointments, and he could be a harsh critic. He dismissed H. A. Jones's "Dancing Girls" as "stupid and nasty."[29]

The Asquiths employed a nonconformist nurse "of rather rigid principles" to care for their children; yet as with many parents who revolt against their own upbringing, Asquith rebelled against the rules of strict Victorian child raising. Again, according to Beb, he never showed "any inclination to interfere with the freedom of his children: on the contrary, his attitude was usually one of mellow and spacious indulgence. . . ."[30] Nevertheless, Asquith always followed the affairs of his children, and when Asquith moved to the center stage of law and politics and his children were off at school, he found time to write them once a week. He visited Raymond in school at Winchester in the middle of a cabinet crisis in 1893, and his diary records with pride that "R. came back from school—3 prizes."[31]

For the most part, the Asquiths' social circle remained nonconformist in the Hamstead years, but Asquith was already beginning to move away from his nonconformist faith as he widened his circle of acquaintances. He never became a regular member of the new Congregational church in Lyndhurst Road in Hamstead, even though he did take an active interest in its affairs, joining with local residents in inviting a fellow of New College, Oxford, Robert Horton, to become minister. The two men soon became friends, and Asquith always admired Horton's efforts to have his church work in poorer areas of London.[32]

A much more significant friendship began in the beginning of 1882 with Richard Burdon Haldane. They first met at a dinner at Lincoln's Inn. Haldane was ill, and Asquith graciously invited the bachelor to convalesce at the Asquith home. This sealed the friendship. After his recovery, Haldane became

Asquith's best friend, and they saw each other almost every day and dined together once or twice a week.

Haldane was four years younger than Asquith. The grandson of the religious writer James Alexander Haldane, he received his early education at the Edinburgh Academy. His parents wished to send him to Balliol, but as strict Presbyterians, they were concerned over the Anglican influence at Oxford. Instead Haldane attended the universities of Gottingen and Edinburgh, receiving a first-class degree in philosophy. The two young barristers shared many interests—literature, law, and, most important, Liberal politics. Haldane became the closest friend Asquith ever had.

Even with his wife's small private income, Asquith's could not support himself and his family as he wished. Between 1877 and 1885, he wrote a weekly leader for *The Economist* until 1885 for which he was paid £150 a year, but unfortunately since the articles were unsigned and the records of *The Economist* were destroyed in World War II, there is unfortunately no way to discover which articles Asquith actually wrote for the publication.[33]

As early as 1875, he began to write for *The Spectator*, which was owned by Meredith Townsend and Richard Holt Hutton, a friend of Prime Minister Gladstone. Asquith fit in easily with the Liberal bent of *The Spectator*, which had made much of its reputation for attacks on Benjamin Disraeli. Writing for the publication until 1884 when he parted ways over Irish Home Rule, Asquith churned out over forty entries averaging about 2,000 words each on a broad range of subjects from the spread of ruffianism to a remedy for undependable trains. In all these pieces he demonstrated a clear and concise style with an easy flow of argument. The scholarly Asquith's attention to detail is evident. In his review of a new translation of *Annals of Tacitus*, he chides the authors for translating "*duas foenoris partes*" as "two-thirds of the principal" when it should be rendered "two thirds of his capital."[34] Some, including his wife, found his production rather boring. "Herbert has an article in the Spectator this week," she wrote her sister, "but I don't think I will read it, it is so dry he has promised me two guineas for reading it carefully through."[35] He also wrote on legal subjects and issues dealing with the court system, such as civil procedure reform, in addition to obituaries of justices.

By far the most important articles were those on political issues where we first get a picture of Asquith's political beliefs. As H. G. C. Matthew in his review of *The Spectator* articles discovered, these early glimpses of Asquith's political views reveal a pattern that he followed for his entire political career. No matter what the political subject, Asquith tended to support the radical position but always with a tempering dose of realism. To Asquith, both radical and Whig wings of the Liberal Party were critical to its success, and party unity was to be valued above all else.[36] In his fourth article, "The English

Extreme Left," he urged the radicals to remain with the Whigs in the Liberal Party. "By voluntarily severing themselves from the Whig," he wrote "they lose their chance of leavening the Party lump," and, he warned, "Yeast without dough is no better than dough without yeast to a nation which wants bread."[37]

Asquith's breakthrough in his law practice came in 1883 when one of the leading barristers of the day, R. S. Wright, asked him to join his chambers. It has been suggested that none other than Joseph Chamberlain mentioned Asquith to Wright, who was serving as Chamberlain's counsel.[38] Whether or not this is the case—Asquith never acknowledged the fact in his memoirs— Wright may have been attracted to the young barrister for other reasons. Like Asquith, Wright was a classical scholar from Balliol and was one of Benjamin Jowett's favorites. The move to Wright's chambers at this particular time was a real coup for Asquith, because Attorney General Sir Henry James, had recently appointed Wright to the "blue ribbon" position of the junior Bar, that is, Counsel to the Treasury or otherwise known as "the Attorney-General's devil." This meant that Wright had more work than he himself could possibly handle. And so "without any pangs of regret," Asquith moved to Wright's chambers at 1 Paper Buildings in 1883.[39] These premises remained his professional home until his permanent retirement from the Bar in 1905, with the exception of a brief interlude as Home Secretary.

At first, Asquith's work was merely that of "devil" for Wright, that is, assisting the senior barrister in preparation of cases. He also frequently worked at the Attorney General's room in the Law Courts. In addition, Wright had already developed a favorable reputation among the solicitors while representing some of the great railway companies of the day, and much of his practice involved them. Over time, these solicitors gradually got to know the young Asquith and eventually began to give work directly to him, including many cases involving judicial interpretations of provisions of the new Railway and Canal Traffic Act.[40] By the end of 1886, Asquith found he "had the nucleus of a substantial and growing practice of my own."[41]

An expanding client base allowed Asquith to concentrate on the type of practice he liked best—non-jury and appellate work. As his former pupil, John Roskill, recalled, Asquith "did not much care for jury work as he disliked repetition and was impatient of platitudes."[42] According to another great barrister of the day, Charles Russell, Asquith could never "play down" to a jury.[43] With only barely disguised disdain, Asquith himself later related that his practice was "rarely concerned in the more sensational class of litigation which excites the man-in-the-street, and is exploited by the Press."[44] What Asquith truly enjoyed was the role of the advocate, and again according to Roskill, "his mastery of legal principles and of their expression found abundant scope in the non-jury and Appellate Courts."[45]

Some of his most interesting and lucrative cases were tried before the Judicial Committee of the Privy Council, the ultimate Court of Appeal from all parts of the Empire. Along with Haldane, over the years Asquith became one of the best known barristers to handle this type of case, many of which came from India. "I have been fighting hard in the Privy Council for the last two days," he wrote, in a case "between the United States on the one side and Canada on the other." As Asquith told it, "I was for Canada, but I'm afraid the Yankees will win...."[46]

After his practice began to expand, most of Asquith's days were busy with hard work. "Business here is tolerantly brisk," he wrote his uncle in 1887.[47] What made his practice interesting, as with most barristers, was that there was no such thing as a typical case. "I got up at 7 this morning in order to get to London from Althrop in time for my work," he wrote his wife in a typical letter. "I have argued two cases, one in the Privy Council and one in the House of Lords, and since then have had two long consultations."[48] Much of this everyday work Asquith found interesting and rewarding, yet some work he did for the fees paid. After an appearance before the Licensing Committee of the County Council, he confessed, "I was well paid but I don't think I will repeat the experience."[49] He also characterized one of his cases where he was representing the Great Western Railway as "devoid of human interest."[50]

Some cases were more interesting, as when Asquith prosecuted Henry Vizetelly, the London publisher of the novels of Emile Zola, for obscenity. All questionable passages had to be contained verbatim in the indictment. Asquith spent a good part of one holiday "with scissors and pot of paste at hand, in a diligent quest for the most objectionable passages."[51] There was no public trial, and Vizetelly got off with a plea of guilty and the payment of a £100 fine.

A review of the case reports turns up a number of more mundane law suits in which Asquith acted as counsel. Take for instance *Carlill v. The Carbolic Smoke Ball Company*.[52] In this case Asquith represented the company that manufactured a "medical preparation" called a smoke ball. The company advertised in the *Pall Mall Gazette* a £100 reward "to any person who contracts the increasing epidemic influenza colds, or any disease by taking cold, after having used the ball three times daily for two weeks." Mrs. Carlill sued for the reward, having used the product as instructed but still contracted the flu. In the non-jury trial Asquith made several arguments including the clever technical assertion that, even if a contract did exist, it was void under the anti-gambling statutes or was void as an illegal contract of insurance. The trial judge, as well as the appellate court, were not impressed with Asquith's defense and awarded damages to Mrs. Carlill.

Before Asquith became Home Secretary in 1892, there were occasions when special cases or events advanced not only his practice but also his political career. In 1883, for example, the Gladstone government found itself bogged down in what became known as the "Bradlaugh" case. Charles Bradlaugh, a radical republican and, as if that was not enough, an atheist and founder of the National Secular Society, was first elected to Parliament for Northampton in 1880. As an avowed atheist, he was not allowed to take the oath of allegiance and serve. The Liberals attempted to allow his seating with the introduction of an Affirmation Bill. Gladstone turned to his Attorney General, Sir Henry James, and asked for a memorandum detailing the history of the oath of allegiance and otherwise, in Asquith's words, "getting up the legal and historical side of the case." James turned to R. S. Wright and the assignment ended up with Asquith. He "devoted much time and care to the task," and when the memorandum was completed, it gave him "great satisfaction."[53] When James showed the memorandum to Gladstone, the Attorney General did not hide its authorship, and both men were well pleased with Asquith's work, moving the young barrister to the top of their watch list.

Another important opportunity for legal and political advancement was Asquith's authorship of a short manual on the workings of the Corrupt Practices Act of 1883.[54] One of the major achievements of Gladstone's second government was the passage of a Corrupt Practices Act aimed at cleaning up elections. The Attorney General suggested to Asquith that he put together a short manual for election officials to use in implementing the new act at the next election. By March 1884, Asquith was able to write to his uncle, "As to the Corrupt Practices Act my little treatise is now finished," and it was soon published by the Liberal Central Association in 1884.[55] *An Election Guide* was an overwhelming success.[56] As might be expected, the general election of 1885, the first under the new law, brought a number of challenges. With his book now making Asquith an "expert" in the field, most Liberal candidates retained him as their counsel.

Asquith's first real public notoriety as a barrister, however, came in 1887. Although he did not do much criminal work, in that year he agreed to defend Cunninghame Graham, a fellow Member of Parliament (Asquith had been elected in 1886), who had been charged with "unlawful assembly" in Trafalgar Square. The Commissioner of Police, with the backing of the Conservative Government's Home Secretary, Henry Matthews, issued a prohibition against a labor demonstration in Trafalgar Square. Graham, along with John Burns, ignored the prohibition, and both were arrested on what became known in labor circles as "Bloody Sunday." Burns represented himself at trial. Despite Asquith's efforts, the jury found both men guilty, and the court sentenced them to six weeks in prison. Reports of the trial filled the papers, and Asquith was recognized by the Bar and the public at large as an important and well respected barrister of the day.

Of course, even as his law practice prospered, Asquith never gave up on his real interest—politics. From his days at Oxford, if not before, Asquith had no doubt that, if the opportunity ever presented itself, he would stand for Parliament. A colleague in his chambers commented that Asquith "looked upon the Bar as a means of livelihood and his ambition was for political, and not legal, promotion."[57] He was not alone in his ambition. Haldane had been elected to Parliament in 1885 as a Liberal for East Lothian. In that some election, Asquith's friend, Alfred Milner, had stood successfully as a Liberal candidate for Harrow, and Asquith spoke on his behalf. Over the years his contacts with the Gladstone government grew, and he had written many articles supporting the Liberal line. His own chance came in the June 1886. When Gladstone's First Irish Home Rule Bill was defeated with over ninety Liberals voting with the Tories to defeat the measure, Parliament was quickly dissolved, and an election called. The election would be a referendum on Gladstone's Irish policy with some Liberals who had opposed Home Rule running as "Liberal-Unionists."

Despite the opportunity, an opportunity he had long awaited, the decision to run required no little courage on Asquith's part. His law practice was picking up steam, but it had not reached full throttle. A premature decision to run before his practice could easily support him could prove financially disastrous.

On June 17, Helen reported to her sister that "delegations have rained down upon us asking Herbert to stand for various places." At first her husband "had quite made up his mind to resist temptation," but to her disappointment, he had been "bitten by the gadfly of ambition" and now wanted to run.[58] Haldane had made a strong case for him to stand for East Fife in Scotland. Only four days later, apparently Asquith once again changed his mind about running. "I am glad to tell you," Helen wrote her sister, "that Herbert is not standing for anywhere after all," even though he had refused "no less than nine seats, many of them perfectly safe."[59] The die, however, had not yet been cast. Helen's final report to her sister only two days later announced that "Herbert has been coerced into standing for East Fifshire after all & begins his campaign tomorrow."[60]

Composed of small villages in Asquith's day, Fife is a peninsula in eastern Scotland bordered on the east by the North Sea and the Firth of Forth to the south. The lairds of Fife with few exceptions were Tories whom Asquith described as "of the most reactionary and fossilized type."[61] His opponent, however, was not a Conservative at all but a Liberal, John Boyd Kinnear. Twenty-five years older than Asquith, Kinnear was a respected local barrister and legal and political writer. He had first been elected to Parliament only a year earlier but had joined with other Liberals in splitting with Gladstone over Irish Home Rule. As a result of Kinnear's disloyalty, the local Liberal association had certified Asquith as its candidate, and Kinnear was forced to run as a Liberal-Unionist.

It was a hard fight. Asquith retained as his agent the able Mr. Ketchen, a solicitor and banker in Elie, an important town in the district. Ketchen was close to the ground and careful to identify problems for his candidate. Once when Asquith announced plans to take the ferry across the Firth of Forth early one Sunday morning, Ketchen feared the loss of votes of Presbyterian Scots for violating the Sabbath. "I would rather you pay down £100," he pleaded, "than it should be known that you had used the ferry on the Sabbath Day!"[62]

Kinnear had the unquestionable advantage of being a relatively well-known local Scotsman, while his opponent was an unknown Englishman. When push came to shove though, Asquith had the greater advantage of being endorsed by the ever popular Gladstone. "I regard with great interest the canditure of Mr. Asquith," Gladstone wired, "whom I believe to be very highly qualified to uphold in this great struggle the honour of Scotland and the unity of the Empire, gainst those who seem to be to be little able to comprehend either one or the other."[63] Asquith received an added boost from local endorsements. The *Dundee Advertiser* asserted that "In clearness of statement, cogency or argument and effectiveness of illustration" it had yet to see Asquith surpassed.[64]

On polling day, Asquith won by a close but not uncomfortable margin, receiving almost 54 percent of the votes cast. When he returned to Hamstead after the exhausting campaign, his wife and children greeted by him with a banner emblazoned with large vermilion letters "Welcome, M. P."[65]

Asquith's first electoral trial was over, but his speaking debut in Parliament did not occur until nine months later in March 1887. The occasion was the debate on the Conservative government's attempt to put forward yet again another Irish coercion bill. In attacking the Conservatives' measure, Asquith had to argue against a measure similar to one supported by his own party and its leader only a few years before. He solved this problem with candor. Admitting that the earlier Liberal coercion act was a "colossal and disastrous mistake," he asked why Parliament "should repeat the blunder," especially when they only faced a "manufactured crisis," one that the "panic mongers of the Press" had created.[66]

With the Conservatives in power, the bill ultimately passed, but the response to Asquith's maiden speech was favorable. *The Times* reported the speech, and the *Birmingham Daily Post* wrote it was "an uncommonly good maiden speech."[67] Sir Edward Grey later commented that the House "listened to it as to the speech of a leader" and was "about the best 35 minutes I've ever heard, well delivered and fresh and strong to a degree."[68]

As Asquith began to learn how to maneuver his way in Parliament, he formed two groups of friends and associates. The first comprised older leaders of the Liberal Party who recognized his abilities and saw in him the potential for leadership. The other group included younger members of the party who shared with Asquith similar ideas about the future of Britain.

The foundation of Asquith's relationship with the leaders of the party was his exceptional intellect and talent. They noticed early on his capabilities, especially his strength as a speaker and debater in the House. Before his election Asquith had already made somewhat of a name for himself as a bright young barrister with some brilliant court appearances; yet such courtroom brilliance does not always easily convert itself into the ability to hold the attention of the House of Commons. "The outlook of the House is very different from the outlook of the Courts," commented Asquith to his friend Haldane. "If less scientific about details, the House of Commons' mind is wider."[69] Despite these differences, Asquith triumphed in the House from the very beginning. As Haldane noted, "His diction was then faultless, and his voice a powerful one. . . . He rarely made a bad point."[70] Surprisingly, even though he was an early success as a Parliamentary speaker, much of Asquith's reputation as a rhetorician was the result of speeches made outside Parliament. In the seven years between his election and his taking office as Home Secretary in 1892, he only spoke about a dozen times in the House of Commons and many were short speeches. More frequent were his speeches on the hustings with a much wider audience and press coverage. Asquith could whip up of the passions of Liberals with his eloquence, and Liberal leaders Sir William Harcourt, John Morley, and others asked him over and over again to address liberal groups.

It was more than just his eloquence that recommended Asquith to the leadership of the Liberal Party. As he had written in many of his *Spectator* articles, Asquith firmly believed that a key to successful Liberal action was party discipline. He had no time for those who broke ranks. Asquith came close to appearing like Sir Joseph Porter, a character in the popular Gilbert and Sullivan musical of the day, *H.M.S. Pinafore*, who proclaimed, "I always voted at my party's call, and I never thought of thinking for myself at all."[71] The party whips could always count on Asquith, even when his friends Haldane and Grey occasionally strayed from the fold.

Another group of Parliamentary friends among whom Asquith circulated was a collection of young Liberals his own age. Soon after his maiden speech, about a half a dozen of these young Liberal MPs began to coalesce around Asquith and look to him as their leader—Haldane, Grey, Sidney Buxton, Ronald Ferguson, Tom Ellis, Arthur Acland, and others. "They were a working alliance, not a school," as John Morley explained, and "they had idealism but were no Utopians." He added that they "had conscience, character, and took their politics to heart," and Haldane, Asquith, Grey, and Acland also "had the temper of men of the world, and the temper of business."[72]

What brought these men together in a common cause, according to Haldane, was Gladstone's continued lack of interest in social reform, together with the Liberal leadership's (except for Morley) failure to understand the reason for the group's discontent.[73] They sat and acted together in Parliament, and some were looked upon with suspicion by older members of the party. Asquith in his later years claimed the group, exaggerating somewhat to include himself, were regarded as "advanced" and "dangerous," and "inclined to mutiny by the orthodox and experienced greybeards of the Party."[74]

Asquith's loyalty to the party, however, was never really questioned, and Haldane, rather than Asquith, seems to have had greater influence on the group. Grey at the time acknowledged Haldane's influence when a depressed Haldane considered giving up politics. Grey wrote to him that his influence was difficult to measure because of its indirectness. Nevertheless, "If it were not for you," Grey wrote, "I do not think I should have even the hold on public life which I have now. . . . I should say for instance that Asquith owes some of the very best of himself to you. . . ."[75]

Another major influence on this group of young MPs was John Morley who published *On Compromise* in 1874, a clarion call for uncompromising reform, and this work most influenced Asquith and his young Liberal friends. Morley attacked "dwelling exclusively on practical compromises." Without such compromises, "The cause of social improvement would be less systematically balked of the victories that are best worth gaining." Morley made clear his belief in a Whig view of history where civilizations changed for the better and where older institutions were replaced "in favour of others of greater convenience and ampler capacity, at once multiplying and satisfying human requirements." He urged that change for the better be speeded up by avoiding compromise with incremental change. Small reforms he saw as the enemy of greater. "A small and temporary improvement may really be the worst enemy of great and permanent improvement, unless the first is made on the lines and direction of the second." Most importantly to Asquith and his young friends, Morley offered an attractive "progressive" liberalism. Institutions of the past "demand progressive adaptations," he urged. There must be an "equality of opportunity" with the "substitution of Justice as the governing idea instead of Privilege" with wide participation in the political process.[76]

Asquith shared with Morley more than a common political outlook; they were both almost incurable optimists. Much more than Haldane or Grey, Asquith and Morley genuinely believed that the possibilities for improvement of the nation were almost limitless. "The understanding between Asquith and me," Morley wrote in 1893, "from the intellectual and political point is almost perfect . . . we both have in different ways the *esprit positif.*"[77]

For a time Asquith and his Liberal friends even toyed with Fabian socialism, regularly attending Fabian meetings before 1892.[78] One of Beatrice Webb's diary entries describes a meeting with Haldane in 1890 in which he came "to arrange an alliance between the progressive liberals—Asquith, Sir Edward Grey, Arthur Acland and himself and the Fabian socialists," although she was not specific about the terms of the offer.[79] Within the Asquith group, it was Asquith himself who seemed most sceptical of the Fabians. After a follow-up meeting of some Fabians and the progressive liberals, Webb reported that, although the meeting was "pleasant and cordial," it was a failure. "Asquith spoilt it," she wrote, "He was the ablest of the lot, and determined that it should not 'go.'"[80]

It was neither the formation of the young Liberal group nor its ideology, however, that ultimately focused public attention on Asquith as a politician. Public attention burgeoned when, two years after his election, he found himself in the middle of one of the great political controversies of the day, a battle that allowed him to demonstrate his talents and worked to accelerate his already promising political career.

In the spring of 1887 the *Times* published a series of articles linking the Irish parliamentary leader, Charles Stewart Parnell, and others to crimes occurring in Ireland. Under the headline "Parnellism and Crime," the articles detailed connections between Parnell and various criminal incidents. As part of the series, the paper published a letter allegedly signed by Parnell. The letter was dated 15 May 1882, nine days after the infamous Phoenix Park murders, in which Lord Frederick Cavendish, Chief Secretary for Ireland and his undersecretary, Thomas Henry Burke, were killed in Dublin. Disturbingly, while the letter stated that a denunciation of the murders was "the only course open to us" and voiced regret at Cavendish's death, it also stated that "Burke got no more than his just deserts."[81] Parnell immediately and publicly condemned the letter as a forgery, but the letter and others by Irish leaders published in the *Times*' series enraged English public opinion.

Even though he denied the authenticity of the letters, Parnell refused to bring a libel action against the *Times* because he believed a fair hearing in an English court would be impossible. Many attributed his failure to take action to his guilt. One Irish ex-member of Parliament, Hugh O'Donnell, who was mentioned in the articles, did however sue the newspaper for libel. At the trial, Attorney General Sir Richard Webster, in private capacity representing the *Times*, introduced even more incriminating letters apparently written by Parnell. At this stage the Irish leader had no other choice but to try to defend himself in some forum. He immediately sought to have a Parliamentary select committee established, but the Conservative government blocked his efforts. Instead, the government established a special commission of three judges to investigate all the charges contained in the *Times'* exposé. Liberals objected. To Asquith, the idea of a commission was "singularly ill-conceived in the unfitness of the proposed tribunal for determination of such matters." Apparently other MPs believed the same way, and the Conservatives only carried the proposal by "a liberal use of the closure and guillotine." [82]

The commission sat for over four months in the autumn and winter of 1889–1890, with Parnell represented by a fellow Irishman and former Liberal Attorney General Sir Charles Russell. Why Asquith was asked to assist is unclear. Like Asquith, Russell was a member of Lincoln's Inn, and perhaps he had been impressed by Asquith's growing legal reputation and impeccable Liberal credentials. After the affair dragged on month after month, Asquith might well have questioned why he ever agreed to participate. He later remembered that in his entire life he had "never been engaged in any proceeding with which could compare with this for sustained dreariness and futile waste of time, lit up, on perhaps five or six days out of one hundred twenty-nine with scenes of poignant and unforgettable drama."[83]

The "unforgettable drama" occurred on two occasions. Russell and Asquith knew from the outset that the letters the *Times* published were forgeries and by whom they had been forged.[84] They wanted to get this fact out at the very beginning of the proceedings but were thwarted because they did not control the order of the witnesses. They had to bide their time until February, when Richard Pigott, a disreputable Irish journalist, who sold the letters to the *Times* was called to the stand. The former Attorney General was one of the premier barristers of his time, known particularly as a talented cross-examiner. After two days of grueling cross-examination, poor Pigott could take no more. Sir Charles destroyed him. Pigott wrote a note confessing that the letters were indeed forgeries and ran off to Spain where he later, when confronted with arrest, committed suicide.

Asquith's role in the drama came when the editor of the *Times*, Simon McDonald, stood waiting for cross-examination. Russell was to handle the cross examination; however, as the witness took the stand, Russell turned to a totally surprised Asquith and said, "You must deal with this fellow."[85] And deal with him he did. Asquith showed that he could equal even someone like Russell in the art of cross-examination. At the end of the day, McDonald left the stand humiliated. Asquith always fondly remembered these few hours of cross-examination as the greatest step he ever took in his forensic career.[86]

Unlike Russell, Asquith, as was his habit, was greatly concerned with the details of the case. To the Irishman Russell, the commission provided a great stage on which to expose English unfairness. Asquith kept his keen legal mind on the commission—indeed a commission that was unfavorable to the Irish cause—which would report specific findings to Parliament. As the commission drew to a close, Asquith prepared a detailed summary of all the evidence for Russell to use in his summation. Russell initially rejected it out of hand, boasting that he intended to cast his summation "on broad imaginative lines, and to ignore this trumpery farrago of gossip and lies." Fortunately for Parnell, Asquith ultimately did convince his chief counsel to include the details in the summation so as to make them part of the record of the proceeding.[87]

The commission reported its findings in February 1890 and entirely exonerated Parnell.

Asquith's political star was rising rapidly. Sir William Harcourt wrote to John Morley around this time that Asquith "is far and away the best of our youth."[88]

His success in the Parnell Commission case and the general prominence his practice prompted Asquith in 1890 to apply to be appointed Queen's Council or, as more popularly known, to "take silk." Over the years, this designation had become merely honorary; yet it was an honor of some importance. Only about a dozen barristers a year received the appointment by the Lord Chancellor, who nominally advised the Crown after taking advice from counsel and senior judges. The limited number of appointments made this group the elite among the elite. Asquith had not practiced that long, and as he stated, application was "always a hazardous step."[89] His application met with success, and he received the honor along with his friend Haldane. So by the 1890s Asquith was generally recognized along with men like Charles Russell, Henry James, Edward Clarke, Frank Lockwood, and others as one of the top ten or so barristers in England.[90]

Soon after this triumph in the summer of 1891, Asquith took his family on a holiday at the village of Lamlash on the Scottish island of Arran, a picturesque village facing the Firth of Clyde that was becoming a favorite holiday spot for Victorians. The family had grown over the years. Four years after Oc's birth, a daughter, Violet, was born in 1887, followed by a fourth son, Cyril ("Cys") born in 1889. A week after the family arrived at Lamlash, Beb became ill, and two days later Helen came down with typhoid fever. A doctor was called, and when things did not improve, Asquith sent for Helen's sister, Josephine, and her father, who hurried to the scene. Helen lingered a few days and died early in the morning of September 11, the day before Asquith's fortieth birthday. He briefly chronicled in his diary these events concluding with "*Infelis infanstumque iter*" (an unhappy and unfortunate journey).[91]

The subject of Asquith's relationship with his wife Helen has been a delicate one. Some have gone so far as to suggest that in many ways he had outgrown her by the time of her death—that he may have over time come to wish for a more dramatic way of life than Helen desired or could provide.[92] In their fourteen-year marriage his career rapidly advanced, and his circle of friends grew wider and wider while hers remained much the same. By all accounts, Helen was a model Victorian woman; her central desire in life was to be a good wife and mother. She had no ambition for herself and, it appears, little ambition for her husband, regretting his decision to first run for Parliament. While her correspondence indicates some pleasure in her husband's growing number of social engagements, there is also a degree of awe of the people she met there. In describing one party, she wrote confidentially to her sister, "there was an elegance & ease of manner about the women impossible to describe, & many of them were really beautiful & almost all were exquisitely dressed." In the same letter she confessed that "I am glad to say we have 'worked off' all our dinner parties and only have a few left."[93] Asquith himself recognized Helen's ambivalence about their changing life together. "In all that lay outside the home, with its duties and interests," he wrote his friend Haldane after her death, "she was by nature a restraining rather than stimulating force, but she acquiesced loyally and devotedly in every step that I took, although it led me into a sphere which was alien and uncongenial to her." He added, "she was hardly 'in' and never 'of' the new world in which she found herself . . . she knew that I was made of different clay."[94]

There is no doubt that Asquith loved Helen, and her death was one of the great trials of his life. Nevertheless, the stoicism that was so much a part of Asquith's personality immediately emerged to help him endure the blow. Only three days after his wife's death, Asquith, writing Haldane, informed him of her death and told him he was a "different man." "I have opened a new chapter, and the future must be built up of new materials—new ambitions, new interests, new affections." He said, in the same month that his fortune "looked bright and even dazzling," even though he was beset by "so many dark and desponding moments." The most telling part of the letter though is when his stoic outlook emerges. "Whatever happens," he concluded, "I shall push on and do my best to keep my head and play my part."[95] Likewise, in the same vein he told his friend Francis Horner, "so it is, there is nothing to be said or done, but to accustom oneself to the darkness + the solitude, and begin over again with such fortitude as one can command."[96]

NOTES

1. Edward W. Cox, *The Advocate, His Training, Practice, Rights and Duties* (London: John Crockford, 1852), 1:11–22.
2. "The Bar and Its Prospects," *Oxford Undergraduate Journal*, no. 72, (17 Nov. 1870): 862.
3. Cox, *Advocate*, 28.
4. HHA to J. W. Willans, 20 Sept. 1875, BL, F. W. Hirst Box 47.

5. Walter W. R. Ball, *A Student's Guide to the Bar*, 2nd ed. (London: Macmillan, 1879), 41.

6. Asquith, *Memories*, 40.

7. Richard L. Abel, *The Legal Profession in England and Wales* (Oxford: Blackwell, 1988), 61.

8. Ball, *Student's Guide*, 31.

9. Asquith, *Memories*, 70–72.

10. Ibid., 84.

11. Sir Charles Biron, *Without Prejudice: Impressions of Life and Law by Sir Charles Biron* (London: Faber and Faber, 1936), 89.

12. Koss, *Asquith*, 9.

13. J. R. Lewis, *The Victorian Bar* (London: Robert Hale, 1982), 43.

14. Elias, *Asquith*, 56.

15. Raymond Cocks, "Dignity and Emoluments: Thomas Blofeld's Life as a Victorian Barrister," *Kingston Law Review* 8 (1978): 41–42.

16. Augustine Birrell, *Sir Frank Lockwood: A Biographical Sketch*, 2nd ed. (London: Smith, Elder and Co., 1898), 55.

17. BL, HHA cash account book, MS. Bonham Carter 577, f. 98.

18. Asquith, *Memories*, 84, 104.

19. Elias, *Asquith*, 6.

20. HHA to Lady Frances Horner (copy), 17 Oct. 1892, BL, MS. Bonham Carter 619, f. 107.

21. Spender and Asquith, *Life of Asquith*, 1:42.

22. Ibid., 45.

23. Ibid., 43.

24. None of Asquith's letters to Helen Melland survive. Apparently Asquith destroyed them upon her death. Spender and Asquith, *Life of Asquith*, 1:45. Helen Melland to HHA, 16 Jan. 1877, BL, MS. Bonham Carter 623; Helen Melland to HHA, 2 May 1877, BL, MS. Bonham Carter, 625, ff. 6–8, 113.

25. Helen Melland to Josephine Melland (Armitage), 25 Apr. 1876, BL, MS. Bonham Carter 564, f. 2.

26. Herbert Asquith, *Moments of Memory* (London: Hutchison, 1937), 61.

27. HHA Diary, 22 Feb. 1891, BL, MS. Bonham Carter 571.

28. HHA to unknown recipient, BL, MS. Eng. Let. E. 89.

29. HHA Diary, 25 February 1891, BL, MS. Bonham Carter, 51.

30. Asquith, *Moments of Memory*, 24.

31. HHA Diary, 24 Feb. 1893, 28 July 28 1891, BL, MS. Bonham Carter, 571.

32. Roland Quinault, "Asquith's Liberalism," *History* 77 (Feb. 1992): 39.

33. H. G. C. Matthew, "H.H. Asquith's Political Journalism," *Bulletin of the Institute of Historical Research* 49 (1976): 147.

34. "The Annals of Tacitus," *The Spectator*, no. 2489 (11 Mar. 1876): 343.

35. Helen Melland Asquith to Josephine Melland (Armitage), 10 Jul. 1878, BL, MS. Bonham Carter 564, ff. 48–50.

36. Matthew, "H. H. Asquith's Political Journalism," 148.

37. "The English Extreme Left," *The Spectator*, no. 2511 (12 Aug. 1876): 1004.

38. Elias, *Asquith*, 61.
39. Asquith, *Memories*, 1:98.
40. 51 and 52 Vict. c. 25 (1888).
41. Asquith, *Memories*, 1:99.
42. Spender and Asquith, *Life of Asquith*, 1:48.
43. Mallet, "Lord Oxford's 'Life,'" 35.
44. Asquith, *Memories*, 112.
45. Spender and Asquith, *Life of Asquith*, 1:48.
46. HHA to MA, 18 Dec. 1904, BL, MS. Eng. c. 6689, ff. 267–70.
47. HHA to J. W. Willans, 10 Feb. 1887, BL, F. W. Hirst Box 47.
48. HHA to MA, 8 Dec. 1896, BL, MS. Eng. c. 6688 ff. 101–102.
49. HHA to MA, 11 Nov. 1898, BL, MS. Eng. c. 6688 ff. 168–69.
50. HHA to MA, 22 Jan. 1896, BL, MS. Eng. c. 6688 ff. 49–50.
51. Asquith, *Memories*, 106.
52. [1892] 2 QB 484 (QBD), [1893] 1 QB 256 C. A. The case was an important one in establishing certain principles of contract law and is studied by law students to the present day.
53. Asquith, *Memories*, 100.
54. 46 & 47 Vict. c. 51 (1883).
55. HHA to J. W. Willans, 24 Mar. 1884, BL, F. W. Hirst Box 47; Asquith, *Memories*, 102.
56. H. H. Asquith, *An Election Guide: Rules for the Conduct and Management of Elections in England and Wales under the Corrupt Practices Act, 1883* (London: National Press Agency, 1884).
57. Spender and Asquith, *Life of Asquith,* 1:49.
58. Helen Asquith to Josephine Melland Armitage, 17 June 1886, BL, MS. Bonham Carter 564, ff. 49–50.
59. Helen Asquith to Josephine Melland Armitage, 21 June 1886, BL, MS. Bonham Carter 564, ff. 53–54.
60. Helen Asquith to Josephine Melland Armitage, 23 June 1886, BL, MS. Bonham Carter 564, f. 58.
61. Asquith, *Memories*, 128.
62. Ibid., 129.
63. Alderson, *Mr. Asquith*, 36.
64. Spender and Asquith, *Life of Asquith,* 1:50–51.
65. Asquith, *Moments*, 23.
66. *Hansard,* 3, 312, 1393–1400, 24 Mar. 1887.
67. *Times*, 25 Mar. 1887, 8; Alderson, *Mr. Asquith*, 37.
68. Grey, *Twenty-five Years 1892–1916*, vol. 1 (London: Hodder and Stroughton, 1925), xxviii. Keith Robbins, *Sir Edward Grey: A Biography of Lord Grey of Fallodon* (London: Cassell, 1971), 28.
69. Richard Burdon Haldane, *Richard Burdon Haldane: An Autobiography* (London: Hodder and Stoughton, 1929), 70.
70. Ibid., 104.

71. Arthur Sullivan and W. S. Gilbert, *H.M.S. Pinafore; or The Lass that Loved a Sailor*, (1878), Act 1.
72. John Morley, *Recollections* (London: Macmillan, 1917), 1:323.
73. Haldane, *Autobiography*, 92–93.
74. Earl of Oxford and Asquith, *Fifty Years of British Parliament* (Boston: Little, Brown, 1926), 1:170.
75. Robbins, *Sir Edward Grey*, 32.
76. John Morley, *On Compromise* (London: Chapman and Hall, 1874), 98, 159, 176, 7.
77. Morley, *Recollections*, 369, 373.
78. H. C. G. Matthew, *The Liberal Imperialists: The Ideas and Politics of Post-Gladstonian Elite* (Oxford: Oxford University Press, 1973), 10.
79. Beatrice Webb, *The Diary of Beatrice Webb*, Norman and Jeanne MacKenzie, eds., 4 vols. (Cambridge: Belknap Press, 1982–1985), 1:345.
80. Ibid., 356.
81. *Times*, 18 Apr. 1887.
82. Asquith, *Fifty Years*, 1:198.
83. Ibid., 199.
84. Ibid.
85. Spender and Asquith, *Life of Asquith*, 1:62.
86. Asquith, *Memories*, 94.
87. Ibid., 93.
88. A. G. Gardiner, *The Life of Sir William Harcourt* (New York: George H. Doran, 1923), 2:138.
89. Asquith, *Memories*, 110.
90. Ernest Bowen-Rowlands, *In the Light of the Law* (London: G. Richards, Fronto, 1931), 104.
91. Cyril Asquith in the official biography cleaned up Asquith's inelegant Latin and stated that the entry was the more refined *infelix atque infaustum iter*. Spender and Asquith, *Life of Asquith*, 1:72.
92. Jenkins, *Asquith*, 29.
93. Helen Melland Asquith to Josephine Melland Armitage, undated 1888, BL, MS. Bonham Carter, 564, f. 67.
94. HHA to Richard Burdon Haldane, 14 Sept. 1892 (typescript copy), BL, MS. Bonham Carter, 619, ff. 73–75.
95. Ibid.
96. HHA to Francis Horner (copy), 22 Sept. 1891, BL, MS. Bonham Carter 619, fol. 106.

Chapter Three

Home Secretary (1892–1895)

Several weeks after Helen Asquith's death, William Gladstone, addressing a large audience at Newcastle-on-Tyne in October 1891, set forth the Liberal agenda for the next general election. The current Parliament was already five years old, and dissolution and an election were expected within a year. The centerpiece of what became known as the "Newcastle Programme" was Irish Home Rule, but the agenda also contained an assortment of other Liberal plans including church disestablishment in England and Wales, "one man one vote" representation, and local option for the sale of intoxicating liquors. There were even some hints of more radical measures such as payment of members of Parliament and further limitations on hours of work. Asquith was not impressed. Privately he confided to a friend that to the "fastidious eye" the Liberal Party is "a vulgar + stupid lot" that cries for leadership and only gets "fireworks and a sawdust programme from Newcastle."[1] At any rate, the stage was set. The Conservative government limped along into the next year, but in June 1892, Lord Salisbury resigned, Parliament was dissolved, and Britain went to the polls.

Asquith again faced a tough election challenge. As in his first campaign his challenger, this time J. G. Gilmour, was not a Conservative but a Liberal-Unionist. Asquith like most Liberals was not afraid to put the issue of Home Rule at the forefront of his campaign, and he reported to his sister-in-law that he made over forty speeches and answered hundreds of questions on the subject. In his election address he recognized that the "case of Ireland is of paramount urgency" but also maintained rather optimistically that "the claim of Ireland to legislate and administer her local concerns no longer occasions alarm or bewilderment." As with so many political issues, to Asquith's mind, Ireland presented a practical problem to be solved with a practical solution.

"The supposed difficulties in the way of reconciling local autonomy with Imperial supremacy," he claimed, "are academic cobwebs, which do not trouble practical men and which will yield to good sense and good faith."[2] Asquith reported that, by the end of the campaign, the "landowners, farmers, and ministers" who had combined against him were much better organized than his campaign and "were quite confident . . . that they had succeeded. . . ."[3] In the end, however, it was Asquith who prevailed with a majority of 294, eighty fewer votes than in his first election.

The Conservatives barely won the most seats in the election; the Liberals won many more seats than in 1886, picking up most from the Liberal-Unionists. With neither the Conservatives nor the Liberals holding a majority, the Irish Nationalists held the balance, and Lord Salisbury refused to resign. Even so, it was clear the Irish Nationalists would shortly side with the Liberals so that a new government could be formed.

Despite his victory, the election did not leave Asquith in good spirits. "Between you and me (tho' as a hardened optimist I scarcely admit it to myself)," he confided to his friend Francis Horner four days after the election, "I'm not in high spirits about the future—the country's, the party's, my own."[4] Such sentiment is surprising since there had been discussion even before the election that, if the Liberals formed a government, Asquith would be given a position. Well before the election, Asquith met with John Morley and discussed who might be included in the new government and recorded in his diary that Morley "thinks I cannot decline."[5]

Morley touted his young friend to a number of party leaders. As early as six months before the election, he told Gladstone's private secretary, Sir Edward Hamilton, that he believed Asquith was willing to leave the practice of law for a position in a Liberal government, provided it was on the cabinet level. Although Hamilton agreed that Asquith "would no doubt be an excellent infusion of new blood . . . and the position he has made for himself politically would entitle him to a highest post," nevertheless, he was not sure Gladstone "would admit his claim to be jumped into the cabinet straight away. . . ."[6]

Speculation about Asquith serving in the next Liberal government began. As Asquith himself admitted years later, "It was, in the circumstances, not unlikely that I might have the refusal of one of the law officerships." These "law officerships" to which he alluded were non-cabinet positions such as Attorney General. Even though young for a government position, Asquith had become one of the up-and-coming barristers of the day and in addition had given service to the party and demonstrated his ability as a public speaker on numerous occasions. Yet there were things that militated against his serving in the new government as a law officer. For one, although he enjoyed the practice of law and had done well in his profession, his first love was politics.

"The prospect did not attract me," he wrote, "as I had no judicial ambitions; though much interested in the law, I was more interested in politics."[7] There was also the issue of money, or rather the lack of it. Asquith might well be willing to give up his lucrative law practice at least for a while to hold an important cabinet position, but he was not willing to do so for a mere law office. He also understood the demands of party loyalty. Months before the election, he wrote to a friend that for his own selfish interests perhaps he should not enter a government that might be short lived and instead "go on making money." "But if one goes into politics," he continued, "one must play up + be loyal + and do one's duty."[8] In light of all these pre-election reservations and discussions, it is easier to understand his pessimism after the election for it appeared that at most he might be offered a law office, a position he did not seek, but one that he could turn down only with a great deal of embarrassment and harm to his political future.

Asquith and his friends were correct that Gladstone had his eye on him. As the time approached to challenge Salisbury's Conservative government, Gladstone gave Asquith the honor of moving the amendment in Parliament that would topple the government. This decision was by no means a foregone conclusion. On July 22, Gladstone asked Harcourt, "What do you think of Asquith and Sir E Grey to move & second the amendment?"[9] Harcourt preferred two others, arguing in an apparent reference to Grey's and perhaps Asquith's party loyalty, "We don't particularly want good speaking but straight voting."[10] Unmoved, Gladstone chose Asquith but did, however, take some of Harcourt's advice to heart. He told Asquith that he did not want a lengthy oration but instead be a "single assertion, avoiding extraneous matters."[11]

If Gladstone wanted a "speech maker" who could get to the point, Asquith did not disappoint him. The amendment to the address was a simple vote of no confidence in the government. Warming up to his audience, Asquith compared the Queen's address to "grace before meat in which this House expresses in anticipation its gratitude for its legislative bounty of Her Majesty's Government." But on this occasion, Asquith mocked, "the cupboard is bare." In his most lawyerlike manner, he then presented his case, attacking the only two arguments the Conservatives had put forward to reverse the verdict of the nation in the last election. The first was that without "the votes of the Members for Ireland—the majority ceases to be a majority all." Asquith put down such an argument with a simple comparison. "If it is true that the majority depends on the Irish vote, it is equally true to say that it depends on the Scotch and Welsh vote." Is this what the opposition meant by "Unionism," he mockingly asked. Secondly, the Conservatives had alleged the Liberals' victory had been "obtained by illegitimate means." To the contrary, Asquith argued that "never was there a case in which the meaning of the verdict of the country as it has been recorded was more free from ambiguity or from possible mistake." The Conservatives had placed before the electorate the proposition that governing Ireland on Unionist principles had been a success. The electorate had rejected that proposition. "The electors voted with their eyes open, with their minds formed, with their judgement unclouded. . . ." All that remained was for the "House to execute the judgement which the nation has pronounced."[12] The amendment passed, Lord Salisbury resigned, and Gladstone at age eighty-two was once again called to form a new government.

No one was really surprised at Asquith's stellar oratorical performance. Even the *Times* reluctantly praised it. Dorothy Grey, wife of Sir Edward Grey, wrote him that his speech "inspired the best part of confidence."[13] The real surprise came when Gladstone's private secretary, Spencer Lyttleton, arrived at Brook's Club on the afternoon of August 14 to deliver a note to Asquith from Gladstone "writing to propose that you should allow me to submit your name to Her Majesty for the office of Home Secretary."[14] Here was an offer of one of the more important cabinet positions. Even the cool and unflappable Asquith must have felt his pulse quicken. There is almost disbelief in his reply to Gladstone the same day:

> I should have thought it a privilege to have had the opportunity of serving you at this time in any post that you might have seen fit to select. The office you name is of all others the most congenial to me, though I cannot but feel that I have a very inadequate title to such rapid advancement.[15]

Writing many years after the formation of what was to become Gladstone's last government, Haldane casually commented in his memoirs that "it was a surprise to nobody when, on returning to office in 1892, Mr. Gladstone made . . . [Asquith] Home Secretary."[16] Haldane must have meant that most believed Asquith would be given *some* position in the government, for there was certainly great shock at the time that Asquith was elevated to one of the top positions in the government, moving ahead of many more senior Liberal MPs. He was only thirty-nine years old, had served but six years in Parliament, had never held any junior office, and on top of it all possessed no wealth or influence. In hindsight, however, Gladstone's selection of Asquith seems more logical. The young leader did have much going for him. Gladstone's letter asking him to serve mentioned his "character, abilities, and eloquence." Liberal leaders had taken notice of his talents almost from the first day he entered Parliament. Over a year before the formation of the government, H. W. Lucy wrote in his diary, "Mr. Asquith has so thoroughly identified himself with affairs in the House of Commons, and has gained so prominent a position, that it seems hard to believe he took his seat so recently as 1886."[17] More important, Gladstone knew that the centerpiece of his government's upcoming legislative agenda would be the uphill battle for Irish Home Rule. Asquith could be counted on for his proven talent in Parliamentary debate, and he also could help bring along his young group of Liberal MP friends whose influence was growing. With Asquith's and others' cajoling, Gladstone even agreed to include some of Asquith's friends in the government. Arthur Acland was brought in as President of the Board of Education. This especially pleased Asquith, for Acland, he told his friend Margot Tenant, was "the only one who counts." Without explanation, he went on to write that, if Acland had not been appointed, "I should have felt isolated + more or less unimportant."[18] The next day he wrote to her that he was anxious to get his colleague, Sir Edward Grey, a good Under Secretaryship, and "if we succeed the 'gang' will have fared pretty well." Ultimately Grey became Under Secretary for Foreign Affairs, but to all of his friends' disappointment Haldane failed to gain a spot in the new government.

Within days of taking office as Home Secretary, Asquith faced one of the most delicate of situations for any politician—a public dispute between supporters, with the politician being caught in the middle. To make matters worse, the dispute was not of Asquith's making. The difficulty arose out of the fact that the Home Secretary, acting through the Commissioner of Lands, controlled the public use of Trafalgar Square. In the 1840s the Home Secretary, Sir George Grey, declared that public meetings might rightfully be held in the square, and thereafter from time to time public demonstrations had taken place. There was no disorder until 1886, when radical and workers groups began to use the square daily. The square was crown property, and even though there apparently was no legal right of assembly there, the public use of the square for over the past forty years muddied the legal picture. In 1888 after several unruly demonstrations took place in the square, Asquith's immediate predecessor as Home Secretary in the Conservative government, Sir Henry Matthews, caused the Commissioners of the Metropolitan Police to ban all meetings in the square. Following this edict, Asquith himself had unsuccessfully defended radical MP Cunningham Graham, who was tried for "unlawful assembly."

The radicals looked to the Liberals to lift the ban immediately once they came back to power. Interest in the issue was intense. In office less than a week, Asquith received a letter from William Saunders, a radical MP and member of the London County Council, urging him to permit demonstrators in Trafalgar Square. Without such change of policy, a potential conflict might enable the Conservatives to claim only the Tories could maintain order.[19] Asquith knew that the Metropolitan Radical Federation intended to test the ban in court in November, and the Social Democratic Federation might also take action. On the other side of the issue many Liberal supporters owned businesses in and about the square and who were directly financially affected by disorders. It was important that the government not been seen as weak on the issue of law and order. Even the Queen herself inquired as to what Asquith's position would be.[20] As the Chancellor of the Exchequer, Sir William Harcourt, wrote to Asquith, "The Trafalgar sq. meeting is no doubt serious business."[21]

Asquith knew he had to act quickly before the situation got out of hand. He wrote to Margot Tennant as early as August 21 that he had "made up his mind about the principle, but there are all sorts of details to be worked out carefully."[22] To delay might also give the impression of weakness and that an ultimate determination was made under duress. "I don't want to seem to have my hand forced in this matter," the new Home Secretary wrote to Harcourt. He proposed to send a letter to William Saunders or others announcing a lifting of the ban "provided the meeting [was] held for lawful purpose and conducted in a peaceful and orderly manner." Promoters of the meetings would also be asked to give timely notice to the police and work with authorities "in minimizing disturbances to traffic and inconvenience to the public."[23] In response, Harcourt favored allowing the meetings as long as traffic movement was not disrupted but suggested that Asquith check with the commissioner of police in London before acting.[24]

To Asquith's practical mind the issue was, as he later stated, "not one of legal right, but of administrative expediency."[25] The question was simply one of "regulating by reasonable restrictions" the "privilege . . . of public meeting in a particular place."[26] Of course the trick was to make all the parties feel comfortable with such "reasonable restrictions." Before issuing his final instructions, Asquith privately sought the opinions of the concerned parties. His plan was to get their approval prior to announcing a new policy. He called upon his friend W. H. Eldridge to sound out radicals and local labor leaders including the Dockers Union and others to see if some sort of compromise might be reached. Eldridge reported on September 2 that most of those with whom he met accepted Asquith's proposal, but there was a split of opinion. The Social Democratic Federation, according to Eldridge, was dead set on discrediting the government, but he believed "as a force may be ignored." To frustrate the S.D.F.'s efforts, the Metropolitan Radical Federation would be publicly sending a deputation to Asquith to present ideas very much in line with the Home Secretary's.[27]

The final choice for the new Home Secretary was whether or not to bother the Prime Minister with the issue. In many ways it was minor when compared with the many other questions the government faced. Yet it was a problem with the potential to embarrass the government at the very outset of its taking power. While Asquith wanted to appear firm and decisive, he also had no cabinet experience and did not yet have the self-assurance to go it alone. A week before issuing the new instructions, he wrote Gladstone and enclosed his memorandum on the issue.[28] "The question of meetings in Trafalgar Square, though in one sense merely a local matter, excites so much general interest, & before now provided so much serious controversy," Asquith explained, that he was "anxious to be fortified by your approval in any course which I may adopt in regard to it."[29] Gladstone replied the next day that he concurred with the proposed policy because the ban on meetings "seems to me inadmissible." Further, as long as Asquith cleared it with the Chancellor of the Exchequer and the Attorney General, he saw no need for discussion of the matter by the full cabinet.[30]

On October 19 Asquith met with the Metropolitan Radical Federation and announced the new policy. He would lift the ban on demonstrations in Trafalgar Square provided demonstrations would be held during the day on Saturday afternoons, Sundays, and bank holidays when traffic in the area was comparatively small. In addition, the Metropolitan Police had to be given prior notice and could insist on further reasonable restrictions as to the route of the march, etc.[31] As expected, the Federation immediately praised the new policy, and Asquith was pleased to report in a speech to the Liberal Federation two months later that there had been "no incident case of collision between the police and the people."[32]

The important thing for Asquith was that he had performed exceptionally well in a difficult situation and had weathered his first test as a cabinet member, meeting the high expectations of his colleagues. Harcourt immediately wrote and congratulated the young minister on the "masterly manner" he had handled the "thorny question," yet warned him tongue-in-cheek, "Woe unto them for whom the *Times* speaks well."[33] The Foreign Secretary, Lord Rosebery, sent a letter of congratulations, writing, "To have pleased the 'Times' and the 'Star' and indeed everybody, may rank with the achievements of Hannibal crossing the Alps. . . ."[34]

Trafalgar Square was a local issue. The political focus of the entire country and the new government was centered on Irish Home Rule. The octogenarian Gladstone had set his mind on Home Rule as the capstone to his long and distinguished career. Then too, the issue was the key to the very survival of the government. The Liberals did not hold a majority and could only survive as long as they had the support of the Irish nationalists. This one issue predominated the Parliamentary session of 1893, one of the longest in Parliamentary history. In a speech to the City of London Club three months after taking office as Home Secretary, Asquith himself described Home Rule as the "first duty" of the government.[35]

Before the government could address the issue, however, Asquith had to resolve the troublesome and more immediate problem of what to do with fourteen Irishmen sentenced under the last government to life in prison for terrorist dynamiting. Convicted between 1883 and 1885, they had been sentenced to serve twenty years in prison with good conduct. Their plight came to a head in January 1893 just as the government was about to present its Irish Home Rule bill. John Redmond, leader of the remaining Parnellite rump of the Irish nationalists, moved an amendment to the address calling for either the release of his fellow Irishmen or at least a commutation of their sentences. Even though the government foresaw that such a move might be made; nevertheless, it was clear the issue could derail the government before it even had a chance of moving forward on Home Rule.

The Home Office policy on reviewing sentences of convicted felons was well-established. As Asquith explained in a letter to the Prime Minister, only at the end of ten years, and again at the end of fifteen years, did sentences for penal servitude come up for review. Obviously, that period had not been reached for any of the convicted dynamiters. Even more importantly, the Home Office almost never released felons unless there was an overriding medical ground or new evidence had emerged casting doubt of the fairness of the conviction.[36]

After carefully examining each of the cases, Asquith later maintained he "was left without a shadow of doubt as to the guilt, or as to the propriety of the conviction and sentence, of any of the prisoners."[37] As a result, the Home Secretary to his credit made it clear to the Prime Minister as early as October 1892 that he had no intention "to depart in this case from the ordinary rules which govern the home office in dealing with convicted prisoners."[38] He did, however, write that the case of James Francis Egan was "somewhat exceptional." The Home Secretary reported that there had always been "grave doubts" as to whether his conviction was justified, and even the Attorney General in the last Conservative government, Sir Henry James, who prosecuted him questioned whether "the verdict against him was a just one." Even if the conviction was justified, Asquith wrote that Egan's "complicity in the plot was so slight that the sentence is, on the face of it, very harsh."[39] In December, Asquith informed James Bryce in a letter marked "confidential" that he intended to release Egan at the beginning of the year. As he had previously explained to the Prime Minister, he told Lord Bryce, "There has always been doubt about the Justice of his conviction," and his "complicity was so slight that after 8½ years of penal servitude he is sufficiently punished."[40]

On January 23, 1893, Asquith ordered the parole, not the pardon, of Egan. He also ordered the release of two Irish-Americans, Thomas Callan and Michael Harkins, who had been convicted of conspiring to destroy public buildings in London, on the condition that they agree to return to America. There was a public outcry. "Moderate men of all parties," *The Economist* declared, "are condemning the action taken by Mr. Asquith. . . ." The article argued that the government must still believe in the guilt of the men because their release was conditional.[41]

Despite the release of the three prisoners, Redmond pressed forward with his amendment to the address calling for amnesty for all fourteen other prisoners convicted under the "Treason Felony Act" and still being held. The debate on the motion took place in early February. Redmond argued that the men being held were "political offenders" and deserving of "political amnesty." He next questioned the convictions themselves, arguing they had been tried in a "state of mad mania in this country" and some "were tried without being defended, without having the advantage of legal counsel to defend them."[42] Asquith's rebuttal completely checked the attack. In a classic example of Asquith's ability to overwhelm an opponent by detailed preparation and logical argument, a method that earned him the sobriquet "the hammer," he met Redmond's challenge point by point. He noted that Redmond had only mentioned the name of one of the prisoners being held. In stark contrast, the Home Secretary proceeded to give a detailed account of each and every prisoner being held and set forth the overwhelming evidence against them. He saved his most blistering attack for the argument that those being held were "political prisoners." In a passage that seems quaint after the war atrocities of the twentieth century, he declared that when men "resort to assassination and to dynamite, . . . they are putting themselves as much outside the pale of political offenders as the man who in time of war goes and poisons the stream disentitles himself to be treated as a prisoner of war." The British government would give "no consideration of indulgence," he concluded, to "persons who resort to this mode of warfare against Society, who use terror as their instrument, who proceed in their methods with reckless disregard of the life and safety of the weak, the innocent, and the helpless. . . ."[43] When he finished, all of Redmond's arguments had been dismantled, and the issue passed from the public eye.

With the dynamiters behind them Asquith and the government could now focus more of their attention on the centerpiece of the government's legislative agenda, Home Rule. Although there was some early question as to whether a resolution, as opposed to an actual bill, should be used to give Ireland Home Rule, Gladstone decided in favor of a bill and soon appointed a committee consisting of himself, Earl Spencer, Morley, and James Bryce to write the measure. The Prime Minister himself, with weakened hearing and sight, introduced the bill and saw it through every step of its tortured passage through the Commons. One could not help but admire Gladstone's masterful exposition of drive and willpower for someone of his age and condition, but many, including Asquith, wondered whether it was best to have the Grand

Old Man lead the charge. During the height of the debate, Asquith commented to Morley, "It's brutal to put into words, but really, if Mr. G. stood aside more, we might get on better."[44]

The Home Secretary had for years supported what was an advanced idea for the time known as "Home Rule all around." As he explained in a speech a number of years later, "Irish Home Rule must be presented to the country as the first step in a process of devolution and delegation, which must sooner or later be applied, not necessarily in the same form, to the other parts of the United Kingdom." He saw such a program of "devolution" as nothing more than a practical solution to Parliament's growing need to delegate more and more local problems to local authorities. Only by granting greater local autonomy could the Imperial Parliament "be relieved, step by step, of a great mass of purely local affairs which it at present transacts with all the disadvantages of limited time and imperfect knowledge."[45] Assuming that Irish Home Rule was a part of a greater movement toward home rule "all around," Asquith focused on two important considerations: "It must maintain intact the supremacy of Parliament" and must give to Ireland "a liberal and satisfactory, or rather I would say satisfying measure of local autonomy."[46] As to the first consideration, although the Home Secretary supported the notion of home rule "all around," this did not mean that he favored the dismemberment of the Empire. According to one of Asquith's early biographers, most considered him to be the strongest "supremacy" man in the cabinet, that is, the strongest supporter of the ultimate supremacy of the Imperial Parliament.[47] Yet Asquith also believed that, if Parliament granted some form of Home Rule to the Irish, it should not be in "in a stinted or delusory form."[48] As he had explained to the Manchester Reform Club in 1891, it was only "by giving the largest, amplest, and most generous powers to the Irish legislature consistent with the maintenance of Imperial unity" that Parliament could "put a final end to the question. . . ."[49]

No one doubted that the Liberals would introduce an Irish Home Rule bill, but there was much debate as to what the exact form the measure would take. Liberal-Unionist opponents of Home Rule, such as Lord Hartington and the Duke of Argyll, demanded to know the specifics. To them, Parliament could not pass legislation with regard to such an important issue without first referring it to the electorate at large in a referendum. Asquith attacked such a proposition, asking how they would define "important legislation"? "It would be further interesting to know," the Home Secretary mockingly inquired "whether Lord Hartington thinks the referendum unnecessary except when the Liberal Party is in power."[50] Nevertheless, Asquith placed himself with those Liberals who urged Gladstone to come out with the specifics of Home Rule even before the election and do so publicly. This angered some

Liberal leaders, such as Sir William Harcourt, who had convinced Gladstone to delay the formulation of the specific details of a Home Rule plan until after the election.[51]

The debate dragged on and on. The Home Secretary wrote his uncle in March, "We had an exhausting and profitless week." He continued, "The Unionists are in a nasty temper + cannot understand why the country does not rise against the Bill."[52] Asquith played only a secondary role in the push for passage of the Irish Home Rule bill. His principal contribution was making a major speech in mid-April in support of a second reading, and the Home Secretary's performance did not disappoint those who knew him to be one of the best speakers in the House. He focused on the two points that he had always emphasized: first, that the supremacy of the Imperial Parliament be maintained, and second, that Ireland be given real and genuine autonomy. He made clear that under the bill the "Irish House of Commons will not have the right to alter even one letter or comma in an Act passed by the Imperial Parliament." On the issue of genuine autonomy, he cleverly pointed out that, if the bill did not grant sufficient autonomy, it was rather strange that the House had "not heard in the course of the Debate, a single complaint from Irish Members that there is any undue restriction of the powers of either the Irish Legislature or the Irish Executive."[53]

By all accounts, Asquith's performance was a success. Even the *Times* begrudgingly commented that the Home Secretary has presented "perhaps as good a case for his clients as anyone who had yet spoken on the same side."[54] *The Daily Chronicle* was more generous with its praise. Describing Asquith's effort as "remarkable," it asserted, "Mr. Asquith always succeeds. . . . He has the knack of it." The speech was "remarkable above all for its powers of lucid arrangement of very complicated material. The arguments on which he chiefly relied have been used before in the debate. But they have never appeared in so compact a form and so orderly a march of ideas. The delivery was perfect, far more dramatic that Mr. Asquith's usual strong, level method. . . ."[55]

After a hot summer of deliberation and debate, the Commons passed Gladstone's Irish Home Rule bill in September 1893. It was a remarkable achievement. On the eve of the passage, Asquith addressed a Liberal meeting estimated to be as large as 10,000 people at Althorpe in Lincolnshire. The government had overcome its opponents and critics who had said at the outset that Home Rule would either split the cabinet or be destroyed in committee. Part of the cabinet's success, according to the Home Secretary, was due to the tactics of the opposition, particularly Liberal-Unionist Joseph Chamberlain. "The more critical the situation, the more delicate the position of the government, the greater the possibility of snatching a chance division at our expense," Asquith told the Althorpe audience, "the more certain was Mr. Chamberlain to swoop down into the fray, and before he had uttered half a dozen sentences, the waverers rallied, the doubters were convinced, and the unity of the Liberal Party was consolidated and assured."[56] With the passage in the Commons, the issue of Irish Home Rule rested in the hands of the House of Lords, and neither Asquith nor any of his cabinet colleagues harbored any hopes of a successful result. Asquith frankly told the Liberal audience at Althorpe, "For the last two generations, with rare and partial exceptions, [the upper chamber had] rejected when they had the courage, and they have mutilated when they had not, almost every great measure of popular reform."[57]

True to form, only a week after its passage in the Commons, the Lords rejected the bill by the lopsided vote of 419 to 41. Gladstone wanted the government to resign and fight an election over the power of the House of Lords to thwart legislation passed by the democratically elected House of Commons, but this idea found no support in the cabinet. Writing more than thirty years after the event, Asquith admitted that "whether as a matter of tactics he or they were right is, and must always remain, a highly questionable debate." This was written with the hindsight of the bloody battles Asquith himself would have to fight with the Lords when he was Prime Minister two decades later. His reflection seems an honest speculation as to whether or not it might have indeed been better to have had it out in the 1890s on the issue of the power of the upper house.

Undoubtedly, the defeat of the Irish Home Rule bill in the House of Lords put the Liberal government in an awkward position. Their leader wanted to press on with the issue. Many knew this was politically impossible. The difficulty of the situation can be seen in many of Asquith's public pronouncements following the defeat. At Glasgow in October, he blasted the Lords. "There is no greater fallacy than to imagine that the House of Lords affords any effective safeguard against rash and revolutionary legislation," he declared. "So long as you tolerate this system which places this gigantic power in irresponsible hands," an exasperated Asquith taunted his audience, "you have yourselves, and nobody else, to blame. . . ." Despite this attack, the Home Secretary did admit that the government had made no definite plans to reintroduce Home Rule in the next session, lamely explaining, "there are other ways of dealing with the question."[58] Speaking a few days later to the Leeds Liberal Federation, he explained that, even though Liberals remained enthusiastic about Home Rule, it would be futile to spend more than eighty days on the matter in the next session, knowing full well that the Lords would once again veto the measure.[59]

The Conservative opposition was quick to take advantage of the government's dilemma. Soon after his Glasgow address, the *Times* assailed Asquith for saying the government would not bring forward another Home Rule bill and then turning around and making Home Rule the centerpiece of his next speech at East Fife. The *Times* was not far from the truth when it surmised that "Mr. Asquith's function is to discover, if he can, whether the electors will stand any more Home Rule, or whether their hearts are set upon registration reform and local veto."[60]

The defeat of Home Rule in 1893 effectively set aside resolution of the issue until Asquith himself was Prime Minister twenty years later. To continue the debate in 1894 would have meant a direct confrontation with the House of Lords, plunging the nation into a constitutional crisis. Gladstone's cabinet was not willing to go this far. Asquith never changed his views on the underlying issue. Five years later in 1898, as he was about to speak in Birmingham, the *Birmingham Daily Post* called upon him to repudiate Home Rule. Asquith quickly responded, "So far as I am concerned there are no principles which I have professed on this subject which I am in the least degree prepared to recant or disavow."[61] Nevertheless, Asquith realized and often stated publicly that, from a practical standpoint, Home Rule might have to evolve slowly through the more limited scale of local institutions. Even so, he also knew this critical political issue would not go away. As he put it, "You cannot kill it by kindness. You cannot extinguish it by land purchase. You may shut your eyes to it, but it will continue to stare you in the face."[62]

On the day his wife Helen died in September 1891, Asquith took a few moments to write a brief note to his new friend, Margot Tennant. "She died at nine this morning," he began. "So ends twenty years of love + fourteen of unclouded union."[63] Less than three years later, after an intense courtship, Asquith married Margot.

They first met one evening in 1891 at a dinner at the House of Commons given by Lord Battersea. Margot recorded the event in her autobiography. Although he was "unfashionably dressed," she noticed "he had a way of putting you not only at your ease but at your best when talking to him." After dinner they "retired to the darkest part of the Terrace where, leaning over the parapet, we gazed into the river and talked into the night." They met a few days later while dining with Sir Algernon West, and after this, according to Margot, "we saw each other constantly."[64]

Born in 1864, Margot was the sixth daughter of Sir Charles Tennant, a successful businessman and a Liberal MP for a short time. The story of the Tennant family is one of the great success stories of Victorian England. They were a family riding the crest of the Industrial Revolution. Margot's great-grandfather, Charles Tennant, founded the family firm that manufactured bleaching powder in Glasgow. His son John, also a talented businessman, is most remembered for his marriage to a young woman who took the shaving water around the firm's plant. This union produced Margot's father, Charles, generally known as the Bart. Margot accurately described her father as "a man whose vitality, irritability, energy and impressionability amounted to genius."[65] After an apprenticeship in Liverpool, Charles moved to London where he worked for Tennant, Know & Co., which traded in chemicals, copper, steel, and other commodities. He wisely invested in many successful ventures including the Midland Railways and an Australian land company. By 1852 he had made small fortune, which enabled him to purchase Glen Estate in Peeblesshire. On this 4,000 acre property he built a large house which Lord Rosebery described in a letter to Gladstone as "the most perfect of all modern houses, architecturally speaking." In the 1860s he was the moving spirit behind a copper mine in Spain that proved tremendously profitable. At age fifty-five, he entered politics and was elected as a Liberal to Parliament in 1879 and served until 1886.

The Tennants were very much a part of London society. Margot's older two sisters, Charlotte (Charty) and Laura, were the first to take the social scene by storm. Charty married Lord Ribblesdale and Laura became the wife of Alfred Lyttleton. It was Laura who developed a remarkable reputation in society, remembered for her flirtatiousness and charm in meeting all types of people. Margot was especially attached to Laura. When it came Margot's turn to enter society, she made her own splash. She and her sister Laura were "Noel Coward characters waiting to be born."[66] Relatively attractive, rich (with an income of £5,000 a year), and athletic, she was filled with zest and vitality. Her great passions were society and riding. Together with A. J. Balfour, George Curzon, Lady Desborough, Violet Manners, and others, she was part of a small, loosely knit but social group which became famous as "The Souls." They loved to gather at country weekend parties to discuss all manner of topics. Asquith's first wife, Helen, once wrote of this group, "They study Schopenhauer, call each other by their Christian names & have platonic friendships with other peoples' wives & husbands."[67]

Months before his wife's death in 1891, Asquith began what became a passionate correspondence with Margot. By May, he was writing to her, "You may smile, but I can never sufficiently thank you for the brightness + vividness, + inspiration to better things, which you have brought into my life." In July he wrote, "You have made me a different man," and continued, "you are not to suppose because I am 'low' (as I confess I am) that I have not faith in you, or that I have any doubt that you will fulfil your promise, + keep our friendship fresh and living and sacred from intrusion as it is today." He concluded that he knew she would and declared "If I lost faith in you the sun would go out."[68] Asquith had clearly become infatuated. In one of the most telling letters written to Margot before Helen's death, he described the depth of his feeling for her in twelve pages and in so doing revealed much about himself:

> and you know me too well by this time to think (as probably most people do) that I am altogether without heart. The little room of which we have often spoken is, since last night, hung with another picture—the softest and most glowing of them all. I have to keep a curtain over it, lest I should be tempted to look at it too often. Only now and then, when I am quite alone, I lock myself in, and lift the veil, and allow it to "flash upon that inward eye, which is the bliss of solitude."
>
> I said yesterday that I thought more of certain things than were good for me. But I was wrong. When one looks back upon the drab coloured web which forms the groundwork of the kind of life we lead, there are a few (with me, very few) golden threads woven which not only brighten but give worth and value to the whole. This is one of them, and if I can only hope to keep it unbroken, I may yet be able in the "roaring loom" of the work-a-day world, to turn out something noble in design and fitten for working use, than anything that I have hitherto done or attempted. It will be my fault, not yours, if I do not. I don't thank you because I can't. Remember your promises—one and all.[69]

His correspondence with Margot continued and at times was passionate. In June he wrote, "I am not selfish enough to expect you to reserve as large a room as I keep for you; but I should like to think that there was a little nook, with a few thoughts and memories of its own, to which I had exclusive access."[70] He believed Margot had changed him. In late July he told her she had taken away nothing from him "but a bad kind of hardness, and you have made me better and stronger, and (I hope) a little gentler, and a thousand times brighter."[71] In one of his last letters to Margot before his wife's death, written on a train heading to Scotland and posted along the way was "Don't forget me."[72]

Despite the emotional intensity toward Margot this and other letters reveal, there is no doubt that Asquith genuinely loved his wife Helen, and her death was one of the great blows in his life. However, the correspondence suggests that he had become enthralled with Margot months before his wife died. After her death, he attempted to work this all out in his mind with the belief that Helen somehow had sanctioned the feelings he was having for Margot. He wrote to Margot several weeks after Helen's death telling her that he could never cease to love Helen and insisting that "My love for you is not disloyalty to her." To put matters right, he told Margot that, as Helen lay dying, "with the intuition that often comes then, she desired (I am certain) that it was to be, and when she sent the sweet little message to you she sanctioned and blessed it."[73]

With this letter, written only weeks after his wife's demise, Asquith began his courtship of Margot.

One of the many responsibilities assigned to the Home Secretary was to oversee the working conditions in factories and shops and the enforcement of various factory acts that passed since the 1820s. Gladstone's "Newcastle Programme" included vague references to further limitations to hours of work, but generally speaking the Liberal government had no real plan to address labor issues. While he always had shown tremendous sympathy for the plight of the working class, Asquith was not known publicly as one of its principal advocates. Haldane asked him to attend a Trades Union Congress meeting shortly after taking office. He refused because "I don't want people to get the idea that I am a clap-trap minister" trying to ingratiate himself with the working men. Then again, he said the same would be true if he went to a Shipowners' Federation meeting or a meeting of the Suffragists' Union.[74] Avoiding the Trades Union Congress meeting was not from lack of concern for the working class but rather an issue of probity to Asquith. In fact, three days earlier he inspected a coal mine disaster outside of Cardiff and had been greatly moved. One of his most emotional letters on a political subject to Margot, six pages in length, described the scene of the disaster as a "battlefield" in which he watched a young boy die in his father's arms, concluding that he had "never spent such an awful day."[75] From the outset of his tenure as Home Secretary, Asquith's heart led him to take steps to assist the working class; but there were limits, and he never wanted to be seen as merely an unthinking politician who would do almost anything to gain the electoral support the working class.

With his instinct for the practical, the first thing Asquith did was to enforce existing legislation. One of the worst abuses of labor in nineteenth-century England was the sweating system in which materials were supplied to workers—mostly women, children, the elderly, and invalids—who were paid by the piece produced. Most of the work was done in the workers' homes or in small "sweatshops." The Factory and Workshops Act of 1891 attempted to get some control over this abusive system by requiring that owners and operators of factories and workshops keep a list of all workers including "outworkers," that is, those doing sweated work. This list was to be available for inspection by either factory or sanitation inspectors. Asquith's predecessor, Sir Henry Matthews, required such a list of the wearing apparel industry, one of the worst to use the sweating system, but only under pressure a year after the passage of the act. Matthews's requirement was not widely publicized and was for the most part ineffective. The new Home Secretary immediately rejected such a limited policy. Using his powers under the 1891 Act, he actually extended the reporting requirement to "the lowest and most degraded and most suffering classes of our national population," including the furniture manufacturing, upholstery, electro-plating, and file making industries.[76] These additions covered some of the worst cases of sweating.

Asquith's proactive stance toward working conditions was not limited to the sweating trades. After a departmental committee had reviewed various trades and made recommendations, he issued an order declaring a number of trades to be "dangerous," including, among others, chemical works, pottery and earthenware factories, and quarries in North Wales. This designation meant that the Home Office could now promulgate regulations for their safe operation. As Asquith explained to a delegation of china and earthenware manufacturers, even though many large manufacturers followed human practices, there was a "residuum of employers who did not take precautions," therefore making an "abundant and ample case" for the setting down of special rules.[77] He admitted to the delegation, however, that special rules of this kind would only work through cooperation and not through enforcement by penalties in the courts.

Asquith saw the weakness of the Factory Acts resulted from a lack of inspection and enforcement. Asquith was anxious to tackle this problem. Unfortunately, on the eve of leaving office, Sir Henry Matthews had extended the term of the chief inspector until the end of 1893, blocking Asquith's appointment of his own man for the job. Asquith explained to Harcourt, if the reappointment was allowed to stand, "the department will for more than another year . . . be nominally presided over by an absentee and broken down chief."[78] To address this situation, he proposed in December 1892 to increase the number of inspectors and add a new category of "inspector-assistants." Harcourt assured Asquith that his request for an increase in the number of inspectors "shall be regarded with a friendly eye."[79] New positions were added in 1893, and Asquith called for additional increases less than a year later. The original increases were "tentative and experimental in character," he noted in a memorandum, yet had "been fully justified by the results." Even so, the Home Secretary observed, "we are still inadequately equipped for the effective execution of the law." He noted that there were only eighty-six inspectors in the entire United Kingdom to protect a factory employee population of over three and a half million workers. With English understatement he concluded, "it is clear that both the staff and the expenditure are still upon an extremely modest scale."[80]

The problem was not only the number but the quality of inspectors. Asquith wanted a "new class of inspectors" drawn from the working class itself.[81] He hoped these new inspectors would be better informed and would know where to look for the worst abuses. In a bold move, Asquith authorized the appointment of women. Initially only two were appointed, but these appointments received praise from almost all quarters, and Asquith was able to write after only a year, "I cannot express too highly my sense of the beneficial results which have followed from this experiment."[82] It was a significant step for women. Years later, Adelaide Anderson, one of the first women inspectors, recalled that the appointment of women inspectors "gave them their liberal starting-point and a wide field of activity."[83]

Asquith realized, however, that abuse could be rooted out only with the cooperation of the government on all levels. He spoke to the issue of cooperation in inspection in a speech to the London Reform Union. The Factory Acts could be fully enforced only with the "united, intelligent and harmonious action of the central and local power." He admitted that, no matter how much you increased the effectiveness of the system of central inspection, "you cannot lift more than a finger to get rid of this gigantic social evil (sweating) unless you can enlist the co-operation with the officers of the central authority, the various local authorities and the County Council."[84]

After pressing the enforcement of existing legislation about as far as he could, the Home Secretary introduced his own Factory bill in March 1895 during the waning months of the Liberal government. The bill was a broad-based extension of the law regarding government regulation of working conditions and extended factory legislation to include docks, quays, bakeries, and laundries.[85] For the first time there was an attempt to legally define "overcrowding" in the work place. The bill proposed that the minimum space for every employee be 250 cubic feet and for those working overtime, at least 400 cubic feet. It also strengthened the regulation of fire escapes, which had been unsatisfactorily placed under the care of the sanitary authorities under the 1891 Act. There were also sections dealing with the hours of labor, the regulation of work done outside the factory, and the abolition of overtime in cases of those workers under the age of eighteen. Just as the Grand Committee of Trade discussed the bill, another unrelated vote led to the fall of the Liberal government. Although no longer Home Secretary, Asquith continued to see the bill though its final stages in the Commons, and it passed the House of Lords and received royal assent on the very last day before Parliament was dissolved.

While Asquith's Factories and Workshop Act of 1895 was the capstone of his considerable efforts on behalf of the working class, unfortunately his tenure in the Home Office was most remembered by the working men and women of England for what became known as the infamous "Featherstone Incident." On September 7, 1893, a labor disturbance broke out at the Ackton Hall Colliery at Featherstone in West Riding. Two persons were killed and numerous others injured. For years afterward, Asquith would face an occasional jeer from a working-class audience, "Why did you murder the miners at Featherstone in '92?" He often shrugged off the question with the reply, "it was not '92, it was '93," but while such a response would bring laughs from the crowd, it did not explain one of his most difficult moments as Home Secretary and harmed his reputation among the working class.

When workers began to riot, Asquith granted the constabulary's request for troops. After troops arrived on the scene, two workers were shot and killed. A subsequent committee of inquiry selected by Asquith and made up of Lord Bowen for whom he had clerked and his best friend, Richard Haldane, found that the troops were justified in firing on the crowd. This is not to say that he sought to hide wrongdoing. Far from it. Asquith was firmly convinced nothing irregular had happened, but what he wanted to ensure was that the investigation would spell that out in the clearest terms possible. For Asquith's political future, the relatively minor risk of criticism for appointing one's well-respected friends to the committee was worth the insurance that the final report would be a powerful statement of exoneration.

The Committee of Inquiry's report came out in December 1893, and in that same month the cabinet discussed the First Lord of the Admiralty Lord Spencer's request for an additional £4 million to the naval estimates for the next budget. Gladstone opposed the increase and, just after Christmas, made it clear that he would resign rather than accept the proposal. Thus began a two-month struggle for leadership of the Liberal Party that would culminate with the Prime Minister's resignation in March, a struggle in which Asquith played an important role.

The leadership of the Liberal Party faced a dilemma. The two contenders to succeed Gladstone were the Foreign Secretary, Lord Rosebery, and the Chancellor of the Exchequer, Sir William Harcourt. Many of the leaders of the party favored Rosebery, but Harcourt had great support among rank-and-file Liberals. The real fear, as Sir Henry Campbell-Bannerman, the Secretary for War, expressed to Acland, was that Rosebery would become Prime Minister, leaving Harcourt to lead in the Commons, and that they would not be able to work together.[86] If Gladstone resigned while the Liberals were still in power, the Queen would be able to exercise her right to appoint, and her preference would be Rosebery. If the Liberal leadership failed to accept this, she would be more than pleased to then call her real favorite, Lord Salisbury, leader of the Conservatives, to form a government.[87]

Asquith much preferred Rosebery. He told Gladstone's private secretary, Algernon West, at the time that, although he admired Harcourt, he found his overbearing manner intolerable, and he could not consent to his leadership.[88] He later wrote that the "overwhelming verdict" of the cabinet at the time was that Harcourt "was an impossible colleague, and would have been a wholly impossible Chief. . . ."[89] Despite a later description of total disinterestedness throughout the leadership struggle, Rosebery was in close contact with Asquith, Acland, Morley, and Spencer, all working to see that he came out on top. There was even some talk during these discussions of Rosebery being Prime Minister and Asquith, rather than Harcourt, leading in the Commons. Morley for one, according to Sir Edward Hamilton, believed Asquith would make the best leader in the Commons.[90] There was another point during these discussions when Rosebery came up with the odd idea of refusing to accept the premiership if called because this would force the Queen to call Harcourt, who would then be compelled to admit that he could not form a government and thus reinforce Rosebery's position as obvious choice to succeed Gladstone. Asquith wrote to Margot that he "strongly dissuaded him from doing anything of the kind."[91]

Gladstone's last cabinet meeting was held on March 1, and the issue of succession had still not yet been finally settled. In relating the details of this last meeting, Asquith wrote that "Harcourt is still the problem: but he has few cards in his hands. . . . It seems likely that he will have to accept conditions instead of imposing them."[92] Harcourt was willing to become the leader in the Commons with Rosebery as Prime Minister but only under certain conditions such as having a voice in appointments and the right of independent communication with the Queen. Rosebery flatly refused. Asquith believed things could ultimately be worked out. "When he sees how the wind blows," Asquith said of Harcourt, "he will probably trim his sails + haul down the conditions; if not he must stand aside. . . ." If this happened, Asquith, who by this time was fed up with Harcourt's antics, would recommend Morley to take the lead in the Commons.[93] Ultimately Asquith's prediction of Harcourt's capitulation was correct. The Queen called for Rosebery to form a government on March 3, and Rosebery in turn asked Harcourt to take the lead in the Commons with no preconditions. Harcourt had no choice but to go along.

During this cabinet crisis, Asquith's three-year courtship of Margot was coming to fruition. The courtship had been passionate throughout. In December 1891, as the year in which his first wife died came to a close, he explained to Margot that the past year "which has brought to me the greatest sorrow of my life has also brought me its greatest joy + blessing in you."[94] By the next year, the courtship had developed to a point of real intimacy and the sharing of ideas. Margot was teaching him how to pray, and Asquith was explaining that "God, however we try to define him or conceive him, remains as the enduring foundation of our higher life."[95] Asquith showed concern once when Margot suggested he might be without a soul and that all "mystery is confusion" to him. He implored her to not think of him as "a person who revels in maps +

statistics + and all manner of pedantries; and who cannot feel the chorus + inspiration of spiritual twilight."[96]

The road to Margot Tennant's hand was not an easy one. In June 1892 it appears that Margot was about to end their relationship. In August of that year, when he had just been selected as Home Secretary, he wrote to her, "Here I am, full from my earliest days of political ambitions, still young, and just admitted to one of the best places in the cabinet, and yet I undertake to say that there is hardly a man in London more profoundly depressed than I am." Margot told him that she had lost the possibility of ever being in love again.[97] To his friend Francis Horner he revealed the up and down nature of his relationship with Margot. "There have been moments when we were more than lovers," he wrote, "+ then a cloud sweeps down out of the blue, + she seems to be separated from me by the whole width of heaven." In desperation he continued, "Can it be that through her God means to teach me the vanity of hope + the nothingness of human will?"[98]

Ultimately, Asquith's will did prevail, and he became engaged to Margot in January 1894. Margot's father readily approved of the engagement, and all seemed well. Asquith still, however, had to reassure his fiancée about their plans. He told her that he would not take her away from the country life she so enjoyed. Somehow they would arrange it so "it will all come right." He wanted her to feel free. As he explained, "The tie will always be there, to keep us close, but I couldn't bear that it should chafe you."[99]

Margot worried not only about marriage to a cabinet minister and the public life such a marriage would entail, but also becoming a mother to five children. John Morley wrote her two months before the wedding that she was about to marry "one of the finest men in the world, with a great store of sterling gifts both of head and heart, and with a life before him of the highest interest, importance and power." He added that he would not join those who wished her "to improve," rather he hoped she would keep her qualities of "vivacity, wit, freshness of mind, gaiety and pluck." He did warn, however, that "Circumstances may have a lesson or two to teach you. . . ."[100] Margot loved to relate the story of talking with the Gladstones one night after dinner before her marriage. Mrs. Gladstone and some of the other wives present described for Margot the duties she would encounter as the spouse of a possible Prime Minister to such a point that her "nerves were racing around like a squirrel in a cage." Gladstone reassured her and told her he knew of no one else better fitted than Margot to be the wife of a politician.[101]

Asquith and Margot married on May 10, 1894, at St. George's in Hanover Square. It was quite the social event, and a large crowd gathered outside the church. Four Prime Ministers or future Prime Ministers signed the register—Gladstone, Rosebery, Balfour, and of course Asquith. Algernon Cecil once remarked that with Asquith and Margot, "reason and intuition might said to have met."[102] While too simplistic an analysis, Cecil's statement does highlight the fact that in many ways Margot and Asquith were quite different. Certainly Asquith represented the more rational. How much intuition Margot brought to the union is debatable. Yet she did bring to their marriage many things that Asquith lacked. Their grandson, Mark Bonham Carter, captured it best when he remarked that Margot "welcomed life with an everlasting yea: on the hunting field riding horses far too strong for her to control, or in Dresden, in the drawing rooms of London, or dancing in front of Dr. Jowett after tea at Godsford." She injected the "unexpected" into the "rich routine of Victorian society."[103] Also with Asquith, Margot picked up the pace.

Rosebery took command in March 1894, but his government was doomed from the start. Harcourt remained bitter and looked for almost any excuse to challenge Rosebery's leadership. Unfortunately, Rosebery gave him plenty of opportunities.

In his maiden speech as Prime Minister, Rosebery foolishly declared that the English, as the "predominant member of the Three Kingdoms," would have to be convinced of the wisdom of Irish Home Rule before it could happen. In effect, he was saying that Home Rule would have to wait until any English majority approved it. This had never been argued by the Liberals and in Asquith's understated words gave "offense to the Irish" and "exercised some of our own people." Rosebery admitted to Asquith that he had made the statement without thinking and immediately realized the mistake. While there were no recriminations in the cabinet meeting the next day, when Parliament assembled, even though the Liberal leadership tried to "gloss over" what Rosebery had said, Asquith wrote to Margot that the Irish leader, John Redmond, "got up + was as nasty as he could be." It was not an auspicious beginning. Asquith talked with Rosebery the day afterward and reported that "he is still rather perturbed and sore" and "nothing could have been more wounding to a man of his self-esteem than to have fallen on the very first opportunity into a faux pas which a little tact and diplomacy could have avoided." Even at this early stage, Asquith was beginning to have some doubts about the Liberal leader, commenting to Margot that "half the act of speaking" is to avoid remarks that can be "fastened upon and twisted about + he [Rosebery] is just the man who might have been expected to steer clear of such sunken rocks."[104]

A more serious problem arose between Rosebery and Harcourt over the negotiation of a treaty with Belgium. Negotiations had been going on for some time between the British and King Leopold of Belgium over British influence in the upper Nile. The cabinet was not notified that these negotiations were going on, although Harcourt was informed in late March. A secret treaty was signed on April 12, and Harcourt was given a copy a little over a week later. The Chancellor of the Exchequer exploded and immediately raised the issue in the cabinet. He claimed he had an agreement with Rosebery to be kept fully informed of all important Foreign Office activity, and he believed this agreement had been breached. Morley and Asquith supported him, not on the terms of any alleged agreement with Rosebery, but at least as to the wisdom of entering such an agreement that might antagonize the French. Ultimately Harcourt let the matter drop, proving he was more interested in putting Rosebery in an uncomfortable position rather than in closely supervising foreign affairs.[105]

Asquith and other members of the cabinet found themselves in a difficult place. In many respects there was an attitude of a "plague on both your houses." For someone with such supreme discipline, self-control, and sense of party loyalty, Asquith could not understand Harcourt's "lack of any sense of proportion" and lack of self-restraint. Further, Asquith thought that Harcourt had a "perverse delight in inflaming and embittering every controversy," which made "co-operation with him difficult and often impossible."[106] Rosebery was hardly better. He acted as if he were defeated almost from his first day in office. His poor health played a part in the later months of his ministry, but even so Rosebery was shy, aloof, and often seemed disengaged. Three times Asquith, Morley, and Ackland invited him to dine with them and meet and get to know other Liberal MPs, but each time he refused.[107]

In spite of the Rosebery-Harcourt squabbles, Asquith was determined to move forward with the Liberal legislative program that came under his responsibility as Home Secretary. As we have seen, he succeeded in getting the Factory and Workshops bill though Parliament, even after the fall of the government but just before its dissolution. After a great deal of time and effort, he failed to gain passage of two other important pieces of legislation dealing with the disestablishment of the church in Wales and employer's liability/workmen's compensation.

For years Asquith had strongly favored the disestablishment of religious institutions in general. This stance almost certainly was a by-product of his nonconformist upbringing.[108] As early as 1888, in a speech to the Society for the Liberation from Patronage and Control, Asquith pointed out the obvious fact that the "Church was no longer coextensive with the nation." Consistently pragmatic, Asquith described the issue of disestablishment as "essentially a modern practical problem." Once dissent was accepted as a civil right, the position of the established church became untenable.[109] He explained his views in more detail during the height of the debate on Welsh church disestablishment in 1895. "The Church is a spiritual body, commissioned, as she believes and teaches, to preach to mankind the truths that are essential for their happiness and salvation—an institution that neither kings nor lords can create or destroy." An established church has become an anachronism. "Establishment" is merely "a set of legal incidents, some of which no doubt are involved in a remote and obscure historical origin. . . ." The days "when Church and State were but different names of one and the same thing" have long passed. Just as the will of kings and Parliament made the church an "established" church, so could they modify or destroy such relationship with the state.[110] To Asquith, there was simply no issue: the legalization of dissent over the years had made the connection between the church and state obsolete, and Parliament had the power to change the relationship to fit better modern circumstances.

The real importance of this issue for Asquith and the Liberal Party leaders was of course purely political, for it profoundly affected party unity. Wales was overwhelmingly nonconformist, and Welsh Liberals had been calling for church disestablishment for some time. Gladstone had mentioned it in the Newcastle Programme. Once in power, however, the Liberal leaders faced a dilemma. While the leaders wanted to appease Welsh Liberals and had no objection to Welsh church disestablishment in principle, the fact was that the government did not want to waste valuable Parliamentary time on a bill that did not have wide appeal in the nation and more importantly would face certain defeat in the House of Lords.[111]

In February 1893, six months after the new Liberal government came to power, Asquith introduced a Suspensory Bill to prohibit any funds from being allocated for new church livings in Wales. The Home Secretary readily admitted he was asking the House "to take the first step" toward disestablishment.[112] Gladstone reported to his Home Secretary that the Queen feared all of this was a foreshadowing of the disestablishment of the English church, to which Asquith responded that it was "difficult to follow the process of the Royal mind" since his speech clearly stated that only Welsh disestablishment was on the government's agenda.[113] The bill never made it to a second reading and was withdrawn in September. Welsh Liberals grew impatient with the government and began to discuss the formation of an independent party. The Liberal whip Tom Ellis, working with David Lloyd George, avoided the split only when the Liberal leadership promised the Welsh that a disestablishment bill would be produced. This agreement was linked to Ellis's reassurance that Asquith was already drafting a full-scale disestablishment bill. The Home Secretary completed his work on the complicated legislation in November to some extent with the help of Ellis and Lloyd George.[114]

Not until April 1894, however, did Asquith finally have the opportunity to introduce the measure. In a speech lasting almost two hours, reported in fifteen pages of *Hansards,* the Home Secretary claimed the bill rested on "broad principles of justice." It was neither in the interests of the church nor the state to leave the Welsh church as it was. If Parliament failed to act, the status quo would "be a constant source of embitterment and animosity." The church, which represented only a small minority, enjoyed property that was "national property to be appropriated for national purpose." The church's title was only "historical," and such title had "certainly not been strengthened in its hold upon the convictions and confidence of the Welsh people by the events which have since occurred." It was time to "set free" the church's property "for purposes of great and lasting public benefit" to the Welsh people.[115] The speech was one of Asquith's oratorical triumphs. Even the opposition praised the Home Secretary's performance. Balfour described it as "an exposition of lucidity," and the *Times* described the speech as "lucid and comprehensive."[116] People were beginning to recognize Asquith as an important leader in the government. After the speech, a writer for the *Sheffield Daily Telegraph* observed, "I have heard members of his party who used to sneer at his superior person airs admit that he is far and away the ablest man in the Cabinet, and that none of his colleagues could have made the speech he has made tonight."[117]

Under Asquith's measure, the church in the Welsh counties would be disestablished, and ecclesiastical law would no longer be in force at the end of 1895. With disestablishment, Welsh bishops and clergy would no longer sit in the House of Lords or in Convocation. Further, the bill disendowed the church of all benefactions prior to 1703, and the tithe was now vested in the county councils. The proceeds of the tithe were to be earmarked for charitable purposes. Incumbents were to be pensioned off, but curates were not included in the pension scheme. The bottom line was that 83 percent of the Welsh Church's income of more than a quarter of a million pounds was to be placed in secular hands.[118]

Asquith faced opposition not only from the church but also from the more radical Welsh MPs who sought an even stronger bill. Strenuous opposition from the church had been expected, and sure enough all the bishops of the church except one issued a manifesto denouncing the measure. A "Central Church Committee" was formed and set up opposition meetings throughout the country.[119] The radical Welsh MPs were even more of a problem. When Irish MPs forced the government to take up an Evicted Tenant's bill, this pushed the disestablishment measure back on the legislative agenda. Welsh MPs became so exasperated that four of them, including Lloyd George, announced that they would no longer receive the Liberal Whip in what became known as the "Revolt of the Four." With no time left for its passage, Harcourt finally announced the withdrawal of the bill in mid-July 1894.

The following year, Asquith prepared to reintroduce the measure. Tom Ellis, the Liberal Whip, urged him to change the bill as little as possible, and the Home Secretary followed his advice. The bill he introduced in February 1895 was almost identical to the bill introduced the year before.[120] Asquith's speech on the second reading was yet another masterpiece. Speeches often lose much of their punch when reduced to the written page, but one can still see "the hammer" at his best in this one. With its tight organization and well developed themes, the speech destroyed all the opposition's arguments. He recognized that the issues presented were of the "utmost delicacy and gravity," yet he refused to admit the questions were too difficult to solve. Even with this sterling performance before the House, once again neither the Liberal leadership nor Asquith for that matter had their hearts in the fight. To further complicate matters, in committee the bill suffered delay due to disagreement among Welsh MPs over the treatment of church funds, particularly tithes.[121] As it turned out, the Liberals fell from power before the bill could be passed, and Asquith could finally lay down what he himself described as a "thankless task."[122] It was not until the Welsh Church Act of 1914 (going into effect in 1920) passed when Asquith was Prime Minister that the Welsh Church was finally disestablished.

If Asquith was somewhat half-hearted in his attempt to push through Welsh Church disestablishment, such was not the case with employer's liability legislation.[123] The employer's liability bill that Asquith and the Home Office constructed proposed sweeping changes in the law and included almost everything labor had been working to achieve. Its essence was simplicity. The bill abolished employer's defences of common employment and assumption of risk. Employer's liability was extended to the negligence of subcontractors, and no limitation was placed on the amount of damages a worker could recover. Finally employers would not be able to "contract out" of their liability under the act.

From the outset of the debate, Asquith made it clear that the main purpose of the bill was to improve workplace safety. He said that with the possibility of greater liability the employer will have "a hundredfold greater inducements than now to see that his business is carried on with greater care and supervision in the interests of the safety and health of his men."[124]

Ultimately, the legislation had simply met an impasse and had to be withdrawn. Without a contracting out provision, it could not pass, and Asquith would not go along with what he saw as emasculation of the bill with such a provision.

By the summer of 1895 the Rosebery government was hanging by a thread. Amendments to the Welsh Disestablishment bill were defeated by smaller and smaller majorities, in some cases as few as seven. The proximate cause of the fall of the government, however, was a "snap" vote of censure against the head of the War Office, Sir Henry Campbell-Bannerman. The issue was the procurement of cordite, a new smokeless propellant explosive, for the army. When the government lost the vote, the cabinet met to discuss whether to resign and let the Conservatives form a government, call for a dissolution and an election, or attempt to continue to limp along in office.

Of those in the cabinet who mattered, Rosebery and Harcourt in a surprisingly rare show of agreement, together with Baron Tweedmouth, favored resignation. Asquith, Morley, Henry Fowler, and the Earl of Kimberly urged dissolution. Parliamentary Whip Tom Ellis and many party organizers such as Robert Hudson, Secretary of the Liberal Central Office, urged delay. Hudson had written Ellis, "By hook or by crook, we ought if we can to go on." He continued, "We want the autumn & winter for campaigning, & we want a new [voter] Register of which to fight."[125] The delay option, however, was never considered. As Asquith put it, the cabinet had simply had enough of "living from hand to mouth."[126]

Two conditions ultimately tipped the scales for resignation. Campbell-Bannerman decided to resign in any case and, according to Asquith, "the unusual—the almost unprecedented—spectacle" of Rosebery and Harcourt's "cordial agreement" that resignation was the best course to follow made the cabinet give in "to their combined authority."[127] Rosebery thus resigned, and the Queen immediately called for Lord Salisbury to form a new government. Asquith was out of office.

NOTES

1. HHA to MT, 13 Oct. 1891, BL, MS. Eng. c. 6685, ff. 91–92.
2. Alderson, *Mr. Asquith*, 48.
3. HHA to Josephine Armitage, 10 July 1892, MS. Bonham Carter 636, ff. 1–4.
4. Spender and Asquith, *Life of Asquith*, 1:75.
5. HHA Diary, 21 May 1892, MS. Bonham Carter 571.
6. W. R. Dudley Bahlman, ed., *The Diary of Sir Edward Walter Hamilton 1885–1906* (Hull: Hull University Press, 1993), 153.
7. Asquith, *Fifty Years*, 1:224.
8. HHA to Margot Tennant, 15 Nov. 1891, BL, MS. Eng. c. 6685, ff. 156–59.
9. WEG to H. V. Harcourt, 22 July 1892, BL, MS. Harcourt 12, ff. 31–33.
10. H. V. Harcourt to WEG, J25 July 1892, Brit. L, WEGP, Add MS 44202, f. 178.
11. WEG to HHA, 2 Aug. 1892, Brit. L, WEGP, Add MS 44515, ff. 129–30.
12. *Hansard*, 4, 7, 94–106, 8 Aug. 1892.
13. Dorothy Grey to HHA, 21 Aug. 1892, BL, MS. Asquith 9, ff. 19–20.
14. WEG to HHA, 14 Aug. 1892, Brit. L, WEGP, Add MS 44515, f. 148.
15. HHA to WEG, ibid., f. 149.
16. Haldane, *Autobiography*, 104.

17. H. V. Lucy Diary, Mar. 6, 1891, Alderson, *Mr. Asquith*, 51–52.
18. HHA to MT, 15 Aug. 1892, BL, M.S. Eng. c. 6686, ff. 87–90.
19. William Saunders to HHA, 20 Aug. 1892, BL, MS. Bonham Carter 621, ff. 14–15.
20. Arthur Ponsonby to HHA, 22 Aug. 1892, BL, MS. Bonham Carter 620, f. 63.
21. H. V. Harcourt to HHA, 24 Aug. 1892, BL, MS. Harcourt 75, ff. 7–8.
22. HHA to MT, 21 Aug. 1892, BL, M.S. Eng. c. 6686, ff. 105–6.
23. "From H. H. Asquith *Confidential. Trafalgar Square*," BL, MS. Harcourt 75, ff. 5–6.
24. H. V. Harcourt to HHA, 24 Aug. 1892, BL, MS. Bonham Carter 619, ff. 80–82.
25. "National Liberal Federation," *Times*, 21 Jan. 1893, 7a–e.
26. "Mr. Asquith in East Fife," *Times*, 23 Oct. 1893, 12b.
27. W. E. Elderige to HHA, 2 Sept. 1892, BL, MS. Bonham Carter, 619, ff. 38–39.
28. Jenkins incorrectly states that Asquith never communicated with Gladstone on the subject. Jenkins, *Asquith*, 64.
29. HHA to WEG, 13 Oct. 1892, Brit. L, WEGP, Add MS 44549, f. 68.
30. WEG to HHA, 14 Oct. 1892, Brit. L, WEGP, Add MS 44549, f. 26.
31. This policy was identical to that outlined in an undated memorandum entitled "Trafalgar Square" in HHA's hand, written apparently before the public announcement. BL, MS Bonham Carter 667, ff. 1–14.
32. "National Liberal Federation," *Times*, 21 Jan. 1893, 7a–e.
33. H. V. Harcourt to HHA, 20 Oct. 1892, BL, MS Harcourt 75, ff. 1920.
34. Rosebery to HHA, 21 Oct. 1892, BL, MS Bonham Carter 620, f. 67.
35. "Mr. Asquith on Future Legislation," *Times*, 24 Nov. 1892.
36. HHA to WEG, 30 Oct. 1892, Brit. L, WEGP, Add MS 44516, ff. 5–6.
37. Asquith, *Memories*, 1:131–32.
38. HHA to WEG, 30 Oct. 1892, WEGP, Add MS 44516, ff. 235–36.
39. Ibid.
40. HHA to James Bryce, 19 Dec. 1893, BL, MS. Bryce 23, ff. 101–3.
41. "The Release of the Dynamiters," *The Economist*, vol. 51, 28 Jan. 1893, 94.
42. *Hansard*, 4, 8, 922, 929–30, 9 Feb. 1893.
43. *Hansard*, 4, 8, 955, 9 Feb. 1893.
44. Morley, *Recollections*, 2:359–60.
45. Alderson, *Mr. Asquith*, 122.
46. "Mr. Asquith in East Fifeshire," *Times*, 21 Oct. 1893, 6a–f.
47. Alderson, *Mr. Asquith*, 121.
48. *Times*, 21 Jan. 1893, 7.
49. "Mr. Asquith on Home Rule," *Times*, 9 Jan. 1891, 8.
50. "Home Rule and the Referendum," *Times*, 25 Nov. 1891, 3.
51. Ibid.
52. HHA to J. W. Willans, 12 Mar. 1893, BL, F. W. Hirst Box 47.
53. *Hansard*, 4, 11, 335–62, 14 Apr. 1893.
54. Spender and Asquith, *Life of Asquith*, 1:79.
55. Alderson, *Mr. Asquith*, 120.
56. "Mr. Asquith at Althorpe," *Times*, 1 Sept. 1893, 10.
57. Ibid.

58. "Mr. Asquith in Glasgow," *Times*, 18 Oct. 1893, 10.
59. "Mr. Asquith at Leeds," *Times*, 31 Oct. 1893, 6.
60. *Times*, 21 Oct. 1893, 9.
61. Alderson, *Mr. Asquith*, 123.
62. Ibid., 125.
63. HHA to MT, 11 Sept. 1891, BL, MS. Eng. c. 6685, ff. 64–65.
64. Margot Asquith, *The Autobiography of Margot Asquith* (London: Penguin Books, 1936), 1:261.
65. Margot Asquith, *The Autobiography of Margot Asquith*, ed. Mark Bonham-Carter (Boston: Haughton Mifflin Company, 1963), xvi.
66. Feely, *Number 10*, 128.
67. Helen Melland Asquith to Josephine Melland Armitage, 4 Mar. 1891, BL, MS. Bonham Carter 565, ff. 48–50.
68. HHA to MT, 23 Mar. 1891, BL, MS. Eng. c. 6685, ff. 1–4; HHA to MT, May 21, 1891, BL, MS. Eng. c. 6685, ff. 15–16; HHA to MT, 22 Jul. 1891, BL, MS. Eng. c. 6685, ff. 35–37.
69. HHA to MT, 6 Apr. 1891, MS. Eng. c. 6685, ff. 5–10.
70. HHA to MT, 5 June 1891, BL, MS. Eng. c. 6685, ff. 27–28.
71. HHA to MT, 25 July 1891, BL, MS. Eng. c. 6685, ff. 39–40.
72. HHA to MT, 13 Aug. 1891, BL, MS. Eng. c, 6685, ff. 53–56.
73. HHA to MT, 2 Oct. 1891, BL, MS. Eng. c. 6685, ff. 67–68.
74. HHA to MT, 1 Sept. 1892, BL, MS. Eng. c. 6686, ff. 125–26.
75. HHA to MT, 21 May 1892, BL, MS. Eng. c. 6686, ff. 53–56.
76. "National Liberal Federation," *Times*, 21 Jan. 1893, 7.
77. "Mr. Asquith and the Pottery Trade," *Times*, 15 Mar. 1894, 14.
78. HHA to H. V. Harcourt, 7 Oct. 1892, BL, MS. Harcourt 75, ff. 11–12.
79. H. V. Harcourt to HHA, 19 Dec. 1892, BL, MS Harcourt 718, f. 254.
80. "Mr. Asquith's Min. of Dec. 1893 on Increased Factory and Mine Inspecting Staff," BL, MS. Asquith 71, f. 13.
81. "Mr. Asquith in East Fife," *Times*, 23 Oct. 1893, 12.
82. "Mr. Asquith's Min. of Dec. 1893 on Increased Factory and Mine Inspecting Staff," BL, MS. Asquith 71, f. 13.
83. Adelaide Mary Anderson, *Women in the Factory: An Administrative Adventure* (London: John Murray, 1922), 10.
84. Alderson, *Mr. Asquith*, 81.
85. "A Bill [As Amended by the Standing Committee of Trade] to amend and Extend the Law relating to Factories and Workshops," *Parl. Papers 1895*, iii, (Bill 329), 1 July 1895, 133–60.
86. Arthur Ackland to HHA, 16 Dec. 1898, BL, MS. Asquith 9, ff. 133–34.
87. Patrick Jackson, *Harcourt and Son: A Political Biography of Sir William Harcourt, 1827–1904* (Madison: Fairleigh Dickinson University Press, 2004), 235–49.
88. Horace G. Hutchinson, ed., *Private Diaries of The Rt. Hon. Sir Algernon West, G. C. B.* (London: John Murray, 1922), 204.
89. Asquith, *Fifty Years*, 249–50.
90. Bahlman, ed., *Diary of Sir Edward Walter Hamilton*, 184.
91. HHA to MT, 28 Feb. 1894, BL, MS. Eng. c. 6687, ff. 128–31.

92. HHA to MT, 1 Mar. 1894, BL, MS. Eng. c. 6687, ff. 132–34.
93. HHA to MT, 28 Feb. 1894, BL, MS. Eng. c. 6687, f. 130.
94. HHA to MT, 17 Dec. 1891, BL, MS. Eng. c. 6685, ff. 176–77.
95. HHA to MT, 28 Feb. 1892, BL, MS. Eng. c. 6686, ff. 19–20.
96. HHA to MT, 14 May1892, BL, MS. Eng. c. 6686, ff. 45–46.
97. HHA to MT, 15 Aug. 1892, BL, MS. Eng. c. 6686, ff. 87–90.
98. HHA to Francis Horner (copy), 17 Oct. 1892, BL, MS. Bonham Carter 619, f. 107.
99. HHA to MT, 1 Feb. 1894, BL, M.S. Eng. c. 6687, ff. 111–14; HHA to MT, 8 Feb. 1894, BL, MS. Eng. c. 6687, ff. 122–23.
100. M. Asquith, *Autobiography*, 1:239.
101. Ibid., 1:225.
102. Cecil, "Lord Oxford and Asquith," 7.
103. M. Asquith, *Autobiography of Margot Asquith*, xxii.
104. HHA to MT, 14 Mar. 1894, BL, MS Eng. c. 6687, ff. 146–48.
105. Robert Rhodes James, *Rosebery* (New York: Macmillan, 1963), 347–51.
106. Earl of Oxford and Asquith, *Fifty Years*, 1:252.
107. James, *Rosebery,* 357.
108. Quinault, "Asquith's Liberalism," 37–38.
109. Alderson, *Mr. Asquith*, 132.
110. Earl of Oxford and Asquith, *Speeches by the Earl of Oxford and Asquith, K.G.* (London, 1927), 31–32.
111. Bentley Brinkerhoff Gilbert, *David Lloyd George: A Political Life, vol. 1 The Architect of Change* (Columbus: Ohio State University Press, 1987), 113–14.
112. *Hansard*, 4, 9, 204, 23 Feb. 1893.
113. HHA to W. E. Gladstone, 26 Feb. 1893, Brit. L, WEGP, Add MS 44517.54–55.
114. Don M. Cregier, *Bounder from Wales: Lloyd George's Career Before the First World War* (Columbia: University of Missouri Press, 1976), 49.
115. *Hansard*, 4, 22, 1455–85, 26 Apr. 1894.
116. Alderson, *Mr. Asquith,* 139.
117. Ibid., 139–40
118. Kenneth O. Morgan, *Wales in British Politics 1868–1922*, rev. ed. (Cardiff: University of Wales Press, 1970), 145–46.
119. Ibid., 147.
120. Ibid., 149.
121. Creiger, *Bounder from Wales*, 55.
122. Earl of Oxford and Asquith, *Fifty Years*, 1:260.
123. See V. Markham Lester, "The Employers' Liability/Workmen's Compensation Debate of the 1890s Revisited," *The Historical Journal* 44, 2 (2001): 471–95.
124. *Hansard*, 4, 21, 401, 13 Feb. 1894.
125. Peter Stansky, *Ambitions and Strategies: The Struggle for Leadership of the Liberal Party in the 1890s* (Oxford: Clarendon Press, 1964), 170.
126. Earl of Oxford and Asquith *Fifty Years*, 1:261.
127. Ibid., 1:262.

Chapter Four

Waiting in the Wings (1896–1905)

To many the Liberal government of 1893 to 1895 had been a great disappointment. It had not only failed in its primary mission of giving Home Rule to the Irish but also failed to gain passage of many other measures such as the disestablishment of the Welsh Church suggested in the Newcastle Programme. Unlike the government's, Asquith's reputation fared much better. He had proved himself a competent administrator and Parliamentary debater. Sir William Harcourt wrote to him about the "brilliant manner" in which he had "exceeded the high expectations of your friend" and that it "is a mighty strength and encouragement to the Party to have the prospect in the future of such a champion and to look forward with confidence to the spes surgentis luli. . . ."[1] Over and over again, the Liberal government knew they could count on "the hammer" to drive home the winning argument. In short, as the Liberal government came to a close, Liberals viewed Asquith as a rising star with a bright political future ahead of him. There was just one problem. He had to earn a living.

When Asquith accepted Gladstone's invitation to serve as Home Secretary, he had every intention of returning to his private law practice when the government came to an end, but there was no precedent for a former cabinet minister, who was automatically made a member of the Privy Council, returning to active private practice. Asquith knew this was merely a tradition and not law; nevertheless, when the Liberal government fell in 1895, Sir Henry James wrote to Asquith and suggested avoiding criticism by seeking a formal opinion of the Chief Justice to confirm the propriety of the move.[2]

So it was, after making the proper inquiries, that Asquith became the first British cabinet minister to return to the private practice of law. To political diarist Henry Lucy, the famed "Toby, MP" of *Punch*, Asquith had "committed an act of political suicide unparalleled in recent history." To Lucy's mind and in the opinion of most others active in politics, it was impossible to get on in politics, even when out of power, without dedicating your full energies to Parliament. "[A] man cannot serve two masters," Lucy wrote. "The only way to get on in the House of Commons, in whatever capacity, is to live in it."[3] No doubt Asquith would have preferred full-time Parliamentary work, but he had no choice. True, his new wife Margot had a handsome income, but her expenditures were far from modest, and she may have even added to the debit side of Asquith's ledger. With no independent source of income of his own and a large family to support, Asquith had no alternative but to roll up his sleeves and earn a living at his profession.

Almost all barristers in Asquith's day were sole practitioners. They might share chambers with a friend or two, but they did not have partners in the modern sense of the term who could cover for them while they temporarily were in government service.[4] Upon leaving office, Asquith returned to his chambers at 1 Paper Buildings and resumed his law career. In reality this was not as daunting a task at it might at first seem. Even though he had not been in practice for three years, he was well known, not only as a former Home Secretary, but also as a well-respected barrister. Within months he appeared before the Privy Council representing an important client, the Union Bank, in a well-publicized case in which the famous actress Lillie Langtry had sued the bank for loss of her jewels.[5]

As with the Langtry case, most of Asquith's practice during the decade he was out of office involved appellate work before the House of Lords and the Privy Council. He had a keen legal mind well suited for appellate work. Despite his distinctly middle-class background, he could never identify with juries or feel comfortable with the emotional arguments necessary to prevail in a jury trial. As Lord Russell of Killowen told Margot, "Before a cultured tribunal your husband is the finest advocate we have; but he cannot play down to a jury."[6] He had a varied practice handling matters from railway litigation to Indian appeals before the judicial committee of the Privy Council. Typical was his involvement in two related cases, *Hawke v. Dunn* and *Powell v. Kempton Park Race Course*. These cases involved what turned out to be a vital question of the day: whether an unroofed area adjoining a race course which charged admission and allowed betting was a "place kept and used for betting" within the meaning of the penal provisions of the Betting Act of 1853. Remarkably such a seemingly inconsequential issue had to be argued before five different courts with twenty-one judges writing opinions.[7]

Most of the briefs Asquith took during this period, even those dealing with less important matters, almost always paid well. In fact he was one of the highest paid barristers in Britain, earning between £5,000 and £10,000 a year.[8] Just as he was finally able to assume office once again in 1905, this time as Chancellor of the Exchequer in the new Liberal government, he received a retainer of 10,000 guineas to represent members of the family of the ex-Khedive of Egypt in land dispute litigation in Egyptian courts.[9] There is no doubt, however, that Asquith's law practice took time and attention away from politics. After a dinner in 1902 Beatrice Webb wrote in her diary that "Asquith is wooden, he lacks every kind of enthusiasm and his hard-headed cold capacity seems to be given, not to politics, but to his legal cases."[10] Nevertheless with sheer discipline and determination throughout his decade out of power, Asquith was able to prove his critics wrong and actively engage in politics despite the demands of a successful legal career. He showed he could indeed serve two masters.

Soon after the Liberals fell from power and the Conservatives under the Marquess of Salisbury formed a government with the Liberal-Unionists, a general election was called in July–August 1895. Asquith's opponent was again the Liberal-Unionist J. G. Gilmour, who had run against him in the last election. Asquith campaigned hard, speaking to at least four or five meetings a day and remained confident of his own re-election. Early returns from other districts made it clear that the Liberals overall were in for a beating. On July 16 he wrote to Margot, "so far the election has been disastrous, and they are not likely to change for the better." He even went on to muse, "On the whole I would rather they [the Conservatives and Liberal-Unionists] had a decent majority than an even balance." As for his own race he reported, "I find all our people increasingly confident: but it does not do to be too cocksure."[11] As it turned out, he had little to worry about; he easily won the election, increasing his majority by over 400 votes, a majority he reported that was "larger than any of us hoped for."[12]

One of the most pressing issues during the Conservatives' tenure in office between 1895 and 1905 was national education. Stimulated by the "national efficiency" rage, education came to be seen by many British as one of the key factors in their nation's continued dominance of world affairs. Speaking in Oxford in 1896, Asquith argued that "an Empire without an educated people was like a navy without a supply of able-bodied seamen." Britain's one chance as a nation of "maintaining their supremacy, industrially and politically . . . lay in their giving the largest and widest possible development to their system of national education."[13]

After several failed attempts at passing educational reform bills, all vigorously opposed by Asquith and the Liberals, Arthur Balfour, who had succeeded Lord Salisbury as Prime Minister, introduced a new education bill in

March 1902. This comprehensive measure had only the reluctant support of the cabinet, yet Balfour knew that if education was to be truly improved, the entire system was to be overhauled. All school boards were to be abolished, and the responsibility for elementary, secondary, and technical education was to be placed in the hands of county and borough councils.[14]

Asquith mounted an attack on the government's bill both inside and outside of Parliament to the delight of nonconformist supporters of the Liberal Party. The *British Weekly*, an influential nonconformist journal, wrote, "We note with special satisfaction the excellent speeches which Mr. Asquith is delivering in the country on the Education Bill." The article continued, "[n]o politician has better grasped its evil intent, and has exposed it more convincingly," and "No one has more frankly accepted it as the first charge and business of the Liberal Party to undo its iniquitous provisions." Finally, the article concluded, "more of such speaking as Mr. Asquith's would enormously reinforce and revive the Liberal Party."[15]

There is some evidence, however, that Asquith was not as sincere in his opposition to the government's education bill as his public statements might suggest. Beatrice Webb recorded in her diary that Asquith had "worked himself into an unreal opposition to the Education Bill. . . . He is not really convinced of the inequity or unwisdom of the bill he is denouncing."[16] Although Asquith may have had doubts about just how evil the Education Bill was, he still had strong reasons for opposing it. As some have noted, much of his opposition stemmed from his own nonconformist background.[17] For years he had consistently attacked unconditional support for denominational schools. By 1902, however, it was more than his nonconformist background or his principles that led him to oppose the government's bill. Along with many other Liberals, Asquith smelled political blood in the issue of education and quickly moved in for the kill. This was an issue Liberals knew would rally the party faithful. Not only was the measure extremely unpopular among the nonconformists, the mainstay of the party, but it also was an issue, unlike many issues of imperialism, that did not divide the Liberal leadership. As recognized by the *British Weekly*, funding education "would enormously reinforce and revive the Liberal Party."[18]

Throughout all the stages of the bill, Asquith was on the attack. His principal address occurred during the debate on the second reading in May. Asquith opened by saying he agreed in principle with the creation of a single authority for education, but he questioned whether the government's bill actually moved in that direction. He mockingly described the proposed system: "You have one Committee which controls but does not manage; another Committee which manages but does not control; you have above them both the Board of Education, which, whenever they differ, is to determine which is in the right;

and lastly you have the County Council whose sole function is to pay the bill and levy the rate." And so, he declared, "Committee one, Committee two, Board of Education, county Council—that is your one authority!" He went on to challenge the government's plan to allow for separate religious instruction. "But the hour strikes for religious teaching and what happens then?" he asked. "The children are all sorted out into separate theological flocks, and each flock is herded off into a little ecclesiastical pen of its own, there to be grounded and confirmed at the cost of the State in the doctrines, or it may the negations, which are dear to its parents."[19]

There was the public to convince too, and Asquith did not limit his opposition to speeches in Parliament. At numerous public gatherings he tended to play upon the "single school issue" and nonconformist fears of forced religious education. A typical speech was one in London in June to a mass protest meeting. At this gathering, chaired by Lord Rosebery, Asquith raised the spectre of the poor nonconformist child being forced by the power of the state to attend schools dominated by Anglicans. Schools, he argued, even though receiving large government subsidies, would be "managed and directed entirely by private irresponsible persons." Playing to the crowd, Asquith even said that proponents of the bill had confessed that the schools were to be made "vestibules of the church." Again in November Asquith appeared on the platform with Campbell-Bannerman at a mass protest meeting. Admitting that there was no question Britain needed a truly national system of education, he nevertheless attacked the government's bill for not accomplishing this but instead preserving two classes of schools.[20]

Although the government ultimately prevailed and passed the Education Act of 1902, education as a political issue remained, and Liberals did all in their power to keep it before the public. Some of the more radical nonconformists argued that they should even refuse to cooperate with the implementation of the act. Asquith along with many others opposed this tactic, saying that to allow a system "to be poisoned by the miasma of sectarian controversy" was "to be guilty of something like treason to the best interests of the Empire."[21] Speaking at Hull, Asquith urged that "it was clearly their duty to make the most they could of facilities as the new Act gave for the popular control of education."[22]

Education was one of the most volatile political topics at the end of the nineteenth century. Asquith and many others of all political persuasions knew that the British educational system was outdated and in need of reform. Standing in the way of real reform was the question of religious education. To the late Victorian, it was difficult, if not impossible, to think of a complete education without some religious instruction. Asquith never questioned this assumption. What he demanded was financial accountability, together with some protection for nonconformist children who lived in predominantly Anglican areas. Throughout the more than five years of debate on the issue, Asquith was consistent in these demands. While this was a principled response to the measures introduced by the government, Asquith was also well aware of the political gain that could be made for the Liberal Party by playing on the fears of its nonconformist mainstay constituency. He was willing to do all he could to ensure that the Liberal Party gain every political advantage it could by attacking the government's plans. The government eventually prevailed, more through party discipline than a national consensus. As Asquith predicted as early as 1897, without such consensus, legislation does not long survive, and this was certainly to be the case with the Education Act of 1902.

Asquith also locked horns with the Conservative government over employers' liability. When the Conservatives and Liberal-Unionists came to power in 1895, it was Joseph Chamberlain who raised the very issue on which he had earlier thwarted Asquith's efforts while Home Secretary.[23] Chamberlain's interest in the matter pre-dated his 1893 debate with Asquith. As early as 1874 in his "radical programme of the future," he had proposed compensation for injuries caused by negligent employers. As President of the Board of Trade in a Liberal cabinet, he introduced the original employers' liability act in 1880. Over the years, Chamberlain had been influenced by the German workmen's compensation insurance scheme, and after his initial resolution on the subject during the 1893 debates over Asquith's bill, it became a central part of his political program.[24]

Under Chamberlain's bill introduced in 1897, workers injured during the course of employment in specifically limited numbers of businesses and industries could claim compensation without any proof of negligence on the part of the employer or a fellow employee. Compensation was to be paid without recourse to litigation unless the employer alleged the injury was deliberately caused by the worker. In return for this concession, the bill limited the employers' liability to a statutory scale. With a specific limit to liability, Chamberlain hoped employers would easily be able to insure themselves at a relatively low cost. Workers could still proceed with a case at common law or under the Employers' Liability Act of 1880 for unlimited damages, but they would be required to prove negligence and be subject at common law to the formidable defenses not only of assumption of risk but also "common employment," whereby an employer was not liable for the negligence of an employee who caused injury to a fellow employee. The Chamberlain bill became the basis for the modern workers' compensation law. Did Asquith's opposition betray his liberal ideals?

In his initial reply to Chamberlain's bill, Asquith returned to what he saw as the "first question" of worker safety.[25] He had never objected to the principle of "universal compensation"; yet the first concern, Asquith argued, should be "reducing the risks of trade and in diminishing the number of injured workmen who have claimed compensation." The Conservative government's bill, according to Asquith, "does not give the employer any additional incentive to take precautions."[26] As a result, although Asquith generally supported Chamberlain's bill, he led the charge to have the doctrine of common employment abolished. Chamberlain's bill, according to Asquith, failed to fix "a direct personal responsibility on the employer for taking all precautions which skill and foresight can suggest against accident, to raise the level of safety."[27] In 1897, just as in 1893, we see Asquith and Chamberlain taking opposite views of how best to increase the level of worker safety. Asquith led the Liberals in wanting to place greater liability on the employer and increase employer common law liability, as Asquith's bill had proposed four years before.

Chamberlain argued that accidents would not be reduced "by laying on the employer pecuniary liability." In fact Chamberlain saw no real urgency in the issue of worker safety at all, declaring, "I myself have never been convinced that such additional precautions were urgently required." He noted that he had never contended his bill would greatly affect safety precautions, because he believed that "every good employer already voluntarily takes all the precautions that he can be called upon to take."[28]

Asquith and his allies' desperate attempt to amend Chamberlain's bill and abolish the doctrine of common employment was to no avail, and it became law. Chamberlain, having brought his business allies a long way in supporting any kind of compensation scheme, could widen the purview of common law liability, as Asquith suggested, without risking the defeat of the entire measure. Yet before leaving this discussion, it should be noted that Parliament passed the act against a wider political backdrop, particularly the attempt on the part both Conservatives and Liberals to attract the support of the growing ranks of labor voters. Both parties sought essentially the same ends: compensation paid for by employers (or ultimately consumers) for victims of industrial accidents and the political support of workers that might result. To be sure, Chamberlain's plan reflected his readiness to abandon *laissez-faire* notions, while Asquith's reliance on an extension of common law remedies showed greater deference to liberal notions of an economy free from government interference. Nevertheless, it was political pressure, especially from employers, rather than political or economic philosophy, that largely dictated the terms of the Workmen's Compensation Act of 1897.

Throughout Asquith's decade out of power, the Liberal Party and particularly its leadership were in great disarray. The principal cause was the Liberals' failure to coalesce around a successor to Gladstone in 1895. This, together with the clash within the party over the Boer War, left the Liberals more or less splintered until at least 1903. For Asquith, who had his own plans to lead the party sometime in the future, it was a generational problem. The political generation that stood between Gladstone and Asquith, men like Rosebery, Harcourt, and Campbell-Bannerman, could never agree among themselves as to who should lead the party, and as if this were not enough, they later divided over the issue of the Boer War. Such a leadership vacuum was calamitous. Asquith's generation had to stand by, doing what they could to hold things together until they could take control. In Asquith's case, he did what he could to maintain party harmony, continuing to hope that Rosebery would finally take the initiative and grasp the reins, but as the years went by, he realized more and more that this was simply not going to happen.

With the collapse of the Liberal government in 1895, Harcourt continued to lead in the Commons, the Earl of Kimberly in the Lords, with Rosebery acting as the titular head of the party. Rosebery, however, had made up his mind to sever all ties with Harcourt and even refused to attend the first meeting of the ex-cabinet because Harcourt would be there. Over and over again, younger Liberal leaders, including Asquith and Haldane, attempted to patch up the differences between Rosebery and Harcourt. At one point even Gladstone said he would be willing to lend a hand. Many did not realize that Rosebery's attitude toward Harcourt and his reluctance to lead were based not just on a personal dislike of Harcourt. While the former Prime Minister loved power, it soon become apparent to all that he thoroughly detested the political maneuvering necessary if he and the Liberals were ever to regain it. Harcourt's attitude was not much better. Although a capable politician and administrator in many respects, he had always been a difficult colleague and did not suffer fools. Publicly he constantly feigned any interest in the leadership position, even though the opposite was true. As a frustrated Asquith wrote Margot about Harcourt in early 1896, "I never saw a better study of bland and ingenious innocence."[29]

The squabble came to a head in 1896, triggered by an international incident. News reached Britain of Turkish massacres of Armenians to the horror of the public and many Liberals. Gladstone himself came out of retirement to denounce the atrocity and called for the government to take some unspecified action in the matter. Asquith generally supported Gladstone's call for action, and much of the Liberal press and the rank and file called for a vigorous response. Rosebery, however, publicly took a more moderate view. When the *Daily Chronicle* reported that Harcourt had made what the paper described as an anti-Turkish speech, the temperamental and ever-sensitive Rosebery saw it as a challenge to his leadership and used the incident as an excuse to resign as leader of the party. Even though the *Daily Chronicle* had misrepresented Harcourt's talk in which, at least by implication, he had actually supported the Rosebery position, there was no changing Rosebery's mind. Since Rosebery kept his intentions to himself, to the shock of everyone, the press reported on the morning of October 8 that he had resigned.[30]

Asquith happened to be visiting the Balfours at Whittingehame when the news broke. He wrote to a friend that Rosebery had "acted selfishly" in resigning and that, even though he might have helped himself personally, "he has sacrificed the interests of his colleagues and friends."[31] Although Asquith, Haldane, and Sir Henry Fowler immediately traveled to see Rosebery, they were unable to convince him to change his mind.

It is not surprising that news of Rosebery's resignation came to the Asquiths while they were at a weekend party. Asquith's legal profession and political career all took place against the backdrop of his family life, a life that had dramatically changed with his marriage to Margot in May 1894. Margot was raised in London high society, and it was clear from the very beginning of their marriage that Asquith would be trading his quiet society at Hampstead for a life that would be an unending round of social events—dinners, luncheons, weekend parties, and the like. Soon after their marriage, Asquith even left his nonconformist faith and joined the Church of England, a move a contemptuous Lloyd George thought he made for "Society" reasons. Others, however, have questioned whether Asquith's move to Anglicanism was in truth a total betrayal of his nonconformist faith, pointing to the fact that Asquith had been brought up in tolerant nonconformist tradition not too distant from popular Anglicanism.[32] His switch to Anglicanism made little difference to him. Undoubtedly, over the years Asquith had moved from the strict nonconformist faith in which he was raised; however, he never once lost the strong religious beliefs that remained with him for the rest of his life.

An outward symbol of Asquith's new social life was the couple's move to 20 Cavendish Square in London, a Georgian mansion, which today houses the Royal College of Nursing. The maintenance of such a large house was a constant drain on finances and could prove at times bothersome in other ways. Margot was often absent on hunting trips, leaving Asquith to deal with the household. He described to her how he had to reprimand a servant just after Christmas for being drunk, leaving him with the warning "that the faintest recurrence of anything of the kind would lead to his instant dismissal + total ruin of his future."[33]

The Asquiths' account book provides an interesting window into their lifestyle. In 1901, for example, they listed £9,000 of expenses. This was in the day when a skilled worker earned only an average of about £100 a year. Almost half of the Asquiths' expenses went to maintain 20 Cavendish Square, including rent, regular maintenance, and kitchen, nursery, and so on.

No doubt Margot was a large item on the list of expenses with her costly clothes and stables. In fact a whole new line item, "Margot," shows up in the account book in 1902 with £1,348 listed and continues with a similar amount for several years. Asquith, however, was not without his own extravagances. A line item "wine, cigars" was £229 for 1901, and increased each year until a decline in 1905 to £150.[34]

The fact was that the Asquiths always lived on the financial edge. They seem to have blithely gone on their way spending money they knew they didn't have, even with the addition of Margot's £3,000 annual allowance from her father. In late 1898, in an attempt to make ends meet, they even stooped to ask their friend Arthur Balfour to write to Margot's father, Charles Tennant, and ask on their behalf that Margot's allowance be increased. The Bart promptly conveyed his refusal to do so to Balfour.[35] On January 1, 1899, Margot confided to her diary, "Henry had a serious talk with me about expenditure and told me I must spend less as some day he might have to lead the party.... I promised him I would be very careful...."[36] Six years later money was still a problem. In the summer of 1905 Asquith wrote his wife asking that she not distress herself over their financial situation and reassuring her that it would "come out alright." Cuts in expenditure had to be made. Margot's suggestions about reducing her hunting that season were good, but he wrote, "it is not necessary to decide yet what do with the carriage horses."[37] Asquith had come a long way from Morley.

Much analysis of Asquith's marriage to Margot has focused on her as spoiler, using the allure of high society to turn her husband away from the discipline of his youth. Haldane in his autobiography, published after Asquith's death, takes this position. "London Society came, however, to have a great attraction for him," Haldane wrote, "and he grew by degrees diverted from the sterner outlook on life which he and I for long shared."[38] Others made similar observations. Beatrice Webb commented in her diary in 1895 that "Asquith has been ruined by marrying a silly ignorant wife, and there is no other man who has at once capacity, character and conviction."[39] Sir Edward Hamilton, a former private secretary to Gladstone, recorded in his diary in July 1894 a conversation he had with Gladstone's son Herbert about Asquith. Herbert Gladstone thought Asquith did not have sufficient Parliamentary experience then to be leader of the Liberal Party and suspected him "a little of preferring society and amusement to House of Commons work."[40]

Such observations by contemporaries cannot be ignored. Asquith changed in his attitude toward London society after his marriage to Margot. He enjoyed it. Nonetheless, his critics' comments need to be taken in context. Haldane had been very close to Helen Asquith, and while Asquith and Haldane remained close associates, they were never again as close as they had been in the 1880s. In addition, Haldane's impressions of Margot's effect on Asquith were written after the bitter break between the two friends in 1916. Webb was writing in the context of her disappointment in *all* Liberal leaders, not just Asquith. Then too, there seems to be a social bias in many people's view of Asquith after his marriage to Margot. Asquith had clearly married beyond his middle-class social station, and as a result, once he was clearly enjoying his new position, there were bound to be those who felt left behind and who viewed Asquith's new life with jealousy and resentment.

For Margot, marriage led to the usual strains of blending in with a family that already existed. Asquith's oldest son, Raymond, was always his father's pride and joy. From the very beginning, Asquith had great ambitions for his son, many of them along the lines of following Asquith's own footsteps. When he first took Raymond to school at Winchester, he wrote that he was confident he would do well, but that his real ambition for him was that he should get the Balliol Scholarship in a few years.[41] There is every indication that Asquith and his first wife Helen wanted to have, more than anything else, "clever sons." Asquith even admitted to Helen on one occasion that this was the case, and Raymond certainly did not disappoint his father in this regard.[42] He did in fact get a scholarship to Balliol, and his career at Oxford, despite his reputation for high living, was one academic triumph after another. Despite this, Margot observed that, when Raymond went to Oxford, "he cultivated a kind of cynicism which was an endless source of delight to the young people around him; in a good natured way he made a butt of God and smiled at man." She continued that he "was without ambition of any kind" and was never really "keen" about any one thing.[43] Such a description seems harsh for a man who took a first in classical moderations in 1899, a first in "Greats" in 1901, and a first in jurisprudence the following year. He also was actively involved in sports and participated regularly in debates at the Oxford Union, ultimately being elected its President like his father. Asquith had a much different view of Raymond. To him, Raymond was a source of continuing pride. As Raymond's time in Oxford drew to a close, Asquith recorded in his diary that his son had received a first in "Greats" and recorded with pride that one of the examiners had told him Raymond "had a first class work for every paper, + did the best in Latin Prose." For the next entry, recorded months later, Asquith, who was not known for his displays of emotion, wrote in large letters across the entire page "Raymond got the Ireland!"[44] Asquith only came in second for the Ireland. The son had outdone his father.

As for the other children, Beb followed his older brother to Balliol. Like Raymond, he was involved in all sorts of drinking, pranks, and carousing. His academic career was not nearly as illustrious as that of his older brother. He only received a second in "Greats"; nonetheless, he became the third member of his family to become President of the Union. Oc, who went up to Oxford in 1902, took a slightly different path, attending New College rather than his family's favorite, Balliol. Oc had little interest in the debates of the Union or in athletics, and his academic performance was unexceptional.

Over time Margot began to get along well with her three oldest stepsons. These boys had known their mother well and had been devastated by her death. The new family structure must not have been easy for either the boys or Margot. Violet, Asquith's only daughter by Helen, was an entirely different matter. She was an outgoing girl who had been somewhat delicate in her youth. In the tradition of the times, she did not receive a formal education, but she was highly intelligent. From the very beginning Violet and Margot did not get along well with each other. The reasons are unclear, perhaps a mother-daughter rivalry.

Margot had become pregnant with Asquith's and her first child in 1894, but the child was lost in childbirth. Three years later she became pregnant again, resulting in the birth of a daughter, Elizabeth, in February 1897. Elizabeth's birth calmed much of Margot's restlessness. She wanted a girl, and having her own child perhaps helped her understand her stepchildren better, especially the devastation all Asquith's children must have felt at the death of their mother. After a period of relatively good health, Margot lost another child in 1899 and again developed a delicate condition. She was diagnosed at one point with "anaemia of the brain" and prescribed constant nips of brandy to ease her dizziness. Over time, her health improved, and in November 1902, she gave birth to a son, Anthony ("Puffin"), born prematurely but relatively healthy.[45]

Margot and Asquith's relationship was complicated. They both respected each other, but as the years went by, it became apparent that Margot became more and more dependent on Asquith rather than the reverse. Although Margot continually offered political advice to her husband, her suggestions rarely, if ever, caused Asquith to change his mind. Living with and caring for Margot could be trying at times, but Asquith seemed to live through it all with not just a stoic patience but also with a continued general affection for his wife.

As the century came to a close, foreign and imperial policy issues became more and more important for Britain, culminating in the outbreak of the Boer War in October 1899. Throughout his Parliamentary career, Asquith closely associated himself with a group popularly known as "Liberal Imperialists." The term eludes simple definition, even though the group has been extensively studied, most notably in Colin Matthew's excellent work *Liberal Imperialists*. Lord Rosebery, who was seen by most as the leader of the group, declared in 1885, "If a Liberal Imperialist means that I am a Liberal who is passionately attached to the Empire—if it means, as I believe it does, that I am a Liberal who believes that the Empire is best maintained upon the widest democracy, and that the voice is most powerful when it represents the greatest number of persons and subjects—if these be accurate descriptions of what a Liberal Imperialist is, then I am a Liberal Imperialist. . . ."[46] Of course, this is much too simple a definition. Those, like Asquith, Haldane, Grey, and others, who considered themselves Liberal Imperialists had much more in common than imperial policy. More than anything else, the Liberal Imperialist group was an elite group who saw themselves as natural leaders of the party and the nation not just in foreign, but also in domestic affairs. According to Asquith, the more influential Liberal Imperialists tended to inclined toward the left wing in domestic affairs. In many ways on both foreign and domestic issues, they wanted the Liberal Party to get away from beating the same old drums of church disestablishment, Home Rule, and franchise reform and to begin anew with what Lord Rosebery famously called a "clean slate." To this group, such a plan was absolutely necessary to the Liberal Party's future success at the polls. If the Liberals were ever once again to become the dominant political party in Britain, this group believed the party needed to carry out a complete reappraisal of the nature of liberalism. Without such a reappraisal, there could be no revival of the Liberal Party's fortunes.[47] They needed issues, such as a forward imperial policy, that would attract a wider audience. In short, they looked for nothing short of a transformation of the Liberal Party into a truly national party, not just one arguing for particular religious or sectional interests.

The danger of such ideas was that, if carried too far or too fast, they could actually destroy the Liberal Party by splitting it in two. This was a grave concern to Asquith, who more than any of the Liberal Imperialists was the most loyal to the Liberal Party. If anything, Asquith was a Liberal first and an Imperialist second. His long friendship and close association with Haldane and Grey, two of the leading Liberal Imperialists, perhaps made Asquith appear to be closer to the group than he actually was, for the first priority for Asquith throughout this period was the unity of the Liberal Party rather than any Liberal Imperialist agenda.[48]

Strangely, there was never as much unity among the Liberal Imperialists on imperial and foreign affairs issues as contemporaries thought. In fact, for many years imperial issues divided the group. For example, Asquith supported the Conservative government's 1888 Land Purchase (Ireland) bill, even though fellow Liberal Imperialists Haldane, Grey, and Munro-Ferguson opposed the measure. Asquith sharply disagreed with Rosebery's plan for the annexation of Uganda, when they both served in Gladstone's last cabinet. In particular, Asquith objected to Rosebery's anti-French views.[49] Again too, when the Turks attacked the Armenians in 1894 and 1895, Asquith favored breaking off diplomatic relations with the Turks, even though Rosebery opposed such a view for fear it might trigger a general European war.[50]

The South African War, which broke out in 1899, however, put Liberal Imperialism to the test and came close to splitting the Liberal Party. The origins of the war are complex. For almost a century, the British had been in conflict with the Dutch Boer settlers in the southern part of Africa. To add more tension to the situation, Australian prospectors discovered gold in the Witwatersrand area of Transvaal in 1886. The wealth that came from the mines allowed the Boers to become less and less dependent on the British Cape Colony. They soon built a railroad to the Indian Ocean at Delagoa Bay in Portuguese East Africa, allowing them to import and export goods as they wished. This led to the importation of arms from Germany, and there were even rumors that the Boers intended to take over all of South Africa by force. The discovery of gold, however, also meant that the Transvaal was flooded with *uitlanders* (outsiders) mostly coming from Britain. By the mid-1890s, these *uitlanders* outnumbered the Boers, and President Kruger decided to stem the tide by denying the *uitlanders* certain political rights and heavily taxing them.

Cecil Rhodes, who became Prime Minister of the Cape Colony in 1890, thought the *uitlander* unrest a perfect opportunity to attempt to overthrow the Boer government of the Transvaal. In December 1895, with the blessing of Rhodes, Dr. Leander Star Jameson crossed into the Transvaal from Bechuanaland with a small force of volunteers. An uprising of the *uitlanders* was supposed to be coordinated with the invasion, but the uprising failed to materialize, and the Boers easily defeated Jameson's force. The affair humiliated the British and offended not only the Boers in the Transvaal, but also those in the Orange Free State and in the Cape Colony itself.

There was an outcry at home. The Secretary of State for the Colonies, Joseph Chamberlain, denied any prior knowledge of the raid, although this apparently was not the case, and immediately condemned the raid, a step that Asquith characterized as "correct."[51] In a speech at Trowbridge five months after the Jameson raid, Asquith described it as a "reckless and foolish enterprise" that had inflicted "irreparable injury and dishonour upon British interests in South Africa." According to Asquith, the raid unfortunately wiped out whatever sympathy there had been for the plight of the *uitlanders* living under Boer rule. It had created a rift between the British and Boers that "might take years and possibly even a generation to close."[52]

Chamberlain asked Asquith to serve on a Committee of Inquiry into the responsibility for the Jameson raid, but he refused, sensing a trap.[53] Instead, grasping the opportunity for a political advantage for the Liberals, Asquith attacked the government for its failure to investigate properly the Jameson debacle. He challenged any attempt "to throw . . . a cloak or a veil either over individuals or associations who might be shown responsible for what had happened."[54]

Asquith became further enmeshed in the South African situation when the government appointed his friend, Alfred Milner, as High Commissioner for South Africa in 1897. He first met Milner as a fellow student at Balliol, where they sat together at the Scholars' table in hall for three years. In Asquith's words, they "formed a close friendship, and were for many years on intimate terms and in almost constant contact with each other."[55] Even after Milner left for Africa, the two men regularly kept in touch. In November 1897, Milner wrote to Asquith commenting on one of Asquith's recent speeches calling for restoration of good relations between the Boers and British and the protection of natives from oppression, particularly in Rhodesia. Milner challenged him as to why he focused his remarks on Rhodesia, ignoring the plight of the natives in Transvaal. "What I am so anxious that you and other English Statesmen, especially Liberal Statesmen, should understand is that object No. 2 [protection of natives] is the principal obstacle to the attainment of object No. 1 [good relations with the Dutch] . . . ." "I should feel quite confident of being able to get over the Dutch-English difficulty," he concluded, "if it were not so horribly complicated by the Native question." Milner added that Asquith was free to share his letter with Morley "or any other good man and true on your side."[56] Asquith replied that he had shown the letter to Morley and Ripon and, recognizing Milner was operating in a difficult position, told him that he could "be sure that, in carrying out the general scheme of policy which you indicate, we shall all watch you with great sympathy, and with a full disposition to appreciate and make allowance for the fetters upon free action and the checks to rapid progress which the local conditions impose."[57]

In March 1899 the *uitlanders* in Transvaal petitioned Queen Victoria for protection from the political oppression they claimed they were suffering at the hands of the Boers. This plea prompted the Salisbury government to demand changes in the Transvaal's treatment of the *uitlanders*. Kruger and Milner met in June at Bloemfontein, the capital of the Orange Free State, and Kruger offered to give the *uitlanders* the right to vote, provided they met a seven-year residency requirement. The meeting broke up, however, when Milner demanded that the requirement be reduced to five years.

In August, Asquith wrote Harcourt that "everything at present points to a pacific arrangement on the basis of give and take."[58] However, two months later on October 9, President Kruger issued an ultimatum to the British demanding not only the withdrawal of all British troops from the Transvaal boarder, but also insisting that all reinforcements recently brought to the Cape Colony be withdrawn. News of the ultimatum reached London on the day it expired, and the Boers invaded British-held Natal and the Cape Colony itself. As Lord Salisbury told the House of Lords, the Boer government has "liberated us from the necessity of explaining to the people of England why we are at war."[59]

Parliament debated the government's actions the next week, and there was a motion of censure. Asquith questioned the sincerity of Chamberlain's intention to work with the Boers. "If so," Asquith asked, "why any war?" Even so, he told Margot that, if he had been a free agent, he would "probably have voted with the govt.," even though he believed they had bungled the situation. However, Campbell-Bannerman strongly appealed to him to abstain, which he did, and he told Margot, "I was not sorry that I did."[60]

The Boers struck quickly with pre-emptive strikes into British-held territories in Natal and the Cape Colony. Soon the British garrisons at Ladysmith, Mafeking, and Kimberly were under siege. When the war had been underway less than two weeks, Asquith described British losses as "terrible to think of" and in terms of officers lost "unprecedented."[61] Before the end of October, Asquith was saying that there had not been such a disaster for the British army since the American war for independence. Even at this early date in the war, Asquith wrote that he believed the "whole strategy of the campaign so far seems in the highest degree risky + unsound." "No one," he observed, "could have foreseen such a costly blunder as this."[62]

By saying only a month into the hostilities that "no one" could have predicted the morass Britain had walked into, Asquith might well have been attempting to justify his own early support of the Salisbury government. Up until almost the outbreak of hostilities, Asquith's views on South African did not differ from those of other Liberals, like Lloyd George, who would ultimately oppose the war. Apparently what caused him to support the government and split with many other Liberals was the Kruger memorandum. Influenced by Milner, Haldane, Grey, Rosebery, and others who took a forward position on the importance of British influence in South Africa, Asquith stated that the Kruger ultimatum had created a whole new situation. Once Kruger issued his challenge, Asquith saw the issue as whether or not Britain was to remain the paramount power in South Africa. Naively he refused to see any ulterior motive of the government such as suppressing the Boers and annexing the Transvaal outright. In his mind the Boers had forced war on the British, and they had no alternative but to fight. In November, Asquith framed the main purpose of the war in terms of the protection of the *uitlanders*, whom he described as "fellow subjects." With no political rights, the oppressed *uitlanders* had no alternative but to fight.[63] In short, Asquith took the government's position at face value. It is surprising that neither Asquith, nor Haldane, nor Grey—all men of political sophistication—had any clear conception of the situation in South Africa or the government's real policy.[64]

It was not long before the South African War began seriously to divide the Liberal Party. The majority of Liberals opposed the war to one degree or another, but opposition ranged from extreme opponents, like Lloyd George, to the more moderate like Campbell-Bannerman. Lloyd George had never paid much attention to South Africa early in his career. He found the Jameson raid ridiculous and publicly ridiculed it, but like Asquith he did not anticipate the outbreak of war in 1899 and was in Canada when the hostilities began. Unlike Asquith, however, Lloyd George immediately suspected the motives of the Salisbury government. He concluded that the war was deliberately provoked, that it would be costly, and that it could only serve to delay social reforms. Despite these views, Lloyd George believed in the empire. In Lloyd George's mind, his objection to the South African War was not an objection to empire, but a dispute over how the empire should be managed.[65] While Asquith viewed the Salisbury government's decision to go to war as a matter of national honor, on the very eve of hostilities Lloyd George accurately summarized the Conservative government's predicament as purely political: "If they go on the war will be so costly—blood and treasure—as to sicken the land. If they withdraw they will be laughed out of power."[66]

Throughout the autumn and early winter of 1899, the war continued to go badly for the British. Violating the first rule of war, the British commander-in-chief, Sir Redvers Buller, divided his force and attempted to relieve the besieged Ladysmith, Mafeking, and Kimberly all at once. The result was a disaster. In one week in December, dubbed by the public "Black Week," the Boer commander Louis Botha stopped Buller's advance on Ladysmith, the Boers defeated the Kimberly relief force at Magersfontein, and the third force had to retreat after an attempt to take the Stromberg railway junction.

Asquith, like many in Britain, was shocked. Most of our generals, he wrote just after "Black Week," were in a "class of unteachables + incapables."[67] On New Year's Eve 1899, Asquith reported the tenor of British public opinion to Lady Milner in South Africa. Before the string of defeats, the public "buoyed themselves up by an almost pathetic faith in the star and genius of Buller." After the news of the disasters, the mood abruptly changed. "For the moment it looked as if British equanimity would for once break down," he wrote, "and we should begin, after the French fashion,—screaming that we were betrayed and hunting feverishly for a scapegoat." The pain of all this for Asquith, an early supporter of the war, was apparent. Yet Asquith's natural tendency was to want to hold the line in face of panic among the ranks—to stay the course. He continued, "Personally, entre nous, I was rather sorry that the Government there and then resolved to send out Roberts and Kitchener, but public opinion was no doubt in a state of exactingness, for which a coup de theatre of this kind is the most specific." "All the same," he concluded, "I cannot help hoping that Buller will be able to do something really big and effective before Roberts and his lot arrive."[68]

In the face of the disasters of Black Week, Asquith did his best to calm public opinion by urging a steadiness of purpose. Speaking just days after the Boers' repulse of Buller's advances, he warned against giving currency "to hasty impressions founded on imperfect information" and seeking to undermine the confidence of the country and the army in General Buller "on the strength of a single error of judgment, or a single reverse in the field."[69] Despite this public show of confidence, privately Asquith was beginning to have doubts about Buller's competence. In mid-January 1900, he wrote to Margot that "Buller appears to be on the move, + one trembles at the consequences," noting that the general had telegraphed he had "seized a place which is not marked on any map."[70]

After the dispatch of massive reinforcements, the tide of the war finally began to turn, and by September, the British were nominally in control of the Transvaal and the Orange Free State, with the exception of the northern part of Transvaal. The war was over, or so it was thought. The Conservatives naturally wanted to take political advantage of the apparent British victory, and even Asquith admitted it was a "tempting situation" for them. Like all Liberals, even those who for the most part had supported the war, he found himself on the defensive. In an address to the East Fife Liberal Association in September, Asquith charged that the government was anxious for an election "in order that the issue may be artificially narrowed" and patriotic fervor exploited. Of course, this is exactly what the Conservatives wished to do. In response to Chamberlain's accusation that the Liberals had opposed the war, he lamely pointed out that the Liberals had voted for the war supplies necessary to win the war. He was also quick to add that the Liberals supported the proposed annexation of Boer territories.[71] It all seemed rather desperate in face of the Conservative patriotic onslaught.

Asquith was politically astute and mature enough to understand why the Conservatives were taking advantage of what had become a popular war. He could not be silent about Joseph Chamberlain's chauvinistic posturing. He described the Colonial Secretary's handling of the campaign as "the worst fit of vulgar political debauch since 1877–1888." "He has the manners of a cad and the tongue of a bargee."[72] In a speech in East Fife, Asquith challenged Chamberlain's accusations that the Liberals had not supported the Colonial Secretary in his pre-war negotiations with President Kruger. He pointed to his own speech made before the outbreak of hostilities in which he had supported the *uitlanders* to maintain that no one in England could abide a situation where his fellow countrymen were denied political rights. Likewise, Chamberlain's attack on the Liberals for letting things drift during their tenure in office was without merit. Lord Loch, the Liberal High Commissioner in South Africa (1889–1895), had made "strong and forcible" protests to Kruger on behalf of the *uitlanders*.[73]

Asquith's skill as a debater and a political campaigner can be seen in his success in blunting the Conservative attacks. While on the hustings, he charged that the government's record "succeeded in neither preserving peace no preparing for war." It had allowed the Boers to arm themselves, while at the same time failing to provide adequate defense for the Cape Colony. Finally, in all his speeches he attempted to direct voters' attention from the war to a number of domestic issues. It was a lengthy list, including "intemperance, overcrowding, industrial risks of danger, the relations of labour and capital, the wider and fuller organization of municipal action, the more adequate adjustment of our educational system to the exigencies of our economic environment, the ownership and occupation of land," and "the fairer apportionment of the burdens of both Imperial and local taxation."[74]

When all the election results were posted, the country returned the Salisbury government with a sizable majority. Campbell-Bannerman, who had opposed the war, saw his majority reduced; however, Asquith had no problem retaining his seat, doubling his majority over the 1895 election.[75]

The fact was that the Liberal Party was beginning to come apart at the seams over the South African War, and the war was far from over. Defeated on the field, the Boers resorted to guerrilla warfare. Fighting in small groups, they constantly harassed British troops and attacked railway lines. In February 1901 talks between General Kitchener, who had succeeded Roberts as commander-in-chief in South Africa, and the Boer commander Louis Botha broke down. The British then embarked on a policy of "clearing the country." To protect supply lines, thousands of blockhouses were constructed and manned by thousands of troops. The British army targeted everything that could possibly give sustenance to the guerrilla fighters with tactics that included destroying crops, burning homesteads, slaughtering livestock, and poisoning wells. In what was to become the most controversial part of the campaign, the British herded Boers and Africans, including women and children, into concentration camps. Ultimately upward of 20,000 Boer women and children would perish in these camps.[76] Asquith gloomily wrote to Margot that as long as the war lasted, there was no doubt that the Liberals were "paralyzed as a party."[77]

Things came to a head for the Liberals in June. Emily Hobhouse, a friend of Leonard Courtney, who had gone to South Africa to investigate the conditions in the Boer camps, returned to England and met with both Campbell-Bannerman and Lloyd George. She vividly described the horrible conditions under which many women and children were being held.

Campbell-Bannerman was shocked and decided to confront the issue directly in a speech to the National Reform Union at the Holborn Restaurant on June 14. Holding nothing back of his feelings on the subject, he declared to the anti-war audience that included Harcourt and Morley:

> A phrase often used is that "war is war," but when one comes to ask about it one is told that no war is going on, that it is not war. When is a war not a war? When it is carried on by methods of barbarism in South Africa.[78]

Three days later Lloyd George moved an adjournment of the House, so that the treatment of the Boers could be discussed. To ensure that no one misunderstood what he meant in his Holborn Restaurant address, Campbell-Bannerman again used his inflammatory phrase "methods of barbarism" in supporting Lloyd George's motion. The motion was defeated, but Asquith led fifty Liberals, including Grey and Haldane, in abstaining. It looked as if the war was indeed about to split Liberal Party.

On the day following Campbell-Bannerman's "methods of barbarism" speech, Asquith wrote to him that "Through no fault of yours, the proceedings were turned into an aggressive demonstration by one section of the party. . . . I am very glad I was not there, and shall do all I can to discourage reprisals, but I do not know with what success." Asquith's real anger was not so much aimed at the likeable Campbell-Bannerman but at the more radical Lloyd George. He wrote to Sir Robert Perks, leader of the influential Nonconformist Parliamentary Committee at the time, "The banquet last Friday with its incidents and consequences, seems to me to suggest that it is time for those of us who are not willing that the official propagandist machinery should be captured by Lloyd George and his friends . . ."[79]

From the outset of the South African War, Asquith did not want to see the conflict trigger a permanent split of the Liberal Party. Throughout the hostilities, although he generally supported the war, he worked to play down the differences between those in the party who believed as he did and those who did not. He was in a unique position to do this. While he had never had a problem identifying himself as a Liberal Imperialist, he also shared the confidence of many influential leaders in the anti-war group, most importantly, Campbell-Bannerman.

Asquith's public pronouncements during this difficult period were conciliatory, and he wanted those on the other side of the party to know this. "I have kept as silent as I could," he wrote to Campbell-Bannerman in December 1899, "and when I had to speak . . . I pitched it in as low a key as I could."[80] Typical of the public line he took during these difficult days was his speech to the Eighty and Russell clubs in February 1900. He acknowledged that the Liberal Party was going through "one of the most critical periods it its history" and that unlike the Conservatives they did not have a strong party organization. Nevertheless, he urged, the South African War was not "of such a character to affect in any way the possible harmonious co-operation of the party in the future." He believed an "examination of the differences of Liberals on the issue of Imperialism would show these differences to be much more differences of words than thing." Any differences that did exist could be worked out in "friendly conferences."[81] In this address and others, Asquith attempted to calm the party faithful, putting out the hope that as long as both sides remained at least somewhat amicable, the war would be over before it split the party.

The problem with Asquith's strategy was that the war did not end as soon as he had anticipated, and until it did the disagreements among the Liberals continued to fester. To make matters worse, the implementation of the government's harsh measures to defeat the Boers once and for all now meant that Liberals disagreed not just about the origins of the war, but also about the proper prosecution of the conflict. As Beatrice Webb observed in her diary, by July 1901,

> Haldane, Asquith, Grey—had been working at the Bar, enjoying themselves in London Society and letting things slide. Suddenly, they woke up to find the Liberal Party in the House of Commons under the leadership of Lloyd George declaring itself definitely against the war, accusing Milner and the Army of gross inhumanity and asserting the right of the Boers to some kind of independence. Campbell-Bannerman had been captured.[82]

Triggered by the "methods of barbarism" speech, Asquith's formal response came less than a week later at a dinner meeting at the Liverpool Street Station Hotel. The anti-war Liberals had gone too far, and it was time to push back. In the opening of his remarks, Asquith admitted the differences within the party. He and other Liberals "held and still hold that war was neither intended nor desired by the Government and the people of Great Britain, but that it was forced upon us without adequate reason, entirely against our will." The origin of the war, however, was no longer important, he argued, and should be left "to be determined by that which is the only sovereign and ultimate tribunal, the judgment of history." What disturbed him about the events of the past few days is that they "gave the impression that those members of our party who have taken the view which I have taken of the war, are henceforth to regard themselves as definitely and authoritatively branded as schismatics and heretics." He voiced hope that one's views on the war would not become the test of political orthodoxy for his Liberal colleagues. All the same, he took up the challenge and at the heart of his speech said that the recent challenge "makes it all the more necessary for me to say in the plainest and most unequivocal terms, that we have not changed our view, that we do not repent it, and that we shall not recant it." He went on to add that, while he deplored many of the recent actions taken by the government against the Boers, "there is no ground for any general charge against either side."[83] If the anti-war Liberals had wanted to pick a fight, they now had one.

Thus began a series of dinners dedicated to mutual denunciation held by both sides of the Liberal Party. "To dine or not to dine," political journalist H. W. Lucy wisecracked paraphrasing Shakespeare, "that is the question. Whether 'tis nobler to suffer the slings and arrows of outrageous John Morley, or, to take a room at the Hotel Cecil, invite Asquith to dinner and make things hot for our pro-Boer brethren."[84]

As each side defended its respective positions over and over, Campbell-Bannerman sensed that he was in a strong enough position to call for an up or down vote on his leadership of the party. Accordingly, he called for a meeting of all Liberal MPs at the Reform Club on July 9. As Asquith described it, the Liberals crowded into a "stifling hot room" that day. Campbell-Bannerman chaired the meeting and spoke first "with touches of a father about himself." He blamed difficulties and differences on cabals, but as Asquith reported, apparently with some relief, "He did not even remotely allude to me." When Asquith's time to speak came, he paid tribute to Campbell-Bannerman but said that the differences between members of the party over the war were "real differences of conviction." "This brought me to my climax: that I claimed for us absolute freedom to express + act upon our opinions . . . at every stage without any implication of disloyalty." The meeting ended with a unanimous vote for a resolution of confidence in Campbell-Bannerman's leadership. Even so, Asquith did not leave feeling cornered or defeated. "The meeting broke up in great good humour," he wrote to Margot afterward, and "the result is very satisfactory," considering that only recently all but the anti-war faction were "to be excommunicated + drummed out of the party."[85]

For the moment, all seemed to have calmed down a bit. The divide over the war remained, but at least it seemed that neither side was willing to advance its position to the point of destruction. Unfortunately the "war to the knife and fork" had reached a momentum of its own. Even before the unity meeting at the Reform Club, invitations had gone out for a dinner honoring Asquith for his Liverpool Street Hotel speech. Undoubtedly such an affair would be another opportunity for the Liberal Imperialists to protest Campbell-Bannerman's recent speeches. Forty Liberal MPs wrote Asquith, even before the Reform Club meeting, telling him that they could not attend the Asquith salute because they saw it as a threat to party unity. On the day after the Reform Club meeting, Campbell-Bannerman himself appealed to Asquith to postpone the dinner "to a later time when all the Party will join in it, and when it will have lost all that tinge of sectional feeling which undoubtedly will cling to it now."[86] Asquith replied the same day that he had checked with those responsible for the dinner and found that the preparations were too far along to allow a postponement without "cost of enormous inconvenience to people in all parts and countless explanations and misunderstandings."[87]

Campbell-Bannerman read this response as Asquith hoped he would, that Asquith wished he could get out of the engagement but the circumstances made it impossible. There is evidence, however, that Asquith in fact wanted the meeting to proceed. "We are fighting for our lives," Haldane told Beatrice Webb, and "both Asquith and I would attach much importance to Sidney being present at the dinner: we do not like to press it because the whole movement may be a failure."[88] Grey also told Rosebery at the time that Asquith had been annoyed at Campbell-Bannerman's request.[89] As Roy Jenkins has suggested, more than likely Asquith did not want to put off his Liberal Imperialist friends by canceling the meeting, and it might even prove useful in showing Asquith's own strength in the party.[90]

What Asquith and his friends could not have foreseen was a loose cannon on deck—Rosebery. Two days before the Asquith dinner, the *Times* published a letter from Rosebery to the City Liberal Reform Club in which he not only attacked the Campbell-Bannerman position, but argued that there was no room for Liberals to compromise on the issue. "If the war be unjust and its methods uncivilized, our Government and or nation are criminal and the war should be stopped at any cost. If the war be just, carried on by means which are necessary and lawful, it is our duty to support it with all our might in order to bring it to a prompt and successful conclusion." The most damaging part of the letter came when he wrote that the two positions in the party could not "by any conceivable compromise be reconciled" and that until the Liberal "crew make up their mind towards what point they are to row, their barque can never move, it can only revolve."[91] As if this were not enough, on the very day of the Asquith dinner, Rosebery spoke to a luncheon of the City Liberal Reform Club and reiterated his message: "fundamental division . . . exists in the Liberal Party." He even went so far as to hint at a possible split. "For the present . . . I must plough my furrow alone," he declared, "but before I get to the end of that furrow it is possible that I may find myself not alone."[92] Neither Asquith nor his friends knew about this extraordinary move by Rosebery. Perhaps in Rosebery's mind the Liberal Imperialist group was not being confrontational enough on an issue of vital national importance. The *Times* might have come closest to the truth when it wrote several days later that Rosebery "thought his friends so badly in want of shaking that nothing but a couple of surprises would serve the turn."[93]

Asquith was not to be moved by Rosebery's antics. Most of the Liberal Imperialist group could barely believe what they heard. Some, like Griffith-Boscawen, even thought Rosebery's pronouncement had "so exasperated both sides" that it might actually unify the two factions. "[N]othing short of Sir John Gorst on School Boards," he claimed, "could have ever brought them together again."[94] While this was too optimistic, Asquith's speech on the evening of the nineteenth once again followed a theme of party unity. "May I say that . . . I have never called myself a Liberal Imperialist?" he asked his audience. "The name Liberal is long enough, good enough, and distinct enough and always will be for me." Nevertheless he argued that the Liberal Party must be "a national party to which you can safely entrust the fortunes of the Empire."[95] Beatrice Webb viewed the speech from the gallery and recorded that it was "manly and sensible, finely phrased and spoken with considerable fervour. Nonetheless, read in cold blood the next morning it suffered in comparison with Rosebery's artistically sensational utterances."[96]

To Grey, at least, Asquith had saved the day. He wrote to Rosebery after the speech, "Asquith has come through a very trying time and has in my opinion saved the situation, as far as the 'centre' of the Liberal Party is concerned." Grey continued, "Without him, and if he had not stood by us, there would have been a secession of myself and a few, but very few, others from the Liberal Party before you had come back." Grey knew that Asquith was attempting to hold the center and for that reason appreciated his support all the more. "Now, if there is a split, it will be a much less one-sided affair," he predicted. "Asquith has been very staunch to us & we are very chivalrously disposed to him."[97] On the central issue of whether or not the pro-war Liberals could support the government's South African policy without being accused of abandoning the Liberal cause, Asquith had prevailed. Even more than Grey, it was Asquith who had insisted on *e pluribus unum* and had won the day.[98]

Asquith was in a difficult position. To most Liberals, he was seen as the future leader of the party, once Campbell-Bannerman and Rosebery ultimately left the scene. But they had *not* left the scene—far from it—and for the next year there was to be a leadership battle with Asquith left in the middle. He did not think highly of Campbell-Bannerman at the time. Not only did he genuinely disagree with the leader's assessment of the war, but he believed he had a second-class mind. Of the two men, Rosebery was Asquith's choice to lead, but over time Asquith became exasperated, as did many of his friends, with the former Prime Minister's vacillation about directly seeking the leadership of the party. After Rosebery failed to give Asquith or his fellow Liberal Imperialists any warning of his speech in mid-July, Asquith wrote to him that "our old & tried friendship, rooted in such deep soil, can (I hope & believe) never suffer any change. But I hope also that your 'furrow' will prove not to be as divergent, or even parallel, but sooner or later (& sooner the better) to be one in which E. Grey & I & all your real friends & associates can lend a hand."[99]

Rosebery again became the center of attention with his much anticipated speech to the Liberal association in Chesterfield in December 1901. On the stage with him were Asquith, Grey, Fowler, and other Liberal leaders. The former Prime Minister took a somewhat conciliatory stand on the South African War. Even though he defended the concentration camp system as a military necessity, he challenged the government's handling of peace negotiations with the Boers. With regard to the Liberal Party itself, he pointed out that the world was changing, and if the party were to lead, it must become independent of the Irish, "clean the slate," and restate its principles. In his idiosyncratic way, this was Rosebery's invitation for the party to rally to him as its leader. The party had to come to him; he would not actively contend for leadership.[100]

Despite a face-to-face meeting between Campbell-Bannerman and Rosebery a few days after the Chesterfield address, the two opponents were unable to reach any agreement about the direction or the leadership of the party. Months dragged on with speech after speech by Campbell-Bannerman, Rosebery, and their respective supporters. Campbell-Bannerman refused to let go, and Rosebery refused to fight for the leadership role he secretly wanted.

During these difficult days, both Campbell-Bannerman and the more extreme Liberal Imperialists knew that Asquith was in Campbell-Bannerman's own words "the man of real importance."[101] Asquith privately sided squarely with the Rosebery group, but he publicly maintained his position as a strong party supporter. In December he declared in a speech to a local Liberal association, "I was brought up in the Liberal Party, and in the Liberal Party I intend to remain."[102]

One of the effects of the leadership battle was the formation in February 1902 of the Liberal League by leading Liberal Imperialists including Rosebery, Asquith, Grey, Haldane, Munro-Ferguson, and others. Many of the Liberal Imperialists undoubtedly foresaw a formal split in the Liberal Party in the not-too-distant future. They were nervous that their faction would be caught with the formal party organization siding with their opponents, and they would be left isolated. Even back in October, when Grey had agreed to head the Imperial Liberal Council, he had told Asquith that he was doing so because "if the split comes soon it will be well to have some kind of nucleus of an organization to fall back upon."[103] Asquith described the purpose of the meeting to gather "the scattered sheep" and "to push on upon the lines of Chesterfield + our general policy + to be a centre + nucleus for the local organizations."[104]

At the initial meeting, called to discuss whether or not to form a separate organization, Asquith said that MPs who agreed with Rosebery should not allow themselves to be "drummed out" of the Liberal Party by Campbell-Bannerman and his supporters. He urged, however, "not to disturb the existing situation." To his mind they could still act together on important questions without having to form a separate organization.[105] Asquith lost his argument but nevertheless agreed to go along with the formation of the League. Rosebery became President of the newly formed organization, with Asquith, Grey, and Fowler serving as Vice Presidents. More than likely Asquith was willing to go along with the Liberal League project because he understood that he and his friends were in a difficult position with regard to the Liberal Party as a whole and that unity might be their best protection for the moment.[106]

Asquith's reluctance to form the League stemmed from a fear that it would further divide the party. In an attempt to prevent further division, he wrote to the chairman of the East Fife Liberal Association, releasing the letter to the *Times*. He endorsed Rosebery's Chesterfield "clean slate," which he described as putting aside the unattainable and focusing rather on those things "weighty, urgent, and within reach." As for the League, Asquith stated it was "not formed for the purpose of developing and inflaming differences, but to press forward Liberal work in the country."[107]

Since the beginning of the South African War, Asquith had fully understood that the only thing that could truly begin to heal the Liberal Party was an end to the war itself. This finally came about in May 1902 with the signing of the Treaty of Vereeniging. Under this agreement the South African Republic and the Orange Free State became a part of the British Empire but were promised eventual self-government, which was granted a few years later.

In January 1900, at the worst of the Liberal Party's tensions brought about by the South African War, Lord Bryce wrote to Asquith expressing the hope that the Liberal Party could eventually find an issue "on which the whole party can unite." Even though Bryce thought the task possible, he did recognize "it is undoubtedly a delicate task."[108] On May 16, 1903, Asquith gleefully entered his wife's bedroom holding the *Times* in his hand. "Wonderful news to-day," he announced, "it is only a question of time when we shall sweep the country."[109] The issue of free trade was about to turn around the fortunes of the Liberal Party.

Since the mid-nineteenth century, Britain had accepted the notion that the economy of the nation was best served by open borders that allowed the free flow of goods without tariff or duty. For years this policy of free trade benefited Britain because, as the world's first industrial nation, Britain had a competitive advantage over all other countries. By the end of the century, however, other nations, particularly the United States and Germany, were competitive, having built a new industrial capacity behind large tariff walls to protect their markets from the British. Nevertheless, the British correctly saw that much of their nation's prosperity since the mid-century had been the result of free trade.

By 1900, however, some began to question the wisdom of continuing a free trade policy. Now that Britain's competitors challenging her in foreign markets, it seemed foolish to continue a policy of free trade while other countries had protective tariffs. When the cabinet began discussions on the 1903 budget, C. T. Richie, the Chancellor of the Exchequer and a devout free trader, demanded that the small tariff on corn adopted the previous year be removed. He even threatened to resign over the issue. Joseph Chamberlain's view of free trade, however, had moved in the opposite direction. Over the years Chamberlain had come around to the idea that the only way Britain could continue to compete globally was to have its own large protected market, which of course would be the Empire. At this juncture, he decided to bring the issue to a head, and so he argued within the cabinet for not just the retention of the small corn tariff, but for the adoption of a broad policy of imperial preference. Chamberlain lost the argument. The cabinet decided to go forward with Richie's free trade budget. As the cabinet should have known, however, Chamberlain was not the type of man to accept defeat without a fight to the finish. Before informing his cabinet colleagues, Chamberlain decided to go public with his imperial preference plan in a speech at the Birmingham Town Hall on May 15, 1903. This was the speech, reported in the *Times*, that so delighted Asquith who immediately saw the issue that would finally return the Liberals to power.

Chamberlain's Birmingham address caught his Conservative colleagues off guard. On the very same day Chamberlain championed protectionism in Birmingham, Prime Minister Balfour was telling a protectionist delegation that the time was not ripe for colonial preferences.[110] There was no confusion for Asquith. Two days after Chamberlain's address, he wrote Campbell-Bannerman that he had decided to "go bald-headed for J. C. and his swindle of a zollverein," and within a week he was at Doncaster publicly attacking Chamberlain's plan.[111] For several reasons Asquith knew immediately that he and the Liberals must support free trade and defend it against all challengers. It might seem that that a strong imperialist like Asquith would have found at least some attraction in a plan for imperial preference. Asquith, however, grasped the underlying popularity of free trade among the British electorate and perceived its importance as a political issue. Free trade finally gave the Liberals the chance to show for the first time since 1886 that Irish Home Rule was not *the* cause that distinguished the Liberals and the Conservatives.[112]

The Liberals intended to oppose Chamberlain's imperial preference plan and defend free trade to the hilt, but imperial preference had not yet become the policy of the Conservative government. Many Liberals immediately wanted to attempt to turn out the government with an amendment to the budget. Campbell-Bannerman and Harcourt had been in close touch with Sir Michael Hicks-Beach, a Conservative free trader who had only recently resigned as Chancellor of the Exchequer. Harcourt reported to Asquith at the end of May that Hicks-Beach "is full of fight and quite prepared to lead the opposition to the Chamberlain programme on the Government side of the House." Even so, Hicks-Beach strongly urged the Liberals not to move an amendment to the budget, since the budget did not reflect Chamberlain's views and in fact actually proposed to do away with the corn duty. If the Liberals insisted on a frontal assault by way of an amendment to the budget, then Hicks-Beach and his friends would be forced to speak and vote against it. Harcourt's recommendation was to follow Hicks-Beach's advice and drop the idea of an amendment.[113]

Asquith had his own sources in the Conservative party. He had been in communication with Lord James of Herford, suggesting an alliance between the Liberals and the free trade Conservatives. James inquired of his colleagues but found that "the Nonconformists and our Churchmen would never join hands, even to save Free Trade."[114] The Liberal shadow cabinet met in mid-June and issued a statement saying that under the existing circumstances they would not introduce a resolution on Chamberlain's fiscal proposals, but instead they decided to concentrate on a propaganda campaign in the constituencies.[115]

Despite the leadership's declaration, throughout the summer more radical Liberals wanted a censure motion on free trade. Harcourt wrote Asquith in early July, "I have been much disturbed at hearing that there is some danger of the Front Bench giving way to the pressure of hotheads to make a frontal attack upon the Government by a motion in which the great majority will be rallied practically in support of Chamberlain and which will be represented at home and abroad as a defeat of Free Trade." The key, according to Harcourt, was to think more about defeating Chamberlain's plan and less about turning out the government.[116] Asquith replied, "I entirely agree with you as to the supreme ineptitude of the suggested vote of censure." He also noted "an increasing disposition among the more sensible men behind to recognize the wisdom of the course which we have so far pursued, and which I hope we shall adhere."[117]

Rather than fight a battle in Parliament, the Liberals took the issue to the country. As Harcourt wrote to Campbell-Bannerman, he was "strongly in favour" of a strategy "to abstain from challenging a party division and rely upon raising the country upon taxation of food."[118] It was not long before the country began to react. Protectionists formed the Tariff Reform League and the free traders organized the Free Food League to carry their respective messages. Economics professors argued the issue endlessly in the press.

All of this attention on the free trade issue placed Balfour in what seemed to be an untenable situation. Free trade was now splitting the Conservative party, just as the South African War had divided the Liberals. Eventually Balfour, who had seemed to remain neutral, showed his hand. In a document submitted to the cabinet in August, he wrote that he supported "retaliatory" tariffs to attempt to force down foreign duties against British goods. Later Balfour published this document as a pamphlet under his name entitled *Economic Notes on Insular Free Trade*. What Balfour did not publish was his "confidential Cabinet Memorandum" in which he stated that in addition to "retaliator" tariffs he also supported imperial preference and food taxes.[119]

Even though it seemed as if Balfour had bought into the Chamberlain program in its entirety, he nevertheless told Chamberlain that he did not believe it was politically safe for the government to support food taxes just yet. Chamberlain, therefore, offered to submit his resignation, but Balfour kept this offer to himself. A week later, Balfour raised the level of public anxiety by summoning the cabinet to London for a special meeting. After issuing *Economic Notes on Insular Free Trade*, Balfour astonished almost everyone by announcing that he had accepted the resignation of Chamberlain and in addition the resignation of staunch free traders Ritchie, Balfour of Burleigh, and Lord George Hamilton. Balfour attempted to keep the Duke of Devonshire, another strong free trader, in the cabinet, but he resigned a few weeks later. Although Chamberlain left the cabinet, he did not feel alienated or discouraged. As part of the cabinet shuffle, Balfour named Chamberlain's son, Austin, the new Chancellor of the Exchequer. Further, all signs pointed to Balfour eventually accepting Chamberlain's program—the strong free traders had been pushed out of the government; the only thing that seemed to separate Balfour and Chamberlain was a disagreement as to political timing.

Chamberlain's job was now to sell his plan to the country. He began his sales pitch in early October in a speech in Glasgow, followed by an address at Greencock the next day. The former Colonial Secretary's plan was simple: a duty of two shillings a quarter would be imposed on foreign corn (excluding maize), and a 5 percent duty on foreign flour, meat, and dairy produce (excluding bacon). Foreign manufactured goods would have an average 10 percent duty imposed. All colonial produce would be exempt. Recognizing that the working class would need some type of compensation for these "food taxes," Chamberlain proposed that the tax on tea be reduced by three-quarters and the duty on sugar be reduced by half. Coffee and coca would receive similar reductions.

Asquith immediately took to the chase, pursuing Chamberlain around the country challenging the case for protection. It was not easy. Asquith still had to practice law to support his family; the speeches in provincial towns meant that he would have to burn the candle at both ends.

Asquith's campaign against Chamberlain opened at Cinderford on October 8.[120] Chamberlain's plan was clearly a tax on food, he declared. The heart of the plan was retaliation against protectionist countries. Since Russia and the United States were the two most protectionist countries and since 92 percent of Britain's imports from Russia and 85 percent of the imports from the United States were foodstuffs, you "cannot retaliate effectively in this country upon protected countries without imposing a tax upon food or raw material."

Asquith next set out to destroy Chamberlain's argument made recently at Glasgow that the United Kingdom's trade had been "practically stagnant" for thirty years. Reciting impressive economic figures indicating British prosperity for the last three decades, Asquith said that Chamberlain had ignored home trade, looking only at the foreign trade picture. Moreover, Chamberlain had failed to take into consideration the many services such as banking and shipping so profitably performed by the British.

Chamberlain had also raised the specter of the break-up of the Empire unless some form of colonial preference were imposed. Asquith quickly dismissed this argument. Where were the complaints from the colonies? "We give them free admission through our open door into the largest and best market in the world" while "they have at home complete fiscal autonomy." Could Chamberlain be serious in asking the colonies "to stereotype their industrial condition, to arrest their industrial development, in order that the Mother Country may keep and increase the hold she has on their markets . . ."? To Asquith, it was hard to believe such a proposal was "seriously made in the interests of Imperial unity."

To the extent there was a problem with British industry, Asquith said, it was not free trade. "We have seen," he admitted, "industries in which we ought to have maintained our supremacy falling behind, and in some cases entirely taken away from us by our competitors." But these losses could not be attributed to free trade, but rather to "Defective knowledge, inferior processes, lack of sensibility or versatility, [and] a stubborn industrial conservatism."

Chamberlain's opening pitch at Glasgow and Asquith's rebuttal in Cinderford were repeated over and again as the country was treated to a first-class debate on an issue of critical importance to its future. Campbell-Bannerman and others joined in. Harcourt believed that Campbell-Bannerman's speeches were even more effective than Asquith's, but most contemporary opinion (including that of Campbell-Bannerman) gave Asquith the higher marks.[121] Asquith's performances were indeed impressive. He was perhaps at the height of his oratorical power. Free trade was a subject about which he knew a great deal and in which he had an almost blind faith. Such a faith was understandable. He had grown up in a family that had prospered from free trade. His grandfather, William Willans, a wool stapler, had been an active supporter of Cobbden and Bright in the Corn Law repeal campaign of the 1840s, and in fact Willans had chaired Cobden's election committee when he stood for Huddersfield in 1857.[122] Asquith had lectured on economics at the University Extension years before, and the articles he had written for *The Spectator* and *The Economist* in his early career consistently supported free trade.

Chamberlain himself, at least so far as he could ever do so, recognized that he had met his match with Asquith. In a letter to a supporter he admitted that Asquith's argument that the colonies did not want a preference, followed by other Liberals making the same point, had "undoubtedly produced an effect."[123] Asquith's strength in the campaign was the strength of all good lawyers—carefully responding to Chamberlain point by point with overwhelming factual detail and clear logical progression of argument. As an American observer of the free trade campaign put it, Asquith "had none of the arts of the advertiser, but his skill in argument proved the best advertising."[124] And Asquith's advertising was beginning to result in sales.

By 1905 the political skies had begun to clear for the Liberals. The Conservative government was starting to founder on the twin issues of free trade and education, and the Liberals' prospects for returning to power were improving by the day. Asquith seemed in striking distance of his goal of returning to office. The last decade had been a difficult one for Asquith, and there were a number of times his own prospects might have been dashed. He had proven the sceptics wrong who had said it would be impossible to support himself and his family through his practice of law while at the same time remaining politically active. Others scoffed that his marriage to Margot had made him too interested in society to the detriment of his political career; yet he had made perhaps the most effective impact of any Liberal leader in challenging the Conservatives on the issues of education, employers' liability, and free trade. The most dangerous shoals to navigate, however, had been those of the leadership struggle in the Liberal Party, exacerbated by the differences within the party over the South African War.

Asquith knew that, if he was ever to reach his goal of leading the Liberal Party and perhaps one day becoming Prime Minister, the party must remain intact—not a foregone conclusion during the critical time that Asquith waited in the wings. He had to continually work against the forces that threatened to pull the party apart. Although he identified himself with the Liberal Imperialist wing of the party, he never went so far as to let the other side give up on him. While others like Grey and Rosebery did not seem to be frightened by a total split in the party, Asquith knew it would mean disaster, and he did everything in his power to prevent it. As Campbell-Bannerman said at a critical point, Asquith was "the man of real importance." He had been the ballast in the Liberal ship that had made it through difficult waters and was on the eve of making it safely to port of power.

NOTES

1. Sir William Harcourt to HHA, 15 Apr. 1893, Gardiner, *Life of Sir William Harcourt*, 2:233.
2. Sir Henry James to HHA, 27 June 1895, BL, MS. Bonham Carter 619, f. 128.
3. Henry W. Lucy, *A Diary of the Unionist Parliament 1895–1900* (Bristol: J. W. Arrowsmith, 1901), 107.
4. Daniel Duman, *The English and Colonial Bars in the Nineteenth Century* (London: Croom Helm, 1983), 174.
5. Elias, *Asquith*, 67.
6. Spender and Asquith, *Life of Asquith*, 1:126.
7. Earl of Oxford and Asquith, *Memories*, 113; The House of Lords eventually affirmed the lower court and held that the inclosure was not "a place opened, kept, or used" for purposes prohibited by the Betting Act of 1853, *Powell v. Kempton Park Race Course Co.* [1889] A. C. 143 H.L.
8. Spender and Asquith, *Life of Asquith*, 1:126.
9. Earl of Oxford and Asquith, *Memories*, 121.
10. Webb, *Diary*, 2:235.
11. HHA to MA, 16 July 1895, BL, MS. Eng. c. 6688, ff. 21–24.
12. HHA to MA, 19 July 1895, BL, MS. Eng. c. 6688, ff. 29–30.
13. "Mr. Asquith at the Oxford Union," *Times*, 28 Feb. 1896.
14. R. J. Q. Adams, *Balfour: The Last Grandee* (London: John Murray, 2007), 168.
15. Alderson, *Mr. Asquith*, 20.
16. Webb, *Diary*, 2:263.
17. Quinault, "Asquith's Liberalism," 43.
18. Alderson, *Mr. Asquith*, 230.
19. *Hansard*, 4, 107, 1132–38, 8 May 1902.
20. Alderson, *Mr. Asquith*, 233–34.
21. "Mr. Asquith at Barnsley," *Times*, 19 Apr. 1902.
22. "Mr. Asquith at Hull," *Times*, 29 Jan. 1903.
23. Much of the discussion of the employers' liability debate is taken from Lester, "The Employers' Liability/Workmen's Compensation Debate of the 1890s Revisited."
24. Peter T. Marsh, *Joseph Chamberlain: Entrepreneur in Politics* (New Haven: Yale University Press, 1994), 70, 328, 370.
25. *Hansard*, 4, 48, 1434–64, 3 May 1897.

26. *Hansard*, 4, 48, 1434, 3 May 1897.
27. *Hansard*, 4, 49, 748, 18 May 1897.
28. *Hansard*, 4, 48, 1462–64, 3 May 1897.
29. HHA to MA, 10 January 1896, BL, MS. Eng. c. 6688, ff. 37–38.
30. James, *Rosebery*, 386–93.
31. Ibid., 393.
32. Quinault, "Asquith's Liberalism," 39.
33. HHA to MA, 27 Dec. 1894, BL, MS. Eng. c. 6687, f. 179.
34. Account book, 1901–1905, BL, MS. Bonham Carter, 664.
35. Colin Clifford, *The Asquiths* (London: John Murray, 2002), 84; Balfour to MA, 22 Dec. 1898, MS. Eng. c. 6670, ff. 17–18.
36. 1 January 1899, BL, MS. Eng. d. 3203.
37. HHA to MA, 4 August 1905, BL, MS. Eng. c. 6690, ff. 31–31.
38. Haldane, *Autobiography*, 103.
39. Webb, *Diary*, 2:77.
40. Bahlman, *Diary of Sir Edward Walter Hamilton*, 269.
41. HHA to MA, 13 Sept. 1892, BL, MS. Eng. c. 6686, ff. 135–38.
42. HHA to Josephine Armitage, BL, MS. Bonham Carter 636, ff. 1–4.
43. M. Asquith, *Autobiography*, 1:230–31.
44. HHA Diary, BL, MS. Bonham Carter, 572.
45. Daphne Bennet, *Margot: A Life of the Countess of Oxford & Asquith* (New York: Franklin Watts, 1985), 154–56, 165.
46. James, *Rosebery*, 158.
47. Matthew, *Liberal Imperialists*, ix.
48. Ibid., 63.
49. Ibid., 16.
50. Spender and Asquith, *Life of Asquith*, 144–45.
51. Earl of Oxford and Asquith, *Fifty Years*, 286.
52. "Mr. Asquith in Wiltshire," *Times*, 11 May 1896.
53. M. Asquith, *Autobiography*, 20.
54. "Mr. Asquith in Wiltshire," *Times*, 11 May 1896.
55. Earl of Oxford and Asquith, *Memories*, 1:210.
56. Milner to HHA, 10 Nov. 1897, BL, MSS Asquith 9,86.
57. HHA to Milner, 12 January, 1898, MSS Milner 204, ff. 426–28.
58. HHA to W. V. Harcourt, 4 Aug. 1899, Matthew, *Liberal Imperialists*, 39.
59. *Hansard*, 4, 77, 17, 17 Oct. 1899.
60. HHA to MA, BL, MS. Eng. c. 6688, ff. 219–20.
61. HHA to MA, 25 Oct. 1899, BL, MS. Eng. c. 6688, ff. 227–28.
62. HHA to MA, 31 Oct. 1899, BL, MS. Eng. c. 6688, ff. 237–38.
63. Alderson, *Mr. Asquith*, 183–84.
64. Matthew, *Liberal Imperialists*, 176.
65. John Grigg, *Young Lloyd George* (Berkeley: University of California Press, 1973), 259–60.
66. Ibid., 261.
67. HHA to MA, 18 Dec. 1899, BL, MS. Eng. c. 6688, ff. 255–56.

68. Vicountess Milner, *My Picture Gallery 1886–1901* (London: John Murray, 1951), 162–63.

69. Alderson, *Mr. Asquith,* 185.

70. HHA to MA, 13 Jan. 1900, BL, MS. Eng. c. 6689, ff. 3–4.

71. "Mr. Asquith on the Political Situation," *Times,* 17 Sept. 1900, 13.

72. Matthew, *Liberal Imperialists,* 129.

73. "Mr. Asquith's Campaign," *Times,* 27 Sept. 1900, 10.

74. "Election Addresses. Mr. Asquith," *Times,* 29 Sept. 1900, 10.

75. The 1900 election returned 334 Conservatives, 68 Liberal Unionists, 183 Liberals, 77 Irish Parliamentary, and 2 Labour; Asquith's majority increased from 716 to 1,431.

76. John Wilson, *C. B.: A Life of Sir Henry Campbell-Bannerman* (London: Constable, 1973), 344.

77. HHA to MA, 20 Feb. 1901, BL, MS. Eng. c. 6689, ff. 82–83.

78. Gilbert, *Architect of Change,* 200; *Times,* 15 June 1901.

79. Robbins, *Sir Edward Grey,* 90–91.

80. HHA to Campbell-Bannerman, 20 Dec. 1899, Matthew, *Liberal Imperialists,* 48.

81. "Mr. Asquith on the Party System," *Times,* 26 Feb. 1900, 13.

82. Webb, *Diary,* 2:212.

83. H. H. Asquith, *Speeches 1892–1908* (London, 1908), 37–44.

84. H. W. Lucy, *The Balfourian Parliament 1900–1905* (London: Hodder & Stoughton, 1906), 85.

85. HHA to MA, 9 July 1901, BL, MS. Eng. 6689, ff. 118–21.

86. H. Campbell-Bannerman to HHA, 10 July 1901, BL, MS. Asquith 10, ff. 19–20.

87. HHA to H. Campbell-Bannerman, 10 July 1901, BL, Add MS 41210, 208–9.

88. Webb, *Diary,* 2:213.

89. E. Grey to HHA, 12 July 1901, BL, MS. Asquith 10, ff. 23–24.

90. Jenkins, *Asquith,* 127.

91. "Lord Rosebery on the Liberal Party," *Times,* 17 July 1901.

92. "Lord Rosebery on the Liberal Party," *Times,* 20 July 1901.

93. *Times,* 22 July 1901.

94. A. S. T. Griffith-Boscawen, *Fourteen Years in Parliament* (London: John Murray, 1907), 203.

95. "Mr. Asquith and the Liberal Party," *Times,* 20 July 1901.

96. Webb, *Diary,* 2:214–15.

97. James, *Rosebery,* 426.

98. Lucy, *Balfourian Parliament,* 95.

99. James, *Rosebery,* 427.

100. Wilson, *C. B.,* 370.

101. Matthew, *Liberal Imperialists,* 83.

102. "Mr. Asquith on Lord Rosebery," *Times,* 20 Dec. 1901.

103. HHA to MA, 28 Oct. 1901, BL, MS. Eng. c. 6689, ff. 130–33.

104. HHA to MA, 26 Feb. 1902, BL, MS. Eng. c. 6689, ff. 158–59.

105. Matthew, *Liberal Imperialists*, 86.
106. James, *Rosebery*, 439.
107. "The Liberal Party," *Times*, 3 Mar. 1902.
108. Bryce to HHA, 20 Jan. 1900, BL, MS. Bryce 23, 117–18.
109. M. Asquith, *Autobiography*, 2:45–46.
110. Elie Halévy, *A History of the English People in the Nineteenth Century*, vol. 5, *Imperialism and the Rise of Labour* (London: Hodder and Stoughton, 1929), 324.
111. HHA to Campbell-Bannerman, 18 May 1903, Matthew, *Liberal Imperialists*, 100.
112. Matthew, *Liberal Imperialists*, 102.
113. Harcourt to HHA, 25 May 1903, MS. Harcourt, 718.302.
114. George Ranken Askwith, *Lord James Herford* (London: Ernest Benn, 1930), 276.
115. J. L. Garvin and Julian Amery, *Joseph Chamberlain and the Tariff Reform Campaign—The Life of Joseph Chamberlain Volume 5—1901–1903* (London: Macmillan, 1969), 254.
116. Harcourt to HHA, 5 July 1903, BL, MS. Harcourt 718, 312.
117. HHA to Harcourt, 6 July 1903, BL, MS. Harcourt 718, 315.
118. Gardiner, *Life of Sir William Harcourt*, 2:556.
119. Alfred F. Havighurst, *Britain in Transition* (Chicago: University of Chicago Press, 1985), 65.
120. Asquith, *Speeches*, 45–63.
121. Garvin and Amery, *Joseph Chamberlain*, 474.
122. Quinault, "Asquith's Liberalism," 37.
123. Garvin and Amery, *Joseph Chamberlain*, 521–2.
124. Notestein, "The Career of Mr. Asquith," 364.

Chapter Five

Chancellor of the Exchequer (1905–1908)

As Balfour's divided Conservative government continued to stumble along and the possibility of a Liberal government became more and more likely, speculation mounted as to what the composition of a new Liberal government might be. Although Campbell-Bannerman remained the leader of the party, his age and health caused many to wonder whether he would be willing or able to take on the responsibilities of Prime Minister. Herbert Gladstone reported to Asquith as early as 1903 that he and Campbell-Bannerman had had "a long talk about the future" and the Liberal leader had told him "he did not think that he would be able to take any post which involved heavy and responsible work. A peerage and some office of dignity like Presidentship of the Council would be what he would like."[1]

Rumors began to circulate that many in the Liberal Imperialist group were keen on shuffling Campbell-Bannerman off to the House of Lords to make way for new leadership. In September 1903, Liberal MP Earl de Grey, later Lord Ripon, wrote Lord Spencer, "I hear that the intrigues against C.B. have not ceased & that Asquith, Fowler & E. Grey are supposed to be likely to refuse to join a Liberal government if he remains Leader in the House of Commons. Can this be true?"[2] Two years later, Sir Edmond Gosse, poet and historian of the House of Lords, told of Haldane's prediction that Campbell-Bannerman would be elevated to the House of Lords as Viscount Belmont and that he, Asquith, and Grey would stick together so that "C.-B. must take all three or none."[3]

Seven months later, Haldane visited Asquith at a country house Asquith and his wife had rented at Glen of Rothes in northeastern Scotland. On September 11, Haldane and Asquith traveled to see Grey, who was fishing nearby at Relugas, to discuss the formation of a future Liberal government.

They well understood that Campbell-Bannerman, at a minimum, could demand at least the title of Prime Minister, considering his popularity within the party and his decades of service to the Liberal cause. Nevertheless, he was in poor health, having suffered a number of heart attacks, and the Relugas group hoped to convince him to accept the title of Prime Minister but move to the House of Lords and allow the more energetic Asquith to lead in the Commons as Chancellor of the Exchequer. As Grey explained, "our view was that with Campbell-Bannerman as Prime Minister, the leadership of the Commons should be in Asquith's hands." He added, "There had not been differences about foreign policy, but there had been about Imperial affairs such as the South African War and the Soudan, and my view was that Asquith would be more robust and stronger leader in policy and debate in the Commons."[4] "What we believed to be best," Haldane related, "was that Campbell-Bannerman, while remaining leader of the party with which he was very popular, should, if sent to be Prime Minister, take a peerage and occupy that office with his seat in Parliament in the House of Lords. In that case Asquith, as Chancellor of the Exchequer, would lead the party in the Commons."[5]

Asquith, Haldane, and Grey believed so strongly that Campbell-Bannerman must at all costs be blocked from serving as both Prime Minister and as leader of the Commons that they were willing to link their own fortunes together. Any new Liberal government would include Asquith as Chancellor of the Exchequer, and apparently the three decided it would be best for Grey to become Foreign Secretary or Colonial Secretary and Haldane be made Lord Chancellor. They further resolved, according to Haldane, that "Unless our scheme were in substance carried out we resolved that we could not join in Campbell-Bannerman's Government."[6] Among themselves, the three referred to their agreement as the "Relugas Compact." Apparently it was to be one for all and all for one—or so it seemed.

In light of the events that would unfold in the formation of Campbell-Bannerman's government, it is important to remember that, when Asquith, Haldane, and Grey made their agreement at Relugas in September 1905, they assumed that the Conservative government would resign, an election would be called, and if the Liberals won, a government would then be formed, but only *after* the election was held. As will be seen, however, when the Conservatives resigned office, the Liberals decided not to dissolve Parliament immediately, but to form a government *before* an election was held. There is no indication that the sequence of events that actually came to pass was ever considered at Relugas, and unfortunately for Asquith, because of this short-sighted omission, the agreement with his friends was to bring him no end of trouble.

To implement their plan, the Relugas group agreed that Haldane should attempt to bring the King into their plot, while Asquith informed Campbell-

Bannerman of their agreement. Haldane sprang into action. The day after the agreement was reached, he wrote to Francis Knollys, the King's Private Secretary, who was with the King at Balmoral, informing him of the Relugas meeting. If Campbell-Bannerman refused, he told Knollys, he, Asquith, and Grey "could in office render no real service in public affairs, and we have decided, in such a case, that it would be best for us to intimate early to Sir H.C.B. that we should stand aside and leave him with his hands free to follow another lure than ours."[7] Having hatched their plans fishing, the "lure" metaphor is almost too much. The trio might have been better advised to keep fishing and politics separate, and Haldane clearly erred with his remarkably brash communication. As historians have pointed out, it was highly improper for a member of Parliament, not even a member of the government, to attempt to drag the sovereign into a inter-party leadership conflict.[8]

Improper or not, Knollys rose to the bait and responded immediately that he would show Haldane's letter confidentially to the King. He also agreed that "Asquith would be the best man to lead the H. of Commons," since Campbell-Bannerman was "a weak or at all events not a strong man like Asquith, would be inclined to give way to pressure from the extreme left." Nevertheless, the King's Private Secretary cautioned against the Relugas group refusing to serve if Campbell-Bannerman insisted on staying in the Commons. A cabinet without moderates would "be disastrous both for the Country and the Party." According to Knollys, "what the King would desire would be the presence of a restraining influence in the Cabinet, being aware that many members of it would be men holding extreme views, and this could be effected by the presence in it of men like yourself, Asquith and Sir E. Grey."[9]

As a result of this overture, the King asked Haldane to Balmoral to discuss the matter further. In a letter marked "Secret," Haldane triumphantly wrote to Asquith on Balmoral Castle stationery on October 6 that "The plan is thoroughly approved in all details. The consultation has been how to work it out." He believed that the King would see Campbell-Bannerman in November and attempt to convince him that the duties and responsibilities of being Prime Minister and leading from the Commons would be too onerous for a man of his age. Later the King would suggest a peerage. Haldane went on to inform Asquith that the King and Knollys agreed Asquith should go ahead and talk to Campbell-Bannerman but "not to go as far as to let him surmise any connection between your conversation" and what the King was planning to do. Ever the intriguer, Haldane concluded, "They are fully alive to the importance of secrecy and reticence" and that he himself was "quite pleased with the result up to now—If only tongues are held (and I have done all that can be done to secure this) I think we have succeeded in marking out a course of action & that we have secured very cordial and powerful assistance."[10]

Campbell-Bannerman was out of the country at the time, and not until he returned over a month later did Asquith finally have the opportunity to play his role in the drama. In the interim, Lord Spencer, who had very much considered himself to be in the running to be the next Liberal Prime Minister, suffered a cerebral hemorrhage on October 17, leaving the path wide open for Campbell-Bannerman. The only question now was whether he would assume the premiership as a true leader or be elevated to the House of Lords and be Prime Minister in name only.

Asquith met one on one with Campbell-Bannerman on November 13. The most extensive record of the meeting was recorded by Margot Asquith some years later. According to her account, Campbell-Bannerman told Asquith that he believed it looked like things were "coming to a head politically and that any day after Parliament met we might expect a General Election" and that "he would probably be the man the King would send for . . ." The conversation continued:

> Henry said: "C.B. then looked at me and said: 'I do not think we have ever spoken of the future Liberal Government, Asquith? What would you like? The Exchequer, I suppose?'—I said nothing—'or the Home Office?' I said, 'Certainly not.' At which he said: 'Of course, if you want legal promotion what about the Woolsack? No? Well then, it comes back to the Exchequer.'"[11]

Campbell-Bannerman then took the offensive and said that he had heard "that ingenious person, Richard Burdon Haldane" had suggested that he should go to the House of Lords. He made it plain to Asquith that he was not interested in this option. Margot described it, "I could see that the impression left on Henry's mind while he was telling me of this conversation was that it would be with reluctance and even repugnance that Campbell-Bannerman would ever go to the House of Lords."[12] The conversation next turned to the Lord Chancellorship. Campbell-Bannerman had inquired of Asquith's interest in the position. Although it would be a great honor, Asquith had no interest in the position. His interest was politics, and he had no desire to follow the earlier models of Lord Mansfield or Lord Eldon who readily gave up their political careers for the opportunity to sit on the woolsack.

Asquith strongly suggested Haldane be given the position, although it soon became apparent that Campbell-Bannerman thought otherwise. When the discussion turned to the Foreign Office, Asquith urged that Grey be given the appointment, stating that he was the "only man" for the job.[13] Even though Campbell-Bannerman had been thinking of Grey for the War Office, Asquith told his wife that he believed he had "made an impression" with Sir Henry on this point.[14]

In his biography of Campbell-Bannerman, John Wilson alleges that at this meeting Asquith "agreed unconditionally" to become Chancellor of the Exchequer. Likewise the authors of Asquith's official biography state that "It was arranged at this meeting that he should be Chancellor of the Exchequer."[15] If true, it means that at the very first chance he could get Asquith cut his own deal with Campbell-Bannerman and did not stick to his promise to his friends not to serve unless Campbell-Bannerman went to the House of Lords. There is real ambiguity as to whether or not Asquith "agreed unconditionally" to serve under Campbell-Bannerman at their first meeting to discuss the new Liberal government. To begin with, it runs counter to Asquith's well-earned reputation for personal integrity. If Asquith did make such a commitment, there is no evidence that he ever told Haldane or Grey that he had done so, even though there would have been no reason not to tell them, and again, such a deceitful move is totally out of character.

Margot's description of the meeting never even hints that Asquith made this extremely important commitment. In fact, she says that her husband told her that he said nothing when Campbell-Bannerman proposed his taking the Exchequer. The most convincing reason such an early commitment is unlikely is that Asquith's first discussion with Campbell-Bannerman on November 13 happened prior to the Liberal leadership's decision to form a government *before* an election, a decision not made until some weeks later. Margot's description of the conversation implies that both men were assuming an election would come before the formation of a government. In fact two weeks later, Asquith wrote Herbert Gladstone urging that the Liberals should refuse to take office before dissolution of Parliament and an election.[16] The timing of this fact is important because, as will be seen, Asquith joined Campbell-Bannerman's government, even without Haldane and Grey, because of the political ramifications of forming a government before an election. With no decision having been made about when a government was to be formed, there was simply no reason for Asquith to give in to Campbell-Bannerman at this early juncture.

Events now began to move rapidly toward the resignation of Balfour's government. Shortly after the meeting on November 13, Asquith and Grey met with Campbell-Bannerman to hammer out a compromise and bring the party closer together on the issue of Ireland. With all three in agreement, Campbell-Bannerman made a speech to his constituency on November 23. He told them that while he would not totally reject a comprehensive Home Rule measure under any circumstances, he was committed to moving toward Home Rule on a "step-by-step" basis, which is exactly what Asquith had been advocating since 1901.[17]

Out of the blue, Rosebery now entered the fray, as he was often wont to do. In response to Campbell-Bannerman's pronouncement on Ireland, two days later Rosebery made a dramatic speech at Bodmin while on a Liberal League tour of Cornwall. Unaware that Grey and Asquith had actually helped prepare Campbell-Bannerman's remarks, Rosebery took off on his own, declaring that he was adamantly opposed to the Liberals fighting under a banner of Home Rule. For Rosebery such a move weakened the unity around the free trade issue and would postpone badly needed social and educational reforms. He concluded, "I will, then, add no more on this subject, except to say emphatically and explicitly and once and for all that I cannot serve under that banner."[18]

Asquith was livid. "I have just come across Asquith," Morley reported after going to the Athenaeum. "Most furious at the 'bombshell.' . . . I have seldom seen a hardened politician so angry. . . . He ridicules the notion of R now being able on any terms to come into a Liberal Govt."[19] Harry Paulton, a young Liberal League MP, after seeing Asquith two days after Rosebery's speech, reported to Rosebery that he found Asquith "very much put out and, indeed angry"; Asquith, Haldane, and others, tattled Paulton, "regard your utterance as a positive disaster!"[20]

While some claim that Rosebery's Bodmin speech caused Balfour finally to agree to resign, because the Prime Minster saw a possible division in the Liberal ranks, Balfour actually told his cabinet the day before the speech that he would resign. On the day of the Bodmin speech, Balfour wrote a memorandum stating his reasons for proposing to resign without a dissolution of Parliament.[21] The first sure evidence the Liberals had that Balfour was about to resign came when Lord Esher told J. A. Spender on Wednesday, November 29, that Balfour would resign the following Sunday or Monday and asked Spender to relay this information to Campbell-Bannerman. Spender did not record whether Esher said that the government would resign without calling for dissolution.[22] What the Bodmin speech did do, however, was to move the Liberal leadership toward the idea of trying to form a government before an election was called. According to Spender's account of the events, there was great concern that Rosebery's Bodmin remarks might split the party, and as a result, it might be better first to bring the party together in forming a government and then to go to the polls rather than the reverse. On Thursday, November 30, Spender met with Herbert Gladstone and his secretary, Robert Hudson. Spender recorded: "Carefully discussed whether C.B. should accept office & came to the conclusion that in the circumstances & especially after Rosebery's speech he would probably be compelled to do so."[23] While it is not exactly clear when Campbell-Bannerman and the Liberal leadership decided to form a government before dissolving Parliament, it seems clear that it was around the time Campbell-Bannerman returned from Scotland late on Sunday, December 3. This decision to form a government before going to the polls would fundamentally change Asquith's views on the formation of the new government and would mean the end of the "Relugas Compact."

Balfour's resignation was imminent. On Monday, Campbell-Bannerman immediately began consultations with his Liberal colleagues to form a new government. After lunch he met with Grey, and following their meeting, Grey sent a note to Asquith. "Just a line before you see C-B to say that I don't want you to risk your personal position more than you think absolutely necessary." He continued, "C-B gave me the impression that he was quite prepared to form a Government without any of us: he never once suggested that my abstaining would make the formation of the govt. difficult, though I had suggested it might raise difficulties as regards yourself." This statement implies that Grey revealed the "Relugas Compact" to Campbell-Bannerman in one way or another. What is surprising is that, had Asquith already agreed unconditionally agreed to serve back on November 13, why would Campbell-Bannerman not have told Grey? More than likely Campbell-Bannerman reiterated to Grey what he had told Asquith earlier: he did not want to go to the House of Lords. Apparently Grey picked up on Campbell-Bannerman's determination in this regard because Grey was now willing to release Asquith from their compact. "[I]f you go in without me eventually I shall be quite happy outside and I shan't think it the least wrong of you to go in. . . ."[24]

Late that afternoon the King returned to London from Sandringham to meet with Balfour, who submitted his resignation. Campbell-Bannerman was to be sent for the following morning and asked to form a government. Before the evening ended, however, Grey returned to Campbell-Bannerman's house and informed him in no uncertain terms that he would not serve in the cabinet unless Campbell-Bannerman went to the Lords and Asquith was made leader in the Commons. The following day, when Herbert Gladstone reported Grey's conversation with Campbell-Bannerman the evening before to Spender, he stated, "Asquith and Haldane were understood to have come to the same decision."[25]

On Tuesday morning, before going to Buckingham Palace to meet with the King, Campbell-Bannerman met with Asquith. Once again, Asquith pleaded with him not to take on both Prime Minister and leadership in the Commons. "Henry pointed out," Margot recorded, "what a fearful labour C.B. would find the combination of leading the House and being Prime Minister, as they were practically two men's work . . ." As a final argument, Asquith told Campbell-Bannerman that his insistence on staying in the Commons was putting Asquith "in a cruel and impossible position if under the circumstances Edward Grey refused to take Office; he was his dearest friend as well as supporter, and to join a Government without such a friend would be personal pain to him, as they had never worked apart from one another." Asquith was much more diplomatic than Grey had been in presenting their case to Campbell-Bannerman, who later told John Morley how much he appreciated Asquith's delicacy in making his case. The issue was left there for the time being. Asquith told Campbell-Bannerman "that as the matter was one of vital importance to him personally it could not be settled in a day, and that he must be given time to think things over."[26] Campbell-Bannerman then went to Buckingham Palace where the King asked him to form a government. Fortunately, since the King would be leaving London for a few days, the new Prime Minister would have a week to put together a final list of the new government members to present to the sovereign.

The following day, Asquith for a third time met with Campbell-Bannerman in an attempt to convince him to go to the House of Lords. Asquith told Margot that the Prime Minister said to him, "It is no use going over ground again, my dear C.B. I make a personal appeal to you, which I've never done before; I urge you to go to the House of Lords and solve this difficulty." Asquith thought he had made some progress. Campbell-Bannerman told him that his wife was to arrive that evening, and she would be the "final arbiter."[27]

Margot described her husband at dinner that evening as "worn out."[28] Events were moving to a point that there was little room for him to maneuver to effect some compromise. Grey accurately described to his wife Asquith's dilemma. "If I stay out, Asquith will have to decide what he does; if he goes in without me his position will be horrid and people will say he has abandoned me in order to have office." He continued, "If he stays out with me it is considered that the Liberal Party will smash and Free Trade may be beaten at the Election . . ."[29] Despite the difficult personal circumstances, Asquith was not about to let the latter take place. If Campbell-Bannerman insisted on leading from the Commons, Asquith simply could not bring himself to break up the Liberal Party and potentially cause the loss of the election by refusing to serve.

Strangely, a person totally outside the extended discussions so far was to cast the die. Charlotte Campbell-Bannerman talked to her husband on the night of Tuesday, December 6. They were close and had always consulted each other on important matters. Her position was clear. For years she had seen him labor in the ranks to reach this pinnacle of political success. He should stand firm and insist on being a true Prime Minster, not just one in name only, and remain in the House of Commons.[30] This settled the matter.

The next day Campbell-Bannerman told Asquith that his mind had been made up and offered Asquith the Exchequer. Bowing to the inevitable, Asquith accepted. Campbell-Bannerman asked him to tell Grey and Haldane that Grey could have the Foreign Office and Haldane the War Office.³¹ In a letter that same day to Haldane, Asquith explained his decision to join the government with or without Haldane or Grey. He first pointed out that he had "tried ceaselessly for two days" to get Campbell-Bannerman to go to the House of Lords but his efforts had "proved vain." He said he had thought things over during the past forty-eight hours and had concluded that it was best to agree to serve. If he did not, a Liberal triumph in the upcoming election would be put in jeopardy. The situation had dramatically changed since they met at Relugas. "The election is before and not behind us, and a Free Trade majority, still more an independent majority, is not a fact but at most a probability." He saw two possible alternatives if he refused to go in. Either an attempt to form a government would be abandoned, which he did not believe would happen, or "a weak Govt. would be formed entirely or almost entirely of one colour." He concluded, "In either event in my opinion the issue of the election would be put in utmost peril. . . . And the whole responsibility, I repeat, would be mine." The key factor was that the Liberal government was being formed before an election. "If the election were over, and Free Trade secure," Asquith explained, "different considerations would arise."³²

All that mattered now for Asquith was to hold the party together as Campbell-Bannerman finished constructing his government. With their friend now definitely on board, Haldane and Grey began to weaken. The central figure in the drama was now Arthur Ackland, long a close friend of all three of the Relugas group. Meeting with both Grey and Haldane on Thursday evening, Ackland argued they should serve, basing his argument on broad national issues rather than personal ones.³³ Ackland told Spender that night that he believed he had made an impression, and indeed he had. Haldane went to see Campbell-Bannerman that evening and accepted the War Office, and Grey followed the next day, accepting the Foreign Office.

It is easy to describe, as some have done, Asquith's role in the entire episode of the Relugas Compact and the formation of the new Liberal government as that of an ambitious, unprincipled office seeker more than willing to sacrifice Grey and Haldane and his promises to them in order to obtain office. Lord Morley called the transactions involved in the formation of the government "unedifying."³⁴ Historian Stephen Koss has gone so far as to assert that Asquith sacrificed the interests of his friends for his own advantage.³⁵ A close reading of the events, however, shows otherwise. There is no doubt that Asquith, Haldane, and Grey thought it in the best interests of the Liberal Party for Campbell-Bannerman to stand aside and allow Asquith to provide a more energetic leadership in the Commons. All three men were anxious to hold office and to push forward an ambitious Liberal agenda. Their decision to attempt to force Campbell-Bannerman's hand by only agreeing to serve if he went to the House of Lords was premature and unwise. Unwise because events can change. It was made under the assumption that, when Balfour resigned, there would be an immediate dissolution and an election called before the Liberals had to form a government. Under this scenario, with a Liberal victory in hand, it would have made sense to pressure Campbell-Bannerman into taking a lesser role. Asquith agreed to serve as Chancellor of the Exchequer only after he had made repeated requests of Campbell-Bannerman to go to the House of Lords and, more important, after it became obvious that a government would have to be formed before the election. Grey and Haldane knew and understood the implications of this, and that is the reason they never thought the less of Asquith for going forward without them. They knew that Asquith was taking this step only because he thought it in the best interest of the party and not for personal gain. In fact Haldane, whom Beatrice Webb described as "in a state of exuberant delight," told her after he had accepted the War Office that "Asquith, Grey and I stood together; they were forced to take us on our own terms. . . . I have never been so happy in my life."[36] Haldane recalled in his memoirs, "Asquith was deeply attached to us and he was the straightest of men. But there were other influences at work, and it was plain that forces were being exerted to place him in the Cabinet, even if Campbell-Bannerman and not he were its head."[37]

The new Liberal cabinet held its first meeting on December 14. Writing for the first time to Margot on Treasury stationery, Asquith reported, "We had our first cabinet yesterday, which went off in quite a hum-drum fashion."[38] The ministry that Campbell-Bannerman put together was anything but hum-drum. Indeed, it was truly a "ministry of all the talent." Sir Robert Reid, now Lord Loreburn, became Lord Chancellor. Asquith took his position as Chancellor of the Exchequer; Grey, the Foreign Office; and Haldane, the War Office. The left wing of the party was represented in the cabinet by John Morley, who became Secretary for India, James Bryce, who became Chief Secretary for Ireland, and, most significantly, Lloyd George, who took over as President of the Board of Trade. Herbert Gladstone, who had played such an important role in holding the party together during the formation of the government, came in as Home Secretary. Augustine Birrell became President of the Board of Education, and Winston Churchill, who had recently crossed the aisle from the Conservative party, was named Under Secretary of State for the Colonies.

Traditionally the Chancellor of the Exchequer occupied 11 Downing Street, but the house was much too small for Asquith's large family. The Asquiths needed not only a nursery, but also a school room, and Margot thought it impossible to squeeze both into the Downing Street residence. So the family remained at 20 Cavendish Square, and Asquith lent 11 Downing Street to Herbert Gladstone, who had no house in London.[39]

The government's first order of business, of course, was the election. Parliament was dissolved on January 8, 1906, and the polling, which in those days lasted over a period of several weeks, began. Over several weeks, results were announced as they came in, until all polls had closed. By far the most important issue of the campaign was free trade; however, the Liberals had many other issues on which to indict the Conservative administration. These attacks focused on everything from the Education Act, so unpopular with the nonconformists, to the infamous *Taff Vale* decision by the House of Lords in 1901 allowing employers to recover damages against unions for strike activity. Even the introduction of Chinese contract labor into the Transvaal gold mines came under attack by the Liberals.

Asquith's seat at East Fife was considered safe, and this allowed him to campaign for other Liberal candidates throughout the country. Driving home the issue of free trade at St. Andrews on January 19, he pointed to the inconsistency of the Conservatives expressing fears about the "revolutionary" program of Labour when "There was not an item put forward by these Labour colleagues in their programme which involved so fundamental, and certainly not so disastrous, a change in the conditions of life in this country, as the return from Free Trade to Protection."[40]

The growing women's suffrage movement too provided some excitement to campaign events. When making a speech in Scotland, Asquith related that a "woman jumped up in the gallery about ½ way thro' my speech + unfurled her banner + began to shriek." There was a vain attempt to eject her from the hall. Nevertheless, "she kept quiet for the rest of the meeting," he reported.[41]

As the returns began to come in, it became apparent that Liberals were being returned in a landslide. Asquith wrote to Margot on January 18, "The votes are getting almost monotonous: there has been nothing like it since '32." He added, "Some of the misfortunes of our friends give me a malignant satisfaction. . . ."[42] Liberals and their allies gained an overall total of 229 seats. One of the "misfortunes of our friends" Asquith may have been alluding to was Balfour's loss of his own seat in East Manchester, the first Prime Minister in modern times to be defeated in a general election. The only strongholds the Conservatives were able to preserve were the universities, North Ireland, Liverpool, Sheffield, and Chamberlain's Birmingham. The Liberals would have 397 seats in the new House, compared to only 156 for the Conservatives and Liberal-Unionists. The total votes for the Liberals, 49 percent, was not as impressive as the seats gained. Eighty-two Irish Nationalists and twenty-nine Labour members could also be counted on to support the Liberal program. Asquith's majority in East Fife was only thirteen votes more than it had been in 1900, an impressive 59 percent of the votes cast.

As with all Chancellors of the Exchequer, Asquith's first order of business was to prepare and present a budget; however, unlike many of his predecessors, Asquith came into office late and so had little to do with the 1906 budget. As he told the Commons in presenting this first budget, "I had little more than four months in which to survey a large tract of rough and tangled ground," and he was dealing with "finances of one year for which I am hardly at all responsible."[43] Nevertheless Asquith and his Liberal colleagues came into office with definite ideas about government finance, the most notable of which was the retrenchment element of the old nineteenth-century Liberal holy trinity of "Peace, Retrenchment, Reform."

The new Chancellor was a quick study. Sir Edward Hamilton, Permanent Secretary to the Treasury (Finance Division), wrote only a little over a month after Asquith took office, "I am very glad to have Asquith who is as quick a man as I ever had."[44] There is no doubt Asquith's legal training and practice, with its emphasis on quickly getting to the heart of a matter and focus on the facts, was to be of benefit. Even so, as Asquith explained, "Coming into office, as we did, in the month of December, and much occupied during January with the general election, my colleagues presiding over the spending departments could not, with the best will in the world, do much to recast the expenditure of the country."[45] Hamilton's diary records in February Asquith's reluctance to take on a controversial new budget. "I had a talk yesterday with Asquith. He has quite made up his mind to do nothing this year about the gradation of the Income Tax, which I believe to be impracticable, or the taxation of land values which is a very thorny question, and which has always been tremendously exaggerated, notwithstanding deputations which waited the other day on the Chancellor of the Exchequer."[46] As a result, Asquith's 1906 budget was largely unremarkable, even though *The Outlook* described it as "the last word on laissez faire finance."[47] With a £3 million surplus inherited from the Conservatives, the Asquith budget applied £135,000 to school districts and just over £100,000 for improvements to the postal service. Slightly under £2 million Asquith used to eliminate the export duty on coal and to reduce the duty on tea and stripped tobacco. The remainder of the surplus was to be left for "contingencies."[48] Some economies were also realized.

The 1906 budget was only a beginning. Asquith and the Liberal leadership had much more in mind than retrenchment. The new Chancellor of the Exchequer hinted at his plans as he closed his address. "I should like to see, I hope to see," he told the House, "more attempted and more done than I can attempt or do this year in the reduction of expenditure, in the repayment of debt, and in the readjustment of the incidence of taxation."[49] The first two categories were all too familiar, but for anyone who understood politics and listened closely as he finished his address after two hours and twenty minutes, the last category, "readjustment of the incidence of taxation," signaled a call for real reform and the gigantic political battles such reform would entail.

To prepare for the 1907 budget, the first one in which Asquith would have any real impact, the Chancellor of the Exchequer moved for the appointment of a Select Committee on Income Tax, which was duly formed. A 1905 departmental committee on income tax had already found widespread tax evasion.[50] Charged with reporting on the practicability of graduating the income tax and differentiating between "Permanent and Precarious incomes," the new Parliamentary committee, chaired by Sir Charles Dilke, began taking evidence in May and reporting in November.[51] The committee's five important conclusions were to revolutionize the British tax system. First, it found that gradation of income tax was possible, and second, that gradation could partially be achieved through the imposition of a "super tax" on the very wealthy. Most important, the committee concluded that a further improvement could be made in the tax system by differentiating between "earned" and "unearned" income. Finally, the committee suggested two changes in the methodology of tax collection to help with tax evasion: abandonment of collection at the source (adopting a direct personal assessment of the whole of each person's income) and a compulsory personal declaration.

Three months after the Select Committee issued its report, the Treasury circulated a memorandum outlining the government's challenges. The Liberal government's plans for social reforms would undoubtedly call for additional expenditure. There was room for some reduction in the current budget, particularly in defense spending, but these reductions would never generate sufficient funds for new spending, even if combined with indirect taxes, such as taxes on alcohol. As the memorandum wryly put it, "The country refuses any longer to drink itself out of its financial straights." The unavoidable conclusion: "Unless the whole system of our taxation is to be recast, the solution must be found in the increase of direct taxation."[52]

With the backdrop of the Select Committee report and the Treasury memorandum, Asquith began preparing his 1907 budget. The social reforms he and other Liberals advocated would be costly, and he readily accepted the conclusion of the Treasury that the only real possibility of raising anywhere near the sufficient revenue to support such programs would be direct taxation. Asquith, however, was hesitant about increasing direct taxation too far, too fast. He wrote to Sir Edward Hamilton that for the present he opposed the idea of a "super tax" and he thought that a full gradation of the income tax was impractical at this time.[53] To Asquith's mind, the Select Committee's suggestion to differentiate between "earned" and "unearned" income was for the moment the most practical way forward, since many Liberals had strong reservations about a full gradation of the income tax, fearing it would harm the work ethic. These Liberals did not have such qualms about taxing unearned income or unearned increment, such as increased value of land or death duties. They thought this could be done without sacrificing the Liberal sacred cow of protecting individual effort.[54] Ever politically sensitive to just how far he could proceed, the Chancellor of the Exchequer wisely applied a step-by-step approach.

The summer before Asquith took office, the family had been busy with Violet's first London season. It began in May when Margot and her father, Sir Charles Tennant, gave a ball in Violet's honor. There were the required rounds of receptions, parties, and balls until the following month when she was presented at court.

After Asquith's elevation to Chancellor, finances, as usual, were the biggest problem. His new duties precluded his lucrative practice of law. One welcome economy was Margot's gracious decision to give up hunting, which had always been a great drain on their resources. They were relieved when Margot's father offered to pay the rent for 20 Cavendish Square, so that they would not have to live in the cramped quarters of 11 Downing Street. Their financial picture, however, took a turn for the worse five months after Asquith took office when Sir Charles died. Margot's two younger brothers each received capital sufficient to produce an income of £40,000 a year. Her eldest brother inherited the family seat at Glen with an annual income of £80,000. Margot and her sisters received the continuation of their yearly allowance of £3,000. It is hard to believe Margot when she wrote in her diary, "I confess without bitterness of any sort that I think papa made a mistake." She continued, "My brothers have not the size or scope or ease to spend such fortunes—5,000 a year less to each wd have been quite unfelt by any of them and just made the difference to the 3 girls."[55]

Other family members continued to do well. Oc, who Asquith privately admitted was his favorite son, had finally "found" himself. In 1904, to the great disappointment of his father, he had abandoned his classical studies at Oxford and later that year was struck hard by the death of Molly Manners, with whom he was passionately in love. For a while he talked vaguely of going into business. Finally in 1905 he decided to join the colonial service in the Sudan, and after returning to Oxford briefly to master Arabic he was admitted to the service in 1906.[56] His father, always proud of his son's achievements, wrote to Margot bragging that "Oc was one of 12 selected from about 130 candidates, at least 100 of whom were well up to the mark."[57] Even so, it was with a sad heart that Asquith and the rest of the family said good-bye to Oc in September. It would be at least eighteen months before he could return home.

While Oc would be greatly missed, Asquith and Margot were buoyed by the anticipation of a new member of their family. Margot was once again pregnant, and the new child was expected in February. A boy was born two months premature on Christmas Eve. The baby at first appeared healthy yet tragically died the next morning. Asquith composed himself enough to hold a short prayer service to thank the servants for helping the family. Three days later he and Violet traveled to Wanborough to bury the baby next to his sister.[58]

The death of their child had the more profound effect on Margot. Collin Clifford in his study of the Asquith family asserts that her health never fully recovered. Together with the loss of the baby, she had to endure an agonizing bowel operation the following March, to be followed by an even more horrendous operation to cure "acute inflammation" in her ears, apparently without anaesthetic. Her overall condition was so bad that she was sent to Easton Grey to recuperate. Asquith did what he could to assist in her recovery, traveling to see her during her convalescence despite the pressing business of Parliament. His letters to her are filled with concern and encouragement. Her condition became a rollercoaster—improving one day, declining the next. In a typical letter, he wrote, "I am very sorry you felt sick again—but I hope this has already passed away. You must do your best to keep up your spirits."[59] Over time Asquith must have begun to realize that some of Margot's physical condition was linked to her mental state. He seems to allude to this when he wrote, "I am distressed that you still have bouts of sickness, but all your discomforts are eventually connected one with another, and all will go when you get the centre of things right." In the next sentence, however, he told her that he "would not dream . . . of going to a nerve doctor." According to Asquith, "They are mostly quacks, and those who are not live upon guess work. . . ."[60] After a period of difficult recuperation with bouts of insomnia, nausea, and stomach aches, she was only barely able to return for Raymond's wedding in July.

Raymond, now a barrister practicing in London, had fallen in love several years before with Katherine Horner, the younger daughter of the Asquith's friends, Sir John and Lady (Francis) Horner. Despite a small allowance, like his father before him, Raymond was a struggling young barrister with insufficient funds to support a wife and family. Both his father and stepmother enthusiastically supported Raymond's courtship of Katherine, but without additional financial support, marriage was out of the question. Eventually Asquith offered to increase Raymond's allowance, and this was enough to allow the young couple to marry.[61]

As for Asquith himself, Philip Snowden, a new Labour MP, observed at the time, "I had not seen Mr. Asquith until then for twenty years, and the change in his appearance was very striking. Only a little over fifty years old, his hair was quite white. He had lost the pallor of his younger days."[62] Although his physical appearance had changed over the years, his relations with his wife and children during this period continued to show a loving husband and father who was genuinely concerned about their welfare. Whether traveling to see Margot during her convalescence or giving Oc a government dispatch case as a going away present, he seemed always to have their welfare in mind. Even though his time with family members was now more limited, his letters mention having lunch with his children, visiting his sons at school, inquiring as to their health, voicing concern when they were sick and great relief when they recovered. Even so, there was a distance. Cys Asquith perhaps described it best when he observed, "Notwithstanding their cool and casual contacts, the family as a whole were united by a powerful freemasonry, and its members would even on occasion furtively fight each other's battles: but horror of emotional nudism led them to clothe their mutual appreciation with a semblance of judicial indifference, and to deny ordinary expression."[63] An example was when Asquith was saying good-bye to Oc who was about to leave for eighteen months service in the Sudan. As Oc described it, he shook hands with his father in the hall after lunch. Then "we had a little talk in the billiard room before, neither of us venturing beyond money matters and banalities . . . he was nearly crying."[64] The "horror of emotional nudism" did not mean a lack of love.

Asquith introduced his long anticipated 1907 budget to Parliament in April.[65] The Prince of Wales and other dignitaries were in the gallery waiting for a speech that was to be in Haldane's words "in the first rank, worthy to stand with the great performances of the great Chancellors."[66] Asquith began by saying that he thought it important to set out the lines on which the government believed "the finance of the country during the next few years should be directed." To Asquith, the annual budget ought to be considered "an integral part and a necessary link in a connected and coherent chain of policy." This perspective diverged markedly from that of any of his predecessors, for he believed the country had reached the point where, as he put it, "whether we look merely at its fiscal or at its social exigencies, we cannot afford to drift along the stream and treat each year's finances as if it were self-contained." Although he did not admit it outright, he was craftily setting the stage for his step-by-step approach. Yes, he was proposing a budget for 1907, but the implication he wanted to leave was that there would be more to come. As he said, "The Chancellor of the Exchequer, in other words ought to Budget, not for one year, but for several years."

All of this was preparation for an explanation of how he intended to alter the British tax system to pay for the costs of social reform coming in future budgets. He now proposed one of the key elements not only to the 1907 budget, but to all future British budgets, including the famous "People's Budget" of 1909, namely, the principle of differentiation. He described the hypothetical cases of one man earning £1,000 a year from investments "perhaps accumulated and left to him by his father" and another man, perhaps thinking of his own experience, with the same income earned by "personal labour in the pursuit of some arduous and perhaps precarious profession or some form of business." "To say that those two people are, from the point of view of the State, are to be taxed in the same way," he argued, was "flying in the face of justice and common sense." To remove this flaw, "without destroying the essential features or the productive character of the tax," the Asquith budget proposed for the first time to differentiate "earned" from "unearned" income. Under the proposal all "unearned" income up to £2,000 annually would be taxed at the full rate of income tax, then one shilling in the pound. "Earned" income would be taxed at nine pence in the pound, and all existing abatements would be calculated from earned incomes only.

The 1907 budget has been mostly remembered for the introduction of the principle of differentiation, which established a vast new source of revenue for the government. What has been less clearly seen is that the 1907 budget was only part of the Chancellor of the Exchequer's larger plan. He said as much himself in introducing the budget. In 1907 Asquith was more than willing to go along with differentiation and the raising of death duties, but he was not willing, as many Liberals urged, to place the system in shock by also going forward with the introduction of a general gradated income tax. This would still have to wait.

As the number two leader of the Liberals, Asquith involved himself in much more than the budget. Legislation to reverse the infamous 1901 *Taff Vale* decision by the House of Lords sat near the top of the Liberal government's and their Labour allies' agenda.[67] This decision held unions could be held liable for damages resulting from strike activity, a terrific blow to British trade unions, creating a chilling effect on their activities. Unions now feared being financially liable to the extent of most of their assets for even unauthorized activities of their members. Further, even the right to strike had been placed into question by other recent court opinions.

The question for the government was not whether to reverse the decision, but how.

Asquith and Haldane thought the controversy over the *Taff Vale* decision extremely important. In fact, their proposal to deal with the situation was the only plan for any domestic policy when they assumed office.[68] Even though Asquith and Haldane sympathized with Labour's position, almost immediately they disagreed with the Labour Party over the appropriate remedy. From the outset, the trade unions demanded legislation to reverse *Taff Vale* in its entirety, giving unions complete immunity against damages. Asquith's and Haldane's position called for more gradual change. Asquith worried about the public's reaction to giving unions a blanket immunity against damage claims for their activities. Asquith did not want the Liberal Party's response to the *Taff Vale* controversy to appear to the average voter as a Liberal sell-out to the Labour Party. Asquith strongly believed that the Liberal Party, if it was to succeed, must be seen as broadly based and not merely tool of special interests and particularly not the representative of a particular class.[69]

The Prime Minister together with John Burns, the President of the Local Government Board, and a minority of the cabinet supported the simple provision that unions could not be liable for damages.[70] Asquith, leading a majority of the cabinet that included Haldane and others, particularly the law officers, supported the Royal Commission's more nuanced recommendations. To them, amending the law of agency so that trade unions would not be held responsible for the unauthorized actions of minor and subordinate agents was sufficient. Unions, however, would remain liable for tort damages where agency of responsible union officials could be established. This position became the governing principal behind the government's bill.

The Trade Disputes bill was introduced in March 1906 to the disappointment of many radical Liberals and the Labour members of the House who supported a blanket reversal of *Taff Vale*. Under the bill trade unions would be required to set up "executive committee," and union organizations could only be held liable for damages that resulted either from the direct actions of these committees or their agents acting under instructions from a committee.[71] To counter the government's proposal, a private bill, introduced by Walter Hudson, a Labour MP and leader in the National Union of Railwaymen, called for complete immunity for unions in trade disputes. Under the Hudson bill, a union could never be held liable for damages on account of illegal acts by its members. The Attorney General, Lawson Walton, vigorously attacked this bill, and it looked for the moment like the government was holding the line. That is until the Prime Minister entered into the debate. To what must have been the complete surprise of his entire cabinet, Campbell-Bannerman announced his support for the second reading of the Hudson bill. "This was certainly an unusual step" as Campbell-Bannerman's biographer has understatedly admitted. Without any prior explanation to his colleagues, the Prime Minister had thrown his support to a bill closer to his own personal views, suddenly opposing a bill that he and his cabinet had agreed to support. This left his cabinet high and dry.

There was nothing for the cabinet to do but to regroup and reassess its position. Clearly Asquith's idea of limiting the Trade Disputes bill to a modification of agency law was no longer a viable option. Asquith desperately did not want the measure to seem slanted toward the union and looked for some way to make the measure more even handed. Ultimately, the cabinet compromised. The unions as well as combinations of employers would be exempted from liability, and this became the measure the government came to support.

Asquith now had a great deal of face-saving to do in the debate over the government's "new" Trade Disputes bill. F. E. Smith pointedly asked, "What explanation had the Chancellor of the Exchequer given of his change of opinion, except that he could not have controlled his party in the division lobby?"[72] Asquith responded to this and other similar questions as best he could. He tried to explain by differentiating between means and ends. The end was to reverse the *Taff Vale* decision that had overturned thirty years of settled law. He still believed that the best method was to amend the law of agency, yet he realized the majority of those on the government side thought otherwise. The government now proposed a legitimate compromise. He saw nothing "dishonourable or unworthy in deferring to the prevailing opinion of those who after all were the best judges in the matter."[73] The key was that under the new proposal unions were not the only ones to be exempt from liability. He made clear that "he could only assent to an arrangement which established perfect equality as between the combinations of masters and the combinations of men, and his objection in principle on this point was met. . . ."[74]

The government's modified Trade Disputes bill ultimately passed with little trouble. When the bill came up for a third reading, Balfour did not even ask for a division, and with a unanimous decision in the Commons there was little the Conservative-controlled House of Lords could do but to pass the bill. Elie Halévy has concluded that the Trade Disputes Act of 1906 was "a victory not of the Liberals over the Conservatives, but of the proletariat over the bourgeoisie." Right or wrong, this viewpoint is exactly what Asquith feared would be the public verdict on the measure—the growing division of the nation and the Liberal Party along class lines. What Asquith had argued for was a middle road. Unions should be liable, like any other entity, for illegal actions that they actually authorized. He wanted nothing more than a level playing field. Labour and the radical Liberals demanded more and carried the day. What Asquith correctly understood, however, was that if such a trend of setting class against class continued, there would be no room left in the political middle for the Liberal Party.

Looming ominously in the background of the Liberal legislative agenda was the overwhelmingly conservative House of Lords. While the Liberals succeeded in getting the Trade Disputes bill through both Houses, largely because of the Conservatives' policy of not wanting to anger the Labour vote, the government failed to gain passage through the House of Lords between 1906 and 1908 for three other key parts of the Liberal program—the Education bill, the Plural Voting bill, and the Licensing bill.

Just as the *Taff Vale* decision had energized Labour supporters in the 1906 election, the Education Act of 1902 mobilized the nonconformist community into political action. The Liberal government had been only in power a few months when Augustine Birrell, President of the Board of Education, introduced its Education bill in April. Asquith was somewhat nervous about an issue toward which so many had such strong feelings. He wrote to Margot on the day the bill was introduced, "I haven't found out how it is going to be received by our people: the Church of course will be angry."[75] It was a complicated bill that addressed many issues, but to Asquith "the very root and foundation of the whole Bill" was that all schools "shall be under popular control."[76] The practical effect of the measure was that there would be no denominational teaching, although nondenominational teaching, usually referred to as "Bible teaching," would be permitted. Further, nonconformist children in the country districts would no longer be forced to receive Anglican instruction.[77]

The bill passed the Commons in late July by a comfortable margin, even though passage did require the application of cloture. The House of Lords, however, through amendment transformed the measure into something entirely different, including, among other things, authorizing teachers to give denominational instruction in situations not even provided for in the 1902 Education Act. Asquith said it was like exchanging the positives and negatives in the Ten Commandments and still calling it the Ten Commandments.[78] Upon the recommendation of the cabinet, the Commons in December rejected the Lords' amendments *en bloc*. When the Lords insisted on its amendments, the government decided to drop the bill.

Next to education, the most important issue for the nonconformist Liberal supporters was regulation of the drink trade. In 1905 there were almost 100,000 licensed facilities for the sale of alcohol in England and Wales, almost one for every 333 persons.[79] The Unionist government in 1904 reduced the number of licenses, but nonconformists had been infuriated by the amounts paid in compensation to license holders. The new Liberal government, anxious to please its nonconformist constituency, gave a new Licensing bill top billing in the King's speech in 1907. Later the government decided to postpone the measure, because it might well be trying the patience of the Commons to spend an inordinate amount of time on a bill that clearly had even less chance of passing the Lords than the Education bill.[80] The goal of a Licensing bill, however, was far from abandoned. In February the next year, Asquith introduced a measure that he had been working on for some time.

The Chancellor of the Exchequer's Licensing bill of 1908 was so complicated that Asquith's speech introducing the bill runs twenty-five columns in *Hansard*.[81] It was doomed from the start, like the Education and Plural Voting bills before it. It readily passed its second reading in May and sailed through the committee stage largely unaltered. Yet once again the House of Lords had a different idea. When the bill reached the Lords in late November, it was overwhelmingly rejected after only three days' debate.

It is no wonder, then, given the Lord's actions on these measures, that the Liberals felt the constitutional question of the power of the House of Lords could no longer be avoided. One Liberal publication noted that since 1870 the House of Lords had never rejected a bill supported and passed by Conservatives; yet in the same period the Lords had defeated or mutilated twenty-six Liberal measures, eight of which between 1906 and 1907.[82] As the first step in a three-year-long constitutional crisis that will be discussed in detail in the next chapter, the Liberal government in 1907 appointed a cabinet committee to investigate Constitutional alternatives to limit the House of Lord's veto power and put through the Commons a resolution stating that "in order to give effect to the will of the people as expressed by their elected representatives," it was necessary that the power House of Lords to reject bills passed by the Commons "be so restricted by law as to secure that within the limits of a single Parliament the final decision of the Commons shall prevail."[83]

For over two years, the Liberal government had proceeded in their work knowing the precarious health of their leader, Campbell-Bannerman. On February 12, 1908, he held what would be his last cabinet meeting, the following day he suffered a serious heart attack. To add to an already grave situation, he developed influenza, and despite a slight rally late in the month, it became apparent that he would not be able to return to his duties and responsibilities. Although his doctors knew his condition was terminal, this news was kept from him. By the end of March, Campbell-Bannerman realized he would not recover.

Quite frankly the old man had proved many wrong, including the old Relugas group of Asquith, Grey, and Haldane. Far from being feeble and inept, he had shown himself to be an effective leader. In the end, it was the Prime Minister's health, not his abilities, that failed him. Grey wrote to the Prime Minister, perhaps meaning to speak for all the Relugas group, "I have long ago recognized that the difficulties I made when the Government was formed were short-sighted and ill-judged and we all feel now that troubles, which your presence at the head of the Government, kept in abeyance, will have to be faced."[84] Margot recorded in her diary: "On the 27th of March, Henry . . . told me that Sir Henry Campbell-Bannerman had sent for him that day to tell him that he was dying. They had talked for over an hour, and Henry's voice shook as he repeated their conversation to me." In Asquith's relation of his last conversation with Campbell-Bannerman, the Prime Minster thanked him for "being a wonderful colleague. So loyal, so disinterested, and so able." With this, Asquith put his arm around his shoulder and they cried together.[85] A little over a week later on April 5, Campbell-Bannerman resigned as Prime Minister, and the King sent for Asquith.

NOTES

1. Herbert Gladstone to HHA, 29 Oct. 1903, BL, MS. Asquith 10, ff. 98–8A.
2. Robbins, *Sir Edward Grey*, 116.
3. Wilson, *C. B.*, 425.
4. Grey, *Twenty-five Years*, 1:60.
5. Haldane, *Autobiography*, 157.
6. Ibid., 159.
7. Major General Sir Frederick Maurice, *Haldane 1856–1915: The Life of Viscount Haldane of Cloan* (Westport, CT: Greenwood Press, 1937), 1:149.
8. Wilson, *C.B.*, 428–29.
9. Maurice, *Haldane*, 1:152.
10. R. B. Haldane to HHA, 6 Oct. 1905, BL, MS. Asquith 10, ff. 153–56.
11. M. Asquith, *Autobiography*, 2:55.
12. Ibid., 2:56.
13. Ibid.
14. Ibid., 2:57.
15. Wilson, *C. B.*, 433; Spender and Asquith, *Life of Asquith,* 1:172; Jenkins makes no comment on whether or not Asquith agreed to accept the position at this meeting, Jenkins, *Asquith*, 148–49.
16. HHA to Herbert Gladstone, 25 Nov. 1905, in Wilson, *C. B.*, 434.
17. T. Boyle, "The Foundation of Campbell-Bannerman's Government in December 1905: A Memorandum by J. A. Spender," *Bulletin of the Inst. of Hist. Research.* 45 (1972): 289.
18. James, *Rosebery,* 454.
19. Morley to Campbell-Bannerman, 28 Nov. 1905, Wilson, *C. B.*, 436.
20. James, *Rosebery,* 455.
21. Eric Alexander Akers-Douglas Chilston, 3rd Viscount Chilston, *Chief Whip: The Political Life and Times of Aretas Akers-Douglas, 1st Viscount Chilston* (London: Routledge & Kegan Paul, 1961), 331.
22. J. A. Spender, *Autograph Account of Events*, 30 Nov.–8 Dec., 1905 (30 Nov.), BL, Add MS 46388, f. 59.
23. Ibid., f. 60.
24. E. Grey to HHA, 4 Dec. 1905, BL, MS. Asquith 10, ff. 180–81.
25. Spender, *Autograph Account*, f. 63.

26. M. Asquith, *Autobiography,* 2:60.
27. Ibid., 2:61-62.
28. Ibid., 2:61.
29. George Macaulay Trevelyan, *Grey of Fallodon: The Life and Letters of Sir Edward Grey, afterwards Viscount Grey of Fallodon* (Boston: Houghton Mifflin, 1937), 114.
30. Wilson, *C. B.*, 448.
31. M. Asquith, *Autobiography,* 2:62.
32. Spender and Asquith, *Life of Asquith,* 1:174-75.
33. Memorandum by Ackland enclosed in Ackland to Campbell-Bannerman, 17 Dec. 1905, BL, Add. MS. 52518, f. 77-81.
34. Earl of Oxford and Asquith, *Memories,* 1:229.
35. Stephen E. Koss, *Lord Haldane: Scapegoat for Liberalism* (New York: Columbia, 1969), 38.
36. Webb, *Diary,* 3:19.
37. Haldane, *Autobiography,* 168.
38. HHA to MA, 15 Dec. 1905, BL, MS. Eng. c. 6690, ff. 57-58.
39. Bennett, *Margot,* 171.
40. Spender and Asquith, *Life of Asquith,* 177.
41. HHA to MA, 10 Jan. 1906, BL, MS. Eng. c. 6690, ff. 63-64.
42. HHA to MA, 18 Jan. 1906, BL, MS. Eng. c. 6690, ff. 65-66.
43. *Hansard*, 4, 156, 307, 277, 30 Apr. 1906.
44. Bahlman, ed., *Diary of Sir Edward Walter Hamilton,* 461.
45. *Hansard*, 4, 156, 284-85, 30 Apr. 1906.
46. Bahlman, ed., *Diary of Sir Edward Walter Hamilton,* 461.
47. *The Outlook*, 9 May 1906, Julian Amery, *Joseph Chamberlain and the Tariff Reform Campaign: The Life of Joseph Chamberlain, vol. 6, 1903-1968* (New York: Macmillan, 1969), 890.
48. *Hansard*, 4, 156, 306-7, 30 Apr. 1906.
49. Ibid., 307.
50. *Report of the Departmental Committee on the Income-Tax,* Cd. 2575, Parl. Papers (1905) vol. 44.
51. *Report from the Select Committee on Income Tax* (London: H. M. Stationary Office, 1906).
52. Cab. 37/87, No. 22, 26 Feb. 1907.
53. H. V. Emy, *Liberals, Radicals and Social Politics, 1892-1914* (Cambridge: Cambridge University Press, 1973), 199-200.
54. Michael Freeden, *The New Liberalism: An Ideology of Social Reform* (Oxford: Clarendon Press, 1978), 134.
55. 13 June 1906, BL, MS. Eng. d. 3204.
56. Clifford, *Asquiths*, 105-6, 114, 116.
57. HHA to MA, 3 Aug. 1905, BL, MS. Eng. c. 6690, ff. 29-30.
58. Clifford, *Asquiths,* 126.
59. HHA to MA, 7 June 1907, BL, MS. Eng. c. 6690, ff. 105-6.
60. HHA to MA, 19 May 1907, BL, MS. Eng. c. 6690, ff. 99-100.

61. There is some discrepancy as to the source of the increased allowance. Daphne Bennett asserts it was Margot who settled an additional £400 a year on Raymond. Colin Clifford implies that it was Asquith; Bennett, *Margot,* 176; Clifford, *Asquiths,* 130.

62. McCallum, *Asquith,* 52.

63. Spender and Asquith, *Life of Asquith,* 1:222–23.

64. Christopher Page, *Command in the Royal Naval Division: A Military Biography of Brigadier General A. M. Asquith DSO* (Staplehurst: Spellmount, 1999), 7.

65. *Hansard,* 4, 172, 1175–211, 18 Apr. 1907.

66. Spender and Asquith, *Life of Asquith,* 190.

67. *The Taff Vale Railway Company v. The Amalgamated Society of Railway Servants,* (1901) A.C. 426 H.L., 22 July 1901.

68. Matthew, *Liberal Imperialists,* 248.

69. Ibid., 249.

70. Wilson, *C. B.,* 505.

71. Elie Halévy, *The Rule of Democracy 1905–1914 (Book I)* (London: Ernest Benn, 1952), 95.

72. *Hansard,* 4, 163, 1366, 1 Nov. 1906.

73. Ibid., 1368.

74. *Hansard,* 4, 162, 1713, 2 Aug. 1906.

75. HHA to MA, 9 Apr. 1906, BL, MS. Eng. c. 6690, ff. 77–78.

76. *Hansard,* 4, 158, 1411, 18 June 1906.

77. Halévy, *Rule of Democracy,* 65–66.

78. Spender and Asquith, *Life of Asquith,* 1:185.

79. *Hansard,* 4, 185, 77, 27 Feb. 1908.

80. Spender and Asquith, *Life of Asquith,* 190.

81. *Hansard,* 4, 185, 73–98, 27 February 1908.

82. Homer Lawrence Morris, "Parliamentary Franchise Reform in England from 1885 to 1918," *Studies in History, Economics and Public Law* 91, no. 2 (1921): 24.

83. *Hansard,* 4, 176, 909, 24 June 1907.

84. Edward Grey to Campbell-Bannerman, 7 Apr. 1908, Brit. L, Add MS 41230, f. 214.

85. M. Asquith, *Autobiography,* 2:73.

Chapter Six

Prime Minister (1908–1914)

Following his interview with the King at Biarritz on April 8, Asquith boarded a train to hurry home to London. After an overnight stop in Paris, where he refused to make any comment to reporters, he arrived at Charing Cross at six o'clock the following evening. Greeting him at the station was a large group that included Margot, Violet, and Raymond. The news of his appointment was now public, and a large crowd cheered him as he made his way to Downing Street to inquire about Campbell-Bannerman's condition and finally home to Cavendish Square.

Asquith's appointment seemed a forgone conclusion. Yet among Liberal circles there were some questions. After becoming Chancellor of the Exchequer in 1906, Asquith, according to Arthur Ponsonby's diary, had gone through a period of "extreme unpopularity" brought on by his perceived "want of sympathy" and "tendency to ride roughshod over the party & his lack of humanity."[1] According to the Viscount Esher's diary, Morley reported that "The Cabinet might, if polled, support Asquith, but he, Morley, would not serve under him." John Morley discussed the succession with the Viscount in November 1907. According to Morley, Grey "has 'more character,' 'less intellect,' but 'fewer drawbacks.'"[2] Most of the objection to Asquith came from the more radical Liberals, who looked with disfavor on Asquith's stance as a Liberal Imperialist in support of the Boer War. Chief among those questioning the wisdom of making Asquith the new leader was C. P. Scott of the *Manchester Guardian*. He wrote to historian and journalist Goldwin Smith in March 1908 expressing his concerns. "Asquith . . . is a sort of natural successor, and his claim is reinforced by his readiness and force as a leader in the daily Parliamentary scrimmage, but his political record is bad, and the present cabinet with Asquith simply substituted for Campbell-Bannerman could not command confidence in the country, and will, I hope, never be accepted by the genuine Liberals in the cabinet."[3] Scott and others held that Asquith was somehow not a "genuine" Liberal but more of an old-fashioned Whig Liberal, not only because of Asquith's Liberal Imperialist attitudes, but also almost certainly because of his reluctance to put Irish Home Rule at the top of the Liberal agenda.

While the more radical Liberals grumbled, Asquith was the only logical choice to succeed Campbell-Bannerman. The more realistic party faithful understood that Campbell-Bannerman's successor would be taking the reins of a party at a difficult juncture in its history. The momentum of the landslide victory of 1906 had already run its course, and Liberal Party morale was at a low point. Time and again, the House of Lords had frustrated party efforts for social reform. Yet the Conservatives had been shrewd in their tactics, passing some legislation popular with the working class, such as a Trade Disputes Act. Campbell-Bannerman had simply not found a formula to counter these Tory defensive moves. In short Asquith faced what one historian has called a legislative "log-jam," for the Liberals still had on their agenda a Licensing bill, left over from the last session, another Education bill, land valuation, and an old-age pension scheme.[4] To add to all this, an economic downturn in 1907 soured the mood of the electorate. Liberals were losing by-elections. In spite of all these difficulties, Asquith was a proven leader with tremendous abilities, and most Liberals were confident he was their man. As Sir Edward Grey commented years later, "Asquith was the only man who could then aspire to succeed to the post of Prime Minister."[5]

Few could argue that Asquith was one of the more talented and brilliant people ever to become Prime Minister. If it is true, as the Stoics believed, that rational thought is a gift of the Gods, then Asquith was especially blessed. Of all his character traits, Asquith is perhaps best remembered for his intelligence. As Winston Churchill put it, Asquith had "an orderly, disciplined mind" that "delighted in reason and design."[6] It was also a mind that loved history and literature, and throughout his life, Asquith was a voracious reader. Yet, admirably, he was, in the words of one colleague, "a scholar who did not parade his scholarship."[7] A lawyer by training, he could reduce complicated issues to their essence, and the power of his memory was legendary. J. A. Spender recalled an incident at a house party with Asquith.[8] When Spender recited the lines,

> To thee too comes the golden hour,
> When flower is feeling after flower,

and attributed them to Tennyson's *In Memoriam*, Asquith challenged him, saying he didn't think it was Tennyson, and it was certainly not *In Memo-*

riam. Friends retrieved a copy of the poem from the library and, to Spender's pleasure, the lines appeared. Despite what appeared to be incontrovertible evidence on the point, Asquith refused to admit defeat. A few days later, Spender received the following letter,

My Dear Spender,

If you will look at any edition of "In Memoriam" prior to 1870 or thereabouts (mine, e.g. is the 19th edition, dated 1867) you will not find in the poem now numbered XXXIX ("Old Warder of these buried bones"), in which the disputed lines occur. It must have been inserted between 1867 and 1870, with the result that, instead of there being as before CXXX poems, there are since alteration CXXXI.

I regretfully admit that the evidence compels me to withdraw the attribution to you of "flower feeling after flower." But I was right in maintaining that, if it came from Tennyson, it was an afterthought, and no part of the original "In Memoriam."

The "Life" throws no light upon the matter.

Yours sincerely,
H. H. Asquith

Asquith's undoubted brilliance, however, was neither reflective nor original, but was firmly grounded in practicality. Again, Winston Churchill, who knew him well, while acknowledging Asquith must have "communed deeply with himself," thought it was much less than "most men at the summit of a nation's affairs." "On all [subjects] when the need required it," Churchill observed, "his mind opened and shut smoothly and exactly, like the breach of a gun." As a result, "there was also the sense of scorn, lightly and not always completely veiled, for arguments, for personalities and even for events which did not conform to the pattern he had with so much profound knowledge and reflection decidedly adopted."[9] Spender also speculated that Asquith's "certain reluctance to admit a new fact" must have been "extremely irritating to the nimbler minds which leap at new facts and take liberty with old ones."[10]

Augustine Birrell noted that "there was nothing metaphysical about Asquith," and he was the "least speculative of mortals, whose powerful brain operated directly upon questions as they arose before him, and he never seemed to go in search of them."[11] Perhaps the most unkind and inaccurate comment in this regard was that of his friend Arthur Balfour, who scornfully remarked to Lady Rayleigh in 1894, "But for the split in the Liberal Party he [Asquith] would never have been more than a fairly successful lawyer earning his three thousand pounds and ending perhaps a Judge."[12] Lytton Strachey was an even harsher critic. "In Asquith's case the inveterate lack of ideals and imagination seems really unredeemed; when one has peeled off the brown-paper wrapping of phrases and compromises, one finds—just nothing at all."[13]

According to Sir John (later Viscount) Simon, who served in Asquith's cabinet as Home Secretary, even though Asquith consulted others, he "was essentially a man who reached his own conclusion" and had no problem acting on those conclusions once reached.[14] The time it took to reach those conclusions concerned many. Asquith's perceived hesitancy to take quick action became enshrined in one of his most oft quoted remarks, "wait and see." He first employed the phrase in the 1910 debate over the so-called "People's Budget." Viscount Helmsley had inquired, "Are we to understand that if the resolutions sent up from this House fail to pass in another place, the circumstances contemplated by the P.M. will have arisen?" Asquith famously responded, "We had better wait and see."[15] This was lampooned by many including Archibald Stodart-Walker who published the satirical poem "Asquith" in 1914:

> And then, when asked to name the peers to be,
> Self-schooled, self made, self honoured, self secure,
> You use a phrase unguessed at—"Wait and see."
>
> Such snubs the Opposition must endure,
> All questions which they put, all doubts they raise,
> Find their reply in that Asquithian phrase.[16]

The phrase "wait and see" unfortunately stuck with Asquith until the end of his life and was particularly a problem during the war. Yet many thought the idea of Asquith being unnecessarily slow to come to decisions ridiculous. Simon in his memoirs flatly states, "There never was a more absurd misrepresentation of his powers of decision and leadership than the misuse which was made of his phrase 'wait and see.'"[17] These conflicting views may both be true. Asquith was capable of using delay as a deliberate political strategy. Particularly during the war years, in many instances Asquith used "wait and see" as a tactic to gain time for greater political advantage.

More careful observers, while recognizing Asquith's lack of initiative and vision, saw this not much as a liability but rather an asset when combined with his powerful intelligence. Just before Asquith became Prime Minister, J. A. Gardiner wrote a perceptive character sketch of him in the *Daily News*. To Gardiner, Asquith was

> Not a man of visions. He leaves the pioneering work to others and follows after with his levels and compasses to lay out the new estate. No great cause will ever owe anything to him in its inception, but when he is convinced of its justice

and practicability, he will take it up with a quiet, undemonstrated firmness that means success . . . if he is wanting in any essential of statesmanship, it is a strong impulse to action. He has patience rather than momentum.[18]

John Maynard Keynes also recognized Asquith's "absence of originality and creative power." When combined with Asquith's "rapidity of apprehension, lucidity, critical sharpness, a copious and accurate memory, taste and discrimination, freedom from both prejudices and illusion," Keynes viewed the two qualities as a "successful combination." For Keynes, the Prime Minister's mind was "built for the purpose of dealing with the given facts of the outside world; it was a mill or a machine, not a mine or a springing field." Asquith "had no intellectual fancies to lead him astray, no balloons of his own making to lift his feet off the ground." Rather, he was built to "hear and judge" and the political positions he held are best occupied "not by one ingenious to invest and to build, but by one whose business is to hear and judge." Keynes concluded that in this regard Asquith had no equal.[19]

As a logical result of his rational way of thinking, Asquith was eloquent. From a very early age, he demonstrated a remarkable gift for speech that was fluent, forcible, and persuasive, and he fully understood the power of the weapon he possessed. Beginning with the early descriptions of Asquith's schoolboy oratory at the City of London School, through his speeches at the Oxford Union, to his years in Parliament, Asquith was one of the best public speakers of his generation. Those who served with Asquith in Parliament remembered him as the "perfect orator," whose "sequence of argument never flagged" and whose "sentences never came out wrong," the central characteristic of his oratory being "the perfection of its language and form."[20] He developed a renowned command of facts and figures. Once, when he spoke for an hour to a large public gathering on the government's Licensing bill to reduce the number of public houses, his audience sat amazed at his command of detailed facts and statistics. When a woman approached him afterward and asked for his notes as a souvenir, he obliged, handing her a small sheet of paper where all he had scrawled was "Too many pubs."[21] Prime Minister Campbell-Bannerman always knew he could count on Asquith, whom he dubbed "the hammer," to close out debate on an issue. Reading his speeches in *Hansard* today, one is still impressed with the quality of his speeches, although there are few memorable phrases. The power of his eloquence lay in his logic and his unique talent in explaining even the most complicated issues in the simplest of terms, distilling them to their essence.

Asquith's admiration of classical values can also be seen in his disciplined, stoic self-control. Yet he knew the ancient stoic writers well enough to understand that controlling one's emotions did not mean the absence of emotion.

Asquith followed the stoics' advice in suppressing his negative emotions, such as anger, fear, grief, and anxiety, and encouraging his more positive feelings. This led to a countenance that was steady and calm. "In spite of calls on his time," his son Beb related, "he rarely showed any signs of being rattled or worried, or being ridden by that demon of nerves. . . ." Rather, "his attitude was tinged with a kind of mellow fatalism, an economy of worry which was part of his practical philosophy and became closely knit with his nature . . ."[22]

Asquith's ability to control his emotions was largely made possible by the bifurcation of his personality. There was the public persona—disciplined, hardworking, ambitious, no nonsense, sober, nonconformist, and rarely expressing emotion. Then there was the private man—fun loving, kind, not so sober, and romantic. The two personalities, of course, were not always mutually exclusive. Asquith could be the most kind and generous of leaders, while at the same time showing a distinct reserve. Nevertheless, his duality of nature was almost always present. Perhaps his son Beb came closest to an accurate, concise description of his father's emotional nature. He admitted that "it was extremely rare to hear him give any full expression to his feelings and he had no tendency towards emotional display." Yet he explained that "the warm and generous qualities of his heart were masked by a fortress of reserve, which strangers who only had a surface knowledge and little imagination, sometimes regarded as the inner nature."[23]

The public Asquith displayed what the Romans called *gravitas* and, in a non-religious sense, *pietas*.[24] His colleague Duff Cooper remarked that the impression he had of Asquith was always "a man of great dignity, somewhat aloof and Olympian," a man of the Victorian age who "would have thought it ill-bred to discuss current politics at the dinner table, or to criticise other politicians."[25] Some thought he had an air of never having been young.[26]

Asquith's remarkable ability to partition his public and his private lives reflected the bifurcation of his personality. Spender called it "the professional habit," a rarity among politicians, of being able to turn off politics when the day's work was over.[27] Asquith disliked "talking shop out of business hours," observed Churchill, noting that with the Prime Minister "either the Court was open or it was shut."[28] He was able to do this because his brilliant, disciplined mind allowed him to accomplish an incredible amount of work in a short period of time. Lord Beaverbrook was amazed with the amount of business Asquith could accomplish and still relax at the end of the day. He surmised that this time was not wasted and that "his subconscious mind was all the time working and pondering over grave issues and presenting him at the end with a completed process of thought."[29]

In his private world Asquith was much more apt to allow his feelings to come to the surface. There is no question, for example, of his love of his family and the pride he took in his childrens' many accomplishments. His affectionate letters to them show a consistent concern for their well-being and happiness. Examples of his dedication to his wife and children abound as, for example, his consistent and genuine concern for his wife Margot's fragile health or his shedding tears when one of his sons left for war.

His private feelings can also be seen in his religious faith. Although he left the Congregationalist Church of his youth for the Church of England when he married Margot and never wore his religion on his sleeve, he was a devout man. He told Harold Laski in 1925 that, except for a brief time at Oxford, he never remembered being seriously puzzled by religious doubts.[30] Even after he was out of power in the 1920s, visitors reported that he attended a Church of England service every Sunday morning and took Communion once each month.[31]

Also in regard to his emotional make-up, over the years, there has been a great deal of comment and speculation about Asquith's attraction to young women. He himself admitted that he was often credited with "a slight weakness for the companionship of clever and attractive women."[32] Like many Victorian upper-middle-class young men, Asquith spent little time growing up with those of the opposite sex other than members of his family. He married his first love, Helen Melland, at the age of twenty-five, then considered young for matrimony. Even before Helen's tragic death fourteen years later in 1891, Asquith had begun a passionate correspondence with Margot Tennant whom he married in 1894.

In December 1909 Asquith began a friendship with one of his daughter Violet's friends, Venetia Stanley. His relationship with Stanley evolved over the years into a deep attachment, if not love. Michael and Eleanor Brock, editors of the Asquith correspondence with Stanley, are convincing in their assessment that Asquith "never became Venetia's lover in the physical sense; and it is unlikely that he even wished for this." In fact, we will never know, and it is difficult to see any historical significance in the question. Still, there has been endless speculation and questioning as to whether Asquith and Venetia Stanley ever consummated their love relationship.[33] Margot was aware of her husband's infatuation, and at one point, when she believed Stanley was trying to get Asquith to avoid telling her things, wrote, "I'm far too fond of H. [Asquith] to show him how ill and miserable it makes me."[34]

Between January 1912 and May 1915, Asquith wrote Stanley over 560 letters, which have been described as the "most remarkable self-revelation ever given by a British Prime Minister."[35] Unfortunately Stanley's letters to Asquith have disappeared. What remains is a remarkable one-sided correspondence in which the Prime Minister reveals the most remarkable details of his own views and observations together with the most sensitive military and political secrets. This is all the more remarkable since Asquith knew full well that Stanley was preserving the correspondence. It was a reckless slip by an otherwise highly disciplined man. Perhaps the best explanation is the simplest and most obvious: Asquith used his correspondence with Stanley as an outlet or release for the burdens of his office and his passionate, yet always private, emotions. He abruptly ended the correspondence with Stanley in May 1915, when he received word that she had become engaged to Edwin Montagu, one of his Liberal colleagues.

With the news that Asquith was to be the new Prime Minister, attention began to focus on the changes, if any, Asquith might make in the cabinet. He related to Margot, "I told him [the King] I should do as little as possible—probably nothing—to alter the composition of the Cabinet or shift the men, at any rate until the Session was over." More surprisingly, he told the King that he would serve as both Prime Minister and continue as Chancellor of the Exchequer at least for a while.[36] Undoubtedly his desire to continue as Chancellor of the Exchequer stemmed from wanting to put forward not only the budget that had been already prepared under his direction, but also the old-age pensions scheme he was putting together. Some have suggested that he wanted to hold on to the position so that at a later time, when he himself had more authority, he could make his friend Richard Haldane Chancellor of the Exchequer.[37]

A month later in April, however, when Asquith announced his changes to the cabinet, he proposed immediate and major changes, beginning with his own resignation as Chancellor of the Exchequer. More than likely, his reason for reversing himself was more practical. He wanted to keep a balance between the "left" and the "right" in the cabinet. With his representing the "right" side of the party, it was necessary to balance positions with someone from the "left" promoted to the Exchequer.[38]

Almost an equally obvious choice for the Exchequer was David Lloyd George, who with the death of Campbell-Bannerman had taken up the mantle of leader of the "left" wing of the Liberal Party. Lloyd George wanted the position and believed he deserved it as a result of his work at the Board of Trade and other service to the party.[39] Asquith imposed but one condition of Lloyd George's appointment. "The only stipulation that I make," he wrote to him telling him of his appointment, "is that . . . you should leave to me the introduction of the Budget for the present year." He explained that "The change of government has come at a time when it would not be fair, or even possible, either for you or for me, to follow the ordinary course."[40]

The Lloyd George appointment balanced the cabinet politically; two other appointments brought younger, more energetic leaders into the government. For the Admiralty Asquith chose Reginald McKenna who, like Lloyd George, was a member of the next generation of Liberal leaders after Asquith.

For Secretary of State for the Colonies, Asquith chose Robert Crewe-Milnes, Earl (later Marquess) of Crewe, who had served as Lord Lieutenant of Ireland in the Gladstone/Rosebery government and was then Lord President of the Council. Asquith was especially fond of Lord Crewe and years later wrote that he rated Crewe's judgment the best of any of his colleagues.[41]

Another young Liberal star Asquith promoted was thirty-three-year-old Winston Churchill, originally a Conservative MP, who had crossed the aisle to join the Liberals in 1905. Churchill had done an outstanding job as Under Secretary for the Colonies, and so Asquith called upon him to replace Lloyd George as President of the Board of Trade. Asquith had had his eye on Churchill for some time and told the King a month before becoming Prime Minister that Churchill had "behaved very well" when he had twice before been passed over and now "had every claim to Cabinet rank."[42]

These numerous changes in the government did not signal any fundamental change in direction or policy. Yet to be seen was whether or not Asquith could break the log-jam and transform what so far had been a government marked by only minor successes to one of the great reforming ministries in British history.

When the King finally returned from France on April 16, Asquith had his cabinet list complete, and there was the official exchange of the seals of office at Buckingham Palace. Ten days later Campbell-Bannerman died. Asquith returned from an Easter holiday to move the adjournment of the House out of respect for the fallen leader. In eloquent and moving remarks, the new Prime Minister said of the old, "And yet we have not seen in our time a man of greater courage—courage not of the defiant or aggressive type, but calm, patient, persistent, indomitable."[43]

Even before Asquith became Prime Minister, it was clear to almost all in the Liberal Party that the key to its program of social reform was fiscal policy. No reforms were possible unless the means to pay for them could be found. Philosophically the new liberalism espoused by Asquith and his colleagues assumed that, broadly speaking, the nation's resources belonged to the nation and should be effectively and equitably used for social reform and advancement.[44] Then, too, there was the political question: could the Liberal Party finesse the taxation necessary to support its social reforms without overly risking its support among the middle class? Much of the groundwork had been laid. As early as 1894, Liberal Chancellor of the Exchequer Sir William Harcourt had introduced progressive graduation into the death duties. Also, as has been shown, Asquith's 1907 budget had for the first time differentiated between earned and unearned income, opening new possibilities for additional revenue and, just as importantly, beginning to demonstrate that taxation could be used to advance social policy in addition to raising revenue.

As the government began to construct its 1909–1910 budget, famously described by Lloyd George as the People's Budget, two items on the expenditure side of the ledger loomed large: the old-age pension scheme and naval expenditures.

When the Liberals came to power in 1906, they had no policy regarding pensions for the elderly. Earlier an extra-Parliamentary group, the National Committee of Organized Labour for Old Age Pensions (NCOL) had been formed to lobby strenuously for universal old-age pensions paid for through taxation. For the most part, the Treasury was willing to accept a change as long as it did not cost more than about £6 million annually. As Chancellor of the Exchequer, Asquith began to work on a plan to tread the fine line between the demands of the NCOL and the financial limitations insisted upon by the Treasury. Asquith had to come up with a formula using controls of age, income, and past conduct to abide by the Treasury limits.[45]

In his budget speech on May 7, 1908, Asquith announced in the Commons his government's old-age pension scheme. It had been two years in the making. He admitted from the first that it was only a "first step," providing for a pension of five shillings a week for everyone over seventy years old (7s. 6d. for couples) excepting aliens, lunatics, paupers, criminals, loafers, wastrels, or people with incomes of more than £26 a year (or £39 for couples).[46] During the Committee stage, the bill was amended to change the benefit to a sliding scale. The new benefit began with five shillings a week for those with annual incomes of £21 or less to one shilling a week for those with incomes of no more than £31/10s. a year.

Everyone knew that the government's Old Age Pension bill constituted a large and ongoing financial commitment. The great concern was whether the cost of the scheme could be financed without having ultimately to resort to tariffs and abandoning free trade. Asquith displayed an almost innocent optimism about the cost. He assured the Commons that the number of pensioners would not exceed half a million, and the cost would be approximately £6 million annually—well within the Treasury's limitation. Balfour scoffed at these figures, asserting that the true cost could be annually as much as £11.5 million. How, he asked, could the government possibly come up with such a large sum "within the limits of free trade finance"?[47] Although Lloyd George was also sceptical of Asquith's optimistic figures, he nevertheless resolutely defended them. Others like *The Spectator* questioned the limits of government expenditure under free trade finance. Asquith responded in a letter to John St. Loe Strachey, editor of *The Spectator*, explaining, "I have realized from the first that if it could not be proved that Social Reform (not socialism) can be financed on Free Trade lines, a return to Protectionism is a virtual certainty." This axiom was "one of the mainsprings" of his policy as Chancellor of the Exchequer. Nevertheless, he claimed, "I prepared the way by steadily reducing the principal of the debt . . . til I have brought it as the end of this year to the level of 20 years ago . . . Old Age Pensions were inevitable. I have secured an ample fund to meet them without any extra taxation."[48] As will be seen, Asquith was ultimately proven wrong. In March 1910 almost 700,000 pensions were in force at a cost of £8.5 million, more than 40 percent more pensioners than Asquith had originally predicted. By 1912 the cost of pensions had reached almost £12 million, close to the figure Balfour had predicted.[49] Two years later on the eve of the First World War, over a million people were receiving a pension. It is difficult to explain why Asquith, normally so good with numbers, was so far afield on the cost of the old-age pension scheme. It is doubtful that he was deliberately underestimating the cost. More than almost anyone else in the Cabinet, he did not want to stretch the budget to a point that might place free trade finance in jeopardy. He had every reason to be deliberatively conservative in his calculations. Yet, whatever the reason, Asquith or those upon whom he was relying for information grossly underestimated the number of persons who would be claiming a pension and were qualified under the law to do so.

The measure easily passed the Commons that summer, and the Lords reluctantly approved the measure because Arthur Balfour, the Conservative leader, had accepted at least by implication that the bill was a money bill, which could not be amended in the House of Lords. The bill received Royal Assent on August 1 and began to be implemented in January 1909.

Next to funding the Old Age Pension bill, the other great pressure on the budget for the Asquith cabinet was naval expenditure. The financial foundations for Asquith's Old Age Pension bill had begun by clearing the ground for the imposition of new forms of direct taxation, securing a considerable reduction in the national debt, and cutting back Army and Navy expenditures. This delicate balance was about to be disturbed by events beyond the Prime Minister's control. In 1898 Germany had passed a new Navy Law expanding its fleet. As Asquith later wrote, this initial step did not arouse apprehension in Britain, since it "was far from being excessive, either in reference to Germany's naval interest, or the relative strength of other fleets."[50] None doubted that Britain would maintain its naval superiority, even though the German navy had grown, as a result of a subsequent Navy Law in 1900, to second in size behind Britain's. All might have continued as before for another decade or so with the growth of the German Navy being more of a nuisance than a threat to British supremacy but for the launch by the British of the *H.M.S. Dreadnaught* in February 1906.

The *Dreadnaught*'s speed, armament, and firepower were so much greater than any other fighting ship that it now made them all obsolete. With the construction of this remarkably powerful battleship, the British Navy ironically in one stroke reduced is naval superiority to just one ship, for now all the Germans had to do to catch up was to construct their own *Dreadnaught*-class ship. The *Dreadnaught*-class ships were horribly expensive, costing upward of £2 million each, twice that of a traditional battleship. To add to the cost, these behemoths took 1,000 men to man rather than the 700 usually employed on battleships.

At first the Germans responded to the *Dreadnaught*'s construction by merely increasing the armament on the battleships it already had under construction, about all they could do for the time being. However, in April 1908, only two years after the launching of the *Dreadnaught*, the Reichstag passed an amendment to the basic Navy Law that called for the laying down of four new *Dreadnaught*-class ships each year for the next four years with a reduced number after that point. Suddenly, the German navy was transformed from a nuisance to a threat. Asquith later commented, "The amended Law of 1908 made it clear that unless British ship-building was increased Germany might gain a superiority in capital ships in 1914."[51]

Asquith had been a strong "economist" while at the Treasury, cutting expenditures wherever possible. Now that he was Prime Minister facing a new and much more significant German naval threat, he was much more willing to open the purse. In the summer of 1908, Admiral Sir Edmund Slade, Director of Naval Intelligence, recorded in his diary that Admiral Fisher had told him the cabinet was equally divided, "Lloyd George and Churchill standing for a general reduction all round so as to get money for old age pensions; Asquith, Grey, and Haldane standing for keeping up our strength . . ."[52]

By 1909 rumors circulated that the Germans were in fact accelerating their building program. Reginald McKenna, who had been Asquith's Financial Secretary at the Treasury, was now First Lord of the Admiralty and called for a minimum of six new *Dreadnaught*-class ships to be laid down in 1909. On January 3, McKenna wrote Asquith regarding intelligence information about German naval construction. Although he was "anxious to avoid alarmist information," he told the Prime Minister that "German capacity to build Dreadnaughts is at this moment equal to ours." He added that this conclusion "is the most alarming and, if justified, would give the public a rude awakening should it become known."[53] The whole issue was taking a dangerous turn and began to seriously divide the party. Churchill insisted that four new ships were more than enough to meet the threat. Lloyd George warned Asquith in a letter dated February 2, 1909, that the party had pledged in 1906 to reduce arms expenditure, "But if Tory extravagance on armaments is to be exceeded, Liberals who have nothing to hope from this Parliament in the way of redress of their grievances will hardly think it worthwhile to make any effort to keep in office a Liberal Ministry."[54] On February 15, Lloyd George brought a compromise before the cabinet. Under his plan Parliament would enact a multiyear program so as to equalize the burden of expenditure. Although McKenna opposed the plan, Asquith appointed a cabinet committee consisting of himself, Lloyd George, and John Morley to discuss it with the Admiralty.

Asquith wrote to his wife on February 20, "The economists are in a state of wild alarm, and Winston and Ll.G. by their combined machinations have got the bulk of the Liberal press into the same camp." He went on to explain that even though John Morley and Lewis Harcourt were "disinclined" to join with Lloyd George and Churchill, there was nevertheless going to be a "temporary revival of the old pro-Boer animus." Asquith was doing his best to hold things together. As he told his wife, "I am able to keep a fairly cool head amidst it all," and "E. Grey is a great stand-by, always, sound, temperate, and strong."[55]

A conference was held in the Prime Minister's room at the House of Commons on February 23. The Prime Minister, Lloyd George, McKenna, Grey, and Admirals Fisher and Jellicoe were present. Asquith focused on spreading the financial costs over three years. The real concern was that the Germans had a greater capacity to turn out armament than British manufacturers. Asquith remarked that he thought "this is the most disquieting thing I have heard about the whole question." The Prime Minister then laid out the need to ask Parliament and for an authorization for so many ships: "some may not have to be built, but if they do the authorization will be there."[56]

By February 25, Asquith wrote to Margot after the final cabinet meeting on the naval estimates, "A sudden curve developed itself of which I took immediate advantage, with the result that strangely enough we came to a conclusion which satisfied McKenna and Grey and also Ll.G. and Winston." The Admiralty had agreed to sign off on the proposed estimates. Four *Dreadnaught*-class ships would be immediately laid down in the summer and autumn of 1909. Further, components would be gathered so that an additional four could be laid down in April 1910. Although Asquith's official biographers imply that Asquith came up with the compromise, the final terms were almost exactly what Lloyd George had earlier proposed.[57] Even so, it appears that Asquith's efforts in appointing a cabinet committee helped keep Lloyd George's proposal on track with the Admiralty. As Churchill later humorously observed, "In the end a curious and characteristic solution was reached. The Admiralty had demanded six ships: the economists offered four: and we finally compromised on eight."[58] At any rate, Asquith argued to the House on March 29 that the compromise was "not as a middle course between two extreme views, but upon their merits as being at once the most prudent and effective means of promoting the end which all of us on both sides have in view—namely, the maintenance of Imperial security and the unchallenged continuance of our command of the sea."[59]

To cover the expected £16.5 million deficit, Lloyd George's original budget, presented to the cabinet in early April, provided for £13.5 million to be raised by new additional taxation with £3 million coming from the sinking fund. For the entire first weekend in April the cabinet haggled over the tax package and finally reached a conclusion on Tuesday April 6. The new taxes would include a super-tax on the rich consisting of a 6d on the pound for incomes of £5,000 pounds or more. The tax on unearned income above £700 was increased by 2d on the pound, and the tax on all incomes earned and unearned over £3,000 was to be increased by 2d. Also included was a 20 percent tax on the unearned increment of land values, an annual duty of a half penny on the pound on the value of undeveloped land. There were also taxes on motor vehicles, petrol, and liquor licenses. Even with these new sources of income, the income tax was to be increased from 1s. to 1s. 2d. on the pound on unearned incomes and on incomes of more than £3,000. This was combined with increased duties on tobacco and spirits and duties on stamps and estates.

The cabinet heatedly debated the budget during fourteen cabinet meetings from mid-March until the end of April, tediously going over it almost clause by clause and line by line. Through the entire debate, Asquith played the pivotal role. Many in the cabinet had cold feet about this or that element. Runciman thought there were too many direct taxes. Harcourt objected to the scale of duty on settled estates.[60] Yet Asquith stood by his Chancellor every step of the way, joined by Churchill. Lloyd George wrote to his brother at the time, "Budgeting all day. Got on extremely well on one point where the Cabinet was very divided, but on which I was very keen. Prime Minister decided in my favour to my delight."[61] On the critical issue of the land taxes Lloyd George was convinced that the cabinet would have rejected the idea "by an overwhelming majority" had it not been for Asquith's support.[62] Lloyd George always acknowledged that only with Asquith's help had the more controversial parts of the budget survived. He once told his son that when substantial opposition was voiced to one of his proposals, Asquith would still conclude, "Well, there seems to be substantial agreement with Mr. Chancellor's proposal. Next item . . . ?"[63] Shortly after the Cabinet had finally agreed on the budget, Lloyd George readily acknowledged his debt to Asquith in a conversation with his Welsh friend David Daniel in May. According to Daniel, the Chancellor of the Exchequer told him "above all the Prime Minister has backed me up through thick and thin with splendid loyalty. I have the deepest respect for him and he has real sympathy for the ordinary and the poor."[64]

Lloyd George presented the budget to the Commons on April 29 in a marathon speech lasting five hours with only one short break. The Finance bill received its second reading on June 10 and went into committee eleven days later. Asquith and Lloyd George continued to have difficulties with the cabinet, even now only reluctantly supporting the bill. When Lloyd George asked his colleagues on June 16 to endorse a time schedule known as the "guillotine" for the rapid disposition of clauses, it adamantly refused. "The Prime Minister is for it," the Chancellor of the Exchequer reported to his brother, "but I shall have trouble with the rest of my colleagues who hate the Budget and would very much like to see it killed by time but they won't, as the party is behind me."[65] The crisis for the cabinet came on July 16 when J. A. Pease, the Chief Whip, told Lloyd George that he was asking too much of the Commons and requested that he withdraw the undeveloped land tax portion of the budget. Lloyd George said that he would rather resign.[66] Apparently discussion in the cabinet became so heated on this issue that Asquith had to intervene, something he was always reluctant to do. "We are in rough waters" Asquith later told John Burns.[67]

As the summer months passed, there was growing suspicion that the House of Lords might well break with hundreds of years of precedent and reject the budget. There is no evidence that either Asquith or Lloyd George intended that the budget provoke a final crisis with the House of Lords over its powers. Nevertheless, at some point Lloyd George decided that it was to the Liberals' political advantage to press on and put the House of Lords to the test. In 1908 and the first three months of 1909 the Liberals had lost more than nine seats without winning one election. Things began to change in July after Lloyd George introduced the budget, and the Liberals won three bi-elections. Admittedly these were Liberal seats, and the majorities were less than they had been in 1906; nevertheless, Lloyd George may have sniffed out that his program had a particular popularity all its own. By the end of July, he had begun to believe the budget was a sure election winner, even if his cabinet colleagues were not yet on board.[68]

As it became more and more apparent that the House of Lords might actually do the unthinkable and fail to pass the government's budget, Asquith became clear as to what he believed to be the best strategy. At all cost, at least the appearance must be kept that the government believed the Lords would indeed pass the budget without amendment. He did not want to get mired in hypotheticals that with a little luck might not even come to pass. It would be counterproductive to suggest publicly in any way that the Lords might fail in following the Constitution.[69] Asquith may also not have been so optimistic as Lloyd George about the Liberals' electoral chances should the issue be forced.

Lloyd George was determined to take a different path. On July 30, at the invitation of the Budget League, he addressed a packed house of over four thousand in the East End of London at the Edinburgh Castle, Limehouse. Tossing caution to the wind, after initially criticizing "the rich" for dragging their heels to pay for the *Dreadnaughts* they had so vociferously demanded, he proceeded with a lengthy attack against landlords.

Asquith met with the King several days later and found him "in a state of great agitation and annoyance." The Prime Minister wrote to his Chancellor of the Exchequer telling him that the King "sees in the general tone, & especially the concluding parts, of your speech, a menace to property and a Socialistic spirit, which he thinks peculiarly inappropriate and unsettling in a holder of your office." Asquith then attempted to rein in Lloyd George, writing, "I feel very strongly that at this moment what is needed is reasoned appeal to moderate & reasonable men. There is great & growing popular enthusiasm, but this will not carry us through—if we rouse the suspicions & fears of the middle class, & particularly if we give countenance to the notion that the Budget is conceived in any spirit of vindictiveness."[70]

While Lloyd George was more than likely little bothered by the King's reaction, he must have been seriously concerned about Asquith's.[71] Lloyd George's Limehouse address was a play to the working class, an attack on landed wealth and especially against the House of Lords. He made no direct threats to the middle class. While Lloyd George had the pulse of the working class, Asquith was a much better judge of the middle class and realized that irresponsible plays for working-class support might be seen by the middle class as bordering dangerously on "class warfare," which it abhorred. Although the Prime Minister privately had begun to realize that the Conservatives might well defeat the budget in the House of Lords, he publicly refused to recognize such a possibility. If the Lords defeated the budget, the onus would be upon the Conservatives. Asquith the bridge player knew the Liberals had a fairly good hand, but he feared Lloyd George might well be overplaying it.

As the possibility of a constitutional crisis loomed larger, on October 6 the King met with Asquith at Balmoral. Asquith thought rather well of the King. He once told his wife that His Majesty was "a clever man and a good listener, if you aren't too long."[72] "He asked me," Asquith reported in a note, "whether I thought he was well within constitutional lines in taking upon himself to give advice to, and if necessary put pressure upon, the Tory leaders at this juncture." Here Asquith, who before entering government had the reputation of being one of the leading lawyers in the nation and a recognized authority of the British Constitution, could speak with authority. Without hesitation the Prime Minister responded that it was "perfectly correct from a constitutional point of view."[73] The King further inquired if Asquith would be willing to agree that, if the Lords *passed* the budget, the Liberals would call for an election in January. Asquith replied that he would have to consider this but pointed out that there would be little advantage and great disadvantage to the Liberals in an election if the budget passed. Nevertheless, in such circumstances dissolution could not be long delayed.[74]

Asquith was doing all in his power at this stage to avert a constitutional crisis. Immediately after his interview with the King, he wrote to Lloyd George, who was about to make an important speech in Newcastle in two days, imploring him to speak on the assumption that the budget would be approved and above all avoid language that might derail the King's negotiations with the Conservatives.[75]

Despite his attempts to pull the nation back from the brink, in his cabinet letter to the King on November 3 Asquith reported that a veto was now "generally regarded as probable."[76] The budget cleared the House of Commons the following day after seventy-three days of debate. Now assuming that there would be a veto, the cabinet began to plan over the next several weeks how to finance day-to-day government operations in the absence of a budget. There was some discussion of introducing a short bill that would merely declare existing taxes collectable, but with Lloyd George in strong opposition the idea was rejected. Instead the cabinet decided to borrow funds and suspend payments to the sinking fund, combined with a bill in the new Parliament that would make all tax collections retroactive to the dissolution of the old Parliament.[77]

On November 16, Lord Landsdowne confirmed what almost everyone expected by this time, that he would move the rejection of the budget on the second reading. Landsdowne did just that on November 22, and the House of Lords declined a second reading by the overwhelming majority of 350 to 75. The entire budget had now been defeated without even an attempt at amendment.

On December 2, Asquith set the stage for an appeal to the country by moving "That the action of the House of Lords in refusing to pass into law the financial provision made by this House for the service of the year is a breach of the Constitution and a usurpation of the rights of the Commons." All of Asquith's frustration with his Conservative opponents came to the fore in his impassioned speech in the support of the resolution. He began by setting the historical stage. "For the first time in English history," he declared, "the grant of the whole of the Ways and Means for the Supply and Service of the year ... has been intercepted and nullified by a body which admittedly has not the power to increase or diminish one single tax, or to propose any substitute or alternative for anyone of the taxes." He went on to say that in the judgment of the government the Commons "would be unworthy of its past and the traditions of which it is the custodian and the trustee if it allowed another day to pass without making it clear that it does not mean to brook the greatest indignity, and . . . the most arrogant usurpation, to which, for more than two centuries, it has been asked to submit." Recalling the numerous Liberal measures defeated by the House of Lords, he succinctly stated what was at stake. "The real question which emerges from the political struggles in this country for the last 30 years is not whether you will have a single or double chamber system of government," he explained, "but whether when the Tory Party is in power the House of Commons shall be omnipotent, and whether when the Liberal Party is in power the House of Lords shall be omnipotent." Clearly the forthcoming election would be about more than the budget. It would be a referendum on the powers of the House of Lords itself. As Asquith made clear in the conclusion to his remarks, "The House of Lords have deliberately chosen their ground. . . . In so doing, whether they foresaw it or not, they have opened a wider and more far reaching issue." The country was to be asked "to declare that the organ, the voice of the people of this country, is to be found in the elective representatives of the nation."[78]

The resolution overwhelmingly passed 349 to 134, and Parliament was dissolved the next day with an election called for January 14. The stage was now set. As R. J. Q. Adams has written, what was now in place was a series of risks. Asquith was gambling that the budget would revive the government's lagging popularity, while the Conservatives were betting that the people would reject the attack on the Lords and return them to power.[79]

Should Liberals prevail in the election, the government planned to pass another budget bill. Should the House of Lords again reject the measure, the King would be called upon to exercise his prerogative and create as many as 300 new peers suggested by the government, thus tipping the majority in the House of Lords in the Liberals' favor. Less than two weeks after Parliament was dissolved, the King's private secretary Lord Knollys met with Asquith's secretary Vaughn Nash. As Nash reported in a memorandum to the Prime Minister, "the King had come to the conclusion that he would not be justified in creating new peers . . . until after a second general election." The King's justification was that the government's plan was "tantamount to the destruction of the House of Lords" and that such a monumental change should take place only after the country was "acquainted with the particular project for accomplishing such destruction."[80] Thus Asquith entered the campaign knowing that more likely than not it was going to take not one but possibly two elections to limit the powers of the House of Lords.

Asquith opened the campaign for the Liberals on December 10 in a speech to a capacity crowd of 10,000 at Albert Hall. A huge banner was strung from wall to wall above the chairman's table proclaiming "Shall the people be ruled by the Peers?" The Liberal war horses—Asquith, Lloyd George, and Churchill—carried a heavy load during the campaign. Lloyd George led major regional campaigns in Wales and London, while Churchill focused on the

North and Scotland. Despite the burden of his family's grief over the recent death of his daughter Violet's fiancé, Archibald Gordon, Asquith toured a selection of English constituencies that included Brighton, Ipswich, Salisbury, Bradford, and of course his own seat at East Fife.[81]

The election began on January 14 and continued for two weeks. The Liberals entered the election holding 373 seats. The Liberal leadership had begun with a rather rosy picture of the results but shortly before the voting Lloyd George and newspaper owner George Riddell predicted that the result would be a virtual tie between the two parties.[82] This is exactly what happened. The Liberals won only 275 seats to the Conservatives 273. The Labour party MPs were reduced from 46 to 40, and the Irish Nationalists won a total of 82 seats. Even where Liberal candidates prevailed, majorities were down. With the near equality of seats between the major parties, the Conservatives nevertheless received almost a quarter of a million more votes than the Liberals. The Liberal single-party majority was gone.

It is difficult to pinpoint why many voters turned against the Liberals. To do so would require disentangling the effects of the three major campaign issues—House of Lords, free trade, and the budget. The Conservatives took up the Liberal's uncompromising support of free trade, and there is no doubt that many voters at least in some areas had begun to look favorably on import duties on some products. Lloyd George's stridency may also have cost votes. Louis Harcourt wrote to Asquith after the election that he believed Lloyd George's speeches had caused either "alarm" or "disgust" and "probably account for heavy losses in the South."[83] Many factors were at play, but it seems the election represented more than anything else a shift back to the electoral "norm" after the aberration of the 1906 election. Whatever the cause of the results, the real story of the election was of course that the Liberals now had to depend on the Irish to have a majority and form a government.

Did Asquith and the Liberal Party make a political mistake in pressing the issue of the budget? The important point is that sooner or later the Liberals had to challenge the Lords' veto. It was simply impossible for them to govern otherwise. The 1909 budget was perhaps as good a vehicle as they would ever have to ride to the challenge. The government did in fact survive, even though by the thinnest of margins and now only with the support of the Irish. Nonetheless it is difficult to believe the Conservatives would have vetoed the budget unless they believed the subsequent election would be in their favor, and in this sense the election was a Liberal victory.

The new Parliament opened in February 1910, and some historians have argued that until at least mid-April Asquith was not at his best. Roy Jenkins believes that for several weeks in February he "exhibited less sureness of touch that at any other stage in the long constitutional struggle," while John

Griggs, Lloyd George's biographer, believes that the Prime Minister was in a "state of almost cataleptic indecision."[84] There is some evidence for these conclusions. C. F. G. Masterman recorded that "Asquith, so far as anyone could discover, came back with no ideas and no plan of any kind." Further he had been told that Asquith "wandered about utterly wretched and restless, like a man conscious that he is facing a situation too big for him."[85] Whatever his state of mind, the Prime Minister no doubt faced a complicated political situation in the early spring of 1910. It is not difficult to understand Asquith's predicament.

To begin with, now that the Irish Nationalists had leverage, they were not shy in their demands. John Redmond, speaking at the Gresham Hotel in Dublin on February 10, set them forth. What had caused the Irish to support the Liberal Party in the last election was Asquith's pledge that neither he nor his colleagues would ever assume or retain office again unless they were given assurances that they would be able to curb and limit the Lords' veto, which was the key to Irish Home Rule.[86] It was now time to make good on that pledge, and the Irish thought they had a hostage to see that their demands were met—the budget. For Redmond and his supporters, there would be no supporting the budget without a veto bill. On the same day that Redmond spoke in Dublin, Asquith reported to the King that the cabinet had been informed "as a certain fact that the Irish party led by Mr. Redmond would vote against the Budget unless they were assured that the passing of a Bill dealing with the Veto of the House of Lords was guaranteed during the present year."[87] But this was only the half of it. There was a question as to whether the Irish would support the budget without some amendments, even *with* the promise of a veto bill, because it contained license and spirit duties that hit publicans and distillers, some of the strongest financial backers of the Irish National Party.[88] In fact, this had been enough the year before to cause the Irish to oppose the "People's Budget."

The cabinet was in complete disarray as to what was to be done about the House of Lords. Radicals favored what the Irish demanded: remove completely the Lords' veto. This is what Campbell-Bannerman had proposed and received cabinet consent to in 1907. This system to put an end to the Lords' veto would provide that all legislation passed three times by the House of Commons would be treated as if it had been passed by both Houses and would receive Royal Assent. Lloyd George instinctively favored this plan but was much more concerned to see that the crisis be ended quickly, so that the government could move forward with its progressive program of social reform.

Now, however, there was another important group in the cabinet, including none other than Asquith's close friends Grey, Haldane, and Crewe, joined by Runciman and Samuel, who believed Campbell-Bannerman's plan tantamount to single-chamber rule. They argued it would be better to reform the House of Lords by making it more representative without touching the substance of its power. The problem with this idea: as early as February 15, a group of radical Liberals led by Sir Charles Dilke met with the Prime Minister and told him they would oppose any attempt to reform the House of Lords rather than end its veto. Several days later, meetings of Liberal MPs for northern and Scottish constituencies passed resolutions challenging the reform option.[89] As if all this were not enough to stir the pot, Churchill proposed replacing the House of Lords with an elected second chamber with no power to touch money bills.[90]

Asquith's own view is as difficult to ascertain now as it was at the time. This was perhaps just what he wanted. He worked to avoid an open confrontation if possible, but he knew that limiting of the Lords' veto could not long be postponed. Just as likely Asquith, fully realizing the political minefield ahead, wanted to ensure that steps were slowly and deliberately considered before being taken. To achieve this, he simply could not show his hand at this critical point.

Whatever the cabinet would eventually decide, one thing was without doubt: the King had made no commitment to create new peers to ensure acceptance of the government's policy. Some had come to believe incorrectly that Asquith had such "guarantee," which stemmed from Asquith's pronouncement in an Albert Hall speech during the campaign that the Liberals would "not hold office unless we can secure the safeguards which experience shows to be necessary for the legislative utility and honour of the party of progress."[91] Since the Liberals were still holding office, the assumption was that he had the King's pledge. The cabinet had to reassure the King in a note dated February 11 that it did not intend to ask him to exercise his Royal prerogative in appointing peers "in existing circumstances" and indeed would not do so until the "actual necessity may arise."[92]

When the new Parliament opened on February 12, Asquith first made clear he had no guarantees from the King. In what Arthur Murray, Master of Elibank, described as "the very worst speech I have ever heard him make," Asquith admitted, "I tell the House quite frankly that I have received no such guarantee and that I have asked for no such guarantee." To ask in advance for a "blank authority" in regard to a measure that had never been submitted or approved by the House of Commons would be improper. Even so, he made clear that he "would not hesitate to tender such advice to the Crown as in the circumstances the exigencies of the situation appear to warrant in the public interest." According to Murray, Asquith "for the time being lost his customary nerve, strained as he was to the utmost by continual Cabinet meetings and the growing discontent of his Party."[93]

In the same speech Asquith outlined the government's plan. First resolutions would outline the government's proposed relationship between the two Houses. Then a bill would follow. Some hint was given as to what at a minimum would be included in these resolutions when Asquith stated that the Liberals had asked the electorate to approve "the complete and undisputed supremacy of the Commons over finance and the removal of the veto at present possessed by the House of Lords over legislation." Simultaneously with the resolutions, the Prime Minster explained that the Commons would work until the Easter recess to reaffirm the budget and deliberate measures to deal with the financial situation created by its rejection the previous year. After the recess the House would focus its attention on passing a bill founded on the resolutions. Such a process appeared to the government "to be by far the most businesslike way of meeting a very exceptional situation." As he concluded, Asquith announced that the government staked all its credit on passing the budget and the Lords' Resolutions. "We stand or fall by them," he defiantly declared.[94]

And so things stood. For Asquith's government to survive, it had to come together with the Irish on the two issues of the budget and the Lords' Resolutions. Asquith was adamant that the new budget had to be in all essentials the same as had been previously rejected by the Lords.[95] He was not willing to bargain with the Irish on items such as the liquor duties. On this point the Irish were going to have to give in. Asquith's position on the Lords' Resolutions was much more flexible. If a determined move were to define the future relationship between the two Houses *before* the budget was sent to the House of Lords, Asquith had no objection to acquiescing.[96]

On March 29 the government introduced its three Lords' Resolutions. They reflected the Campbell-Bannerman plan favored by the Radicals. The first declared that the House of Lords would have no power to amend any "Money Bill" broadly defined. The second provided that any bill passed in three consecutive sessions by the House of Commons "shall become law without the consent of the House of Lords." A third resolution limited the duration of a Parliament to five years.[97]

Time was running out for both the Irish and the government if anything was to be accomplished for either of them. What finally broke the impasse was the realization that, if the Irish compromised to back away from attempting to amend the budget to remove the whisky duties, those in the cabinet who opposed seeking guarantees from the King in order to remove the Lord's veto might be convinced to allow a call for guarantees. Lloyd George sensed this and on April 12 announced that the whisky tax would not be deleted from the budget.[98] To press the matter, the Master of Elibank reported that, if the Prime Minister would not now make a declaration about the creation of peers, he would resign and side with the Irish.⁹⁹ As C. F. G. Masterman reported, "Suddenly the whole opposition in the cabinet collapsed, the government agreed to the double declaration, keeping the whisky tax and giving promise of the guarantee policy, and to let Redmond do his best or worst."¹⁰⁰ There would be no deal with the Irish. They could take the resolutions and the budget or leave them. Of course, most knew that Redmond had been boxed in. Even Redmond himself admitted to Masterman, "If we vote you out now it is on whisky, where we shall get no sympathy from the priests or the British Radicals."¹⁰¹

Still, the cabinet was not totally sure yet how the Irish would respond. Asquith telegraphed Lord Knollys, the King's Secretary, at Biarritz on April 13 where the King was staying that the cabinet had decided to refuse the Irish demand for reduced spirit duties and to ask the House of Commons to accept substantially the budget passed the previous year. "It is possible and not improbable," Asquith noted, "that in consequence of this decision the Irish Party will vote against the Government" when the budget is presented, and "If they do Government will be defeated and a crisis of extreme urgency will at once arrive."¹⁰² The same day Asquith wrote to the King that the Irish might vote against the budget, in which case the government would resign. "A crisis of an unexampled + most embarrassing kind would therefore arise. How is your Majesty's Government to be carried on? by whom? And with what Parliamentary majority?"¹⁰³

Still uncertain how the Irish would react, Asquith the following day rose to announce to the Commons that he had a short statement of policy. He recognized that it was unusual for the government to announce a policy in regard to contingencies that had not yet arisen, but he stated that they were confronted with "an exceptional and perhaps unique case." Unless the Lords' Resolutions became law, he declared, "there is no legislation except the Budget and substantially non-contentious matters which we [the government] can without risk of futility, and even ridicule, undertake." Accordingly, if such resolutions did not become law, "we shall either resign our offices or recommend the dissolution of Parliament." Then came the crux of the announcement. Asquith pronounced that the government in no case would recommend a dissolution "except under such conditions as will secure in the new Parliament the judgement of the people as expressed at the elections will be carried into law."¹⁰⁴ In short, the government would seek the King's commitment that if the Lords refused to pass the legislation curbing its power, he would use the Royal Prerogative to create enough new peers to ensure its passage.

Asquith and his cabinet had to wait in suspense another four days until April 18, when the Prime Minister finally put forward the guillotine resolution to cut off further debate on the reintroduced budget. The Irish now had to choose. "There is not a man sitting on that [the government] bench who knew, either directly or indirectly, what decision the Irish party would come to until the meeting of the Irish party was held today." Redmond announced that his Irish faction would support the government's motion to end debate and hence support the budget. "I have given no guarantees to the Government. . . . They have asked for none," Redmond declared, "and therefore there was absolutely no bargain." Nevertheless, the Prime Minister's declaration during the election that once the House of Lords' veto was abolished the government would take up the issue of Irish rule was "a sufficient guarantee that this movement will go on now full speed ahead."[105] With the support of Redmond's Irish faction (O'Brien's group opposed it), the guillotine motion passed. The budget moved swiftly through the House and passed its Third Reading on April 27 by a majority of 93. The following day the House of Lords approved it without a division, and the budget of 1909 finally received Royal Assent and became law on April 29, one year after it had been originally introduced.

It was a major victory for Asquith and the Liberals, and they knew it. Jack Pease reported in his diary that there was a "very cheery happy" cabinet meeting on April 20, their first gathering after they learned the Irish were to support the budget. The Prime Minister was "radiant."[106] Yet Asquith and his colleagues knew full well the battle was far from over.

In Biarritz since early March, the King returned to London on April 27 and had an audience with his Prime Minister the following evening. Asquith reported to Margot that he had had "a good talk with the King . . . and found him most reasonable."[107] The Prime Minister did not realize that this was to be his last audience with Edward VII. Shortly afterward Asquith attended a dinner at the Savoy hosted by Lloyd George to celebrate the passage of the budget, leaving early to travel to Portsmouth to board the Royal Navy yacht the *Enchantress* and head to the Mediterranean. Several days later, the King fell ill. Margot worried, when the King's condition worsened, that her husband might not be able to be reached in an emergency. When Sir Charles Hardinge, Permanent Under Secretary at the Foreign office, told her that he had just left Lord Knollys in tears and asked her to send her husband a telegram, she immediately wired via the Admiralty cipher, "Advise your returning immediately. The king seriously ill: all London in state of well-founded alarm."[108] Lord Knollys also sent a message: "Deeply regret to say the King's condition is now most critical." As soon as the *Enchantress* reached Gibraltar on May 6, Asquith ordered that they immediately sail for Portsmouth, but at three o'clock on the morning of the seventh Asquith received a wire that the King had died. "I went up on the deck," he recalled, "and I remember well that the first sight that met my eyes in the twilight before dawn was Halley's comet blazing in the sky.... I felt bewildered and indeed stunned. At a most anxious moment in the fortunes of the State, we had lost, without warning or preparation, the Sovereign whose ripe experience, trained sagacity, equitable judgment, and unvarying consideration, counted for so much.... What was the right thing to do? This was the question which absorbed my thoughts as we made our way, with two fast escorting cruisers, through the Bay of Biscay, until we landed at Plymouth...."[109]

The day after his return, the Prime Minister had his first audience with forty-four-year-old King George V, and Margot recorded that he came away "deeply moved" by the new King's "modesty and common sense." The House of Commons assembled on the eleventh to hear eulogies by its members. Asquith was always at his best on these occasions. He praised the monarch whom he had served for two years as Chief Minister: "He loved his people at home and over the seas. Their interests were his interests, and their fame his fame. He had no self apart from them." Given Asquith's character, it is not surprising that he also praised the late King's "tact in the management of men, and a judgment of intuitive shrewdness as to the best outlet from perplexed and often baffling situations."[110] After the King's funeral Asquith resumed his cruise, this time heading by way of Pembroke Dock to Skye. Yet it was a working holiday; "I spend most of the day alone reading, or writing at a long memorandum which I am preparing for the King."[111]

With a new King on the throne, the cabinet thought one more attempt to avoid involving the monarch in a constitutional crisis concerning the power of the House of Lords advisable. As a result, Asquith called for a Constitutional Conference with Conservative and Liberal representatives to see if some compromise might be reached. The Prime Minister, Lloyd George, Lord Crewe, and Augustine Birrell, who served as Chief Secretary for Ireland, represented the government. Lloyd George opposed the idea of the conference, Lord Crewe supported it.[112] Balfour, Lord Lansdowne, Austen Chamberlain, and Lord Cawdor, who had been First Lord of the Admiralty in the last Conservative government, represented the opposition. The Irish and Labour were not asked to attend. Asquith later explained that the Irish "were content to leave the negotiations in the hands of their Liberal allies" and, much less convincingly, that there was really no distinction at that time between the Liberals and Labour, there not being more than three or four cases where a Labour candidate for Parliament had opposed a Liberal.[113]

The first meeting of the Constitutional Conference took place in Asquith's room at the House of Commons on June 17. The group held eleven more meetings before Parliament's break for summer holiday at the end of July. Further meetings took place in mid-October and early November. All in all the conference met twenty-one times, and the proceedings in Asquith's words "from the first to the last were secret and informal, and it is hardly necessary to say that the seal of confidence was strictly respected."[114]

Very early in the negotiations the Liberals put forward what had become known as the "Ripon Plan."[115] In Liberal cabinet discussions in 1907, Lord Crewe and Asquith formulated the proposal named for Lord Ripon, Liberal Leader in the House of Lords. In the event of a difference between the two Houses, the disputed bill would be brought in the next session by a joint vote of the House of Commons and a delegation of 100 members of the House of Lords, including all members of the government who were peers (not to exceed twenty) supplemented with others chosen by the House of Lords. On July 19, Asquith read a paper at the conference entitled "A Suggested Scheme for Dealing with Deadlocks," which placed what was basically the Ripon Plan front and center in the deliberations, where it remained until the break for summer holiday.[116] The Conservatives responded by accepting it only regarding what Balfour termed "ordinary" legislation in addition to financial and constitutional legislation.[117] For "financial" issues, the Conservatives were willing to surrender the Lords' power to reject money bills provided such bills were narrowly defined. For "constitutional" issues, which they defined as all questions "affecting the machinery by which legislation was turned out," the Conservatives demanded a public referendum. It was quite clear that this definition was intended to include Irish Home Rule, which made it unacceptable to the Liberals. Asquith wrote Balfour that the Unionist definition "is entirely unknown to our Constitution: it discriminates between legislative projects on the ground not of their real importance and the seriousness of their consequences, but according as they do or do not touch the law-making machinery." The real issue was Irish Home Rule. Asquith continued in his note to Balfour that the referendum on "constitutional" issues "would render the new system totally inapplicable to a large number of the proposed changes to which our supporters attach the greatest value, and in which deadlocks are likely to occur."[118] He might just have easily used just three words: Irish Home Rule.

The conference nearly broke apart when it looked to the Conservatives that the Liberals would insist that the issue of legislative process be settled independently of and before any discussion of reforming the House of Lords. Disaster was barely adverted when Chamberlain directly asked Asquith if this was the case. The Prime Minister responded, "oh no, no, certainly not."[119] Before the House adjourned for holiday, Asquith was able to report "the result is that our discussions have made such progress, although we have not so far reached an agreement, as to render it, in the opinion of all of us, not only desirable but necessary that they should continue. In fact, I may go further, and say that we should think it wrong at this stage to break them off."[120]

On October 14, Asquith reported to the King that "the prospect of agreement is not so favourable as it appeared to be at the beginning of the week," but he had "not altogether abandoned the hope that some *modus vivendi* may yet be discovered." He explained to the King that the "point of divergence" was whether or not "constitutional" issues such as "Home Rule, the franchise, redistribution" should be excluded from the procedure of joint sessions (i.e., the Ripon Plan) and be submitted to a popular referendum. He said that the government would never accept such a plan "not only on its merits, but because they know that it would be quite impossible to induce the Liberal Party to agree to it."[121]

The conference continued, but on November 8 Asquith forwarded to Lloyd George a note he had received from Balfour stating that he saw no use in continuing the meetings and regretting this conclusion because he had "hoped for better things."[122] He wrote the King on the same day that there was "an apparently irreconcilable divergence of view."[123] Two days later the Commission met for the last time, and Asquith reported the failure of negotiations to the cabinet.

Asquith always believed the conference worth the effort even though it ended in failure. He believed that the circumstances were unfortunately not right for compromise. On November 10, he informed his wife that the conference was about to hold its last meeting, "as we are very near the parting of the ways." He continued, "It will be a disappointment if we fail, but nobody's fault."[124] At the time the conference broke up, Almeric Fitzroy, clerk of the Privy Council, wrote that Asquith had held the more radical element of his own party in check while "going a long way towards making every possible concession to the views and feelings of their opponents" in an attempt to find a compromise. Although Fitzroy believed a "substantial accord was in an ace of being concluded," other evidence indicates this was not the case.[125] The Liberals could never agree to a compromise that would endanger the ultimate passage of Home Rule for Ireland, and the Unionists could never agree to a compromise that would lead to Home Rule. It was as simple as that.

What next? The cabinet faced several alternatives. One was to allow the Parliament bill ending the Lords' veto to be passed through all its stages in the Commons and then have it rejected by the Lords. Asquith believed this to be a waste of time and supported the idea of an immediate dissolution and election, as did Alec Murray the Chief Whip. The Parliament bill had been introduced in the Commons and was before the country. In addition, the resolutions upon which the measure was based had been fully debated. The issue was simple, and the nation's electorate was in a position to make an informed decision. Nonetheless, there could be no election unless it could mean a final decision on the issue. The King must promise before the election that should the Liberals prevail, he would exercise his prerogative to ensure passage in the House of Lords. To delay an election might increase the chances that the King would become involved in the electoral struggle and perhaps subject him to public controversy.[126] Based upon these arguments, Asquith and other supporters of an immediate election prevailed, and on November 10 the cabinet agreed to ask for an immediate dissolution.

The next day Asquith headed to Sandringham to meet with the King. As recorded in his memorandum written immediately after their meeting, Asquith explained to the King that if the nation was to be put through another election, "in the event of the Government obtaining an adequate majority in the New House of Commons, the matter should be put in train for final settlement." He went on to make clear that after the election, should the Lords still be of a mind to reject a Parliament bill passed by a majority in the Commons, final resolution of the constitutional crisis could only be accomplished "by the willingness of the Crown to exercise its prerogative to give effect to the will of the nation." To reassure the King, Asquith told him that the constitutionality of the use of the prerogative was "undoubted" and cited its use in the eighteenth century and King William IV's agreement to use it on a wide scale in 1832. Further the Prime Minister told the king that in his opinion the mere knowledge that the King was prepared to exercise his prerogative would be sufficient without it actually having to be employed.[127] Fully realizing that he was asking the new King to take an almost unprecedented step, Asquith did not ask for his immediate commitment. Time was running out.

On November 15 the cabinet met again and prepared a memorandum for the King. In words strikingly similar to Asquith's earlier account of his conversation with the King, it stated on behalf of the cabinet what Asquith had told the King five days earlier. "H. M. Ministers cannot . . . take the responsibility of advising a dissolution unless they may understand that in the event of the policy of the Government being approved by an adequate majority in the new House of Commons, H. M. will be ready to exercise his constitutional powers (which may involve the prerogative of creating Peers) if needed, to secure that effect shall be given to the decision of the country."[128]

The next day Asquith met with the King at Buckingham Palace. Asquith found His Majesty "without obstinacy, both plucky and reasonable."[129] The Prime Minister said that it was impossible to let things drift as they were doing and finally obtained the King's promise that should the Liberals be returned in the forthcoming election with an "adequate majority," then the King would create a number of peers sufficient to pass the Parliament bill limiting the Lords' veto. The promise was to remain for the time being strictly confidential. The King did insist that the Parliament bill be submitted to the House of Lords before the election, to which Asquith agreed. When he was about to take his leave, the King said to him, "Is this the advice that you would have given my father?" Asquith replied, "Yes, Sir; and your father would have taken it."¹³⁰

The second Parliamentary election of 1910 was held between November 17 and December 20 and was in Asquith's words years later "conducted everywhere with the utmost vigour and enthusiasm, and in some quarters with not a little bitterness."¹³¹ The campaign was hard fought like the January election, but this time there was a single issue—the House of Lords. In the two weeks leading up to the election, Asquith spoke all over the country; yet despite his and others' efforts, few were surprised by the election results. As Asquith put it, the election left the "distribution of the forces in the House of Commons practically unchanged."¹³² Asquith's own majority of 1,799 in East Fife was more than comfortable but down from the 2,059 eleven months earlier. Liberals were returned with 272 seats with the Unionists the same. Labour retained 42, but the Irish still held the balance of power with 84 seats. The die was now cast. The Liberals with the unquestioned support of the Irish and Labour had a working majority of 126 to pass the Parliament Bill.

The King opened Parliament on February 6, and the government introduced its Parliament bill a little over two weeks later. The bill was in exactly the same form introduced the year before. Under Asquith's leadership and direction, it made its way through the various stages and finally passed the House of Commons on May 15.

From the beginning of the crisis, Asquith had believed that the House of Lords, when confronted with certain defeat, would not force the King to create the new peers. This is what Asquith told the King directly on November 10 before the dissolution was announced. "If we are beaten at the General Election, the question will never arise," he repeated to Margot that same evening, "and if we get in by a working majority the Lords will give way, so the King won't be involved."¹³³ It must have been with some surprise to him when, as events unfolded, he realized that the Conservatives would not be willing to surrender without hearing publicly the King's pledge.

By mid-July the Lords had amended the Parliament bill out of recognition. In Asquith's words it was "as completely transformed as though no General Elections had been held."¹³⁴ One of the amendments provided that measures of "grave importance," specifically including Irish Home Rule, must be referred to a direct vote of the people. Once the Committee stage in the House of Lords was completed, the event Asquith had hoped to avoid had become unavoidable. The cabinet minuted the King on July 14 that it would soon "be the duty of Ministers to advise the Crown to exercise its Prerogative so as to get rid of the deadlock and secure the passing of the Bill."¹³⁵ Several days later the cabinet was informed that the King would accept the advice of his ministers.

After some discussion as to whether the King himself should announce his intention, Asquith's position that the announcement should come from the government prevailed. So that constitutional proprieties would be strictly observed, the Prime Minister wanted it to be absolutely clear that the King was acting on the advice of his ministers and that all the responsibility belonged to them.[136] Accordingly on July 20 Asquith wrote to Balfour and Lord Lansdowne, "I think it is courteous and right, before any public decisions are announced, to let you know how we regard the political situation." After telling the Conservative leaders that the House of Commons would reject the Lords' amendments, he then made the announcement he had hoped to avoid. "In the circumstances, should the necessity arise, the Government will advise the King to exercise his Prerogative to secure the passing into law of the Bill in substantially the same form in which it left the House of Commons; and His Majesty has been pleased to signify that he will consider it his duty to accept, and act on, that advice."[137] The letter was published in the press two days later. The word was now out. The Conservative camp had increasingly divided over what to do when the moment that was now upon them arrived. There were the "ditchers," who were willing to die in the last ditch to defend the House of Lords' veto. Cooler heads, known as the "hedgers," were more willing to accept the inevitable.

Asquith first appeared in House of Commons after the announcement on July 24. When the Prime Minister attempted to address the House, he was howled down by angry Conservative MPs led by Lord Hugh Cecil and F. E. Smith. This went on for half an hour until Asquith finally gave up and the session was adjourned. Despite this demonstration of poor taste and poorer judgment, the Parliament Bill moved on to a final vote in the House of Lords on August 18. Landsdowne led the "hedgers" in abstaining, and the "ditchers" kept their promise to oppose the measure till the bitter end. Even so, the bill passed by a mere seventeen votes.

C. F. G. Masterman summed up this historic battle best. It had been the "biggest constitutional Revolution since 1688 and equally bloodless," and to "the dogged determination of Mr. Asquith the credit belongs of accomplishing a work which thus seemed incredible to the wise."[138] With the Parliament Bill of 1911 ending the Lords' veto, the government could now turn its attention to Home Rule for Ireland.

With the defeat of Gladstone's third Irish Home Rule bill in 1893 and the return to power of the Unionists in 1895, self-governance for Ireland had been moved to the back burner of politics. Asquith had loyally supported Gladstone's last effort, but once it failed, he saw little future for the Liberals in being tied to the issue. Under Asquith's influence the Liberal Party refrained from directly pledging itself to Home Rule in the 1901 and the 1906 elections.[139] Campbell-Bannerman did, however, pledge to the Irish leaders John Redmond and T. P. O'Connor in 1905 just before the election that should the Liberals be returned to power, they would introduce some type of interim measure to serve as a half-way house toward ultimate Home Rule for Ireland. The Irish leaders accepted this and even told the Liberal leader that they would have no objection if the new government waited until as long as its third year in office to bring the measure forth.[140]

In the spring of 1908, as Campbell-Bannerman was near death and Asquith was for all intents and purposes the head of the government, Redmond introduced a resolution in the House of Commons calling for Home Rule, thus placing the Liberals in the rather embarrassing situation of declaring unequivocally their position. Asquith was not about to let his hand be forced. Speaking against the motion, he pointed out that the resolution did not contain the one element that he had always believed to be the "governing condition" in the matter—imperial supremacy. "In my opinion," he told the House, "the recognition of the claim of Ireland for self-government must be accompanied by the express statement that whatever is granted must be granted subject to the dominant and paramount supremacy of this Imperial Parliament." He did say that the goal of Home Rule was "certain and inevitable"; otherwise, he asked, "are we to go on, generation after generation, treading with blind steps the same old well-worn hopeless track which zig-zags between coercion and conciliation, and which always returns in a vicious circle to the point from which it started?"[141] The House passed the resolution only after adding an amendment making Home Rule "subject to the supreme authority of the Imperial Parliament."[142]

As has been seen, all of 1909 was taken up with the controversy over the "People's Budget," culminating in January in the first parliamentary election of 1910 that left the Liberals dependent on the Irish Nationalists for a majority. During the campaign, Asquith stated at Albert Hall on December 10 that he favored a "policy which while explicitly safeguarding the supreme and indefeasible authority of the Imperial Parliament, will set up in Ireland a system of full self-government in regard to purely Irish affairs." He went on to declare that the new House of Commons in the hands of a Liberal majority would consider itself free to put forward such a proposal.[143] Of course Asquith naturally disliked the idea of having to depend on the Irish for a majority. Speaking to voters in his home district of East Fife on January 18, he declared, "I promise no legislation of any kind in the next Parliament until we have settled our conclusions with the House of Lords," a proposition the Irish could hardly disagree with, considering any hope of Home Rule depended on reforming the Lords.[144] With the removal of the House of Lords' ability to veto legislation in August 1911, Asquith's government now turned its attention to Home Rule.

The government's Home Rule bill put together during the winter of 1911–1912 followed the lines laid down by Gladstone as early as 1886. Purely Irish matters were to be handled by an Irish Parliament, while matters such as treaties and foreign relations together with custom duties and other such matters touching the Crown would be reserved for the Imperial Parliament at Westminster. Although a common treasury would continue, the new Irish Parliament would be given the power to raise new Irish taxes to a certain limit. The number of Irish members of the Imperial Parliament was to be reduced to forty-two members able to speak and vote on all matters before the body. Finally the Irish Parliament was to be barred from endowing any religion or imposing any religious disabilities.

The northern counties that comprised Ulster, some with Protestant majorities, were the fly in the ointment, and Asquith and his cabinet fully understood this. Would these counties be included in the Home Rule bill, and if so, to what extent? As an opening gambit, the cabinet decided to included all of Ireland in the initial bill. Asquith, who preferred and recommended this approach was also a practical politician. He wrote to the King on February 6, 1912, that "the Government held themselves free to make changes, if it became clear that special treatment must be provided for the Ulster Counties, and that in this case the Government will be ready to recognize the necessity either by amendment or by not pressing it [the Bill] on under the provision of the Parliament Act."[145]

As the government prepared to introduce its Home Rule Bill, the situation in Ireland continued to go from bad to worse. In September 1911 the Ulster Unionist Council had announced its intention to prepare a constitution and declare a "Provisional Government" for Ulster should Parliament ever pass a Home Rule bill. When Winston Churchill went to Ulster on behalf of the government to explain the Home Rule bill in February 1912, he was able to speak publicly only under military protection. Thus began what Asquith later described as the "opening chapter" of the "complete Grammar of Anarchy."[146]

On April 11 Asquith rose in the House to face an angry opposition. It was to be one of his most lawyer-like performances, lucidly enumerating all the provisions of the bill. Describing the measure as "the most urgent and the most momentous step towards the settlement of the controversy which, as between ourselves and Ireland, has lasted for more than a century," he told the House that it "will give to the Irish people a free and ample field for the development of their own national life and at the same time bind them to us and the Empire by a sense of voluntary cooperation, and, as I believe, in sincere and loyal attachment." He also made a point to note that the bill contained what he had always considered a key to the success of Home Rule—"the supremacy, absolute and sovereign, of the Imperial Parliament." To this point in his speech his message had concerned the bill itself, but he then turned on Bonar Law, the leader of the Conservatives. According to Asquith, Law had made a speech in Belfast earlier in the week in which he had claimed the government had sold itself to hold on to office. Such irresponsible statements the Prime Minister derisively described as "the new style." When Law interrupted Asquith to reaffirm his accusation even to the point of stating the government had no convictions, Asquith's quickly retorted, "We are getting on with the new style." Asquith concluded by pointing out that the opposition had offered no alternative "beyond the naked veto of an irreconcilable minority, and the promise of a freer and more copious outflow to Ireland of Imperial doles." He continued by asking whether with twenty to thirty self-governing legislatures in existence already under allegiance to the Crown, "Are we going to break up the Empire by adding one more?"[147]

Just as the government began to focus its attention on Ireland, it was distracted by what became known as the Marconi scandal. The Sixth Imperial Conference of 1911 had called for the construction of an "Imperial wireless chain" throughout the Empire. This resulted in a tender to the government by the English Marconi Company. During the summer rumors began to circulate that cabinet ministers had made immense profits dealing shares in the English Marconi Company, which had been awarded a contract in February 1912 for the erection of a chain of wireless stations. With rumors rampant, it was finally decided in October to set up a Parliamentary select committee to investigate. Lloyd George and Rufus Isaacs during the debate on the appointment of the select committee denied they had ever had any interest, direct or indirect, in the *English* Marconi Company.

When the three ministers finally testified before the committee the last week of March, it became clear why their statements in October were far from the whole truth. Isaacs admitted that he had purchased shares in the *American* Marconi Company and had sold some to Lloyd George and the Master of Elibank.[148] Lloyd George subsequently sold some of his shares for a profit. Ultimately, the investigation showed no corruption. Using no privileged knowledge, the ministers involved had purchased their shares after the government contract had been made public. Even so, the whole episode seemed suspicious for a number of months.

To his credit, Asquith stood by his ministers. He refused to accept their offers of resignation in January 1913. Roy Jenkins has put it well: the Prime Minister, even though "he felt an instinctive distaste for the process of money-making," at the same time "was never harsh towards human frailty."[149] Even so, there is some question as to exactly when Asquith learned of his Ministers' unwise actions. Postmaster General Herbert Samuel always maintained that he told the Prime Minister of the exact nature of the transactions in June

1912. From this some have argued that Asquith should have pressed Isaacs and Lloyd George to be more direct in their statements in October before the select committee was seated. Asquith, however, told the King that he first heard the complete story in January 1913 and found it "lamentable" and "so difficult to defend."[150] Although it does not settle the matter, it is true that Asquith wrote to his friend Venetia Stanley on January 7, "I am bothered with various things—the latest being certain follies wh. Rufus Isaacs & Ll. George have committed in regard to Marconi shares," and this seems to indicate he had just learned the full story.[151] What he knew and when is not nearly as important as his standing by his colleagues. It was an episode neither Isaacs nor, more importantly, Lloyd George would forget.

In July 1912, as the Home Rule bill was making it through the various stages of passage, Asquith decided to go to Dublin himself. He was determined to work to moderate the increasingly hostile rhetoric about civil war openly employed by Ulstermen and Conservative and Liberal-Unionist leaders. Addressing his Irish audience, he declared, "I find it difficult to find any justification whatever for incitement to rebellion and civil war." Acknowledging that minorities have rights, he said that they had no right "before any actual wrong has been or can be done to them . . . to thwart and defeat the Constitutional demand of a vast majority of their fellow-countrymen to frustrate a great international settlement."[152]

The Conservative response was swift. Only a few days later, Bonar Law declared at a mass meeting at Blenheim, "In our opposition to them we shall not be guided by the considerations, we shall not be guided by the bonds, which would influence us in an ordinary political struggle." He continued, "We shall use any means, whatever means seem likely to be most effective. . . . I can imagine no length of resistance to which Ulster will go in which I shall not be ready to support them."[153] Asquith was thoroughly disgusted with Law's remarks, describing such demagoguery as "unparalleled in the language of any responsible statesman within living memory" and a "declaration of war against Constitutional Government."[154]

Later that September, Edward Carson led nearly half a million Ulster Protestant men and women in signing a Covenant stating they would resist "using all means which may be found necessary to defeat the present conspiracy to set up a Home Rule Parliament in Ireland." When Asquith met with the King the next month, the King was "not pleased with Carson and his antics" and had "begun to realize the difficulties of the situation." When he suggested some sort of conference, Asquith told him that such a meeting "at this moment & under existing conditions—even if you could get the necessary people into the room—would degenerate either into a tea party or a beer-garden."[155] As the New Year dawned, the Ulster Unionist Council began to raise a Volunteer Force, giving formal organization to paramilitary forces that already had been formed.[156]

On January 16, 1913, the Home Rule bill passed its third and final reading in the Commons, but as expected two weeks later the measure was defeated in the House of Lords by a margin of more than four to one. Under the Parliament Act of 1911, if the Home Rule bill was passed by the House of Commons in three consecutive sessions, it would become law with or without the concurrence of the House of Lords. The House of Commons moved much faster on the second passage of the bill. By the time Parliament recessed for the summer in 1913, the Home Rule bill had once again been passed by the Commons and again rejected by the Lords.

Undoubtedly by the autumn of 1913 the question of Ireland was about to reach its climax. One more passage of the Home Rule bill by the Commons and it would be law. Asquith prepared a private memorandum to the King setting out his views of the situation. He had no doubts about the seriousness of the situation. If the Home Rule bill became law, "there will undoubtedly be a serious danger of organized disorder in the four north-eastern counties of Ulster." He continued, "I have not the least disposition to minimize the gravity of the situation which will probably arise." Even so, he believed that the consequences of turning back from Home Rule at this juncture would be far worse. In such a situation "Ireland would become ungovernable—unless by the application of forces and methods which would offend the conscience of Great Britain, and arouse the deepest resentment in all the self-governing Dominions of the Crown."[157] The King conveyed his appreciation for the memorandum and said he was "very glad to hear that you have not shown the paper to any of your colleagues and are treating it as a personal communication between ourselves."[158]

In early October Asquith was visiting the King at Balmoral and with the King's approval decided to contact Bonar Law directly to see if they could meet face to face. On October 14 the two leaders met secretly at Sir Max Aitken's country house Cherkley, near Leatherhead in Surry. Despite a friendliness of tone, the discussion defined for both men the almost insurmountable problem they faced. If the government prevailed, it would almost certainly be faced with the coercion of Ulster. Likewise, if there was dissolution and the Conservatives returned, they would have to face the coercion of southern Ireland.

The two met again on November 6. They agreed that both sides were becoming entrenched and the opportunity for compromise was fast slipping away. Law suggested the possibility of an election, but Asquith quickly dismissed the idea. To Law's mind, even though there was little possibility of an election changing the composition of the Commons, it might still drive home the point of the inevitability of a compromise. To Asquith, another partisan campaign would just make for more bad blood. The discussion then turned to the possibility of excluding Ulster from Home Rule. Law said that Carson would insist on the exclusion of the entire province, to which Asquith responded, "out of the question." Donegal, Monaghan, and Cavan counties were overwhelmingly Nationalist with Tyrone and Fermanagh about evenly split. The best Law could hope for was to hold out for the latter two provinces to join with the remainder of Ulster to be excluded. According to Asquith, they departed "in good will but in no very sanguine spirit."

A week later on November 12, Lloyd George proposed that an area of Ulster, unspecified at the time, should be allowed to opt out of Home Rule for a period of five or six years. The idea was to allow two general elections to take place before inclusion. In other words, kick the can down the road. There was a good deal of support for the idea in the cabinet, which permitted Asquith to raise the idea with Redmond on November 17.[159] If Asquith had any hope that the concept would be well received, he was quickly disabused. Redmond told the Prime Minister that he "could conceive of no proposal which would array against it a more compact and united body of sentiment in Ireland, both Nationalist and Unionist."[160] Such a proposal would split the Irish Party, and he would only consider it as a last resort as a price of an agreed settlement. He countered Asquith's suggestion with a plan of what Sir Edward Grey had described as "Home Rule within Home Rule." Ulster would remain part of a united Ireland granted Home Rule, but would be granted a great deal of local autonomy, including a local Ulster Council and greater representation in the new Irish Parliament.

Asquith actually favored some type of "Home Rule within Home Rule" formula and in his last private meeting with Bonar Law proposed the idea of a "Federal" solution. Under this scheme there would be Home Rule all around, perhaps even including Scotland and Wales, with an Imperial Parliament over all. This in many ways was grasping at straws. Law rejected the idea and clung to the idea of a definite exclusion of a part of Ulster with an option to come in later.[161]

At this point Asquith on his own authority decided to contact Sir Edward Carson directly. He wrote to him on December 23 suggesting a plan whereby "no legislation in the Irish Parliament on any matter of importance should become effective in the Ulster area against the will of a majority of Ulster representatives unless submitted to and approved by the Imperial Parliament."[162] Carson rejected the overture, refusing anything less than the full exclusion of Ulster. He wrote to Asquith, "So far as I am concerned I cd. not feel justified (& indeed it wd. Be useless) in submitting these terms to my colleagues and associates in Ulster, as however guarded, the basis is the inclusion of Ulster in the Irish Parlmt."[163]

When Parliament convened on February 10, the King's speech expressed the wish that "the good will and cooperation of men of all parties and creeds may heal the dissention and lay the foundation of a lasting settlement"—wishful thinking at best.[164] Asquith had again approached Redmond a few days earlier on February 2 with the Prime Minister's favorite plan of "Home Rule within Home Rule," but this time with even greater powers granted Ulster. Apparently Asquith was also thinking of the political implications of the negotiations. According to Redmond's description of the meeting, Asquith told him "that for the safety of Home Rule it is essential that he should make an offer to Ulster of such a character that in the event of their refusal of it—and he thinks at this stage any offer he makes short of the exclusion of Ulster would be rejected—it would deprive them of all moral force."[165] Asquith's refusal to give up on some formula of "Home Rule within Home Rule" indicates that this is where he thought the middle ground could be reached. Despite rejection from both sides of the Irish issue, he continued to hang on. Not until March did Asquith, as he later related, part from the idea "with regret and reluctance," for "it had not commended itself to any of the parties concerned."[166]

Compromise was now sought with a plan that would allow part of Ulster, yet undetermined, the opportunity to opt out of Home Rule for a defined period of time. Lloyd George and Augustine Birrell worked with Redmond and were able to gain his reluctant consent—in Redmond's words in a letter to Asquith—as "the price of peace."[167] The cabinet endorsed the plan on March 4, and five days later the Irish Home Rule bill began its third and final journey through the House of Commons. At the same time Asquith announced the government's intention to introduce an amending bill giving Ulster counties the right to vote themselves out of Home Rule for a period of six years.

As it became more and more apparent that the Irish Home Rule bill was indeed going to become law that summer, the government began to make preparations. Over the previous year, the War Office had received reports that the issue was causing some problems of discipline within the army.[168] The King himself had warned Asquith that if the Home Rule negotiations broke down, many officers might resign their commissions rather than fight against Ulster.[169] In early December 1913, Sir John French, Chief of the Imperial General Staff, and Sir Spencer Ewart, Adjutant General, reported to Colonel J. E. B. Seely, who had replaced Haldane as the Secretary of State for War in 1912, so that "many efforts were being made to seduce officers and men from their allegiance that there was a real danger of indiscipline in the army."[170] On December 16 Seely met with the general officers commanding at the War Office and reassured them there would be "no question of enforcing the Home Rule Act on Ulster by force of arms for years to come, and indeed such an event would probably never happen." Nevertheless he made it clear that they had to face the possibility of "action being required by H. M.'s troops in supporting the civil power and protecting life and property when the police were unable to hold their own."[171] Subsequently, Sir Arthur Paget, the Commander-in-Chief in Ireland, obtained from the Secretary of State and the Army Council the concession that should the Army have to confront challenges by the Ulster Volunteer Force, officers from Ulster would be permitted to "disappear" without harming their prospects for promotion.[172]

In early March the cabinet received the news that according to police reports, there might well be an attempt by the Ulster Volunteer Force to seize police and military barracks and depots of arms and ammunition.[173] By March 7 instructions had been sent to Paget to take precautionary steps to safeguard the weapons and supply depots in some parts of Ulster. Upon receipt of these instructions and knowing that such a move might meet with resistance by the Ulster Volunteer Force, Paget thought it prudent to gather his senior officers at Curragh on March 20 to ascertain their view of the situation. It is not clear exactly what was said at the meeting, but the impression given was that all officers, not just those domiciled in Ulster, were being asked to declare their intentions based on a purely hypothetical set of circumstances. One of the most distinguished officers, Brigadier-General Hubert Gough, an Ulsterman and commander of the 3rd Calvary Brigade, and fifty-seven other officers (out of a total of seventy in his brigade) stated that if their duty involved the initiation of active operations against Ulster, they would prefer to be dismissed.

General Gough and some of the other officers who had expressed doubts of their ability to carry out lawful orders were summoned to the War Office in London for consultation. The cabinet prepared a carefully worded memorandum that was issued as an Army order stating that no officer would be questioned about nor should any officer inquire about "orders dependent on future or hypothetical contingencies." More importantly, the order specifically reminded officers and soldiers that it was their duty "to obey all lawful commands, either for the safeguarding of public property, or the support of the civil power in the ordinary execution of its duty, or for the protection of the lives and property of the inhabitants in the case of disturbance of the peace."[174]

Even after the order was issued, General Gough persisted in requesting a clarification as to whether officers would be called upon to enforce the Home Rule bill as part of "maintaining law and order." In response, Seely added two paragraphs to the copy of the cabinet memorandum he forwarded to General Gough. Seely stated that the government had no intention of taking advantage of the armed forces "to crush political opposition to the policy or principles of the Home Rule Bill."[175] Both Sir John French and Sir Spencer Ewart initialed Seely's additions.

Later the same day, Asquith was shown the response to Gough and was surprised to discover the additional paragraphs. The Prime Minister acted decisively. He immediately commanded that General Gough and others be informed that the two additional paragraphs were inoperative. As Asquith later explained, "I held, as did my colleagues, that if it was not right to ask an officer what he would do in a hypothetical contingency, still less could it be right for an officer to ask the Government to give him any assurance."[176]

The consequences of what became known as the "Curragh Mutiny," or as Asquith preferred to call it, the "Curragh Incident," were immediate. Sir John French and Sir Spencer Ewart immediately resigned their positions, not because they disagreed with the government's action, but because they had initialed the canceled part of the cabinet memorandum. Seely also resigned, as he told the House of Commons, so that "it might not even appear that any Minister of the Crown had made a bargain with any of the Crown's servants as to the terms of service under which they should serve."[177]

The situation was serious enough that Asquith decided that he himself should take over as Secretary of State for War in addition to his duties as Prime Minister, and he did on March 3. J. A. Spender observed that although Asquith was reluctant to take control and until he did so thought himself "unequal" to the occasion, nevertheless Asquith admitted when he did take over that he was "both formidable and resourceful."[178] Taking this new cabinet position required him to vacate his seat in Parliament and seek reelection, which he did, unopposed. Speaking in Fife at Ladybank on April 4, he set forth his position. Determining what was in the best interest of the public was the duty of Parliament, not the Army. "The Army," he said "will hear nothing of politics from me, and in return I expect to hear nothing of politics from the Army."[179]

Asquith continued discussions with the Conservative leadership, and over the next few weeks it was provisionally agreed that as a last resort, an option for the northern counties to come in would be substituted for a compulsory inclusion at the end of a waiting period.[180]

Negotiations continued, but the parties were only drifting farther apart. On June 9 Redmond announced that the Irish Nationalists had taken steps to encourage their friends to support the volunteer force forming in the south to counter the Ulster volunteers.[181]

Asquith had only one option left—ask the King to call a conference of the interested parties. The conference, chaired by the Speaker of the House, consisted of Asquith and Lloyd George representing the government, Lord Landsdowne and Bonar Law for the opposition, Redmond and Dillon for the Irish Nationalists, and Carson and Captain Craig for the Ulster Unionists. It met on July 21 and held sessions on each of the following three days. Asquith stated that the "discussions were carried on in a courteous and friendly spirit, and with a real desire to find a way to agreement," but in the end, it foundered on the same rocks that had sunk previous negotiations.[182] The parties simply could not agree either as to the boundary of the territory to be excluded from Home Rule or the length of time for such exclusion.

Asquith now informed Redmond and the other Irish leaders that the government intended to go forward with an Amending bill that would allow all the counties of Ulster the option to opt out for an indefinite period. Under protest Redmond and Dillon agreed to submit this plan to their supporters. By the time the Amending bill was set down for its second reading in the House on July 30, events on the continent had caught up with and surpassed the importance of Ireland. By mutual agreement with Bonar Law, Asquith announced to the House that issues of peace and war were "hanging in the balance, and with them the risk of a catastrophe of which it is impossible to measure either the dimensions or the effects." Under such circumstances, it was critical to "present a united front, and be able to speak and act with the authority of an undivided nation."[183] With the willing concurrence of the opposition, the Irish controversy was suspended for the duration of the conflict.

When the First World War broke upon Britain in August 1914, Asquith had been Prime Minister for a little over six years. What did he have to show for it? One historian argues that the Liberals "muffed" the opportunity the landslide of 1906 presented. The Liberals fought three general elections between 1906 and 1910 and in not one of these contests did they present a systematic Liberal program of social reforms. The result, once the Liberals took office, was a hotchpotch of measures. Even the "People's Budget" of 1909 resulted more from events than the force of radicalism. There simply was no attempt to devise and put on the statute books a clear-cut program that mirrored Liberal values.[184] While for the most part factually correct, this view misses the forest for the trees.

It is true that Asquith and his colleagues passed only a few pieces of specific social legislation during the six years leading up to the war. In 1908 the Liberals' Licensing bill was rejected by the House of Lords, and their Education bill, their last attempt to settle the education problem, had to be withdrawn. Even if these bills had become law, it is doubtful they would have had had much effect in ameliorating the deep social problems Britain faced. Yet Asquith's government was able to pass a Coal Mines Regulation Act and a Children Act, establishing a new system of juvenile courts throughout the country and abolishing the imprisonment of children. The 1909 session was almost totally taken up with the budget, nevertheless Labour Exchanges and trade boards in "sweated" trades were established, and an Irish Land bill and a housing and town planning bill were passed in modified forms.

The Liberals also avoided some important issues, most notably women's suffrage. Although a majority of Liberal MPs, including Liberal leaders such as Grey and Lloyd George, supported giving the women the right to vote, Asquith had opposed the idea since the beginning of his political career. Asquith's opposition seems to run counter to his overall liberal tendencies. A number of "Conciliation" bills extending the franchise were introduced throughout 1910–1911, but none of them could muster a majority because they included limitations based on age and property, and many Liberals feared adding Conservative voting wealthy women to the voter lists. In 1912 Asquith's government came forward with a bill to abolish plural voting (the right of a voter who owned land in several constituencies to vote in more than one) and to extend the male franchise from 7.5 million to 10 million voters. Over Asquith's objection, the cabinet decided that it would accept any amendment to the Reform bill adopted by the House that would add the vote for women. As expected, such an amendment was proposed. To everyone's surprise, the Speaker of the House ruled that if the women's amendment was adopted, it would so change the bill as to necessitate its withdrawal. This ruling meant that a new bill would have to be introduced, and there would be no chance of its passage in the current session. Even Asquith was surprised, writing to the King, "This is a totally new view of the matter which appears to have occurred for the first time to the Speaker himself only two or three days ago, and is in flat contradiction of the assumptions upon which all parties in the House hitherto treated the bill."[185] He predicted to a friend, "The Speaker's *coup d'état* has bowled over the Women for this Session: a great relief—but I dare say the militants will now take again to the war-path...."[186]

In the 1913 session a new Reform bill was introduced incorporating the vote for women. It was defeated on the second reading 268 to 221 with Asquith speaking and voting against the bill. Although such views are dated and quaint today, Asquith's main reason for opposing the women's franchise was his Victorian sense of decorum and chivalry. In his speech opposing the bill he began by asking rhetorically: "Would our political fabric be strengthened, would our legislation be more respected, would our social and domestic life be enriched, would our standards of manners—and in manners I include the old fashioned virtues of chivalry, courtesy, and all the reciprocal dependence and reliance of the two sexes—would that standard be raised and refined if women were politically enfranchised?" The answer to him was obviously "No." Further, he saw no evidence of a "settled demand for the change by an overwhelming majority of women," nor that the denial of votes for women had "caused or was causing a neglect by Parliament of the special interests and needs of women."[187]

Despite these failings, Asquith's peacetime premiership is remarkable, and he himself deserves a great deal of the credit. His pioneering proposals in the

1907 budget and the People's Budget of 1909 fundamentally changed the British system of taxation. Even more important, for almost three decades before Asquith assumed the reins of power in 1908, two major issues darkened the political horizon: the power of the House of Lords and Irish Home Rule. All during this period those who understood the British political system realized that sooner or later these major constitutional issues would have to be resolved. Session after session of Parliament ignored them, hoping that they might go away but knowing they would not. Both issues were so politically disagreeable that even Asquith and his Liberal supporters shied away from them until events forced a resolution. When that time did come, under Asquith's skillful leadership the Liberal party did face up to the challenge of these nearly insoluble constitutional issues. In adjusting of the constitutional powers of the House of Lords, the result was almost complete success. The Constitution was changed to reflect a more democratic society without the entire system coming apart at the seams, which many had predicted. The result regarding Irish Home Rule is not nearly so clear. Had the First World War not intervened, there surely would have been civil war in Ireland in 1914. The bloody events after the war confirm that violence in Ireland could not have been avoided. Yet Asquith and many of his colleagues understood that Home Rule could no longer be postponed no matter what the price, and they tried mightily to resolve it. The compromise hammered out in the summer of 1914 was as good as circumstances permitted, not the best solution, but probably the only realistic one.

Britain was fortunate to have a leader with Asquith's particular skills during this difficult period. As a lawyer he understood the major constitutional implications of the actions his government was taking. He could advise the monarch with the sure authority of one who had made an almost scholarly study of the issues. Sometimes his efforts were mistakenly seen as weakness. Yet some knew otherwise. When Reginald McKenna complained of Asquith's weakness during the budget controversy over the number of *Dreadnaught*-class ships, Viscount Esher wisely responded that twenty years of experience had taught him that "P.M.s—even the strongest—Mr. G. [Gladstone] and Lord Beaconsfield are all called 'weak' when they try to keep their Cabinet or Party together."[188] When one looks at these conflicts and sees the raging forces locked in combat, be they "last ditchers" in the House of Commons or radical Liberals in the cabinet, one sees above the smoke and the din of battle the calm, patient figure of Asquith. Over and again in the tough negotiations and complicated political maneuvering of the period, it was the Prime Minister who held things together, sometime by a thread, until a compromise could be reached or a way forward found. Asquith's government could not pass a comprehensive Liberal program, but given the realities of the period, no government could have. By facing the tough, key political issues of the day, Asquith could lay claim to leading one of the great reform governments in British history. Asquith had demonstrated remarkable talents in holding together and leading his cabinet and the Liberal Party to achieve what they did. He now faced in the summer of 1914 the stern test of his leadership skills: a world war.

NOTES

1. Ponsonby diary, BL, MS. Eng. Hist. c. 653.
2. Reginald Viscount Esher, *Journals and Letters of Reginald Viscount Esher vol. 2 1903–1910*, ed. Maurice V. Brett (London: Ivor Nicholson & Watson, 1934), 256.
3. Wilson, *C.B.*, 617.
4. Bruce K. Murray, *The People's Budget 1909/10: Lloyd George and Liberal Politics* (Oxford: Clarendon Press, 1980), 51, 58–59.
5. Grey, *Twenty-five Years*, 1:67.
6. Churchill, *Great Contemporaries*, 140.
7. John Viscount Simon, *Retrospect: The Memoirs of the Rt. Hon. Viscount Simon* (London: Hutchison, 1952), 141.
8. J. A. Spender, *Life, Journalism and Politics*, 2 vols. (New York: Frederick A. Stokes, n.d. [1927]), 1:153–54.
9. Churchill, *Great Contemporaries*, 137, 141.
10. Spender, *Life, Journalism and Politics*, 1:155.
11. Augustine Birrell, *Things Past Redress* (London: Faber and Faber, n.d.), 249–50.
12. Max Egremont, *Balfour: A Life of Arthur James Balfour* (London: Collins, 1980), 134.
13. Michael Holroyd, *Lytton Strachey: A Critical Biography, vol. 2 The Years of Achievement (1910–1932)* (New York: Holt, Rinehart and Winston, 1968), 331.
14. Simon, *Retrospect*, 141.
15. *Hansard*, 4, 14, 972, 3 Mar. 1910. Asquith may have been making an indirect reference to Quintaus Fabius Maximus (280–203 B.C.) nicknamed "Cunctator" translated as "Wait and see" in John Dryden Plutarch and Arthur Hugh Clough, *Plutarch's Lives* (London: Samson Low, 1859).
16. Archibald Stodart Walker, *The Oxford Book of English Verse 1340–1913* (London: Eveleigh Nash, 1914), 129.
17. Simon, *Retrospect*, 141.
18. Koss, *Asquith*, 90.
19. John Maynard Keynes, *Essays in Biography* (New York: W.W. Norton, 1951), 46–47.
20. John Vincent, ed., *The Crawford Papers: The Journals of David Lindsay Twenty-Seventh Earl of Crawford and Tenth Earl of Balcarres 1870–1940 during the*

Years 1892 to 1940 (Manchester: Manchester University Press, 1984), 526; Simon, *Retrospect*, 141.

21. Cassar, *Asquith as War Leader*, 32–33.
22. Asquith, *Moments*, 78, 104.
23. Ibid., 90.
24. D. W. Brogan, "Last of the Romans," *New York Times Book Review*, June 27, 1965, 1.
25. Duff Cooper, *Old Men Forget* (London: Rupert Hart-Davis, 1953), 54.
26. Lucy, *Balfourian Parliament*, 87.
27. Spender, *Life, Journalism and Politics*, 151.
28. Churchill, *Great Contemporaries*, 140–41.
29. Beaverbrook, *Politicians and the War*, 216.
30. Mark DeWolfe Howe, ed., *Holmes-Laski Letters: The Correspondence of Mr. Justice Holmes and Harold J. Laski 1916–1935,* 2 vols. (Cambridge, MA: Harvard University Press, 1953), 1:725.
31. Sir Oswald Mosley, *My Life* (London: Nelson, 1968), 94; Howe, ed., *Holmes-Laski Letters*, 1:725.
32. "Scene—The Infernal Tribunal" (undated), Michael and Eleanor Brock, eds., *H. H. Asquith Letters to Venetia Stanley* (Oxford: Oxford University Press, 1982), 471.
33. For a detailed description of the speculation on this subject, see Naomi B. Levine, *Politics, Religion and Love; The Story of H.H. Asquith, Venetia Stanley and Edwin Montagu, Based on the Life and Letters of Edwin Samuel Montagu* (New York: New York University Press, 1991), 231–35.
34. MA to Edwin Montagu, 21 Mar. 1914, Brock, *Letters to Venetia Stanley*, 13.
35. Ibid., 3, 13.
36. HHA to MA, 1 Mar. 1908, BL, MS. Eng. c. 6690, ff. 153–54.
37. John Grigg, *Lloyd George: The People's Champion 1902–1911* (Berkeley: University of California Press, 1978), 133.
38. Gilbert, *Architect of Change*, 331.
39. Grigg, *People's Champion*, 133.
40. HHA to Lloyd George, 8 Apr. 1908, Grigg, *People's Champion*, 133–34.
41. Earl of Oxford and Asquith, *Memories*, 2:88.
42. HHA to MA, 1 Mar. 1908, BL, MS. Eng. c. 6690, ff. 153–54.
43. *Hansard*, 4, 187, 1034, 27 Apr. 1908.
44. Freeden, *New Liberalism*, 133–45.
45. E. P. Hennock, "The Origins of British National Insurance and the German Precedent 1880–1914," in W. J. Mommsen, ed., *The Emergence of the Welfare State in Britain and Germany 1850–1950* (London: Croom Helm, 1981).
46. The bill also excluded all people who received poor relief during the year prior to the statute's effective date.
47. *Hansard*, 4, 192, 184–85, 9 July 1908.
48. Gilbert, *Architect of Change,* 341.
49. Ibid., 342.
50. H. H. Asquith, *The Genesis of the War* (New York: George H. Doran, 1923), 115–16.

51. Ibid., 122.
52. Ruddock F. Mackay, *Fisher of Kilverstone* (Oxford: Clarendon Press, 1973), 409.
53. McKenna to HHA, 3 Jan. 1909, BL, MS. Asquith 21, ff. 22–25.
54. Gilbert, *Architect of Change*, 386.
55. HHA to MA, 21 Feb. 1909, BL, MS. Eng. c. 6690, ff. 183–84.
56. "Minutes of Conference," 23 Feb. 1909, BL, MSS Asquith 21, ff. 110–54.
57. Spender and Asquith, *Life of Asquith,* 253–54; Gilbert, *Architect of Change*, 368.
58. Winston S. Churchill, *The World Crisis* (New York: Charles Scribner's Sons, 1923), 33.
59. *Hansard*, 5, 3, 129, 29 Mar. 1909.
60. Runciman to HHA, 12 Apr. 1909; Harcourt to Runciman, 24 Mar. 1909, Grigg, *People's Champion*, 177.
61. William George, *My Brother and I* (London: Eyre & Spottiswoode, 1958), 223.
62. Lucy Masterman, *C. F. G. Masterman: A Biography* (New York: Augustus M. Kelley, 1969), 133.
63. Richard Lloyd George, *My Father Lloyd George* (New York: Crown Publishers, 1960), 120; for a similar description see diary entry for 30 May 1936, A. J. P. Taylor, ed., *Lloyd George: A Diary by Frances Stevenson* (New York: Harper & Row, 1971), 323.
64. Grigg, *People's Champion*, 178.
65. George, *My Brother and I*, 228.
66. Gilbert, *Architect of Change*, 382.
67. Ibid., 382.
68. Ibid., 383.
69. Grigg, *People's Champion*, 201.
70. Ibid., 209.
71. Ibid., 212.
72. M. Asquith, *Autobiography*, 2:93.
73. Spender and Asquith, *Life of Asquith*, 1:257.
74. Ibid., 258.
75. Gilbert, *Architect of Change*, 393.
76. HHA to Edward VII, 3 Nov. 1909, BL, MS. Asquith 5, ff. 167–68.
77. Gilbert, *Architect of Change*, 397.
78. *Hansard*, 5, 13, 546–81, 2 Dec. 1909.
79. Adams, *Balfour*, 241.
80. Spender and Asquith, *Life of Asquith*, 1:261.
81. Murray, *People's Budget*, 244–46.
82. Riddell, *More Pages*, 18.
83. Louis Harcourt to HHA, 26 Jan. 1910, BL, MS. Asquith 12, f. 79A.
84. Jenkins, *Asquith*, 204; Grigg, *People's Champion*, 246.
85. Masterman, *C. F. G. Masterman*, 158–59.
86. Spender and Asquith, *Life of Asquith,* 1:272.

87. HHA to Edward VII, BL, MS. Asquith 5, f. 180, 10 Feb. 1910.
88. Gilbert, *Architect of Change*, 404.
89. Spender and Asquith, *Life of Asquith*, 1:272.
90. Grigg, *People's Champion*, 245–46.
91. Spender and Asquith, *Life of Asquith*, 1:272.
92. Ibid., 1:273.
93. Arthur C. Murray, *Master and Brother: Murrays of Elibank* (London: John Murray, 1945), 39; *Hansard*, 5, 14, 56, 21 Feb. 1910.
94. *Hansard*, 5, 14, 53–61, 21 Feb. 1910.
95. Spender and Asquith, *Life of Asquith*, 1:274.
96. Ibid.
97. Ibid., 1:277.
98. Grigg, *People's Champion*, 253, Gilbert, *Architect of Change*, 407.
99. Murray, *Master and Brother*, 46.
100. Masterman, *C. F. G. Masterman*, 162.
101. Ibid.
102. Spender and Asquith, *Life of Asquith*, 1:278.
103. HHA to Edward VII (copy), 13 Apr. 1910, BL, MS. Asquith 5, ff. 208–9.
104. *Hansard*, 5, 16, 1547–48, 14 Apr. 1910.
105. *Hansard*, 5, 16, 1762–64, 18 Apr. 1910.
106. Murray, *People's Budget*, 285.
107. M. Asquith, *Autobiography*, 2:100.
108. Ibid., 2:101.
109. Asquith, *Fifty Years*, 100–10.
110. *Hansard*, 5, 17, 794, 11 May 1910.
111. Spender and Asquith, *Life of Asquith*, 282.
112. Corine Comstock Weston, "The Liberal Leadership and the Lords' Veto, 1907–1910," in Clyve Jones and David Lewis Jones, eds., *Peers, Politics and Power: The House of Lords, 1603–1911* (London: Hambledon, 1986), 503.
113. Earl of Oxford and Asquith, *Memories*, 1:236.
114. Ibid.; No official records of the conference have been found and the only historical record are notes taken by Chamberlain and Lansdowne. See Weston, "The Liberal Leadership and the Lord's Veto, 1907–1910," 504, n. 4.
115. For a detailed discussion of the Ripon Plan and its place in the Constitutional Conference, see Weston, "The Liberal Leadership and the Lord's Veto, 1907–1910."
116. "A Suggested Scheme for Dealing with Deadlocks," NA., 21 July 1910, CAB. 37/103/34.
117. Weston, "The Liberal Leadership and the Lords' Veto, 1907–1910," 508.
118. Spender and Asquith, *Life of Asquith*, 289.
119. Weston, "The Liberal Leadership and the Lords' Veto, 1907–1910," 527.
120. *Hansard*, 5, 19, 2529, 29 July 1910.
121. Spender and Asquith, *Life of Asquith*, 1:290.
122. HHA to Lloyd George, 8 Nov. 1910, Gilbert, *Architect of Change*, 426.
123. Spender and Asquith, *Life of Asquith*, 1:291.
124. HHA to MA, 3 Nov. 1910, BL, MS. Eng. c. 6690, ff. 240–41.

125. Sir Almeric Fitzroy, *Memoirs* (New York: George H. Doran, 1925), 2:422.
126. Spender and Asquith, *Life of Asquith,* 1:295–96.
127. Ibid., 1:296.
128. Ibid., 1:297.
129. M. Asquith, *Autobiography,* 2:109.
130. Ibid., 2:110.
131. Earl of Oxford and Asquith, *Memories,* 1:238.
132. Ibid.
133. M. Asquith, *Autobiography,* 2:109.
134. Asquith, *Fifty Years,* 2:111.
135. Spender and Asquith, *Life of Asquith,* 1:310.
136. Ibid., 1:312.
137. Ibid., 1:312–13.
138. Masterman, *C. F. G. Masterman,* 153.
139. John Grigg, *Lloyd George: From Peace to War* (London: Methuen, 1985), 109.
140. Peter Rowland, *The Last Liberal Governments: The Promised Land, 1905–1910* (London: Barrie & Rockcliff, 1968), 132.
141. *Hansard,* 5, 187, 223–28, 30 Mar. 1908.
142. Ibid., 237.
143. *Times,* 11 Dec. 1909, 8.
144. *Times,* 19 Jan. 1910, 10.
145. Spender and Asquith, *Life of Asquith,* 2:15.
146. Asquith, *Fifty Years,* 2:152 using a phase employed in his speech to his constituents on 5 Oct. 1912. *Times,* 7 Oct. 1912, 9.
147. *Hansard,* 5, 36, 1424–25, 11 Apr. 1912.
148. Testimony also showed that the Master of Elibank had invested Liberal Party funds in 3,000 American Marconi shares.
149. Jenkins, *Asquith,* 252.
150. Harold Nicholson, *King George V: His Life and Reign* (London: Constable, 1952), 210.
151. Brock, *Letters to Venetia Stanley,* 22.
152. Spender and Asquith, *Life of Asquith,* 2:19–20.
153. Asquith, *Fifty Years,* 2:153.
154. Ibid., 2:154.
155. HHA to MA, 7 Oct. 1913, BL, MS. Eng. c. 6691, ff. 81–82.
156. Grigg, *From Peace to War,* 116.
157. "Most Secret–Government of Ireland Bil," September 1913, BL, MSS Asquith 38, f. 164 (entire document quoted in Spender and Asquith, *Life of Asquith,* 31–32) (King's response is BL, MS. Asquith 38, ff. 202–9).
158. George V to HHA, 19 Sept. 1913, BL, MS. Asquith 38, ff. 175–76.
159. Grigg, *From Peace to War,* 117.
160. Spender and Asquith, *Life of Asquith,* 2:36.
161. Ibid., 2:37.
162. Ibid., 2:36.

163. Ian Colvin, *Carson the Statesman* (New York: Macmillan, 1935), 267.
164. *Hansard*, 5, 58, 52, 10 Feb. 1914.
165. Denis Gwynn, *Life of Lord Redmond* (London: George C. Harp, 1932), 250.
166. Asquith, *Fifty Years*, 2:162.
167. Spender and Asquith, *Life of Asquith,* 2:37.
168. Ibid., 2:40.
169. Grigg, *From Peace to War*, 120.
170. Spender and Asquith, *Life of Asquith,* 2:41.
171. Ibid.
172. Ibid.
173. Ibid., 42.
174. Asquith, *Fifty Years*, 2:167.
175. Spender and Asquith, *Life of Asquith,* 2:46.
176. Asquith, *Fifty Years*, 2:168.
177. *Hansard*, 5, 60, 842, 30 Mar. 1914.
178. Spender, *Life, Journalism and Politics*, 2:2.
179. Asquith, *Fifty Years*, 2:171.
180. Spender and Asquith, *Life of Asquith,* 2:50.
181. Ibid., 51.
182. Asquith, *Fifty Years*, 2:175.
183. *Hansard*, 4, 65, 1601, 30 July 1914.
184. Rowland, *Last Liberal Governments,* 342–44.
185. HHA to George V, 25 Jan. 1913, BL, MS. Asquith 7, ff. 7–8.
186. HA to VS, 27 Jan. 1913, Brock, *Letters to Venetia Stanley*, 27.
187. *Hansard*, 4, 52, 1911–12, 6 May 1913.
188. Esher, *Journals and Letters*, 2:378.

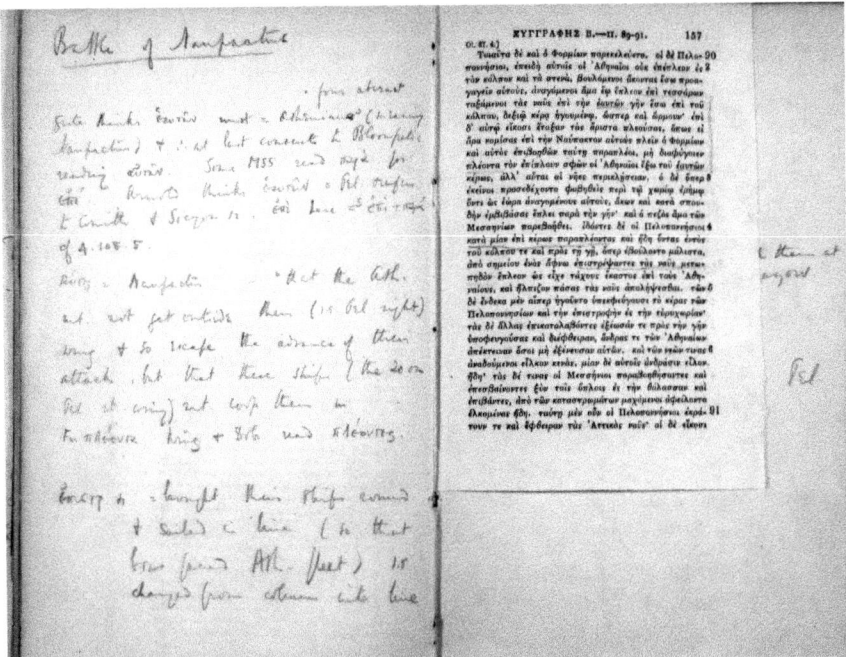

Asquith's copy of Herodoti Historia with his marginal notations, Balliol College, 1873. Author's personal collection.

The young barrister—Asquith in 1876. © Alamy.com/Paul Brown.

Helen Melland, Asquith's first wife, 1877. © Alamy.com/Pictorial Press.

The Home Secretary—Asquith in 1894. © Alamy.com/ Cassell's Century Edition History of England after a photograph by John Thompson.

Margot Asquith (née Tennant), Asquith's second wife, 1910. © GettyImages.com/Bentley Archive/Popperfoto.

Asquith, cartoon by "Spy" (Leslie Ward) from Vanity Fair, *London, July 1904.* © Alamy.com/World History Archive.

Sir Edward Grey, Secretary of State for Foreign Affairs, 1905–1916. © Alamy.com/ Hilary Morgan.

David Lloyd George, c. 1910. © Alamy.com/GL Archive.

Asquith leaving the Board of Trade, 1911. © Alamy.com/PA Archive.

Winston Churchill, First Lord of the Admiralty (left) and Admiral John Fisher, 1st Baron Fisher, 1913. © Alamy.com/PA Archive.

Field Marshall Herbert Kitchener, 1st Earl Kitchener, Secretary of State for War, 1914–1916. © Alamy.com/ GL Archive.

Asquith watching soldiers adjusting fuses, France, 1916. © Alamy.com/Historica Graphica Collection.

Asquith leaving Richmond Barracks after conversations with captured Irish republicans, May 1916. © Alamy.com/PA Archives.

1st Earl and Countess of Oxford and Asquith, c. 1926. © Alamy.com/Scherl/Süddeutsche Zeitung.

Chapter Seven

Family Troubles and the Road to War (1905–1914)

When Asquith became Prime Minister in April 1908, his work intensified considerably. Each and every day Parliament was in session was filled with public duties and responsibilities. Then there were those countless and never-ending cabinet meetings, private conferences, public meetings with delegations, and committee meetings. Despite the heavy burdens of his office, he found time for his family, friends, and other relaxations, made possible largely by keeping to his long habit of leading a compartmentalized life. He completed his work with incredible efficiency, almost always within the normal office hours. Completely separate was the remainder of the day strictly reserved for the pleasures of his private life.

Asquith had lost the spare frame of his youth and had become somewhat portly, which gave him the appearance of a rather prosperous Edwardian. Almost all the photographs from the period show him in need of a haircut, his white mane flowing out from underneath his hat. Although not perhaps in as good physical shape as in his youth, he continued to have a constitution that he himself described as equally made up of iron and leather. He was rarely ill except for an occasional cold and went to a dentist only twice until he was well into his sixties. His constitution did not include competence at mundane activities. He could almost appear clumsy at times—Margot often said he couldn't even strike a match. But he was a fairly good at billiards, and at one of his most favorite pastimes, golf; although his drives left much to be desired, his performance on the putting green was always impressive.

Contemporaries commented often on his drinking habits. This was particularly true of his enemies, who alleged that he drank to excess, derisively referring to him as "Squiff." Even his friends at one time or another became concerned about the level of his drinking. In 1904 Haldane voiced concern about the amount of champagne he was drinking, and during the committee stage of the 1911 Parliament bill some claimed he appeared on the front bench too drunk to speak.[1] In the spring of 1912 he experienced one of his few illnesses while Prime Minister, a near physical collapse that frightened Margot so much as to call a physician to examine him. The diagnosis: "blood pressure on an exhausted brain while eating and drinking the same amount as if he had not been using his brain to the very utmost." His doctor urged him to cut back on his drinking, and Margot even threatened to leave him unless he cut back. This had a sobering effect, and although he never quit drinking, he did cut back substantially.[2]

No doubt Asquith could on occasion drink a great deal of wine and brandy at the dinner table, and there were rare occasions when he appeared late at night in Parliament somewhat worse for the wear. As others have noted, the tales of his drinking bouts are almost certainly exaggerated. Even if one accepts them as true, his enemies admitted that Asquith inebriated could still be quite a force to reckon with. The Earl of Crawford entered in his diary in December 1912: "Asquith remains the master hand, and the only gentleman of the lot: 'he can speak better drunk than any of us can speak when sober'—a comment of B. L. [Bonar Law] the other day when Squiff shuffled through an intricate problem with skill and éclat notwithstanding the obvious effects of copious libations."[3] There is also evidence of actual moderation, particularly after 1912. Visiting The Wharf in December of that year, J. A. Pease noted, "All Asquith took for dinner in the way of liquor was a whisky and soda and a glass of mild port from the wood; at 12 a tumbler of perrier water; and I am told except when dining out he rarely takes more."[4] The real proof, however, that Asquith was never in any real danger of letting his drinking get the best of him was the prodigious work load that he carried day in and day out almost until the end of his life. There is no evidence—indeed contemporaries who commented negatively about his drinking never alleged—that either the quantity or the quality of his work was ever any the worse for his drinking. Neither is there any indication he was ever intoxicated at any of the numerous cabinet meetings, personal interviews, or other important conferences. Perhaps the most telling bit of evidence is, as Colin Clifford has noted, that all of the many letters he wrote to his friend Venetia Stanley and other confidantes, some late at night, are perfectly lucid and legible.[5]

The Parliamentary recesses in late summer always provided Asquith and his family with the opportunity to get out of London for an extended period. For the late summer and early autumn of 1908, the family went to the Earl of Erroll's Slains Castle on the Aberdeenshire coast in Scotland. The trip was marked by an incident where Violet, walking alone, slipped off a cliff onto a ledge below and lay unconscious. She was finally discovered after a frantic search. Violet had given her father and her stepmother quite a scare, but she survived the incident unharmed. The national papers were filled with the incident.

This otherwise insignificant episode once again aggravated the already tense relationship between Margot and Violet. As Violet had grown older, she and her stepmother crossed swords more and more often. Asquith of course was caught in the middle of these frequent disputes between two strong-willed women. It this particular case, Margot decided that Violet was enjoying the publicity surrounding the incident too much and proceeded to tell some of her stepdaughter's friends exactly that. Word got around to Violet, and Margot had to take all kinds of steps to mend the situation.[6]

The family suffered another shock with Violet late November the next year when they learned that one of Violet's serious suitors, Archie Gordon, the twenty-five-year-old youngest son of the 7th Earl of Aberdeen, had been seriously injured in an automobile accident near Winchester. Archie happened to have been the young man who carried Violet back to the house after she had her fall the year before. Violet immediately hurried to Winchester, but Archie was too injured to be seen by anyone but his parents. Although Asquith was in the middle of preparations for the first Parliamentary election of 1910, he traveled to Winchester with his son Beb to comfort a distraught Violet. While there, Asquith wrote a revealing letter to Margot.

> It is a grief to me that the two women I care for the most should be on terms of almost chronic misunderstanding. Violet is no doubt often self-centered and inconsiderate, and it may be that a little more coercion would have been good for her. But she is at present suffering acutely—more than she has ever suffered in her life—and showing on the whole admirable self-control (as Lady Aberdeen assured me) though she is constantly on the verge of breaking down. No one could have seen her yesterday—when almost the last gleam of hope was vanishing—without being deeply moved.[7]

It soon became apparent that Archie was about to die. When Violet was finally allowed to see him on December 14, although both knew that there was little hope of his survival, the two became engaged. Asquith arrived later that afternoon, and when Violet told him of their engagement, her father held back tears and congratulated both of them, saying, "I've always wished it Archie—I've always wished it." Archie then asked to be kissed and blessed, after which Asquith departed, saying "divine man" and remarking to the nurse, "there goes the finest man alive!"[8]

This episode became yet another occasion for renewed conflict between Margot and Violet. Although Margot thought it a mistake, the day after Archie's death, an announcement appeared in the newspapers of his deathbed engagement to Violet. At the funeral, Violet sat behind the coffin between her father and Archie's mother, Lady Aberdeen. After the funeral, the drama and sadness of the previous few weeks was almost too much for Violet, who began to unravel. She came dangerously close to becoming addicted to veronal, a barbiturate used as a sedative. When Margot confronted Asquith with the news of Violet's excessive use of veronal, he refused to believe her. This resulted in the first serious quarrel in the Asquiths' married life. "Henry spoke to me for the first time in his life cruelly and harshly," Margot reported in her diary. She told him "that there was no kindness in never telling the truth to Violet or standing up to her." The storm apparently passed. As he campaigned in the West Country during the Parliamentary election a bit later, he took a moment to write to Margot on January 6: "I am delighted at the better reports and that you and Violet have had a really good talk. I never said or thought that you were hard. No one knows as well as I do the warmth and tenderness of your heart. It was simply a question of how to deal most gently and wisely with a particular phase in Violet's condition." He ended the letter with an almost pathetic plea, "I long for each to understand the other, and I believe you will."[9]

During this period, Asquith's other children were not nearly as difficult to manage as Violet. His oldest son, Raymond, was successfully building his practice as a barrister in London. In October 1908, Raymond's wife Katherine gave birth to a daughter, Asquith's first grandchild, christened Helen after Raymond's mother. Writing to Margot, Asquith described the child as "a very healthy little creature weighing 9 lbs, wreathed in fat, and with good complexion considering its age."[10] Like all young barristers, even though the son of the Prime Minister, Raymond progressed at the Bar slowly, and he did not particularly enjoy his profession. In 1910, however, he was appointed to the legal team representing Britain at an arbitration in the Hague concerning a dispute between Canada and the United States over Newfoundland fishing rights. At the Hague a second daughter, Perdita, was born.

Beb, three years younger than his brother Raymond, was also practicing law in London. In 1904 he had met and fallen in love with Cynthia Charteris, daughter of Lord and Lady Elcho, later the 11th Earl and Countess of Wemyss. At first Cynthia had been much more interested in Beb's younger brother Oc, but she eventually turned her attentions to Beb. The Charteris family happened to be strongly Tory in their politics and did not approve of the Asquiths. With patience Beb eventually prevailed over Cynthia's parents' misgivings, and the couple married in July 1910. Beb appears to have disliked the Bar even more than Raymond but eventually came to deal with his misgivings. The couple had a son, John, born in May 1911.

Oc continued in his civil service job in the Sudan, and although he enjoyed his work and was well-respected not just by fellow civil servants but also by many Sudanese, he longed to return to England. Violet was able to visit him in the winter of 1910–1911.

While his older brothers were making names for themselves in the world, Cys was accumulating an outstanding academic record at Oxford. A student at Balliol, he earned a first in Mods, and like his brother Raymond won the coveted Ireland Prize in 1911. As if that was not enough, he trumped both his brother and his father when he was awarded the prestigious Hertford Prize in classics, an achievement they had never attained. Bursting with pride, Asquith wrote to Margot that "Cys has really done splendidly," adding that his son's achievement was "a record."[11]

Asquith and Margot took an important step in their lives toward the end of 1911 when they acquired the Mill House, the neighboring structure, "The Wharf," and outbuildings, including a barn in the village Sutton Courtenay, a few miles down the Thames from Oxford. The property, for which they paid £1,300, was in rough condition, but their architect Walter Cave reassured them that for another £3,000 the property could be fully restored and remodeled. As always, however, the Asquiths were short of cash. In what would shock modern sensibilities of political propriety, Margot approached a person who had substantial dealings with the British government, her friend the famous American financier J. Pierpont Morgan, who more than gladly advanced them the £3,000 they needed to improve their new country home. The original buildings dated back to the early nineteenth century. The Asquiths' extensive renovation converted The Wharf, which became their residence, into a two-story, timber-framed house of red and random gray brick in English bond style with an old plain-tile hipped roof. Margot also remodeled the old barn directly on the river to serve as accommodation for the overflow from their many weekend parties.

The Wharf became yet another venue for the Asquiths' almost compulsive and certainly lavish entertainment of colleagues, friends, and family. In many ways this was masking troubling problems the couple faced. For despite the outward appearances of normalcy, whether they themselves recognized it or not, Asquith and Margot's relationship had deteriorated. To begin with there was the problem of Violet. Both Violet and Margot adored Asquith, and he them, but the two women endured each other in a state of constant friction. Even more significant than this difficulty, Margot's behavior over the years had become more and more erratic, and this was beginning to erode the Asquiths' amity. Margot had always been a high-strung, nervous woman, but her health in recent years had declined, especially since the loss of her child in 1906. She constantly suffered from major and minor illnesses, some real and some imagined. A "sort of nerve break-down," as she described it, that she suffered soon after the Marconi scandal, was typical of these medical episodes. "I looked and felt ugly," she complained, and "I was irritable, over-wrought and useless."[12] She even lost her power of speech for a period of time. All these bouts with illness could not help but affect her personality in a negative way. She became almost constantly critical of those around her. Reginald McKenna's wife, Pamela, confided to a friend, "Margot I find rather trying as a visitor, she criticizes everything incessantly . . . and always in the unkindest way; . . . but I know she never means to be wounding and I do feel so sorry for her, as she makes herself terribly unhappy."[13] Unfortunately, the criticisms were not limited to Margot's social acquaintances; she also found herself in trouble for her harsh critiques of cabinet members and other politicians. Living with her became increasingly a trial for Asquith. She was always impatient when, while relaxing, he tended to retell tales she had heard before. To a man like Asquith, who liked to compartmentalize his work and his relaxation, he found it particularly annoying to put up with Margot's political commentary while trying to get away from it all. He told Violet, "I have sometimes walked up and down that room till I felt as tho' I were going mad. . . . When one needed to rest to have a thing like the *Morning Post* leader flung at one—all the obvious reasons for and against things more controversially put even than one's colleagues."[14]

In January 1912, Asquith took a holiday in Sicily with Edwin Montagu, his former Parliamentary Private Secretary, now serving as the Under Secretary of State for India. Joining the two men, in what Asquith later described as "one of the most interesting and delightful fortnights in our lives," were Violet and her friend, twenty-four-year-old Venetia Stanley, youngest daughter of Edward Lyulph Stanley, 4th Baron Sheffield and Stanley of Alderley.[15] Since 1907 Venetia had been part of a group of vivacious, clever, and attractive young women with whom Asquith enjoyed surrounding himself. These included the actress Viola Tree, daughter of the Asquiths' friends Maude and Herbert Beerbohm Tree; Dorothy Beresford, eldest daughter of the Rector of Easton Grey; Margot's niece, Lillian Tennant; and Pamela Jekyll, who later married Reginald McKenna. Margot derisively referred to them in her diary as her husband's "little harem."[16] Two years before the trip to Sicily, Venetia had endeared herself to Violet and to Asquith because of her helpful care and support for Violet at the time of Archie Gordon's death.

Venetia came from a leading Liberal family and happened to be a first cousin of Winston Churchill's wife, Clementine. She was physically attractive, although not one of the great beauties of the day. Her friend Sir Lawrence Jones described her as having "dark-eyed, aquiline good looks and a masculine intellect."[17] Like most women of her class educated by governesses and tutors, she had no formal education, but she was nevertheless intelligent and widely read. She also had a number of outdoor interests and was an avid bird-watcher. As she matured into her twenties, she developed a knack for providing relaxing, entertaining, and yet non-threatening company to men, particularly men who were looking desperately for a respite from the pressures of demanding political responsibilities. Many contemporaries commented on her almost uncanny ability to comfort, to listen to, and to empathize with these leaders. Brendan Bracken, close friend of Winston Churchill, once said that Venetia was one of the few people who could bring Churchill out of his famous periods of depression. She "used to laugh at Winston, and take him by the scruff of the neck and tell him not to go on looking at his plate like a booby."[18]

Shortly after their return from Sicily, Venetia was a weekend guest of the Prime Minister at Hurstly, a house lent to him near Lymington. Writing several years later, Asquith revealed, "I was sitting with her [Venetia] in the dining room on Sunday morning—the others being out in the garden or walking—and we were talking and laughing just on our old accustomed terms." He then confessed, "Suddenly, in a single instant, without premonition on my part or any challenge on hers, the scales dropped from my eyes; the familiar features & smile & gestures & words assumed an absolutely new perspective; what had completely hidden from me was in a flash half-revealed, and I dimly felt, hardly knowing, not at all understanding it, that I had come to a turning point in my life."[19]

Thus began what can only be described as a romantic relationship between Asquith and Venetia that was to last for just over three years. Despite Asquith's description of the "single instant" at Hurstly, it took some time for the relationship to develop. Toward the end of the year, she made her first visit to The Wharf. "It was delicious seeing him again. I hadn't any kind of talk with him since the end of the summer. He was in very good spirits I thought in spite of the crisis [Ulster]. He didn't as you can imagine talk much about it and our conversation ran in very well worn lines, the sort that he enjoys on these occasions and which irritate Margot so much by their dreariness. I love every well-known word of them—with and for me familiarity is a large part of the charm."[20] At first he wrote to her only occasionally, but as the editors of his correspondence to her have accurately observed, in early 1914 when the pressures of his office caused by the situation in Ireland began to increase considerably, the character and the number of the letters began to change. In his own words, Asquith said that they reached "the stage in our drives when we began to talk not only of persons & books but of things, & of my interests, politics &c; and I began to acquire the habit, first of taking you into confidence, & then of consulting & relying on your judgment."[21] By the spring of 1914 he was writing to her about three times a week, almost always prefacing his notes with "My Darling." Although her correspondence to him has been destroyed, the cache of over 560 letters from Asquith to Venetia, comprising approximately 300,000 words, constitutes without a doubt what the editors of the letters have described as "the most remarkable self-revelation ever given by a British Prime Minister."[22]

Asquith's close relationship with Venetia largely remained a secret. In those days the press was much more discreet and never commented on the frequency with which the Prime Minister was seen with Miss Stanley. Suspicion was also thrown off by the fact that Asquith already had a reputation for enjoying the company of young women, and so Venetia must not have stood out among the many young women that socialized with the Prime Minister. Margot, however, apparently knew of her husband's infatuation with Venetia almost from the very beginning and was far from happy about it. She wrote to Edwin Montagu in March 1914, "If Venetia had an ounce of truth and candor . . . I should smile; but she is even teaching Henry to avoid telling me things . . . I'm far too fond of H. to show him how ill and miserable it makes me . . ."[23]

Remarkably, throughout the time of her relationship with Asquith, Venetia was also able to encourage the amorous intentions of Edwin Montagu. Since their trip to Sicily, the young Liberal leader had also been in love with Venetia and even proposed to her in the summer of 1912. She accepted but later changed her mind. The great complicating factor in their relationship, however, was that Montagu's father, Lord Swaythling, who died in 1911, had left all his wealth in trust for his children with the proviso that if any of them abandoned the Jewish faith or married a gentile, they would be disinherited. If she were to marry Montagu, she would either have to change her faith or live in comparative poverty. Eventually in May 1915 she decided to marry Montagu and convert to Judaism. Asquith immediately ended his correspondence and relationship with Venetia.

Until 1914, domestic politics and policy had always been the central focus of Asquith's political career. The index of his two-volume work *Fifty Years of British Parliament* lists only one reference to France and no reference whatsoever to Germany. Even when he became Prime Minister, on matters of foreign affairs he largely deferred to his close friend Sir Edward Grey, the Foreign Secretary. Asquith himself admitted, "Between him and myself there was daily intimacy and unbroken confidence. I can hardly recall any occasion on which we had a difference of opinion which lasted for more than half an hour."[24] A close examination of the historical record reveals that Asquith did in fact have definite views on foreign policy, particularly European affairs, and his actions as Prime Minister were specifically designed to ensure that British foreign policy was in line with his understanding of events and their implications.

When the Liberal government came to power in December 1905, it was immediately confronted with a serious dispute between Germany and France, what became known as the First Moroccan crisis. Over the previous two and a half decades, Germany had been pursuing a more and more aggressive foreign policy. It had garnered colonies in South West Africa, the Cameroons, and East Africa, and its policy of *Drang nach Osten* advanced German interests in the Middle East. All of this, combined with an ambitious naval rearmament, was leading to an ever more dangerous political atmosphere in Europe. Beginning in 1905 the Germans set out to challenge the French position of dominance in Morocco, the economic and political status of which Asquith described as "a smouldering, international firebrand, which after intervals of quiescence, leapt from time to time into flame."[25]

Just as the Liberals assumed office in December 1905, the Moroccan crisis again heated up. Germany called up reserve units on December 30, and the French responded by moving troops to the German border on January 3. At this crucial juncture the French Ambassador, Paul Cambon, asked Grey, the new Foreign Secretary, if France could count on British armed support should France and Germany go to war. Grey could not answer the question without cabinet consultation, and such consultation was impossible until the end of the current election the Liberals had called. Grey and Cambon also discussed the advisability of direct communication between the military authorities of both nations as to contingencies for cooperation in case of war. Secretary of War Haldane met with Campbell-Bannerman and obtained the Prime Minister's permission to allow military discussions to take place, provided both sides clearly understood that such discussions would in no way commit the British government to support France in case of war. And so British staff officers began discussions with their French counterparts on January 16. Unbeknownst to those involved at the time, these discussions marked the first step down the road to Britain's joining France in war with Germany in 1914.

Later there was a great deal of controversy over the fact that Campbell-Bannerman and Grey never told the entire cabinet that military discussions with the French had been authorized and continued to take place even after the First Moroccan crisis subsided in May 1906. Only the Prime Minister, Grey, Haldane, the Marquess of Ripon (Lord privy seal), Baron Fitzmaurice in the Foreign Office, and Asquith knew.[26] It is not clear exactly when Asquith learned about the need for discussions with the French or that they were taking place. Asquith's official biographers, J. A. Spender and Cyril Asquith, claim that he did not learn about the discussions until after they were under way because he was out of London and not one of the ministers directly involved. In sharp contrast, Haldane's recollection implies that Asquith was informed even before the French were approached.[27] Whenever Asquith learned of these discussions, there is no doubt that he was included in the small group in the know, and that Campbell-Bannerman deliberately kept the rest of the cabinet in the dark, knowing that many ministers would strongly oppose his decision. Apparently the Prime Minister was willing to risk later criticism, convinced that Grey and the French fully understood that the talks meant no political commitment.[28] It was never Asquith's place to reveal this step to his colleagues. Years later, on the eve of Britain's entry into the First World War, when the existence of the discussions became highly controversial, both Asquith and Grey regretted that the full cabinet had not been informed. Even so, there is no question that from the outset both men fully approved. For Asquith, the advantages were obvious. "We had, indeed, a direct interest in the strategic aspects of an unprovoked German invasion of France: almost as direct as, and far more likely to become actual than, a German invasion of our own shores. . . ."[29]

Just six months after Asquith became Prime Minister in the fall of 1908, the British government faced its second major European political crisis. On October 6, Emperor Franz Joseph unilaterally announced Austria-Hungary's annexation of Bosnia-Herzegovina, leading to what became known as the First Bosnian Crisis.

The destabilization caused by the Austro-Hungarian annexation was immediate. Although it is unclear whether Germany had been informed prior to its ally's action, the Kaiser's government stood firmly behind their ally. Threatened, Serbia mobilized its army on October 7, demanding that the annexation be reversed or that Serbia receive some territorial compensation of its own. Russia believed that the Austro-Hungarians had dealt with them in bad faith and had hurriedly carried out the annexation before Russia's interests could be met. France and Italy favored some kind of Conference to settle the differences.

The position of Asquith, Grey, and the entire cabinet was resolute from the onset. On the very day Bulgaria announced its independence, Grey wrote to Sir Edward Goshen, British Ambassador in Berlin, setting out the government's policy. "A deliberate violation or alteration of the Berlin Treaty, undertaken without previous consultation with other Powers, of which Turkey is the most affected could never be approved or recognized by His Majesty's Government."[30] In this early statement, Grey alludes to the two principal ideas behind British policy. The first was Asquith's and Grey's abiding belief in the sanctity of international agreements. They were indifferent to territorial alterations, provided they took place in a legal manner with the approval of all signatories to the 1878 Treaty of Berlin. As Grey described it, "we felt that the arbitrary alteration of a European Treaty by one Power without the consent of the other Powers who were parties to it struck at the root of all good international order."[31] The second factor was Turkey. Asquith's government was sympathetic with the "Young Turks" who had overthrown the despotic regime of Sultan Abdul Hamid earlier in 1908 and wanted, if at all possible, to protect the struggling new government from unnecessary foreign policy humiliations. At the very least, the Ottoman Empire should be consulted and perhaps compensated for alterations in the status quo. To address the growing crisis, Grey proposed a conference of all the Treaty of Berlin's signatory powers for the purpose of addressing the issues raised by the rapidly changing situation.

It happened that in October Russian Foreign Minister Alexander Isvolsky accompanied the Tsar on his yacht to Cowes to meet with King Edward. This gave Asquith and Grey the opportunity to have a long conversation with Isvolsky about the growing tensions. Isvolsky favored a conference, but he further proposed altering the Treaty of Berlin to allow Russian warships to travel through the Straits of Constantinople. This was not a surprise. Grey later wrote, "I had foreseen from the beginning that, if we were to maintain friendly relations with Russia, we must abandon the policy of blocking her [Russia's] access to the sea."[32] Asquith reported to the King on October 12 that after much discussion, the cabinet concluded "(1) that Mr. Isvolsky should be informed that, in our opinion, it is highly inopportune to raise this question at the present juncture, and (2) that public opinion in Great Britain would not support any Government which, for no consideration to us, abandoned what has always been regarded here as a valuable Treaty right. The proper consideration of course would be that we and other nations should have a reciprocal right of ingress to the Black Sea."[33]

Grey got nowhere with his conference proposal. Austria-Hungary rejected the idea, and Germany stood firmly behind her ally in also refusing to participate. On November 6, Arthur Balfour related to Lord Landsdowne that Asquith was "extremely perturbed about the European situation, which, in his [Asquith's] view, was the gravest of which we have had any experience since 1870."[34]

Asquith used the occasion of one of his earliest public speeches as Prime Minister on November 9 at the Guildhall to call upon the great powers to work to preserve the peace of Europe. He asked his audience, "May I submit to you and to others outside these walls, there should be no talk at such a time of isolation, of hostile groupings, or rival combinations among the Powers, those Powers who are the joint trustees of civilization and of its greatest and paramount safeguard—the peace of the world." According to Asquith, Britain had only three objectives: "to maintain the public law of Europe, to secure for the new Turkish *regime* in Turkey just treatment and a fair chance and to promote the varied interests and susceptibilities which are involved as will present a disturbance of peace. . . ." He ended his remarks proclaiming that

Britain had "neither animosities to gratify nor selfish interests to advance" and would not "be reluctant to grasp the hand that is extended to us in goodwill and in good faith."[35]

Diplomatic negotiations merely continued to heighten tensions throughout the winter of 1908–1909. In January, the Austro-Hungarians were able to buy off the Turks by agreeing to pay an indemnity of £2.5 million, allowing the Turks to increase their custom duties, and agreeing to totally evacuate the Sanjak of Novi Pazar in the territory of present-day Montenegro, Serbia, and Kosovo. Germany informed the Russians that unless they recognized the annexation of Bosnia-Herzegovina, Germany would give Austria-Hungary a free hand, which would almost certainly mean a war involving all the European powers. With this threat Russia backed down, and the Bosnian Crisis finally came to an end.

This was no victory for British foreign policy. What Asquith and Grey had sought was a regularized and more formal alteration of treaty obligations with all powers participating in the negotiation process. What happened was far from it. Individual states, acting on their own, had worked out the best deal they could for themselves under the circumstances. Russia was left humiliated. Britain, together with France and Italy, appeared helpless to avoid this haphazard end to the crisis.

In the summer of 1911, the "smouldering, international firebrand" Morocco once again ignited. A rebellion broke out against Moroccan Sultan Abd al-Hafid, and by April the Sultan was besieged in his palace in Fez. In support of the regime and to protect European lives and property, the French dispatched troops to Fez in late April to assist in putting down the rebellion. To ensure its own interests in Morocco, Spanish forces in June occupied Larache and later Ksar el-Kebir in northwest Morocco. Suddenly on July 1 the German gunboat *Panther* appeared at the port of Agadir. The Germans had once again in Asquith's term "rung the bell."[36] The Germans claimed that the presence of the *Panther* was merely to defend German nationals and property threatened by the rebellion. However, Agadir was not open to trade, and as Asquith put it, the Germans were defending "non-existent German interests against imaginary perils."[37] What was clear to Asquith and the British Admiralty from the outset and what they feared was that the Germans ultimately aimed to develop Agadir as an Atlantic naval base to be used at some point to threaten British trade.

The cabinet met, and Home Secretary Winston Churchill reported to his wife, "We decided to use pretty plain language to Germany and to tell her that if she thinks Morocco can be divided up without John Bull she is jolly well mistaken . . ."[38] The Germans held that the French movement of troops into Fez had altered the status quo in Morocco established by the Algeciras agreement in 1906, and as a result Germany was due some compensation. The British position was that, while Germany was perhaps due something, it must be reasonable and *not* include an Atlantic naval base. Grey met the German Ambassador, Count Metternich, on July 4 and told him that the British "attitude could not be a disinterested one with regard to Morocco" and "could not recognize any new arrangement which was come to without us."[39] Further he warned that if German demands were so unreasonable that no French government could accept them, then Britain public opinion would side with France.[40]

Normally the Foreign Secretary would have received an almost immediate reply after the Ambassador had had the opportunity to check with his government. In this case three weeks passed with no German response. On July 21 Lloyd George approached Grey with the idea of using his speech that evening at the Lord Mayor's annual dinner for the bankers of the City of London to raise indirectly the Moroccan issue and even presented a proposed text of his speech to the Foreign Secretary. Grey thought the idea a good one and approved the text. Almost certainly Asquith at some point was let in on the plan. He stated in *Genesis of the War* that, facing no German response, "it seemed to be necessary to make it clear that we were not to be ignored," and accordingly Lloyd George was given the green light.[41] A few days later, after Lloyd George's speech, the German Ambassador had told Grey that there could be no response from Germany to the British statement of policy.[42]

The crisis ultimately passed without further British intervention. Franco-German negotiations ultimately led to the Treaty of Fez. Nevertheless, the incident became the basis for a cabinet shuffle. Throughout the events of the summer of 1911, Winston Churchill, even though he was Home Secretary, vigorously engaged in military and naval matters. In letters and memoranda, he repeatedly offered his opinions on decisions well outside his purview. On September 13 he wrote to Asquith, asking, "Are you sure that the ships we have at Cromarty are strong enough to defeat the whole German High Sea fleet? If not they shd be reinforced without delay."[43] This insight and display of detailed knowledge impressed Asquith and convinced him that Churchill should replace McKenna at the Admiralty.

So it was in late September the Prime Minister invited Churchill to stay with him at Archerfield in Scotland. Before Asquith came to his final decision on moving Churchill to the Admiralty, Haldane had come to Archerfield to convince the Prime Minister that Haldane himself should become First Lord. Since Haldane had carried out the reorganization of the Army, he was the most qualified to handle the anticipated reorganization of the Navy.[44] Asquith listened but ultimately chose Churchill. As they were returning from golf,

Asquith abruptly asked Churchill if he would like to go to the Admiralty, to which he responded without hesitation, "Indeed I would."[45]

One of the great foreign policy conundrums for the British in the decade and a half leading up to the First World War was the Anglo-German naval race, discussed previously in the context of the battles over the budgets. When Asquith became Chancellor of the Exchequer in late 1905, he was determined to carry out economies to reduce or at least limit the growth of government expenditure. The Navy was to be no exception, and Asquith worked hard to keep naval estimates as low as possible. In July 1906, the Liberal government announced that it intended actually to reduce battleship construction by 25 percent, destroyer construction by 60 percent, and submarine construction by a third.[46]

About the time Asquith became Prime Minister, the Reichstag passed another naval law reducing the replacement period for ships from twenty-five years to twenty years. The practical effect of this measure was to increase the annual building program to four capital ships a year. When all the calculations were made, this new law meant that unless the British government increased its warship building program substantially, Germany might well have more capital ships than Britain by 1914. This threat along with the Liberals' desire to advance social programs, as we have seen, led to the need for much greater revenue and the introduction of the "People's Budget" of 1909. As to naval construction, the cabinet accepted Asquith's compromise to lay down four *Dreadnaught*-class battleships immediately and four additional ships within the same financial year or earlier if it became necessary.

Asquith and his cabinet were not about to let Germany gain naval superiority, but this resolve to maintain a dominant position came at a high price. The Liberals saw the increased naval expenditures as funds that could be better used for social reform. It seemed the only way out of this dilemma was to convince Germany to work with Britain to reduce the size of their respective fleets or at least slow the pace of naval construction. Time was of the essence. As 1912 dawned it was no secret that Germany was about to introduce yet another naval law, this time increasing their fleet with the creation of a third eight-battleship squadron. Even more seriously, if enacted such a program would mean that 80 percent of the entire German fleet would be ready for war at any given time. Not only was time short, but also there was what Asquith viewed to be a unique opportunity with the German Chancellor, Theobald von Bethman-Hollweg, whom Asquith believed shared the British cabinet's hope of decelerating the naval race.[47]

In January 1912 "some influential members of the Cabinet," according to Haldane, who did not name them, prepared a memorandum with suggestions for improving Anglo-German relations. Sir Ernest Cassell, a German-born merchant banker and capitalist, took the memorandum to Berlin and discussed it with Albert Ballin, a German businessman and general director of the Hamburg American line respected and admired by the Kaiser. Asquith may have had a hand in writing the memorandum or even knew that it had been given to Cassel. In any case, Cassell was a good friend of Asquith, and the Prime Minister was not averse to back channels. Through Ballin contact was made with the Kaiser, and Cassel returned to London with an invitation for the British government to send one of its members to confer with German ministers in Berlin.

For a number of years, the Kaiser had hoped that the British would send Sir Edward Grey to Berlin for discussions, but the cabinet, as Asquith informed the King, "while most anxious to take the fullest advantage of this or any other opportunity for a fresh start toward more cordial relations between the two countries," thought it premature to send the Foreign Secretary. Grey himself proposed and the cabinet agreed to send Haldane, an obvious choice because he spoke fluent German, was close to Asquith, had a friendly relationship with the Kaiser, and as Secretary for War was familiar with military affairs. In addition, the informality of the discussions could be preserved since Haldane in his role as Chairman of the London University Commission had an excuse to go to Germany at this time to look at German methods of clinical teaching. Asquith told the King this would present the opportunity for Haldane "at the same time to see the Emperor & the Chancellor, and, on the basis of the communications . . . to feel the way in the direction of a more definite understanding."[48] As a precaution, Grey informed French Ambassador Cambon of the project and assured him that no agreement would be made that would tie Britain's hands.[49]

Arriving in Germany, Haldane met first with Chancellor Bethman-Hollweg, whom he found "sincerely desirous of avoiding war," but Haldane told him that Britain "could not sit still if Germany elected to develop her fleet to such an extent as to imperil . . . [British] naval protection" and that Britain would continue to lay down two keels to match every one Germany laid down. His next meeting was with the Kaiser himself and Admiral von Tirpitz. They gave Haldane a copy of the draft naval law being prepared, and again he responded with the British position that a "fundamental modification was essential if better relations were to ensue."[50] The purpose of the Haldane mission was not to reach a specific agreement but to determine whether there were areas where some progress could be made. The result was disappointing. Germany was interested in reducing the pace of its naval program only if Britain was willing to agree to neutrality in the event of war between Germany and France. For the British this was out of the question, since such an agreement would be, in Grey's term, "the height of dishonour" and the end of the Britain's *Entente Cordiale* with France.[51] Although a few additional unofficial contacts with the Germans were made that summer, Germany would not back away from its demand for British neutrality, and so no agreement was ever reached. That summer the Reichstag passed the Naval Law of 1912, under which the German fleet would quickly grow to five squadrons of eight battleships each.

With the failure of the Haldane mission, Asquith and his cabinet now faced a very real and growing German naval threat. One possible response was naval cooperation with France, and already that spring the French naval attaché had inquired about possible cooperation in the event of war. France might prove useful to the British in a coordinated disposition of each nation's naval forces. Since 1904 the British had begun to concentrate naval forces in home waters as part of the Cawdor-Fisher reforms. Admiral Fisher and the Admiralty were able to carry out this concentration by bringing home an assortment of ships doing nothing more than "showing the flag" around the world. By 1912 the only way to further concentrate the fleet would be to withdraw capital ships from the Mediterranean. Before the failure of the Haldane mission, it was still thought possible that the British naval force in the Mediterranean could actually be *reinforced*. In January Asquith had forwarded to Churchill a memorandum by Lord Esher arguing for just such reinforcement. The Prime Minister thought the memorandum had "some good sense in it," although Churchill strongly disagreed and was already urging a greater concentration of forces closer to Britain, the only way to form a badly needed third battle squadron in home waters.[52] If this could be accomplished without too much risk, eventually enough ships could be constructed to replace the ones removed from the Mediterranean. With the French naval attaché pressing Grey and Churchill for an answer as to the question of coordination, the cabinet discussed the matter at length in May where, as Asquith told the King, "it became apparent that the whole Mediterranean situation must be resurveyed from the point of view of both policy and strategy." No commitment to the French was made at this time.[53]

A debate ensued both in the cabinet and in the Committee of Imperial Defence between those who supported a force divided between the North Sea and the Mediterranean and those who supported concentration in the North Sea. Eventually the latter position won out. On July 4 the Committee of Imperial Defence agreed that "there must always be provided a reasonable margin of superior strength ready and available in the Home waters."[54] In August the cabinet authorized naval conversations with France, which eventually led to an agreement signed on February 10, 1913. Under its terms British battleships would be withdrawn from the Mediterranean and concentrated in the North Sea. The French would do the reverse. The agreement made plain that this was not an alliance; it was merely to maximize efficiency *should* Britain decide to enter a war on the side of France.⁵⁵ This had been earlier reinforced in correspondence between Grey and Ambassador Cambon in November 1912, in which Grey wrote that both nations understood the military and naval conversations between the two nations did "not restrict the freedom of either Government to decide at any future time whether or not to assist the other by armed force."⁵⁶

Although not a formal alliance, the 1913 Anglo-French naval agreement had momentous implications. While it is true, as Churchill wrote to Asquith in August 1912, that even "If France did not exist, we should make no other disposition of our forces" than to concentrate ships in home waters. France had left itself highly vulnerable in the North Sea and English Channel.⁵⁷ Asquith wrote after the war that as a result of the agreement "France undoubtedly felt that she could calculate, in such a contingency [a German unprovoked attack of France], upon our vetoing any attack by sea upon her Northern and Western coasts, which were practically denuded of Naval protection by her concentration in the Mediterranean."⁵⁸ This is exactly what would happen in August 1914 and became the basis for Asquith's and Grey's strong support for Britain's entry into the war.

A redeployment of the fleet was not enough to meet the growing German naval threat. More ships would have to be built, and they were becoming more and more expensive. Churchill proposed to the Germans a "naval holiday" in March 1913, during which Britain and Germany would agree to postpone the planned construction of battleships. He repeated the offer in a speech in Manchester in October, but the Germans rejected the idea. As a result the First Lord of the Admiralty warned in a speech at the Guildhall on November 10 that the next naval estimates would be much larger due to the naval race with Germany.⁵⁹ As we saw in the last chapter, a bitter fight within the cabinet ensued over the naval estimates. Lloyd George opposed the proposed increases and made public his argument that such increases were unnecessary, particularly when Anglo-German relations were actually improving. Churchill and the Sea Lords threatened resignation if larger naval estimates were not accepted.⁶⁰ Asquith wrote to Margot on January 20, 1913: "I find the political affairs very much entangled, as Ll. G. And Winston are still poles apart over the Navy, and it looks as if it might eventually come to a breaking point." The situation was so serious that he went on to say that if the end of the government was inevitable, he would rather dissolve Parliament and have an election rather than suffer "smash-up" and resignation.⁶¹ Less than a week later there seemed to be some hope, and Asquith was able to tell Margot that it looked as if "LL.G. and Winston are anxious for an accommodation."⁶² Yet Churchill remained firm. "I do not love this naval expenditure & am grieved to be found in the position of taskmaster," he wrote Asquith on February 2. Nevertheless he was "the slave to facts & forces wh are uncontrollable unless naval efficiency is frankly abandoned."[63] Eventually a compromise was reached. Churchill got most of what he wanted in the naval estimates, thanks to what Churchill later described as the "unwearying patience of the Prime Minister, and his solid, silent support."[64] Naval estimates were increased by 5.7 percent over the original 1913–1914 estimates with a promise of a substantial reduction in the following year.[65]

Churchill's proposal of a "naval holiday" caught the attention of an important spectator to this series of events—the Americans. For months, the American Ambassador to Britain, Walter Hines Page, had been urging Woodrow Wilson to make a goodwill trip to England, but the President had been unable to do so because of the pressing affairs of a near-war with Mexico and tariff and currency battles in Congress. In December 1913 Colonel Edward House, close confidant to President Wilson, suggested to Sir William Tyrrell, private Secretary to Sir Edward Grey, that the United States together with Germany and Britain might still be able to bring about the "naval holiday" Churchill had suggested back in March. Tyrrell, according to House, thought "there was a good sporting chance of success."[66] Soon House's suggestion had grown into the possibility of an Anglo-American-German alliance. On January 14 House confidently wrote to Ambassador Page the "general idea is to bring about a sympathetic understanding between England, Germany, and America, not only upon the question of disarmament, but upon other matters of equal importance to themselves, and to the world at large."[67] Asquith greatly admired Page, describing him as "a loveable man, with a shrewd and penetrating judgment, and by no means a sentimentalist." Page was skeptical of the mission, but Wilson gave it his blessing, and House was soon on his way to Germany, then to France, and finally to London.[68]

House arrived in Berlin in the last week of May. He met with many important officials including Admiral von Tirpitz and was finally able to obtain an interview with the Kaiser on June 1. House, however, was discouraged by his talks with the Germans. The Kaiser seemed to be unstable, and Wilson's advisor deemed the militaristic clique the real threat. He was convinced that the military was determined to have its way and might even overthrow the Kaiser if he showed any intention of seeking a more peaceful future for Germany.[69]

House's talks with French officials proved no more encouraging. France was focused on domestic issues, and the government was so unstable as to make any discussion of a long-term solution to international tensions impossible.[70]

In contrast House received a warm welcome in London. He had sympathetic interviews with the leadership of the government including Grey, Lloyd George, and Asquith. The timing of the visit was unfortunate. Asquith and his cabinet had almost all their attention focused on the Irish Home Rule problem that was about to reach a critical juncture. Although House later told the President "how enthusiastically it [his plan] was received by the British Government, and how much they thought it would do toward bringing about a better understanding between the Great Powers," the President's advisor was apparently convinced that the British leadership simply did not see the urgency of the situation with Germany.[71] This can be borne out in House's description of a visit with Asquith after dinner on July 2. The two men discussed a wide variety of topics, mostly centered on the similarities of the Conservative opposition Asquith and President Wilson faced. The Prime Minister agreed with House's conclusion that "if the Conservatives of the two countries had their way, the end would probably be that many of them would be stripped of their wealth and hanged to lamp-posts." Yet there is no mention of the growing tensions in Europe.[72] Perhaps it is true that British officials, including Asquith, did not see the immediacy of the danger of war. However the British government had to be extremely careful in any discussions with Germany and America so as not to ruffle the sensibilities of the French and the Russians, who were rightly sensitive about any talks without them between Germany and Britain. Evidence comes from Grey's last request of House before the outbreak of the war. He asked President Wilson's representative to convey to the Kaiser his impressions of his discussions with the British. Grey was careful to point out to House that "he did not wish to send anything official or in writing, for fear of offending French and Russian sensibilities" and that he "thought it was one of those things that had best be done informally and unofficially."[73] This House did, but before there could be a response, war had broken out.

On June 28, Archduke Franz Ferdinand of Austria-Hungary was assassinated in Sarajevo, setting into motion a chain of events that would eventually lead to the outbreak of the First World War in August. Remarkably Europe remained relatively calm until the last week of July. As expected the Austro-Hungarian press stirred up outrage over the murder of the heir to the throne, and the Serbs for their part condemned the incident and promised cooperation in apprehending those responsible for the crime. It seemed European public opinion had become almost immune to the constant turmoil in the Balkans. Sir Edward Grey made it clear that Britain was willing to press Russia to consent to satisfaction of reasonable Austro-Hungarian demands on the Serbs. There was no alarm when the previously planned test mobilization of the British Third Fleet began with a grand review by the King of the whole fleet at Spithead in mid-July. If Asquith's regular letters to Venetia Stanley are to be believed, the Prime Minister himself at this point was unconcerned about the situation on the continent. He briefly referenced an "obituary" of the Archduke and his wife on June 30, but there is no mention of any incipient crisis until three weeks later on July 24. No doubt Asquith's main focus was on Ireland, even though Grey was keeping him closely informed of developments on the continent.

At the cabinet meeting on the afternoon of Friday, July 24, however, things began to change. This was the same day that the Buckingham Palace Conference on Irish Home Rule had ended without result. "Austria has sent a bullying and humiliating ultimatum to Servia who cannot possibly comply with it," Asquith wrote that day to Venetia, "and demanded an answer within 48 hours—failing which she will march." He continued, "This means, almost inevitably, that Russia will come on the scene in defence of Servia & in defiance of Austria and if so it is difficult both for Germany & France to refrain from lending a hand to one side or the other." He concluded that Europe was "within measurable, or imaginable, distance of a real Armageddon which would dwarf the Ulster & Nationalist Volunteers to their true proportion." He had immediately grasped the implications. Yet ever the optimist, he went on, "Happily there seems to be no reason why we should be anything more than spectators."[74] The following day Asquith reported to the King that the ultimatum "may be a prelude to a war in which at least four of the great Powers might be involved." He also stated that Grey was going to suggest to the German Ambassador the possibility of a "mediating group" comprising Britain, Germany, France, and Italy be organized.[75] On Sunday July 26, Grey formally invited representatives of these governments to meet in London.

Asquith's lawyer-like mind recognized that the Austro-Hungarians had a good case, but as he learned on July 26, even though Serbia was willing to give in on most points of the ultimatum, Austria-Hungary wanted a complete capitulation. He wrote that day, "The curious thing is that on many, if not most, of the points Austria has a good & Servia a very bad case," continuing, "[b]ut the Austrians are quite the stupidest people in Europe (as Italians are the most perfidious), and there is a brutality about their mode of procedure which will make most people think that this is a case of a big Power wantonly bullying a little one." To Asquith, however, Russia was the real culprit, "trying to drag us in."[76]

The cabinet met again on Monday afternoon. Grey reported that Austria considered the Serbian reply to its ultimatum a rejection of its conditions and that he had urged the German ambassador to try to get his government to persuade Austria-Hungary to take a more favorable view of the Serbian response. He also told the cabinet that while France and possibly Italy would agree to his call for a conference, Germany seemed "more than doubtful."[77] Asquith recorded, "We seem to be on the *very brink*."[78] In light of the grim news, the cabinet approved the action of the First Lord of the Admiralty taken the day before to postpone the dispersal of the First and Second fleets. Britain found herself between a rock and a hard place. Asquith perceptively and distinctly summed up Britain's predicament in his letter to the King the next day: "Germany says to us, 'If you will say at St. Petersburg that in no conditions will you come in and help, Russia will draw back and there will be no war.' On the other hand, Russia says to us, 'If you won't say you are ready to side with us now, your friendship is valueless, and we shall act on that assumption in the future.'"[79]

The cabinet now was meeting at least once and many times twice a day as the crisis accelerated. Grey continued his efforts to set up a conference to mediate the crisis, but time was fast running out. On Tuesday, July 28, Austria-Hungary declared war on Serbia and rejected Russia's suggestion to discuss the conflict directly with Russia. Asquith believed the only hope at this point was for Austria-Hungary and Russia, the two hollow empires, to iron out their differences.[80] As Asquith and the cabinet had understood from the very first, a war between Austria-Hungary and Russia would almost immediately draw Germany and France into the conflict. Further it was no secret that German war plans likely involved an invasion of France through Belgium, the neutrality of which had been guaranteed by Britain, France, and Germany in the 1830s. The next day the cabinet began to investigate the implications of such a violation. Their conclusion was that the Treaty of 1839 was somewhat unclear as to a nation's obligation to *maintain* Belgium's neutrality should one or more of the guaranteeing powers refused to respect it. All the cabinet was willing to do at this point was to instruct France and Germany that "at this stage we were unable to pledge ourselves in advance, either under all conditions to stand aside, or in any conditions to join in."[81] Asquith explained to Venetia in a letter that evening, "Of course we want to keep out of it, but the worst thing we could do would be to announce to the world at the present moment that in no circumstance would we intervene."[82]

That same day Grey met with the German Ambassador and warned him that he should not conclude from the cabinet's current viewpoint that Britain would not intervene under any circumstances. While he could not describe under exactly what circumstances Britain would feel compelled to go to war, "if the issue did become such that we [the British Government] thought British interests required us to intervene, we must intervene at once."[83]

That afternoon Churchill and his First Sea Lord, Prince Louis of Battenberg, decided it was necessary to send immediately the First Fleet from Portland into the North Sea to thwart any possible attempt by the Germans to attack the east coast. This maneuver would also signal the Germans that Britain was prepared if necessary to enter the war. Churchill feared, however, that the cabinet might reject the plan, "lest it should be mistakenly be considered a provocative action likely to damage the chance of peace." So he decided to take the matter up directly with Asquith that evening. After he had explained his plan, according to Churchill's later recollection, Asquith "looked at me with a hard stare and gave a sort of grunt. I did not require anything else." By July 31 the First Fleet had slipped undetected through the straits of Dover and was ready at its battle stations.[84] Following his meeting with Churchill, Asquith conferred with his closest friends, Grey and Haldane, until one o'clock in the morning, "talking over the situation, and trying to discover bridges & outlets."[85]

The next day, Thursday, July 30, Bonar Law reached Asquith by telephone and asked him to meet him and Edward Carson at Law's house in Kensington. When Asquith arrived, Law proposed that there should be a postponement of the Second Reading of the Irish Home Rule Amending bill "in the interest of the international situation." According to Asquith's version of the meeting, Law "thought that to advertise our domestic dissentions at this moment wd. weaken our influence in the world for peace &c."[86] Asquith was amenable and after checking with Grey, Lloyd George, and Redmond agreed that a postponement was in the best interests of the nation. In what Asquith described as "the first time in my experience of him," Redmond made a "really useful suggestion," which Asquith accepted, to suspend the operation of the Home Rule bill (now soon to be put on the Statute book) until the Amending bill could become law.[87]

Also that Thursday the Germans offered in Asquith's words to "buy our neutrality during the war by promises that she will not annexe French territory (except Colonies) or Holland & Belgium."[88] Grey was livid over the offer and replied to the Germans the next day that the British government would not "bargain away whatever interest we have as regards the neutrality of Belgium."[89]

On Friday morning the cabinet met once again at eleven o'clock and discussed the growing crisis and particularly what might happen if the Germans violated Belgium's neutrality. That afternoon Grey had what Asquith termed a "rather painful meeting" with the French Ambassador. Grey told him Britain was under no obligation, could give no pledges, and that Britain's actions "must depend upon the course of events, including the Belgian question and the direction of public opinion here."[90] That same day, with the Russians mobilizing their army and fleet, the Germans announced *Kriegsgefahr* (imminence of war) and sent an ultimatum to the Russians demanding the demobilization of its forces. If Russian demobilization did not begin to take place within twelve hours, the Germans would consider it necessary to mobilize totally its forces on both the Russian and French fronts.[91]

Soon after this Asquith received a message from Berlin to the effect that German Ambassador Lichnowsky's peace efforts had been frustrated by the

Tsar's decree calling for full mobilization. Asquith, working with his private secretaries and Sir Eric Drummond, drafted a direct appeal from King George to the Tsar. When completed at one thirty in the morning, Asquith rushed with Tyrrell to Buckingham Palace by taxi to be greeted by the King in his dressing gown over his night shirt. Asquith read to him the initial message and the proposed answer, which the King immediately approved. Asquith and Tyrell did, however, suggest that the letter be made more personal and direct by beginning "My dear Nicky" and signing it "Georgie."[92]

Unfortunately the King's message was too late. On Saturday, August 1, when Germany did not receive an answer to its ultimatum to the Russians, it ordered full mobilization and declared war on Russia. As expected this action triggered French mobilization which would, of course, mean war with Germany. Meeting that day, the cabinet focused its attention on Belgium. As Asquith put it, "The main controversy pivots upon Belgium & its neutrality."[93] He described the various positions at this critical moment:

> Ll. George—all for peace—is more sensible & statesmanlike, for keeping the position still open. Grey, of course, declares that if an out & out and uncompromising policy of non-intervention at all costs is adopted, he will go. Winston very bellicose & demanding immediate mobilization. Haldane diffuse . . . and nebulous.[94]

By Sunday the Germans had invaded the Grand Duchy of Luxemburg and delivered an ultimatum to Belgium demanding access through its territory. Asquith wrote at the time, "Things are pretty black," for there was no longer any doubt that Germany was about to invade Belgium. That morning at breakfast Count Lichnowsky, the German Ambassador, paid Asquith a call. He appeared to the Prime Minister to be "very émotionné" and agitated. As he wept, he begged Asquith not to side with France, arguing that with France and Russia against her Germany was now the underdog. Asquith once again reiterated that Britain would not intervene, provided Germany did not invade Belgium and did not send the German fleet into the English Channel to attack France.[95]

Later that morning the cabinet again met for three hours beginning at eleven. It was plain to all that Asquith's government was about to come apart. There was an intense debate over whether Grey should reassure the French that Britain would not allow the German fleet to enter the English Channel to attack France. At one point during the meeting, Asquith received a letter from Bonar Law and Lord Landsdowne pledging their support and that of their Conservative colleagues for the government in favor of France and Russia.[96] John Burns immediately announced his resignation but agreed not to go public until the cabinet met again that evening. By this point the cabinet had divided into three groups: those who opposed intervention no matter what; opposite stood Grey, Asquith, and Churchill, who were not going to let the French ports be attacked; somewhere between were Lloyd George, Crewe, McKenna, and Samuel.

All along Asquith had worked hard to keep the cabinet together and the country united. He had a lever of which all must have been aware and which never had to be mentioned. If Belgium neutrality was violated and Belgium sought Britain's assistance, in reality Britain was going to war no matter what the Liberal cabinet decided. For if Belgium's neutrality was compromised and a majority of the cabinet decided *not* to intervene, Asquith, Grey, Churchill, and perhaps others would resign. They could then with relative ease join the Conservatives in a coalition government supported by enough members of Parliament to carry the nation into the conflict. So for the Liberals, if the country were going to war anyway, it would be much better to be led by the existing Liberal government rather than a coalition of Liberal leaders and the Conservatives.

At this juncture Asquith had a clear picture of what he considered British interests and obligations and what he thought "right and wrong." He set this all out in a lawyer-like fashion to Venetia at the time, which he later read in another version to the cabinet and included in his reply to the Conservatives. His six points deserve to be quoted in their entirety in order to reveal his clear-headedness about the issues and interests involved at this moment of extreme crisis:

(1) We have no obligation of any kind either to France or Russia to give them military or naval help.
(2) The dispatch of the Expeditionary force to help France at this moment is out of the question & wd. serve no object.
(3) We mustn't forget the ties created by our long-standing & intimate friendship with France.
(4) It is against British interests that France shd. be wiped out as a Great Power.
(5) We cannot allow Germany to use the Channel as a hostile base.
(6) We have an obligation to Belgium to prevent her being utilized & absorbed by Germany.[97]

In the Sunday cabinet meeting, Asquith and Grey were able "with some difficulty" to convince the cabinet at least of Asquith's fifth point, and so Grey could tell Cambon in a memorandum that "if the German fleet comes into the Channel or through the North Sea to undertake hostile operations against the French coasts or shipping, the British fleet will give all protection in its power." Even with this assurance, Grey told Cambon that the government could not yet bind itself to declare war upon Germany if war broke out between Germany and France the next day.[98] As this message was being delivered, the Admiralty sent word to the fleet that German ships should not be allowed to pass into the English Channel and to "Be prepared for surprise attack."[99]

By the time the cabinet came together again that evening, the situation was rapidly changing. There was confirmation that Germany had invaded Luxemburg, signaling an imminent invasion of Belgium. The cabinet decided that the government's policy should follow Gladstone's principle of 1870: If there were a "substantial" violation of Belgium's neutrality, Britain would act.

When the cabinet met the next morning, Monday, August 3, a Bank Holiday, it worked on the statement that Grey was to make to the House of Commons that afternoon. Since it was clear by this time the government intended to go to war if there was a "substantial" violation of Belgian neutrality, four ministers announced their intention to resign—Lord Morley, Sir John Simon, Lord Beauchamp, and John Burns. Asquith held out some hope that they might reconsider in light of events, and he reported this to the King.[100]

That afternoon Grey gave his now famous speech to the Commons explaining the government's position. Events had continued to move rapidly. That morning Belgium refused the German ultimatum demanding passage, and Belgian King Albert had telegraphed an appeal to King George asking for diplomatic intervention (since the German invasion had not yet taken place). Grey masterfully set out the events that had brought Britain to this juncture. He announced the Channel guarantee given to France and the government's policy regarding a violation of Belgian neutrality.

As word spread of impending war, crowds began to gather in front of Parliament and to cheer the King at Buckingham Palace late into the night. As always Asquith was not impressed by such public displays of emotion. "War or anything that seems likely to lead to war," he wrote to Venetia, "is always popular with the London mob." He reminded her of Sir Robert Walpole's remark, "'Now they are ringing the bells, in a few weeks they'll be wringing their hands,'" concluding "How one loathes such levity."[101]

The next morning the British Ambassador to Belgium informed Grey that German troops had in fact entered Belgian territory. The cabinet agreed that an ultimatum must now be addressed to the Germans, and Asquith and Grey were given the job of drafting it. The British Ambassador in Berlin soon informed the German government that unless assurance was received by midnight that evening that Germany would respect Belgian neutrality, "His Majesty's Government [would] feel bound to take all steps in their power to uphold the neutrality of Belgium and the observance of a treaty to which Germany is as much a party as ourselves."[102]

Although Britain had to wait until the midnight deadline, there was no doubt that it was about to enter a terrible conflict. That evening Asquith sat with his wife, Grey, Tyrrell, and Churchill as the last minutes of peace passed. At midnight the Admiralty send the message to all His Majesty's ships and naval establishments, "COMMENCE HOSTILITIES AGAINST GERMANY."[103]

"The whole thing fills me with sadness," Asquith confessed to Venetia.[104] Earlier that day, Margot found her husband in the Prime Minister's room in the House of Commons, and she asked, "So it is all up?" He replied, "Yes, it's all up." When she approached him and leaned her head against his, the man whom so many saw as totally void of emotion could not speak for tears in his eyes.[105]

NOTES

1. Brock, *Letters to Venetia Stanley*, 10.
2. Clifford, *Asquiths*, 193.
3. Vincent, *Crawford Papers*, 292.
4. Brock, *Letters to Venetia Stanley*, 11
5. Clifford, *Asquiths*, 193.
6. Ibid., 143.
7. Ibid., 154.
8. Ibid., 156.
9. Ibid., 162.
10. Ibid., 143.
11. Ibid., 188.
12. Ibid., 214.
13. Brock, *Letters to Venetia Stanley*, 9.
14. Ibid.
15. "Chapter of Autobiography," 4 Apr. 1915, Brock, *Letters to Venetia Stanley*, 532.
16. Ibid., 1.
17. L. E. Jones, *An Edwardian Youth* (London: Macmillan, 1956), 214.
18. Charles Lysaght, *Brendan Bracken* (London: Allen Lane, 1979), 332.
19. "Chapter of Autobiography," 4 Apr. 1915, Brock, *Letters to Venetia Stanley*, 532.
20. Levine, *Politics, Religion and Love*, 194–95.
21. HHA to VS, 5 Apr. 1915, Brock, *Letters to Venetia Stanley*, 534.
22. Brock, *Letters to Venetia Stanley*, 13.
23. Ibid.
24. Asquith, *Genesis of War*, 17.
25. Ibid., 142.
26. Wilson, *C. B.*, 530.

27. Spender and Asquith, *Life of Asquith,* 1:179; R. B. Haldane, *Before the War* (London: Cassell, 1920), 30.
28. Wilson, *C. B.*, 530–33.
29. Asquith, *Genesis of War*, 101.
30. Grey, *Twenty-five Years*, 1:170.
31. Ibid., 1:169.
32. Ibid., 1:172.
33. HHA to Edward VII (copy), 12 Oct. 1908, BL, MS. Asquith 5, f. 51A.
34. Spender and Asquith, *Life of Asquith,* 1:243.
35. *Times*, 10 Nov. 1908, 9.
36. Asquith, *Genesis of War*, 145.
37. Ibid., 145.
38. Randolph S. Churchill, *Winston Churchill: Volume II 1901–1914 Young Statesman* (Boston: Houghton Mifflin, 1967), 504.
39. Sir Edward Grey to Count de Salis, 4 July 1911, Grey, *Twenty-five Years*, 1:214.
40. Grey, *Twenty-five Years*, 1:212.
41. Asquith, *Genesis of War*, 215.
42. Churchill, *World Crisis*, 1:44.
43. R. Churchill, *Winston S. Churchill: Young Statesman*, 513.
44. Haldane, *Autobiography*, 230–31.
45. Churchill, *World Crisis*, 1:66.
46. Asquith, *Genesis of War*, 121.
47. Ibid., 153.
48. HHA to George V (copy), 3 Feb. 1912, BL, MS. Asquith 6, ff. 92–92A.
49. Grey, *Twenty-five Years*, 1:242.
50. Haldane, *Before the War*, 57–72.
51. Grey, *Twenty-five Years*, 1:242; Spender and Asquith, *Life of Asquith,* 66.
52. R. Churchill, *Winston S. Churchill: Young Statesman*, 563.
53. HHA to George V (copy), 17 May 1912, BL, MS. Asquith 6, ff. 139–139A.
54. R. Churchill, *Winston S. Churchill: Young Statesman*, 575.
55. Ibid., 579.
56. Grey to Cambon, 22 Nov. 1912, Spender and Asquith, *Life of Asquith,* 2:72. Cambon confirmed this was France's understanding. Cambon to Grey, 23 Nov. 1912.
57. Asquith, *Genesis of War*, 133.
58. Ibid., 133–34.
59. Chris Wrigley, *Winston Churchill: A Biographical Companion* (Santa Barbara: ABC-CLIO, 2002), 8.
60. Ibid.
61. HHA to MA, 20 Jan. 1914, Spender and Asquith, *Life of Asquith,* 2:76.
62. HHA to MA, 25 Jan. 1914, ibid., 2:77.
63. R. Churchill, *Winston S. Churchill: Young Statesman*, 660.
64. Churchill, *World Crisis*, 1:188.
65. Wrigley, *Churchill*, 8–9.

66. Edward M. House to Walter Hines Page, 13 Dec. 1914, Burton J. Hendrick, *The Life and Letters of Walter H. Page* (Garden City: Doubleday, Page, 1922), 1:277.
67. Edward M. House to Walter Hines Page, 4 Jan. 1914, Hendrick, *Life and Letters of Walter H. Page*, 1:281.
68. Asquith, *Genesis of War*, 234.
69. Hendrick, *Life and Letters of Walter H. Page*, 1:295–96.
70. Ibid., 1:297.
71. Edward House memorandum of conversation with President Woodrow Wilson, 30 Aug. 1914, Charles Seymour, *The Intimate Papers of Colonel House* (Boston: Houghton Mifflin Company, 1926), 1:275.
72. Ibid., 1:268–69.
73. Edward M. House to Woodrow Wilson, 3 July 1914, ibid.
74. HHA to VS, 24 July 1914, Brock, *Letters to Venetia Stanley*, 122–23.
75. HHA to George V, 25 July 1914, Spender and Asquith, *Life of Asquith,* 2:80.
76. HHA to VA, 26 July 1914, Brock, *Letters to Venetia Stanley*, 125–26.
77. In fact, unknown to the Grey or the cabinet at the time of the cabinet meeting, Germany rejected Grey's offer of mediation that day.
78. HHA to VS, 27 July 1914, Brock, *Letters to Venetia Stanley*, 128.
79. HHA to George V, 28 July 1914, Spender and Asquith, *Life of Asquith,* 2:81.
80. HHA to VS, 28 July 1914, Brock, *Letters to Venetia Stanley*, 129.
81. HHA to George V, 30 July 1914, Spender and Asquith, *Life of Asquith,* 2:81.
82. HHA to VS, 29 July 1914, Brock, *Letters to Venetia Stanley*, 133.
83. Sir Edward Grey to Sir E. Goshen, 29 July 1914, James Brown Scott, ed., *Diplomatic Documents Relating to the Outbreak of the European War, Part II* (New York: Oxford University Press, 1916), 951.
84. Martin Gilbert, *Churchill: A Life* (New York: Henry Holt, 1991), 268; R. Churchill, *Winston S. Churchill: Young Statesman*, 695.
85. HHA to VS, 29 July 1914, Brock, *Letters to Venetia Stanley*, 132.
86. HHA to VS, 30 July 1914, ibid., 136.
87. Ibid.
88. Ibid.
89. Ibid., 137, n. 6.
90. Earl of Oxford and Asquith, *Memories*, 2:10.
91. Sir F. Bertie to Sir Edward Grey, 31 July 1914, Scott, *Diplomatic Documents*, 978.
92. HHA to VS, 1 Aug. 1914, Brock, *Letters to Venetia Stanley*, 140.
93. Ibid.
94. Ibid.
95. HHA to VS, 2 Aug. 1914, ibid., 146.
96. R. C. K. Ensor, *England 1870–1914* (Oxford: Clarendon Press, 1936), 493.
97. HHA to VS, 2 Aug. 1914, Brock, *Letters to Venetia Stanley*, 146.
98. Sir Edward Grey to Sir F. Bertie, 2 Aug. 1914, Scott, *Diplomatic Documents,* 1000.

99. Admiralty to Commander-in-Chief, Home Fleet, Vice Admirals, 2nd and 3rd Fleet, Commander-in-Chief, Home Ports, 2 Aug. 1914, R. Churchill, *Winston S. Churchill: Young Statesman*, 695.

100. HHA to George V, 3 Aug. 1914, Spender and Asquith, *Life of Asquith*, 32.

101. HHA to VS, 3 Aug. 1914, Brock, *Letters to Venetia Stanley*, 148.

102. Sir Edward Grey to Sir E. Goschen, 4 Aug. 1914, Scott, *Diplomatic Documents*, 1000.

103. Admiralty to all HM ships and Naval Establishments, 4 Aug. 1914, R. Churchill, *Winston S. Churchill: Young Statesman*, 706.

104. HHA to VS, 4 Aug. 1914, Brock, *Letters to Venetia Stanley*, 151.

105. 4 August 1914, Brock, *Margot Asquith's Great War Diary*, 13; M. Asquith, *Autobiography*, 2:144.

Chapter Eight

Leading a Liberal Government at War (August 1914–May 1915)

Once hostilities commenced, important and immediate decisions faced the Prime Minister and his cabinet. British war plans called for dispatching an expeditionary force to France but only after the German fleet had either been defeated or bottled up in its ports and safe passage for the force secured. Otherwise the force might not make it to France and Britain be left open to invasion. The German advance was moving so rapidly and successfully that the French desperately needed immediate support and were calling for every available man the British could provide. Fortunately the Admiralty had already set up a cordon in the Straits of Dover and was prepared to guarantee a crossing. The War Office awaited the signal to send all six of the divisions of the Expeditionary Force, the Admiralty having waived its requirement that two divisions be saved in reserve for defense against possible invasion. Asquith called a meeting on the afternoon of August 5 at Downing Street to discuss the issue. Included in the discussions were a number of military and naval commanders, Haldane, Grey, Churchill, and Lord Kitchener, who had just joined the cabinet as Minister of War. Some members of the cabinet hesitated, clinging to the hope that British participation in the war could be confined to naval activity. Once the Prime Minister and others were assured of the safe crossing of the Expeditionary Force, the question remained as to how large a force should be sent. Kitchener wanted to keep two divisions in Britain to protect against a possible invasion. Asquith supported this idea not because he feared an invasion, but because he wanted to have a force available should the economy collapse and civil unrest result.[1] With the unanimous support of the military, the decision was made to recommend an Expeditionary Force of four divisions immediately be sent to France, a recommendation approved by the full cabinet the following day.

The other important initial decision taken on August 5 was the appointment of the sixty-four-year-old Field Marshall, Lord Kitchener, as Secretary of State for War. Kitchener was the empire's most famous soldier, having fought the famous battle of Omdurman in 1898 and ended the Boer guerrilla war in 1900. He subsequently served as commander-in-chief of the British Army in India for seven years (1902–1909) and was currently posted as Agent and Counsel-General for the British in Egypt. All of these years of distinguished service made Lord Kitchener more than a national hero—he was a national institution.[2] Asquith had barely known Kitchener before the war, because the famous Field Marshall was rarely in England. It was the Prime Minister's practice to invite Kitchener to Committee of Imperial Defence meetings when the Field Marshall was home, and the two men saw each other when Asquith once made a visit to the Mediterranean with Churchill.

The Field Marshall happened to be in Britain when the war broke out. On the morning of August 3, after Kitchener had already boarded a Channel steamer to begin his journey back to his post in Egypt, he was recalled to London to participate in the Council of War to be held two days later. At this point, Asquith's mind was still open about elevating Kitchner to the cabinet.[3] Since the Curragh incident in March, Asquith himself had been serving as Secretary of State for War, and now that Britain was involved in a European conflict, it would be impossible for one man to carry out the duties of both offices effectively. As soon as Britain went to war, the Northcliffe press and even the liberal *Westminster Gazette* began to call for Kitchener's appointment. Such a move would obviously have large public appeal.

Asquith always maintained that "the only person whom I ever thought of as my successor was Lord Kitchener," and this may well have been true.[4] Even so, there must have been some concern at the time as to whether or not Asquith would make the move. Balfour, in response to pressure from party leaders, sounded out the Prime Minister on the subject on the morning of August 3 and received a sympathetic hearing but no commitment.[5] That same morning Churchill, at Balfour's urging, had an interview with the Prime Minister. In an unpublished note among his papers, Churchill recorded that he asked Asquith to consider Lord Kitchener for the War Office and wrote, "I could see by Mr. Asquith's reception of my remarks that his mind was moving, or had already moved, along the same path."[6] Two days later, after the Council of War meeting, Asquith asked Lord Kitchener to take over the reins at the War Office, and he accepted. It seems doubtful the Prime Minster was forced into this decision by the press. Asquith was rarely, if ever, persuaded by the press. As a politician, however, he understood the popularity of such a move, and there was the simple fact that no one else at the time could immediately command the confidence of the people as Kitchener could. All the same, as

Asquith confessed to Venetia Stanley, "It is a hazardous experiment, but the best in the circumstances, I think."[7]

The next day with less than five minutes of preparation Asquith rose to address the House of Commons in what many believed to be one of the greatest speeches of his career. The government was asking for a £100 million credit to support the war. Up to this point the Prime Minister had yet to address the House in any detail about how the war had come about or why Britain had entered the conflict. He reviewed in some detail Grey's efforts to reach an amicable settlement. While "never derogating for an instant or by an inch from the honour and interests of his own country, he has striven, as few have striven, to maintain and preserve the greatest interest of all countries—universal peace." He had nothing but derision for Germany's "infamous proposal" to respect French national territory (not her empire) and Belgian neutrality in return for Britain's neutrality. Britain was asked to accept a promise—a promise "given by a Power which was at that very moment announcing its intention to violate its own treaty and inviting us to do the same." At the highpoint of his address, Asquith asked rhetorically, "What is it we are fighting for?" His answer was simple and direct. Britain was fighting for two things. First, it sought "to fulfil a solemn international obligation" to Belgium. Second, and more important, Britain was fighting "to vindicate the principle that small nationalities are not to be crushed, in defiance of international good faith, by the arbitrary will of a strong and overmastering Power." He concluded, "I do not believe any nation ever entered into a great controversy . . . with a clearer conscience and a stronger conviction that it is fighting in defence of principles the maintenance of which is vital to the civilization of the world."[8] He thought at the time with a bit of false modesty that he had made a "fairly successful speech."[9] Even members of the press who had not been great supporters of the Liberal government in the past warmly praised it. The *Spectator* said that he "rose to a height of eloquence, and also of convincing persuasiveness, never surpassed"; the *Daily Graphic* called it "one of those marvellously concise speeches for which the Prime Minister is famous."[10]

Events in France moved rapidly. To the credit of all involved, the Expeditionary Force was quickly assembled and made it safely to France in a matter of days. Asquith wrote to Margot on August 13, "all the machine is working with truly beautiful smoothness."[11] The British met the Germans for the first time on August 23 near the Belgian town of Mons. After a fierce struggle, and with the fall of the supposedly impregnable fortress at the Belgian city of Namur, both the British and the French armies were forced to fall back in the direction of Paris. This retreat led to one of the first major tactical controversies of the war. British commander Field Marshall Sir John French, distrusting the French, who he believed had left him exposed at Mons, suddenly announced on August 30 his intention to withdraw the entire British Expeditionary Force from the line to rest and refit behind the Seine.

The next day the cabinet debated French's planned withdrawal. Kitchener saw no reason for the move and thought that it might well not only leave a serious gap in the line, but also have a disastrous effect on relations with France. Asquith supported Kitchener's view and adamantly argued that there could be no retreat from the line of battle. Although the issue was "hotly debated," in the end the cabinet was nearly unanimous in ordering the Expeditionary Force to stay in the line.[12] In his masterful *Asquith As War Leader*, George Cassar argues that deciding to overrule Field Marshall French Asquith "rendered inestimable service to the Allied cause." For one thing, with the British remaining in the line the Allies were eventually able to counterattack at the Marne and ultimately halt the German advance, preventing an early defeat.[13]

In addition to the normal burdens of a war-time Prime Minister, Asquith had to deal in September and October with the additional chore of managing the antics of Winston Churchill, antics that caused the Prime Minister to begin to doubt the First Lord of the Admiralty's judgment. The first episode occurred in the third week of September. Without consulting Asquith, Churchill arranged with Kitchener to send a Marine Brigade and a Yeomanry force, the Oxford Hussars, to Dunkirk, at the request of the French commander General Joffre, who wanted to deceive the Germans about the strength of the Dunkirk garrison. When Asquith learned of the deployment, particularly the deployment of the Oxford Hussars, he was immediately sceptical. He told Venetia Stanley, "if they encounter the Germans in any force, I fear we shall see very few of them back again."[14]

This incident adumbrated a much more serious lapse of judgment on Churchill's part. On October 2, while Asquith was speaking in Cardiff, King Albert I of the Belgians informed the British that his government had decided to abandon Antwerp. If this happened, the Germans might then sweep down the coast and threaten Calais. The Allies desperately needed more time to get their defenses in order, and so the city needed to be held at least so as to buy time for the Allies. In Asquith's absence, Grey called together a midnight conference with Churchill and Kitchener. They decided to reinforce Antwerp with a Marine brigade and a small detachment of regular troops; Churchill, heading to Dunkirk anyway, would go on to Antwerp to convince the Belgian government to hold firm. Informed of the decision, Asquith wrote to Venetia Stanley that Churchill would "try to infuse into their backbones the necessary quantity of starch." Clearly Asquith supported the idea of the Churchill mission at this point, for he said in the same letter, "I don't know how fluent he [Churchill] is in French, but if he was able to do himself justice in a foreign tongue, the Belges will have listened to a discourse the like of which they have never heard before." He concluded, "I cannot but think he will stiffen them up to the sticking point."[15]

Asquith was right. Churchill accomplished his mission. By October 4 the Belgian Prime Minister Baron Charles de Broqueville informed the British that the Belgians were "determined whatever the cost, to hold Antwerp"; it was for them "a national duty of the first order."[16] Asquith reported to the King the next day, "Mr. Churchill has been in Antwerp since Saturday afternoon & has successfully dissuaded the King and his Ministers from retiring to Ostend." He went on to inform the King that Churchill reported that "the town can hold out certainly for 3, and perhaps for as long as 10 days, if the resistance is backed up."[17]

All would have been fine if Churchill had at that moment accepted the success of his mission and headed home. Yet the First Lord of the Admiralty had become intoxicated with the smoke of battle and had convinced himself that the successful defense of the city largely depended on his presence. He wired Asquith, "If it is thought by HM Government that I can be of service here, I am willing to resign my office and undertake command of relieving and defensive forces assigned to Antwerp in conjunction with the Belgian Army, provided I am given necessary military rank and authority, and full powers of a commander of a detached force in the field." Such an arrangement "will afford the best prospects of a victorious result." Leaving out no detail, he ended the wire, "Runciman would do Admiralty well."[18] Asquith was quick to nix Churchill's absurd suggestion. He explained at the time:

> Then comes the real bit of tragic-comedy. I found when I arrived here this morning the enclosed telegram from Winston, who as you will see, proposes to resign his Office, in order to take command in the field of this great military force! Of course without consulting anybody, I at once telegraphed to him warm appreciation of his mission & his offer, with a most decided negative, saying that we could not spare him at the Admiralty &c.[19]

Asquith had worked with Churchill enough to understand that praise should accompany unwelcome news. Even so, Asquith's patience with his First Lord of the Admiralty was wearing thin. Although he had not planned to tell the Cabinet of Churchill's proposal and protect his protégé from embarrassment, when the cabinet pressed him that day to say when Churchill would return, he revealed the contents of Churchill's message (without the suggestion of Runciman as his successor). The cabinet greeted it with a "Homeric laugh." The Prime Minister's humor over his colleague's escapade almost turned to anger several days later when he received a first-hand account of the British marines' engagement at Antwerp. Churchill had assured Asquith that the main body of troops provided to help the Belgians would be seasoned reserves. This was not the case, and many were raw troops with little or no experience who suffered heavy casualties. He confided to Venetia Stanley, "I can't tell you what I feel of the *wicked* folly of it all."[20]

Another challenge Asquith faced almost from the opening days of the war was the conflict between Lord Kitchener and Sir John French, two Field Marshalls who in Asquith's words were "an extraordinarily disparate couple and not born or moulded to work easily together."[21] In August, when French wanted to withdraw from the line of battle, Asquith and Kitchener had overruled him. By November, the relationship between the two soldiers had deteriorated. Asquith wrote on November 3, "I had a long visit from K. [Kitchener], who is far from happy about what is going on at the Front." The problem was the mounting casualties even as the French demanded more and more men. Asquith wrote on October 29, "The losses in the 7th Division, which ... was the last to go out, have been terrific—at least 4000 out of about 12000 men & officers—in these last few days ... if the Germans go on lavishing lives at their present rate, and projecting wave after wave to the front, we shall have to give French all the men we can without being too fastidious as to their quality."[22] A few days later word reached Asquith that General French had heard that Kitchener while in Dunkirk the week before had asked the French officers whether they were satisfied with Field Marshall French and had even suggested Sir Ian Hamilton as a successor. Asquith at the time wrote, "I do not believe there is a word of truth or even a shadow of foundation for the story," yet French sent "Freddie" Guest, former Deputy Chief Liberal Whip and now aide-de-camp to the Field Marshall, to meet with Asquith about the affair.[23] Asquith told Venetia Stanley, "it is all important that French should be kept in good heart," and so to smooth things over, Asquith immediately wrote to French with perhaps some exaggeration that Kitchener "never fails in appreciation of and loyalty to you." He further reassured the Field Marshall, "As the head of the Government I wish you to know that you possess in the fullest measure our absolute and unreserved confidence" and that the country is "fortunate in having at the head of the gallant forces, a Commander who has never been surpassed in the capital qualities of initiative, tenacity, serenity, and resource."[24]

Several weeks later in late December, Asquith called both Field Marshalls to meet with him at Walmer Castle, one of his weekend retreats. If Asquith had hoped to reconcile the two men, his hopes were dashed. There had been "a battle royal which I had to compose."[25] He asked them to meet first for about half an hour by themselves, and then he later joined them. French was in his usual optimistic mood and, as Asquith recorded, "convinced that the Germans have lost their best troops and officers." At this same meeting French suggested General Henry Wilson to replace General Archibald Murray as Chief-of-Staff of the Expeditionary Force. Asquith wasn't about to agree with this suggestion. Wilson had been at the center of intrigue at the time of the Curragh incident the previous March, and Asquith held him largely responsible for the extent of the conflict. Kitchener too objected because Wilson had on occasion been critical of the War Office polices. The Prime Minister crisply noted at the time that French "after a little talk has now quite dropped it, and Murray (who is an excellent tho' slightly jumpy man) will go on." Eventually Sir William Robertson replaced Murray.[26] Try as he might, Asquith simply could not get the two Field Marshalls to bury the hatchet at Walmer Castle, and he would have to continue to keep them at arm's length from each other.

Only three months into the war, it had become clear that the system of managing the conflict had to be altered. When the war broke out, a practice developed whereby the Prime Minister, Churchill as First Lord of the Admiralty, and Kitchener as head of the War Office made the day-to-day operational decisions. The Committee of Imperial Defence or "War Council" was called into play only when there were major changes in policy or to assist in joint strategic operations. Asquith was sensitive to the requirements of cabinet government, and when it met he allowed the twenty-one cabinet members to discuss whatever it wished about the war. In one of the first cabinet meetings of the war, Asquith reported vigorous debate on a number of relatively minor actions, including smaller schemes for taking German ports and wireless stations in East Africa and the China seas. He told his cabinet that they "looked more like a gang of Elizabethan buccaneers than a meek collection of black-coated Liberal Ministers."[27]

This system proved cumbersome and simply could not keep pace with the fast moving events of the war. The difficulty, as Asquith described it, "was how to combine rapid and effective executive action in the various theatres with the maintenance of Cabinet responsibility and control."[28] As early as September, Asquith began to work on the problem and floated the idea with the cabinet on September 22 that two committees be formed, one to handle the conduct of the war and the other handle financial issues. The cabinet accepted this idea in principle, but when it came to working out the details, conflict arose. Not until late October had a definite plan for the most part been agreed to. Under the proposal a three- to five-man War Committee of the cabinet would deal exclusively with the conduct of the war. This committee from time to time would ask other members of the cabinet to assist them both in discussing and deciding issues where particular departments were concerned. More important, as Asquith told his colleagues at the time, the entire cabinet was "to be kept constantly informed of the decisions and actions of the Committee, and in all questions which involve a change or new departure in policy to be consulted before decisive action is taken."[29]

Eventually in late November Asquith established a new committee also known as the "War Council" to assist the cabinet, which still held ultimate responsibility for the conduct of the war. The original War Council was composed of Kitchener, Churchill, Lloyd George, and Grey with the Prime Minister serving as chair. Also included was Arthur Balfour to represent the opposition, chosen because of his long association with the Committee for Imperial Defence (CID) and his friendship with Asquith. Others attended meetings in an advisory capacity including General Wolfe-Murray, Chief of the Imperial General Staff (CIGS), and Admiral Fisher, the First Sea Lord. Eventually the War Council grew to thirteen participants when Crewe, Haldane, Harcourt, McKenna, and Admiral Sir Arthur Wilson were brought in.[30]

As has been observed, the establishment of the War Council in 1914 did not really affect the conduct of the war. Although it met at least weekly, like its predecessor, it was too large and lacked executive authority. The cabinet still had to duplicate important policy discussions before a final decision could be made, and the day-to-day operation of the war remained in the hands of the service minsters, Kitchener and Churchill, in consultation with the Prime Minister.[31]

As 1914 drew to a close, it was apparent to all that the Western Front had for the most part been stabilized. Many people looked for another path to victory. Lord Fisher, the First Sea Lord, proposed an alternative to the slaughter of frontal assaults on entrenched positions. He suggested to Asquith in a letter on December 29 the invasion of Schleswig Holstein, a territory on the Baltic seized by Germany from Denmark in 1864. If successful, the Allies would threaten the Kiel Canal and perhaps bring Denmark into the war on their side. If this were to happen, conceivably Russian forces under cover of the British fleet could be landed in the north of Germany less than ninety miles from Berlin. Asquith was willing to consider the bold idea, but the military establishment soon discovered too many difficulties to consider the operation feasible.[32]

Lloyd George too had become convinced of the futility of assaulting the fortified German lines on the Western Front. In January 1915 he came forward with a plan to withdraw the major part of the British Expeditionary Force from France and transfer it to the Balkans, where it would be reinforced by new troops as they became ready. He argued that such a move could save Serbia from what appeared to be imminent Austro-German attack and perhaps bring Greece, Bulgaria, and Romania to the Allied side. This would in turn knock Turkey out of the war and seriously threaten Austria. Again the military experts gave the move little chance of success, and more importantly both British and French commanders at the Western Front argued that any weakening of their troop strength for such a diversion invited a German breakthrough in the west.³³

A third alternative was to attack Turkey, which had joined the war on the side of the Central Powers. The concept gained momentum when in November the CID began looking at the defense of Egypt and the Suez Canal. In the very first meeting of Asquith's new War Council, in the context of defending Egypt, Churchill floated the idea of an attack on the Gallipoli Peninsula at the entrance to the Dardanelles, which if successful would give the British control of the straits and knock Turkey out of the war. He was careful to say, however, that such a plan "was a very difficult operation requiring a large force." Asquith made no comment, but Kitchener remarked that while it might be necessary at some point to carry out a diversionary attack, "the moment for it had not yet arrived."³⁴

With the New Year, the new War Council was confronted squarely with two schools of thought as to the correct strategy to win the war. On the one hand, Field Marshall French was requesting large reinforcements to begin offensive operations in coordination with the French army on the Western Front. This request was strongly supported by those who saw Germany as the main enemy. The only way to win the war was to defeat Germany by direct attack on the Western Front. These "westerners" also saw a reciprocal danger in lessening to any degree the troop strength in France. Just as the war could only be won on the Western Front, it could also be lost by an irretrievable defeat there at the hands of the Germans. On the other hand, as more and more leaders were beginning to believe that assaults on the German line in France were hopeless, the Allies needed to rethink their position. To this group, 1914 had shown that any future frontal assaults would carry heavy losses that would not be worth the gains. These "easterners" wanted another theater of the war.³⁵

By January 1915 the "easterners" were in the ascendancy. After the war Asquith wrote that, with one exception whom he did not name, the entire War Council thought that "The continued concentration at that moment of all effort and resources on the West—leaving the East, so far as England and France were concerned, practically derelict—might have been fatal to the general cause of the Allies."³⁶ Even so, it would not be correct to describe Asquith as a totally committed easterner. He clearly understood that ultimate victory could only be brought about on the Western Front. Nonetheless, he believed that Britain could neither totally neglect nor, in his words, leave "derelict" the east, for it too could be an important component in weakening the Central Powers and winning the war.

At this juncture, Asquith understood the overall strategic picture and immediate dilemma for the British—either concentrate on the Western Front and endure heavy casualties with little chance of a quick end to the war, or open one or more new fronts elsewhere and risk defeat in France. The next six months were to prove trying to Asquith, as cabinet politics and personal problems added to his burdens of a Prime Minister leading a country at war.

Those who supported some sort of an eastern campaign had a number of choices in the beginning of 1915. On the very first day of the year, Lloyd George called for a two-fold operation in the east: support a Serbian attack against Austria in conjunction with a smaller attack against Turkey.

On January 13, Churchill first came forward with the idea of forcing the Dardanelles by the naval operation, a plan put together by Admiral Sir Sackville Hamilton Carden. The fleet would concentrate fire on the entrance forts. Once these were demolished, the inner forts could be dealt with and the mine fields cleared to allow the fleet to proceed to Constantinople. The Admiralty, Churchill reported, believed that "a plan could be made for systematically reducing all the forts in a few weeks." While Asquith at first expressed no opinion on the idea, Lloyd George and Kitchener said they liked it and thought it was worth trying.[37] If successful, the Turkish government could then be overturned and Turkey would sue for peace. There would be other benefits. A warm water supply route would be opened to Russia, and the Balkan states that still remained neutral might swing over to the Allied cause, presenting a united front against Austria-Hungary. All of this might be accomplished by the Navy acting alone with no troops siphoned from the Western Front.[38] It seemed almost too good to be true, and it was.

Lord Fisher objected to Churchill's idea, and the two took the matter to Asquith. When presented with this dispute, Asquith decided to keep the Fisher-Churchill conflict hidden from the War Council. His reasons for making this important decision are not known for sure. It is true that Asquith at this point favored the Dardanelles plan, but it seems unlikely he was trying to keep an alternative view from his colleagues. More than likely, Asquith was attempting to maintain unity, and publicizing the disagreement would not help in this regard. Asquith's decision has been described as an obvious error in judgment but such a conclusion seems unnecessarily harsh considering the full context, especially the overriding need for unity.[39] Asquith never feared open discussion and almost always encouraged it, some thought to a fault. His decision appears to be an attempt to preserve unity rather than an attempt to deceive.

In the meantime, a possible campaign against Austria through the Balkans had not been forgotten. Asquith always thought the plan had real possibilities. On January 15 he had the opportunity to speak with Charles and Noel Buxton who had recently returned from Bucharest. The Buxtons had been sent by Churchill and Lloyd George nominally to attend the funeral of King Carol of Romania, but the hope was that they might put together some kind of Balkan confederation to support the Allies. After the interview, Asquith wrote to Venetia Stanley recognizing that all the Balkan states "hate one another & are as jealous as cats—particularly the Serbians & Bulgarians." Nevertheless he was optimistic. With regard to the problems of the Serbians and Bulgarians, he wrote that the Allies could "save them from the repulsive necessity of fighting side by side, by putting them back to back—the Serbs going for Austria & the Bulgars for Turkey." He told her that such an effort, combined with the Dardanelles plan, "might conceivably make a huge & even decisive diversion" and would "certainly compel Italy to come in."[40]

The Prime Minister seems to have become more and more convinced that the Balkan play was more promising than the Dardanelles. On January 21 he met with Lloyd George and Kitchener, and both the Prime Minister and the Chancellor of the Exchequer argued strongly for the Balkan option. The immediate problem the Allies faced was that the Germans were reinforcing the Austrians to carry out a death blow against Serbia. Kitchener was impressed with their arguments and admitted that if Serbia were overrun, any chance of a pro-Allied coalition would be dashed. Kitchener's problem, however, was where to find the troops. He estimated it would perhaps take as much as a corps to do the job.[41] Asquith had already urged Grey to put the strongest possible pressure on Romania and Greece to join the Allied cause and to tell them, if they did so without delay, they could count on a British force to join them.[42]

At this juncture, Asquith wrote on January 21 that "There are two fatal things in war—one is to push blindly against a stone wall, the other is to scatter and divide your forces in a number of separate & disconnected operations. We are in a great danger of committing both blunders. . . ." He also believed that at this point "all our 'side shows'—Zeebrugee, Alexandretta, even Gallipoli—ought to be postponed" for the Balkan campaign.[43] The next day Asquith met with Grey, Lloyd George, and Colonel Maurice Hankey, Secretary of the CID and the War Council. The Balkan situation was rapidly deteriorating and an Austrian attack against Serbia was imminent. In early February the War Council authorized Grey to offer the 29th Division, the last remaining regular division in Britain, to Greece. By then it was too late. The Bulgarians were already moving in the direction of joining with the Central Powers. The Greeks, worried about the Bulgarian threat, would not commit unless Romania also joined with the Allies. With recent German victories in Poland, the Romanians were sitting tight.[44] And so the Balkan campaign had to be shelved, but it was not forgotten.

On the morning of January 28, the day the War Council was to meet to make a final decision about the Dardanelles proposal, Asquith received a note from Lord Fisher reporting that he would not attend the War Council meeting scheduled for that afternoon because of his disagreements with Churchill. He stated that both the Dardanelles plan and the proposed bombardment of the Belgian port of Zeebrugee as purely naval operations were "unjustifiable."[45] He even hinted that he would resign over his disagreements not wishing to remain as a "stumbling block."[46] Churchill found a similar note from Fisher on his desk the same morning and hurried over to 10 Downing Street, where he found Asquith furious at the Admiral. Churchill hastily sent the following note to Fisher: "The Prime Minister considers your presence at the War Council indispensable & so do I. He will receive us both at 11:10 so that we can have a talk beforehand." It was not a request, it was an order. Asquith proposed a compromise which both men accepted: Churchill would give up for the present, the bombardment of Zeebrugee in return for Fisher's withdrawing his opposition to the Dardanelles plan.[47] With not a minute to spare, the Prime Minister, Churchill, and Fisher went to the War Council meeting.

Apparently, all had not been worked out. The War Council Minutes show that when Churchill began to discuss the Dardanelles plan, Fisher interrupted. Asquith responded that the War Council could not delay a discussion. Fisher then got up to leave the room and remained only after Kitchener persuaded him to stay. The council then adjourned for lunch, while Churchill worked on Fisher and persuaded him to support the Dardanelles attack as a purely naval operation. When the War Council reconvened, Churchill was able to announce that with Fisher's approval the Admiralty had decided "to undertake the task with which the War Council has charged us so urgently."[48] The Dardanelles campaign, as a purely naval operation, was then unanimously given the green light by the War Council.

After the war, Asquith wrote in his *Memories and Reflections*, "I assert unhesitatingly that at this time the whole of our expert naval opinion was in favour of a naval operation."[49] This statement leaves out the fact that "the expert naval opinion" supported such an operation only if it were to have support from the Army. Hankey, who had himself visited the Dardanelles in 1907, recorded in his diary, "On the first day proposal was made I warned P.M., Lord K., Chief of Staff, L. George and Balfour that Fleet could not effect passage without troops and that all naval officers thought so."[50] He at some point told the Prime Minister that every naval officer at the Admiralty strongly opposed a solely *naval* operation in the Dardanelles. "The First Lord still professes to believe that they can do it with ships" he wrote, "but I have warned the Prime Minister that we cannot trust to this."[51]

Along with other members of the War Council, Asquith bears responsibility for not listening more carefully. Part of the problem was Asquith's leadership style. As Lloyd George told his friend George Riddell at the time,

"The P.M. [Asquith] is unrivalled in giving speedy and accurate decisions on matters submitted to him, but he has not got the art of probing into things for himself and cleansing and restoring weak places."[52] Then too there was the sense of urgency to do something to avoid the certainty of heavy casualties on the deadlocked Western Front. With cabinet government it cannot be said that Asquith was ultimately responsible for letting the plan go forward as it did. Nonetheless he knew that Churchill, while a genius in many respects, was also susceptible to being carried away by his own enthusiasm. This alone, in hindsight, should have placed Asquith on the alert and caused him to probe more deeply. It was perhaps his greatest mistake as war leader.

It did not take Asquith long to become convinced of the correctness of Hankey's view. Churchill too now began to take the view that troops should be waiting in reserve in the Mediterranean, to take advantage of what he still believed would be a successful naval operation. The War Council, at the urging of Churchill, agreed on February 16 to send the 29th Division to the Greek island of Lemnos as soon as possible and to make arrangements for additional troops to be sent from Egypt, all "to be available in case of necessity to support the naval attack on the Dardanelles."[53]

When the War Council met four days after the attack had begun, Asquith reported, "We are all agreed (except K. [Kitchener]) that the naval adventure in the Dardanelles shd. be backed up by a strong military force." Even Kitchener supported the idea in principle but, as Asquith wrote, "is very sticky about sending out there the 29th Division, which is the best we have left at home." The Prime Minister had become convinced that the risk of throwing full support for the Dardanelles campaign was well worth it. "One must take a lot of risks in war, & I am strongly of the opinion that the chance of forcing the Dardanelles, & occupying Constantinople, & cutting Turkey in half, and arousing on our side the whole Balkan peninsula, presents such a unique opportunity that we ought to hazard a lot elsewhere rather than forgo it." Even so, he was reluctant to buck Kitchener. "If he [Kitchener] can be convinced, well & good; but to discard his advice & overrule his judgment on a military question is to take a great responsibility."[54]

In the meantime the bombardment of the outer Turkish forts was moving along successfully. On the day the cabinet was debating the fate of the 29th Division, the British fleet under the command of Vice Admiral Carden successfully entered the mouth of the Dardanelles, and six days later on March 2 the last of the outer defenses had been put out of commission. Things continued to look up, especially when Kitchener on March 10 finally agreed that the situation on the Western Front was sufficiently secure to allow the 29th Division to be sent to the Dardanelles. Two days after Kitchener agreed to send reinforcements, Asquith wrote, "I have just been reading the Admiralty secret report of the operations so far; they are making progress, but it is slow, and there are a large number of howitzers and concealed guns (not in the forts) on both shores wh. given them a good deal of trouble, and have made a lot of holes in the ships, tho' so far the damage done is not serious."[55] "The Admiralty have been over-sanguine as to what they cd. do by ships alone," Asquith concluded. "Every night the Turks under German direction repair their fortifications: both coasts bristle with howitzers and field guns (outside the forts) in concealed emplacements; and the channel is sown with complicated & constantly renewed mine fields."[56]

Weather temporarily delayed a further attack, and on March 23 both Churchill and Asquith were shocked to learn that Admiral De Robeck had postponed any further attack until it could be taken in conjunction with the Army. Since troops would have to be organized, this could well mean that another attack might not be possible until mid-April, all element of surprise having been lost. Churchill wanted to instruct the Admiral immediately that an attack should resume at the first favorable opportunity. Asquith supported Churchill, but even so, he was unwilling to overrule the Sea Lords. In this matter Asquith certainly acted properly. To have insisted upon a further attack, in opposition to the unanimous recommendation of not only the commander on the spot but also the Sea Lords, especially after the Navy had already incurred significant losses, would not only have been irresponsible, but would have risked political suicide should the mission further fail.

The Dardanelles campaign was not the only ball Asquith had to juggle in the spring of 1915. In late February, Lloyd George once again brought to the forefront the issue of munitions production. This controversy once more called into play Asquith's particular skill of patching together what was admittedly a compromise but one that would keep the war effort on track. In a memorandum circulated to the cabinet on February 22, the Chancellor of the Exchequer claimed that he did not believe "Great Britain has even yet done anything like what she could do in the matter of increasing her war equipment." He went on, "I sincerely believe that we could double our effective energies if we organized our factories thoroughly." He recommended that "full powers should be taken . . . to mobilize the whole of our manufacturing strength for the purpose of turning out, at the earliest possible moment, war material."[57]

Munitions production had been a problem since the beginning of the war. The British War Office simply did not have large enough arsenals to equip the enormous armies Britain was now raising. As a result, private industry had to be called into play. By early 1915 the War Office had contracts with 2,500 firms that had never produced arms before.[58] This meant that Kitchener, who hated to delegate authority, had to yield at least some control over armament production. Friction mounted to a point that only two months into the war in mid-October 1914 Asquith had to establish a special Munitions Committee consisting of Haldane; Lloyd George; McKenna; Churchill; Walter Runciman, President of the Board of Trade; and Lord "Bron" Lucas, President of the Board of Agriculture. This committee was to act in coordination with Kitchener.

This did not end the controversy, and Asquith again had to referee a dispute between a cabinet member and the military. On the one side was Lloyd George, defending the manufacturers and repeatedly attacking General Sir Stanley von Donop, the Master-General of the Ordinance, who critics claimed refused to listen to manufacturers, missed opportunities to obtain material, and was the worst of bureaucrats. On the other side stood the indomitable and irascible Kitchener, staunchly defending von Donop. In a typical letter to Asquith he praised his subordinate for having "the complete confidence of every member of his Department" and in seeing that the guns and ammunition obtained were of a quality to ensure "adequate safety" and of avoiding material "too far below the accepted standards."[59] Asquith, more than anyone else, understood that neither side in the dispute could totally prevail. A compromise had to be reached.

A week after the circulation of Lloyd George's February 1915 memorandum, Asquith convened a conference at 10 Downing Street to discuss the matter. Present were Kitchener, Lloyd George, General von Donop, McKenna, Crewe, and others. Afterward Lloyd George sarcastically reported to Balfour, who could not be present, "Once more we decided . . . to take the step in industrial organization which we resolved upon in October and which until recently we were all under the impression had actually been taken." The shocking news: "The War Office admit that they were deplorably short of shells, of rifle ammunition and of fuses; they also admit that they can do nothing this year in this country to supply the deficiencies of our allies."[60] Lloyd George urged Asquith to create a special body to take complete control of munitions production.[61]

The stakes were high, and a misstep might mean disaster. Asquith pondered several options. One would be to appoint an Army contracts directorate with a person of ministerial rank placed in charge. One of the great proponents of this plan was Edwin Montagu, who had recently served as Lloyd George's junior minister at the Treasury and now was in the cabinet as Chancellor of the Duchy of Lancaster. Asquith's protégé and former private secretary, Montagu, was one of the persons considered for the post. The difficulty was that whoever was selected would have to stand up to the formidable Kitchener. The only person that could even begin to do this was Lloyd George, but the Chancellor of the Exchequer would never consider such a position unless he was given full authority for munitions production, which Kitchener of course would never accept.[62]

The Prime Minister's other option was to create an entirely new munitions committee with greater authority. To set the stage for such a plan, Asquith's government rushed through Parliament an amendment to the 1914 Defence of the Realm Act specifically authorizing the government to take over any factory or workshop and control its production of war material. Authority also was given even to cancel contracts that stood in the way of effective production.[63] As early as March 18, Asquith told Venetia Stanley, "I may create a new office for Ll. George ('Director of War Contracts' or something of the kind) and relieve him of his present duties."[64] A few days later, Asquith met with Lloyd George, Balfour, Churchill, and Montagu to discuss the composition and powers of the wholly new munitions committee. Not surprisingly, Kitchener was deliberately excluded. As Asquith related, "The discussion was quite a good one, & I think we came to some rational (and unanimous) conclusions." Even so, he realized, "we may have some difficulty with K [Kitchener]...."[65] As expected Asquith chose Lloyd George to chair the committee and left its composition for the most part up to the new chairman. After the meeting, Asquith did, however, write to Lloyd George that it was "essential to its [the committee's] working that Kitchener should be brought in," and that he thought "that (on the political side) in addition to yourself and A. J. B. [Balfour] you should have a working financier, such as Montagu." Asquith also made suggestions of specific naval and military officers to be included.[66]

The dispute between Asquith's Chancellor of the Exchequer and his Secretary of War, however, was not to be so easily solved. To placate Kitchener, whom he knew would not be pleased with the arrangement, Asquith, when he told the Field Marshall of the new committee, assured him that there would be little interference with the work of the departments. Kitchener did not disagree in principle with a committee, provided it did not interfere with existing War Office contracts or divert labor from firms registered with the War Office to provide war supplies. Asquith understood that the Field Marshall was naturally suspicious of anyone intruding onto his turf and interfering with plans and arrangements already made.[67] Lloyd George thought Kitchener's conditions would make the committee powerless and nothing more than an advisory body. The deadlock put the matter back into the hands of the Prime Minister. As Edwin Montagu summed it up in a memorandum to him at the time, "it really seems to me that there is a difference of principle which cannot be bridged except by you. The responsibility is now yours. George's view or Kitchener's must prevail."[68]

It all came to a head on March 28 when Kitchener threatened to resign if the committee were given executive authority; not to be out done, Lloyd

George threatened to resign if the committee were *not* given such authority. "There is a truly royal row on the stocks between Kitchener & Lloyd George in regard to the proposed Committee on munitions," Asquith explained to Venetia Stanley, "Neither is disposed to give way: K. threatens to give up his office, and Ll. G to wash his hands of the whole business. . . ."[69] To avoid not just the controversy itself but perhaps even bringing down the government, Asquith quickly had to find some compromise. What he came up with was hardly workable, but it was the best he could do under the circumstances. Asquith's strength was understanding the limitations of the situation and forging a plan that would at least avoid a leadership breakup that would stall the war effort. On April 8, the Prime Minister announced the formation of a Munitions of War Committee to be chaired by Lloyd George. Its charge sounded impressive: to "ensure the promptest and most efficient application of all available resources of the country to the manufacture and supply of Munitions of War for the Army and Navy." As it turned out, the committee was never actually in control of munitions production, because the War Office had all the technical information and final approval for all contracts.[70]

There were those, including perhaps Edwin Montagu, who were greatly disappointed in Asquith's decision to cobble together a compromise with regard to the new munitions committee rather than take a firmer stance against Kitchener. Montagu and others failed to realize that the government simply could not risk the public uproar that would certainly accompany a Kitchener resignation. Perhaps Asquith and Lloyd George were testing Kitchener. There is no real evidence Lloyd George ever seriously considered at the time resigning over this issue, despite his threat, and he might well have been willing to bide his time until a more opportune moment to clip Kitchener's wings. For the moment, however, the Field Marshall had stood firm, and the Prime Minister and his Chancellor had backed down.

Even after the formation of the new Munitions Committee, Field Marshall French kept up his constant complaints that a shortage of shells for his field guns was depriving him of the means necessary to make a breakthrough on the Western Front. At home the rumors of shell shortages were eroding confidence in the Asquith government. By early spring the united front that had thus far supported the government in the war was showing signs of breaking down. Even Liberal newspapers were starting to join in the chorus of complaint.[71] To quell the rising concern about adequate supplies for the troops, Asquith decided it was time for him to make some public statement. He was scheduled to speak in Newcastle to the North East Coast Armaments Subcommittee on April 20. This body consisted of representatives from service departments, together with employers and trade unions engaged in munitions production, and seemed to be the perfect audience for an address concerning the supply of shells. Before he headed to Newcastle, the Prime Minister asked Kitchener for a report on the current state of ammunition from Field Marshall French. Asquith received a note from Kitchener stating, "I have had a talk with French. He told me I could let you know that with the present supply of ammunition he will have as much as his troops will be able to use on his next forward movement."[72] Asquith now had his own ammunition.

Addressing the Newcastle audience, Asquith refuted the charges that the government had been lax in providing the troops with the supplies they needed. "I do not believe that any Army or Navy has ever either entered upon a campaign or been maintained during a campaign," he asserted, "with better or more adequate equipment." He went on, "I saw a statement the other day that the operations not only of our Army but of our Allies were being crippled, or at any rate hampered, by our failure to provide the necessary ammunition. I say there is not a word of truth to that statement."[73] This was obviously an uncharacteristic overstatement by Asquith of what he had been told by Kitchener—one for which he would soon pay dearly.

Just as the munitions debate was heating up, Asquith had to concern himself with rumors of a possible leadership challenge in his own party led by Churchill. Balfour was beginning to have a greater and greater influence on Churchill. Edwin Montagu, returning to Walmer Castle from London, reported to Asquith on March 21 his concern about Balfour's ascendency. He told the Prime Minister that Churchill had even suggested that Balfour, who was not even a member of the cabinet, stand in for Grey who would be on his fishing holiday the following week. Montagu thought Balfour was secretly hostile to the Prime Minister. Realizing Balfour was a sounding board for those in the cabinet who opposed Kitchener, particularly Lloyd George and Churchill, Asquith did not appear to be overly concerned.[74]

The situation grew more serious several days later when Margot Asquith told her husband that H. W. Massingham, editor of the *Nation*, had warned her that Churchill was intriguing to have Balfour replace Grey as Foreign Secretary. As Asquith noted, this was much different than the "milder version of the same story" he had received several days before. Later that day, the Prime Minister met with Lloyd George and asked him face to face about the rumors. To his surprise Lloyd George told him that he believed they were "substantially true" and that he thought that "Winston has for the time at any rate allowed himself to be 'swallowed whole' by A. J. B. . . . ." Asquith's reaction was one of pity that "Winston hasn't a better sense of proportion, and also a large endowment of the instinct of loyalty."[75]

The rumors of intrigue soon shifted toward Lloyd George when the *Daily Chronicle* published an article implicating him rather than Churchill in a plot against the Prime Minister. That same day, McKenna met with Asquith and related "a tragic history of intrigue." According to McKenna, the Northcliffe press had been engineering a campaign to replace the Prime Minister with Lloyd George, and he was certain that not only Lloyd George but also Churchill were party to the effort. Asquith didn't believe it, although he confided to Venetia Stanley that McKenna had "a certain amount of evidence as to Ll. G to go upon," which he could not write down in his letter.[76] After the interview with McKenna, Asquith met with Montagu, who, not a fan of McKenna, suspected him of playing the part of a "mischief maker." Interestingly, Asquith asked Montagu what would happen if indeed he was forced to leave office, to which Montagu replied without hesitation that "the whole Cabinet, including Ll. G. And Winston, would go with me [Asquith], & make any alternative impossible." Although Asquith told Stanley in the same letter that he was "fairly indifferent to press criticism" and did not "care one damn" about it, clearly he was more concerned than he let on.[77]

He confirmed his concern in an interview that same afternoon with Lloyd George. In what only can be described as a bizarre confrontation, Asquith brought up the subject rather mildly at the end of their discussion, stating that he had heard the "sinister and . . . absurd interpretations" in the press. Lloyd George's reaction was immediate and emotional, and he almost went overboard in his protestations of loyalty to the Prime Minister. He blasted McKenna, whom he believed was being driven by his animosity toward Churchill and was "the villain of the piece & the principal mischief-maker." Then he went on to attack Kitchener, who in spite of every warning had neglected munitions production. The press, rather than attack the Field Marshall, was making Lloyd George the target of their criticism. Finally, as Asquith reported, in an outburst of emotion Lloyd George "declared that he owed everything to me; that I had stuck to him & protected him & defended him when every man's hand was against him; and that he wd rather (1) break stones (2) dif potatoes (3) be hanged & quartered (these were metaphors used at different stages of his broken but impassioned harangue) than do an act, or say a word, or harbour a thought, that was disloyal to me." Asquith had never seen him so moved with his "eyes wet with tears." The Prime Minister responded warmly and assured him, whether truthfully or not, that he had never for a moment doubted him.[78]

The drama continued the next afternoon when Lloyd George and McKenna were both brought before the Prime Minister. The interview in Asquith's words was "at first & for some time a thoroughly disagreeable interview, wh. I do not wish to go through again." Lloyd George accused McKenna to his face of getting Robert Donald, the editor of the *Daily Chronicle*, to write the article, an accusation McKenna "hotly denied." "There was a lot of hitting & counter hitting between them," Asquith reported, "but I am glad to say that in the end I not only lowered the temperature, but got them into first an accommodating & in the end as almost friendly mood." Asquith was good at this sort of thing. He would sit back, let his colleagues have it out, and then step in to repair the damage and bring them together. He confessed that he thought it "always wise to have these things 'out' at once & not allow the personal virus to curdle, or get inflamed, by suppression, or half-hearted approaches at compromise."[79] And so, as Asquith wrote to Venetia Stanley late that evening in his third letter to her that day, the "silly 'plot' is done with."[80]

All of this intrigue within the cabinet, with charges and counter-charges of disloyalty, plainly reveals, as with any government even in peacetime, grumbling and dissatisfaction among the country's leaders. Asquith's careful, deliberative, and exacting leadership style no doubt at times frustrated those in the cabinet more inclined to speedy or even hasty decisions. As an experienced politician who had known years of political intrigue, Asquith surely knew all this. He also knew his base of support was solid at this point in the war, for in the end the unmistakable consensus still held that Asquith, despite his quirks, was doing a good job. As the Postmaster-General, Charles Hobhouse, recorded in his diary on March 23, "The P. M.'s abilities are as transcendent as ever: his qualities more noticeable. Temper, tact, courage, quite marvellous."[81]

Meanwhile, the situation in Gallipoli had gone from bad to worse. Despite efforts to land troops on the peninsula as soon as possible, it was not until April 25 that General Hamilton finally invaded. After days of heavy fighting with at least 20,000 casualties, all that could be secured were two small toeholds on the tip of the peninsula and one a little further north. By May 8 General Hamilton's last offensive had run out of steam and failure of the entire mission became a real prospect. Success in the Dardanelles was going to require more resources, and the harmful consequences of withdrawal were almost immeasurable. Asquith favored continuing the attack. Kitchener feared the negative reaction in the Muslim world should the British withdraw.[82] Out on a limb in support of the campaign, Churchill could not even contemplate withdrawal.

Even before General Hamilton's final May push stalled, Hankey reported to the Prime Minster that trouble was brewing in the Admiralty. Apparently Admiral de Robeck requested permission to attempt another naval action to force the straits now that the Army had failed. Churchill wanted to encourage the Admiral, but Fisher strongly objected and threatened to resign if any attempt was made to force the straits by the Navy alone. When informed, Asquith said it was a "foolish message" and authorized Hankey to reassure Fisher that "separate naval action would not be taken without F's [Fisher's] concurrence."[83] This was only the beginning of a series of episodes revealing that Lord Fisher was becoming more and more unstable.

Wednesday, May 12, began what would perhaps be one of the most challenging weeks in Asquith's entire life. To his headaches over Gallipoli, munitions, and cabinet intrigue was now added the heartache of a purely personal note. A letter from Venetia Stanley surprised him with the news that she had become engaged to Edwin Montagu, a man who had worked closely with Asquith for some time. For well over a year Asquith had been in love with Venetia Stanley, writing to her sometimes three times a day and sharing candidly with her all the burdens of his office. She was half his age, and he surely realized that someday a younger man would capture her attentions. In April she had let him know that things might be moving in that direction. In response, Asquith wrote, "It is quite true that you have (as no one ever could have) the 'potentiality of making me wretched.' I have long known this." Still, he explained, "you have given me, & continue to give me, the supreme happiness of my life; which has been a different & far richer & nobler thing since I have shared it with you. So that if to-morrow you were to be taken from me—I don't mean by death, but by some veil or barrier, wh. necessarily made our confidence less free & entire and complete—I should still bless you as the chief joy & the real Saviour of my life." Nevertheless, he realized, if she did become engaged to someone, "the difference it would make—not in love; that wd always remain to my last living breadth—: but in expression, in intercourse, in confidence, in the thousand things big & little, grave & gay, light or serious, which have been woven into the web of our unique & divine intimacy."[84]

The blow of Venetia's engagement was hard on Asquith. He immediately wrote to her.

> Most Loved—
> As you know well, this breaks my heart.
> I couldn't bear to come and see you.
> I can only pray God to bless you—and help me.[85]

It did not help matters that Asquith believed Montagu to be utterly unworthy of Venetia. Not only this, but her marriage would entail renouncing her Christian faith. Montagu's father's will required that he marry someone within the Jewish faith to receive his inheritance. Asquith wrote to Sylvia Henley, one of Venetia's sisters, the same day he received the news about the engagement. He told her that he "never had any illusions" and that it was "obvious and inevitable." "But this!" he exclaimed. Asquith's usual politeness and graciousness left him for the moment. "It is not merely the prohibitive physical side (bad as that is)—I won't say anything about race & religion, tho' they are not quite negligible factors. But he is not a man: a bundle of moods and nerves & symptoms, intensely self-absorbed, and—but I won't go on with the dismal catalogue."[86]

Asquith and Venetia exchanged only a few more anguished letters, but they both knew that the old intimacy had come to an end. Venetia resented his advice to "take time" before making a final decision to marry, and she could not help but read a tone of reproach in Asquith's last letters to her. They had a final face-to-face meeting on May 23. For her part, Venetia was greatly affected by Asquith's unhappiness. She wrote to Montagu the day after her final meeting with the Prime Minister, "For three years he has been to me the most wonderful friend & companion, and to see him just now made wretched by me is, and should be if I pretend to any heart at all, a real sorrow."[87]

Many have speculated that Venetia's engagement left Asquith psychologically unbalanced during the critical events about to happen in the week to come. If his last letters to her are to be believed, he was crushed by the thought of her marrying Montagu—even more—his losing her as an intimate sounding board for his thoughts and emotions. Nevertheless, his actions in the days to come belie any such handicap. Even as he was suffering emotionally over the loss of Venetia, he exercised all his many political skills in the most difficult of situations as masterfully as ever.

Only two days after Asquith learned of Venetia's engagement, on Friday, May 14, the *Times* ran a story by its military correspondent, Lieutenant-Colonel Charles Repington, with the headline, "NEED FOR SHELLS. BRITISH ATTACKS CHECKED. LIMITED SUPPLY THE CAUSE. A LESSON FROM FRANCE." The provocative article asserted that in the recent abortive attack against Aubers Ridge an insufficient supply of high-explosive shells for the field guns had cost the lives of many troops. An editorial entitled "Shells and the Great Battle" in the same issue concluded, "The Government, who have so seriously failed to organize adequately our national resources, must bear their share of the grave responsibility."[88] The political danger for Asquith was obvious to all. If the accusations were true, then Asquith's assertion in his Newcastle speech only weeks before that "there is not a word of truth" to allegations of supply shortage was a deception of the greatest magnitude.

The week was not over. The *septimana horribilis* had only just begun. Early on the morning of May 15, Churchill rushed in to tell the Prime Minister that Fisher had resigned, confirmed a bit later by a note from Fisher to Asquith stating that he was "leaving at once for Scotland so as not to be embarrassed or embarrass you by any explanation to anyone."[89] At first Asquith was not too concerned. Fisher had threatened to resign on occasions too many to count, and this seemed to be just another feint. Lloyd George came across Fisher by chance that afternoon, learned of his resignation, and immediately went to 10 Downing Street to discuss it with the Prime Minister. Asquith told him, "Fisher is always resigning. This is nothing new." Lloyd George responded that Fisher might really mean it this time.[90] This caught Asquith's attention, and so he asked Lloyd George; his private secretary, Maurice Bonham Carter; and several aides to track down the First Sea Lord. Eventually he was found in the Charing Cross Hotel, where he was handed the following note: "Lord Fisher, In the King's name, I order you at once to return to your post. H. H. Asquith."[91] Fisher was also asked to meet with the Prime Minister that afternoon, which he reluctantly agreed to do.

Asquith and his family had planned to go to The Wharf for the weekend, but he waited until, as his daughter Violet described it, "Finally he [Fisher] was found, caught, carried in a retriever's mouth and dropped—bloodshot and panting—at the door of the Cabinet Room." Asquith's hour-long meeting with Fisher that afternoon did not go well, although he told his daughter that the Sea Lord "had been very friendly and mellow but complained that he found W. quite impossible to work with."[92] This time Fisher was serious. He had had enough of Churchill. The only promise the Prime Minister could wring out of the old admiral was that he would stay in London; however, he would not agree to withdraw his resignation or return to the Admiralty. Asquith still believed that he might have "shaken" Fisher's resolve to resign, and so he sent for Churchill and told him to do all he could to bring Fisher back into the fold.[93]

The interview with Fisher completed, Asquith headed to The Wharf. Traveling to Oxfordshire that evening, Asquith must have understood that he had three options before him.[94] The first would be to let Churchill take the fall for the crisis in the Admiralty. The Conservatives and even some Liberals would be more than pleased with such a move, and it might well speedily end the controversy. There is some indication that Fisher himself thought this was what the Prime Minister was about to do. Second he could accept Fisher's departure, batten down the hatches, and weather the Parliamentary storm that would surely ensue. This is almost certainly what Churchill believed would happen when he arrived at The Wharf the next afternoon, Sunday, May 16, with the news that Fisher's decision to resign was final. Churchill offered to resign. Asquith's response was: "No, I have thought of that. I do not wish it, but can you get a board?" Churchill had already started an attempt at damage control. He replied that the other members of the Board of Admiralty were prepared to remain at their posts, and Admiral Sir Arthur Wilson would agree to take over Fisher's position as Second Sea Lord. Churchill hoped that by quickly announcing the resignation the next day, together with the reasons for Fisher's resignation and the formation of a new Board of Admiralty, the crisis would quickly pass.

Asquith knew better. He had more than likely been secretly considering a third option for some time, hinted at later that day when Bonham Carter mentioned to Churchill that the Prime Minister thought "the *combination* of Fisher's resignation and the munitions crisis was so serious that the leaders of the opposition would have to be consulted on the steps that would need to be taken."[95] Asquith was thinking about the unthinkable for many Liberals—forming a coalition government.

Unbeknownst to Asquith at this time, Fisher had leaked his resignation to Balfour, who in turn alerted Bonar Law. Early Monday morning, as Asquith was traveling back to London from The Wharf, Law met with Lloyd George, who confirmed that Fisher had indeed resigned. Law told Lloyd George that the Conservatives could not sit by with Churchill remaining at the Admiralty, and if he wasn't removed, it would trigger a break of the political truce and an attack by the opposition on the government's conduct of the war. After some discussion, they both agreed that there was no other alternative but a coalition government.[96] It is unclear why Lloyd George, rather than readily agreeing with Bonar Law as to the necessity of a coalition government, did not at first attempt to diffuse the political situation by playing down the events of the past few days and placing a more positive spin on Fisher's resignation.

Lloyd George asked Law to wait while he went to 10 Downing Street to see the Prime Minister. According to Lloyd George's own account of their meeting, Asquith "at once recognized that in order to avert a serious Parliamentary conflict, which would certainly lower the prestige of the Government, if it did not bring about its defeat, it was necessary to reconstruct the Cabinet and admit into it some of the leaders of the Unionist Party."[97] The key phrase was "at once."

Asquith's ready agreement to the suggestion of a coalition, together with his intimation of its necessity the day before, strongly suggests that he almost certainly had already concluded that a coalition government had to be formed long before it was demanded by Law. In one of his two letters to his cabinet later that day, he indicated that his mind had been moving in the direction of coalition for some time. He wrote, "I have *for some time past* come, with increasing conviction to the conclusion that a continued prosecution of the War requires what is called a 'broad based' Government" [emphasis added]. This, despite having only the previous Wednesday declared in the House of Commons that a coalition was not being contemplated.

The question remains, however, why Asquith began to think a coalition government might be necessary well before the twin crises of the munitions scandal and the Fisher resignation. Asquith himself always denied that the pressure of immediate events influenced his decision and rather maintained that the determination to form a coalition government "had come by me quite independently in the exercise of my own judgment."[98] Martin Pugh has convincingly argued that the key to the puzzle is the fact that Asquith was focused on the threat of a general election.[99] The political parties at the beginning of the war had never agreed to suspend future Parliamentary general elections for the duration of the conflict, and by law one would have to be called no later than January 1916. With the growing unpopularity of the Liberal government's management of the war, the chances of a Liberal victory at the polls looked slim indeed. In addition, the Liberals might well have to fight such an election seriously divided among themselves on such issues as conscription and the treatment of aliens. There was also the major downside of increased party warfare, dissolution of Parliament, and a general election while in the midst of the great trial of war. As an alternative, if the Conservatives would join a coalition government, it would destroy any case for an election, keeping the Liberals still largely in power. The Conservatives could hardly turn down the offer. Such a move would almost certainly be seen by a large part of the public as unpatriotic. Asquith then apparently saw the current twin crises as just the excuse he had been needing to spring his strategy of a coalition government and save himself and the Liberal Party from almost certain defeat in the unavoidable election.

With Asquith's coalition strategy firmly in place, things moved quickly. He knew that for such a plan to work he had to keep it secret even from many of his friends until it could be presented as a *fait accompli*. This was because he knew that many in his party would almost certainly prefer to take their chances with an election rather than suffer a coalition with the Conservatives. Once Asquith informed Lloyd George of his determination to form a coalition government, Law was brought in, and the three men briefly discussed the formation of a new government. Law would immediately send Asquith a letter calling for a change of government. The resulting letter was far from a harsh ultimatum by the Conservatives, as it has often been described, but actually nothing more than a statement following a joint decision by Asquith and Law to cooperate with each other in one way or another.[100]

Soon afterward Churchill arrived for a prearranged appointment and presented his list of the new Board of Admiralty that he wished to announce. According to Churchill, Asquith responded, "No, this will not do. I have decided to form a National Government by coalition with the Unionists, and a very much larger reconstruction will be required." Before he had to end the meeting hurriedly when information was received that the German fleet had put to sea, the Prime Minister told Churchill that as part of the reorganization of the new government, he would have to give up the Admiralty.[101] Crewe and Grey, his closest confidants, were then let in on the decision. Grey was outraged and wanted to resign, and only with a great deal of difficulty did Asquith persuade him to stay on.

The Prime Minister then sent two letters to his cabinet, the first asking for their resignations in preparation for the formation of the new government. In a second letter he explained that if Fisher's resignation and the munitions crisis were exploited in the House of Commons at this point, it would have "the most disastrous effect on the general political and strategic situation." He ended with a plea to his old colleagues made with "infinite reluctance" to help him "in the discharge of a most repugnant but most imperative duty."[102]

At the end of this momentous day, Violet Asquith found her father in the Cabinet Room and was told of the formation of a new government. According to her diary, he said to her "All this butchery I have got to do." Even Haldane had to go. "[I]t is a shameful sacrifice to have to make—but they insist on it." He told her that he himself thought of resigning, but it would mean a "complete breakup." As he explained to his daughter, "we couldn't have a public brawl between Fisher and Winston at this moment—with Italy on the brink of coming in." When the two finally said good-night to each other, he told her "This has been the unhappiest week of my life."[103]

The task now before the Prime Minister was to work out the allocation of positions in the new government. Before this could take place, however, he had to dampen the revolt in his own party. The Liberals in the house had not been consulted, and many were outraged when they heard the news. A group of back benchers seethed under the leadership of W. M. R. Pringle and others and discussed the possibility of a vote of no confidence in the Prime Minister. When he got word of what was going on, Asquith, who never lacked for personal courage, went to the meeting himself and to the surprise of all, entered the room as the motion was being debated. He described it at the time to a friend as "one of the most curious experiences I have ever had." "I was of course unable to tell them the whole, or even half the truth, so I had to go more for their affections than reason." Asquith was never easy equivocating or shading the truth. "I can assure you it was a difficult job" and recounted that he "'pulled out all the stops.'" Nevertheless he had "good reason to be satisfied with the effect." After a little speech lasting about ten minutes he reported, "Several of them were on the verge of tears, and they all rose & cheered wildly & declared that they were absolutely satisfied! So far, so good."[104] Turning the backbenchers around so quickly and without revealing important factors in the decision is a testament to Asquith's continued personal appeal within the party. It also perhaps shows that not only Asquith, but also many Liberals regarded a general election with dim prospects of success and, while frustrated with a coalition, were astute enough to go along with one. Most realized that the war had become a fight-to-the-death conflict demanding a united government and nation.

With his base now covered, Asquith turned to the task of putting together his new cabinet. The Conservatives began the negotiations demanding ten positions or half the cabinet, and this was agreed to at least in principle in the initial negotiations among Bonar Law, Lloyd George, and Asquith. The preliminary discussions called for Lloyd George to replace Kitchener at the War Office, Law as Chancellor of the Exchequer, Balfour as First Lord of the Admiralty, Lansdowne as Lord President of the Council, and Chamberlain as Colonial Secretary. Considering Irish sensitivities, Asquith surprisingly said there might even be a spot for Carson.[105]

Several things made these exploratory plans unrealistic. First Asquith and the others must have known that even if they wanted to get rid of Kitchener, public opinion would not stand for it. The Northcliffe press launched a vicious campaign attacking the Secretary of War, but it backfired, merely releasing an outpouring of sympathy and support for the beleaguered Kitchener. Second, if Kitchener was to remain at the War Office, it would be necessary to use the opportunity of a new government finally to move the responsibilities for the manufacture of munitions from the War Office to a separate new entity headed by Lloyd George as Minister for Munitions. Asquith also had second thoughts on elevating Bonar Law, a man for whom he had little personal respect, to one of the two important positions, Chancellor of the Exchequer or Minister of Munitions. Giving Law such power would only heighten the influence of the Unionist leader.

At a conference of the leaders of the two parties Asquith proposed Lloyd George to head the new Minister of Munitions and Law to head the Colonial Office. The Unionists had no problem with Lloyd George becoming the new Minister of Munitions but objected to Law being given the Colonial Office rather than the Treasury. The Liberals argued that it would be impossible to have a protectionist such as Law in charge of the Treasury with such a large Free Trade majority in parliament. They suggested McKenna be moved from the Home Office to the Treasury. The meeting ended without any final decisions.[106]

Negotiations continued, but the country needed a government without delay. At one point Law threatened to leave the coalition unless his conditions were met. Asquith countered with his own threat. He reportedly instructed Lloyd George to tell Law: "There are my terms, you can take them or leave them." With both men staring at each other, Law blinked and reluctantly agreed to go to the Colonial office. Law later warned Asquith, "You mustn't think I am doing this because I am compelled to." He explained: "I know very well I can have what I want simply by lifting my little finger. But I won't fight. I am here to show you how to run a coalition Government by forbearance and concession."[107]

For Asquith, the most distasteful part of the process was removing one of his oldest friends, Richard Haldane, as Lord Chancellor. For years the press had maliciously attacked Haldane as pro-German. From the first, the Conservatives insisted that Haldane be removed as part of the restructuring. Yet the more the Conservatives called for his resignation, the more many Liberals came to his defense. At one point Grey wrote to Asquith, "I think Bonar Law should be told that it is at least doubtful whether I shall stay if Haldane goes."[108] Whether Haldane's removal resulted from Conservative pressure or the mechanics of finding enough spaces for people in the coalition (Haldane was eventually replaced by a Liberal, Sir Stanley Buckmaster), Asquith was criticized for callously abandoning his old friend. Asquith, who was always careful to write notes to all those leaving the cabinet, never communicated in any way with Haldane. Perhaps he was just too ashamed to do so, an uncharacteristic lapse of character. As a result, their long and productive friendship would never be the same. Despite how closely the two men's careers had paralleled each other for almost thirty years, sadly Asquith's name does not appear in the index of Haldane's autobiography. Their friendship became yet another in the growing list of war casualties.

Somewhat surprisingly, considering Admiral Fisher's recent antics, Asquith did make an attempt to keep him on board with the new coalition government. Technically, he had never accepted the old Admiral's resignation, and on May 17, the same day he first agreed with Law that a coalition needed to be formed, he wrote to Fisher asking him to hold tight.[109] As if he needed to prove yet again his instability, Fisher sent the Prime Minister two days later a list of six "conditions" to be met before he would resume his duties and "guarantee a successful termination of the War." He must be given virtual dictatorial powers over the Admiralty. All the current Sea Lords would have to be replaced, and he would not serve under Balfour. The new First Lord of the Admiralty would have to serve like a Parliamentary Under-Secretary. For good measure, he wanted Churchill totally removed from the cabinet.[110] The demands were absurd, and Asquith wrote to the King that Fisher's message "indicates signs of mental aberration."[111]

An unhinged Fisher was a loose cannon on deck. There was no telling what he might say in public. Asquith asked J. A. Spender, editor of the *Westminster Gazette* and an old friend of Fisher's, to tell him personally that Churchill was to be replaced by Balfour in the new cabinet and to otherwise see what could be done. The interview was not encouraging. Fisher ranted and raved, and "All his pent-up bitterness and accumulated grievances against politicians came pouring out." There was nothing to be done; Spender reported that nothing could bring Fisher back into the fold.[112]

In only seven days, Asquith had put together a new coalition government with Liberals dominating the more important positions. The effort had taken its toll. His daughter-in-law, Cynthia Asquith, noted in her diary a visit to the Prime Minister soon after the formation of the new government. "Mr Asquith generally presents the most extraordinary mellow serenity to the world, and is an imperturbable buffer between himself and all crises private and public." She had "never before seen him look either tired, worried, busy, or preoccupied" despite "weathering a good many storms." But this time was different, for "he looked really rather shattered with a sort of bruised look in his eyes." She thought what "a fearful situation for him—the necessity of carting colleagues and the difficulty of yoking a heterogeneous team."[113] The relatively few spoils the Conservatives gained in the new coalition government is further proof that the coalition did not result from any Conservative "ultimatum" foisted on Asquith, but rather came about through the deft maneuvers of the Prime Minister himself.[114] Grey did not follow through with his threat to resign as Foreign Secretary, even though Haldane had to be axed. The long-standing munitions problem seemed at last to be moving toward a solution with Lloyd George now taking over in the new powerful and important position of Minister of Munitions. Further, although a coalition government had to be formed, it was one dominated by the Liberals. McKenna replaced Lloyd George as Chancellor of the Exchequer, and Simon replaced McKenna as Home Secretary. The highest position the Conservatives acquired was Balfour's move to First Lord of the Admiralty. Asquith liked Balfour and had been working with him throughout the war. Law, as previously mentioned, shuffled off to Colonial Secretary. Other Conservatives were of course included, Walter Long as head of the Local Government Board and Chamberlain in the India Office. Lord Landsdowne, the Unionist leader in the House of Lords, was made Minister without Portfolio. Although Asquith had hoped to keep Curzon out of the cabinet, he was made Lord Privy Seal. Redmond, although asked to serve in the new government, refused. Edward Carson became Attorney General. Filling out the coalition was Arthur Henderson of the Labour Party who agreed to serve as head of the Board of Education.[115]

In hindsight, Asquith weathered the "worst week in his life" rather well. There was nothing he could do about Venetia. She was gone and would not return. Undoubtedly her loss had an emotional impact upon him, but Asquith was ever the stoic. Edwin Montagu, in what must have been an uncomfortable first meeting with Asquith after the engagement had been made known, wrote, "He was just too noble and splendid for words."[116] In his farewell letter to her two days before her marriage, he included one of his favorite lines from an Ode of Horace, which he often quoted, "Not heaven itself upon the past has power."[117] He would forever have his memories, but he must, and could, move on.

Despite his personal grief, Asquith's political decision making was unimpaired. He correctly decided to create a coalition government and deftly and cleverly moved to see that it came about. He had great control over his own political destiny and the destiny of the Liberal Party, control much greater than his contemporaries realized. Through a clever strategy of turning the twin crises of the munitions scandal and the Fisher resignation to his own advantage by readily accepting the idea of a coalition, an idea he had pondered for some time, he was able to avoid the almost certain defeat of the Liberals in a general election. More important he saved the nation from the party strife that could only harm the war effort.

NOTES

1. Cassar, *Asquith As War Leader*, 40.
2. Violet Bonham-Carter, *Winston Churchill: An Intimate Portrait* (New York: Harcourt, Brace & World, 1965), 257.
3. Ibid., 257.
4. Earl of Oxford and Asquith, *Memories*, 2:97.
5. Cassar, *Asquith As War Leader*, 39.
6. Martin Gilbert, *Winston S. Churchill, vol. III 1914–1916, The Challenge of War* (Boston: Houghton Mifflin, 1971), 28.
7. HHA to VS, 5 Aug. 1914, Brock, *Letters to Venetia Stanley*, 157.
8. *Hansard*, 4, 65, 2073–80, 6 Aug. 1914.
9. Asquith, *Memories*, 2:31.
10. Brock, *Letters to Venetia Stanley*, 159.
11. HHA to MA, 13 Aug. 1914, BL, MS. Eng. c. 6691, ff. 155–56.
12. HHA to VS, 31 Aug. 1914, Brock, *Letters to Venetia Stanley*, 209.
13. Cassar, *Asquith As War Leader*, 48.
14. HHA to VS, 19 Sept. 1914, Brock, *Letters to Venetia Stanley*, 247.
15. HHA to VS, 3 Oct. 1914, ibid., 260.
16. Gilbert, *Churchill: The Challenge of War*, 110.
17. HHA to George V (copy), 5 Oct. 1914, MS. Asquith 7, f. 212.
18. Gilbert, *Churchill: The Challenge of War*, 111–12.
19. HHA to VS, 5 Oct. 1914, Brock, *Letters to Venetia Stanley*, 262–63.
20. HHA to VS, 13 Oct. 1914, ibid., 275.
21. HHA to VS, 20 Dec. 1914, ibid., 331–32.
22. HHA to VS, 29 Oct. 1914, ibid., 295.
23. HHA to VS, 6 Nov. 1914, ibid., 311.
24. Ibid.; HHA to Sir John French, 6 Nov. 1914, Spender and Asquith, *Life of Asquith*, 2:109.

25. HHA to Hilda Harrison, 10 Dec. 1916, Desmond MacCarthy, ed., *H. H. A.: Letters of the Earl of Oxford and Asquith to a Friend, First Series 1915–1922* (London: Geoffrey Bles, 1933), 13.
26. HHA to VS, 20 Dec. 1914, Brock, *Letters to Venetia Stanley*, 333.
27. HHA to VS, 6 Aug. 1914, ibid., 158.
28. Earl of Oxford and Asquith, *Memories*, 28.
29. Ibid., 29.
30. Cassar, *Asquith As War Leader*, 54.
31. Ibid., 54–55, 134.
32. Spender and Asquith, *Life of Asquith*, 2:152–53.
33. Ibid., 2:153.
34. Secretary's Notes of a Meeting of a War Council, 25 Nov. 1914, NA, CAB 42/1/4.
35. Spender and Asquith, *Life of Asquith*, 2:154.
36. Earl of Oxford and Asquith, *Memories*, 105–6.
37. Secretary's Notes of a Meeting of a War Council, 13 Jan. 1915, NA, CAB 42/1/16.
38. Cassar, *Asquith As War Leader*, 58.
39. Ibid., 59.
40. HHA to VS, 15 Jan. 1915, Brock, *Letters to Venetia Stanley*, 380–81.
41. Cassar, *Asquith As War Leader*, 64.
42. HHA to VS, 21 Jan. 1915, Brock, *Letters to Venetia Stanley*, 388–89.
43. Idid., 389.
44. Cassar, *Asquith As War Leader*, 65–66.
45. A bombardment of the Zeebrugge lock-gates under cover of a smoke-screen was studied by Vice Admiral Sir Reginald Bacon, Commander of the Dover Patrol and the Admiralty.
46. Gilbert, *Churchill: The Challenge of War*, 268–69.
47. Earl of Oxford and Asquith, *Memories*, 2:107; HHA to VS, 28 Jan. 1915, Brock, *Letters to Venetia Stanley*, 405. In his note to Churchill that day Fisher also said his objection to both the Zeebrugge and the Dardanelles plans was only because they did not have a military component. Gilbert, *Churchill: The Challenge of War*, 269.
48. Cassar, *Asquith As War Leader*, 60.
49. Earl of Oxford and Asquith, *Memories*, 2:106–7.
50. Hankey Diary, 19 Mar. 1915, Brock, *Letters to Venetia Stanley*, 374.
51. Hankey to Balfour, 10 Feb. 1915, Brit. L, Add MS 49703, f. 166.
52. 17 Jan. 1915, Lord Riddell, *Lord Riddell's War Diary, 1914–1918* (London: Ivor Nicholson & Watson, 1933), 53.
53. War Council minutes, 16 Feb. 1915, NA, CAB 42/1/35.
54. HHA to VS, 23 Feb. 1915, ibid., 445–46.
55. HHA to VS, 12 Mar. 1915, Brock, *Letters to Venetia Stanley*, 474.
56. HHA to VS, 18 Mar. 1915, ibid., 488.
57. David Lloyd George, "Some Further Considerations on the Conduct of the War," NA, CAB 37/124/40, p. 5.
58. Spender and Asquith, *Life of Lord Asquith*, 136.

59. Kitchener to HHA, 12 July 1915, BL, MS. Asquith 14, f. 106.
60. Lloyd George to Balfour, 6 Mar. 1915, Brit. L, Add MS 49692, f. 234–35.
61. Cassar, *Asquith As War Leader*, 85.
62. Grigg, *From Peace to War*, 240.
63. George, *War Memories*, 159.
64. HHA to VS, 22 Mar. 1915, Brock, *Letters to Venetia Stanley*, 497–98.
65. HHA to VS, 18 Mar. 1915, ibid., 488.
66. HHA to Lloyd George, 22 Mar. 1915, George, *War Memories*, 161.
67. HHA to VS, 24 Mar. 1915, Brock, *Letters to Venetia Stanley*, 506.
68. Montagu to HHA, (no date mentioned), George, *War Memories*, 164.
69. HHA to VS, 28 Mar. 1915, Brock, *Letters to Venetia Stanley*, 514.
70. Cassar, *Asquith As War Leader*, 85–86.
71. Ibid., 87.
72. Kitchener to HHA, 14 Apr. 1915, BL, MS. Asquith 14, ff. 25–26.
73. *The Times*, 4 Apr. 1915, 9.
74. HHA to VS, 21 Mar. 1915, Brock, *Letters to Venetia Stanley*, 495.
75. HHA to VS, 25 Mar. 1915, ibid., 508.
76. HHA to VS, 29 Mar. 1915, ibid., 517.
77. Ibid.
78. Ibid., 519.
79. HHA to VS, 30 Mar. 1915 (ii), ibid., 522.
80. HHA to VS, 30 Mar. 1915 (iii), ibid., 523.
81. Edward David, ed., *Inside Asquith's Cabinet: From the Diaries of Charles Hobhouse* (London: John Murray, 1977), 229.
82. Cassar, *Asquith As War Leader*, 91.
83. Hankey Diary, 11 May 1915, Martin Gilbert, *Winston S. Churchill, Companion Volume III, Part 2 May 1915–December 1916* (Boston: Houghton Mifflin, 1973), 858.
84. HHA to VS, 19 Apr. 1915, Brock, *Letters to Venetia Stanley*, 533–34.
85. HHA to VS, 12 May 1915, ibid., 593.
86. HHA to Sylvia Henley, 12 May 1915, ibid., 596.
87. VS to Edwin Montagu, 24 May 1916, ibid., 597.
88. *The Times*, 14 May 1915, 8, 9.
89. Asquith, *Memories*, 2:109.
90. Riddell, *War Diary*, 93.
91. HHA to Lord Fisher, 15 May 1915, Gilbert, *Churchill, Companion Volume III, Part 2*, 888.
92. Bonham-Carter, *Churchill*, 318.
93. Ibid., 320.
94. Martin D. Pugh, "Asquith, Bonar Law and the First Coalition," *Historical Journal* 17 (1974): 826–27.
95. Churchill, *World Crisis*, 466.
96. Beaverbrook, *Politicians and the War*, 106–7; George, *War Memories*, 201.
97. George, *War Memoirs*, 201. Churchill claims without attribution in *The World Crisis* that Lloyd George, when he met with Asquith, threatened to resign if a

coalition government was not formed. Neither Lloyd George nor Asquith ever mention such a threat being made. Churchill, *World Crisis*, 466.
  98. Asquith, *Memories*, 2:116
  99. Pugh, "Asquith, Bonar Law and the First Coalition," *passim*.
100. Ibid., 828.
101. Churchill, *World Crisis*, 467.
102. Asquith, *Memories*, 2:114–15.
103. Bonham-Carter, *Churchill*, 323.
104. HHA to Sylvia Henley, 19 May 1915, BL, MS. Eng. lett. c. 542/1, ff. 18–19.
105. Cassar, *Asquith As War Leader*, 102.
106. Ibid., 104.
107. Beverbrook, *Politicians and the War*, 134–35.
108. Grey to HHA, 21 May 1915, Asquith, *Memories*, 2:122.
109. HHA to Fisher, 17 May 1915, Cassar, *Asquith As War Leader*, 107.
110. Lord Fisher to HHA, 19 May 1915, Marder, *Correspondence*, 241.
111. Cassar, *Asquith As War Leader*, 107.
112. Spender, *Life, Journalism and Politics*, 2:71.
113. Diary entry, 21 May 1915, E. M. Horsley, ed., *Lady Cynthia Asquith Diaries 1915–1918* (New York: Alfred A. Knopf, 1969), 25.
114. Pugh, "Asquith, Bonar Law and the First Coalition," 830.
115. Cassar, *Asquith As War Leader*, 108.
116. Edwin Montagu to VS, 31 May 1915, Brock, *Letters to Venetia Stanley*, 600.
117. HHA to VS, 24 July 1915, ibid., 606.

Chapter Nine

Leading a Coalition Government at War (May 1915–December 1916)

Few thought Asquith's new coalition government would last. Before the new cabinet had even gathered, Lloyd George told Lord Riddell that he was doubtful it could survive for long. He questioned whether the new cabinet could ever work with the closeness of the old, which had been a "very friendly body," for Asquith had proved "a very good-tempered person and had imparted that quality to his Cabinet."[1] Now in a coalition government political opposites had been thrown together and were expected to trust each other. After the war Hankey asked Bonar Law about the lack of unanimity in this first coalition. "It had been regarded merely as a stop-gap arrangement," Law explained, "and both parties were watching each other closely all the time."[2]

In the year and a half Asquith led what became known as the First Coalition, from May 1915 to December 1916, his government faced arguably the most difficult years of the war. As with all wars, it daily presented innumerable problems dealing with all aspects of the conflict. Asquith and his new cabinet had to contend with three major issues in their time together. First was to extricate Britain from the Dardanelles campaign, which continued to prove a dismal failure. Second was to solve the growing problem of manpower. The Western Front had shown an insatiable appetite for troops, and by 1915 there were no longer enough volunteers to meet military requirements. Finally the cabinet, but more particularly Asquith, had to keep the various personalities of the war leaders, both political and military, working together in at least a semblance of harmony. Making things even more complicated, all of these issues had for the most part to be handled simultaneously.

With the new coalition in place, Asquith decided it was necessary for him to meet face to face with British commanders and make an on-site inspection of the front. On the evening of May 30, the Prime Minister, supported by a retinue of civil and military advisors, crossed the Channel to Calais, ultimately arriving at the General Headquarters at Saint-Omer. The next day he traveled to the Second Army Headquarters near Ypres, where he had conversations with General Sir John Du Cane, commander of the Artillery, and General Sir Herbert Plumer, the overall commander of the Second Army, whom Asquith described as "competent though not clever." The Prime Minister and his entourage then proceeded to a high point several miles from the town. Through field glasses he surveyed the entire scene and noted that "Not a soldier was visible, and except for a little cloud of shrapnel in the sky pursuing an aeroplane, not a shot was fired." Later that day he appeared at a hospital and reported, "the cases I saw were very bad ones, mostly head wounds, and one officer dying of the gas."[3]

The second day of this tour was dedicated to a visit to the First Army, commanded by General Sir Douglas Haig. Asquith lunched with many of the officers and toured the headquarters area and some of the trench system. Military commanders appreciated that Asquith with his legal training and experience always distinguished between the military decisions of the High Command and the political decisions of the cabinet. If a general had Asquith's confidence, as did Haig, the Prime Minister did not interfere with the commander's ad hoc military decisions. As a result, Haig had the highest opinion of Asquith and thought he had "much more capacity and brain power than any of the others."[4] The next morning Asquith had a long visit with Field Marshall French. Before his departure from London, Asquith had been given a memorandum prepared by Hankey at Kitchener's request setting out the arguments against additional offensive operations in 1915 and arguing that a policy of attrition should be pursued. Hankey told Asquith, "The whole tenor of Lord Kitchener's remarks to me was that he was most anxious that you not commit him in any way to the dispatch to France of any part of the "New Armies" at any particular date, or give any hint that you would wish this to be done."[5] Following the instructions in this memorandum, Asquith relayed Kitchener's view to French that any New Armies that were being massed should be held in reserve for other theaters or to be readily available for some emergency on the Western Front. French disagreed. The experience of the past year had proved to him that the German line could be penetrated, and he believed it could be done even more successfully again with more men and ammunition. Asquith knew that this difference of opinion between the two Field Marshalls had to be resolved, and when he broached the topic of reconciliation, French offered to try to settle their differences. They agreed that French should leave immediately for London with Asquith to follow, so that French would appear to be acting of his own accord and not being led by Asquith back to London.[6]

That afternoon Alexandre Millerand, French Minister of War, joined by Generals Joffre and Foch, came to see Asquith. The French wanted to know when they could count on the arrival of the New Armies. Asquith responded that the decision was Kitchener's. Despite French arguments that the Germans had been weakened by the spring offensives and by the commitments to the Russian Front, Asquith held firm, made no promises, and returned to London in the early hours of June 4.[7]

The tour of the front and the conferences had been successful. Asquith had done exactly as Kitchener had instructed; no commitments had been made to the French. Even before departing France, the Prime Minister wrote glowingly to Field Marshall French that he found the British Army "from the top to the bottom—from those in the highest commands to the latest arrivals among the rank and file—animated by the same spirit, united in the same purpose, and inspired by the same confidence."[8] Despite this rosy description, Asquith was not totally satisfied with what he saw, for his report to the cabinet recommended that there should be an immediate study to determine the state of the Army's "lines of defence & retreat." In addition, French should come to London to discuss his "general strategy of the coming months' policy for the next few months" and after this was done a conference on strategy should be held with the French military.[9]

As soon as the new government was formed, Asquith moved to establish what was called the "Dardanelles Committee" to replace the War Council. Belying its name, this new committee considered policy not only for the Dardanelles but for all war theaters, because at this point any action taken in the Dardanelles almost always affected other theaters of the war.[10] It consisted of thirteen members, six Liberals, six Conservatives, and one non-party member.[11] It was originally designed to work as a pre-war cabinet committee, and for the first few months of its existence, there were no service members, and the Chiefs of Staff or other technical officers rarely were asked to attend.[12]

Asquith's earlier recommendation of a meeting with Field Marshall French in London came to pass in the first week of July, when the cabinet engaged in a thorough review of military policy with the British commander. As Asquith recorded at the time, French told the cabinet that "Joffre's recent offensive had not been a complete failure, & alarming us all by his announcement of a new offensive movement concerted between Joffre & himself." French also informed the cabinet that he had agreed with Joffre to mount a joint offensive sometime in August. The Generals feared that if they waited until 1916, there was a good chance Russia might be defeated and the Germans could concentrate of the Western Front.[13] French got the affirmation he wanted that the west was the dominant theater, but the cabinet was only willing to go so far. Asquith's summary of the views of the cabinet written at the end of the deliberations states, "In view of the still imperfect equipment of our New Army in the matter of artillery ammunition, and the uncertainties of the strategic situation, it should be strongly represented to the French that they should defer in offensive operations." If, however, the French insisted on an offensive, "Sir John French will lend such cooperation with his existing forces as, in his judgment, will be useful for the purpose, and not unduly costly to his army." The overriding principle for the cabinet was that "We must keep our hands free in view of the unforeseeable contingencies of a war which is being carried on in so many different theatres."[14]

Within days after the strategy conference, Asquith again crossed the Channel to meet with French officials, this time at Calais. The talks began at ten o'clock on the morning of July 6. He wrote that none of the French spoke English, and he "opened the proceedings with a carefully typewritten harangue in French, and then we proceeded to a full and free discussion of all sorts of important things. . . ."[15] In his opening presentation he outlined the British hope for no further large-scale Western Front offensives in 1915. Apparently though it was Kitchener who carried the day, at least in Asquith's view. "On the whole the man who came out best, not only linguistically, but altogether, out of the whole thing was K," he wrote at the time. In the end, the French agreed to all the major points the British put forward, including giving the Dardanelles priority over the Western Front for the time being.[16]

After an overnight stay at the General Headquarters at Saint-Omer, Asquith and his party traveled again to Ypres, where the Prime Minster, Kitchener, and "a bevy of Second Army generals and officers, including Allenby, whom I found the most intelligent of the lot" walked through the trenches and dugouts. The Prime Minister was moved by the scene. He wrote, "It is one of the most wonderful and tragic sights in the world, or I should think in history: not a single house has escaped, and there is not an inhabitant left." Even before he made this inspection tour, he of course knew that there had been enormous loss of life for little gain. Looking at Ypres, he observed, "it must have cost us the better part of 50,000 casualties and the Germans probably many more, and nothing can ever repair the damage." He also understood the larger ramification: "Unfortunately it has now become almost a point of honour with both sides."[17]

Apparently, Asquith's unease over defending a piece of land being as a "point of honour" must have been picked up by some at a dinner that night with Sir John French and officers. When meeting with Asquith the next day, French asked the Prime Minister whether he had reservations about defending the Ypres salient. Asquith responded that he knew nothing of strategy and left such a decision to French. Apparently, however, he did not endorse the strategy either. French also was bold enough to raise the recent flap over ammunition and asked whether or not Asquith thought that he had misled him. According to French's recollection, the Prime Minister graciously gave him "quite satisfactory insurances on this point."[18]

When Asquith and Kitchener returned to England on the afternoon of July 8, both men could find satisfaction in their trip. The French had been brought around to the British position on overall strategy in a diplomatic way with no ruffled feathers. In addition, Asquith had the opportunity to spend time in serious conversations with French. The Field Marshall was sensitive and required a high degree of maintenance. Asquith knew this and knew time with his field commander was always well spent.

Asquith and all his cabinet had earlier in June approved of a new summer offensive in the Dardanelles and understood its success was critical, for far too many troops and supplies had already been committed to the project. The attack began on August 6 with a main thrust carried out by Anzac troops to take a high ridge in the center of the peninsula. It was all over rather quickly. Only eleven days later, General Hamilton had to report that the attack had failed. With so much at stake, Asquith like everyone else was greatly disappointed. He had sent Hankey to the Dardanelles prior to the opening of the summer offensive, and Hankey reported many mistakes after the attack had taken place, particularly the landing at Suvla Bay of British forces which were supposed to support the main Anzac attack. Rather than advance, the troops had consolidated their position, even though they faced little or no opposition. In an uncharacteristic loss of patience, Asquith wrote to Kitchener on August 20, "I have read enough to satisfy me that the generals and staff engaged in the Suvla part of the business ought to be court-martialled and dismissed from the army."[19] J. A. Spender saw the Prime Minister several days after the news that the attack had failed and reported, "he went backwards and forwards over the operation on the map, commenting rather grimly on certain phases of it and pointing to where it came within a hairbreadth of success." He told Spender that it was "exasperating" and his worst disappointment since the war began.[20]

The situation in the east became even more complicated in September. In a letter to the King dated October 2, Asquith reported that the "last chance of preserving the neutrality of Bulgaria has now disappeared." Bulgaria had finally agreed to join the Central Powers in return for the promise of territorial gains at Serbia's expense. "The result," Asquith wrote, "unhappily, is likely to be that Serbia will move in her own defence upon Bulgaria—a step which will unite the whole Bulgarian army & nation, now much divided and discontented at the prospect before them." Asquith knew exactly where the blame lay. "The discredit for the result," he wrote, "must be divided between Russia, but for whom Bulgaria wd. probably have been brought in months ago, & Serbia whose obstinacy and cupidity have now brought her to the verge of disaster."[21]

Things then went from bad to worse. At first Asquith instructed Grey to withhold any British consent for Serbia to make a preemptive strike against Bulgaria. His reasons were those he had mentioned to the King, that is, a fear that such a move would only unite the Bulgarians behind their King. Only a few hours later, he changed his mind, concluding that Serbia should be allowed to take strategic advantage of the situation by forestalling a Bulgarian attack and no message should be sent "which could be interpreted either encouraging or restraining Serbia."[22] The cabinet agreed. With Serbia under immediate threat, Greek Prime Minister Eleftherios Venizelos asked the Allies for 150,000 men, so that his nation could fulfill its treaty commitment to aid Serbia should it be attacked by Bulgaria. Britain's part of this number was 75,000 men, and unfortunately it could be only met by withdrawing troops from the Gallipoli Peninsula. Asquith was hesitant. The British General Staff assessment made in late September had concluded that reinforcements could best be used to enable the Greeks to protect the Serbian flank and the line of communication with the Greek city of Salonika.[23] The French, however, at once agreed to the request and immediately ordered a division sent from Cape Hellas. As Asquith explained to the King, "It was impossible for us in the circumstances to hold back," and so, after Hamilton was consulted, the 10th Division from the Dardanelles and a cavalry regiment from Egypt went to Greece.[24]

As the Allied troops began to land at Salonika on October 5, suddenly King Constantine dismissed Venizelos and declared Greece's intention to remain neutral. Asquith, who had doubted the wisdom of the Greek reinforcement plan from the outset, urged that the troops immediately withdraw from Salonika, which was also the opinion of most of his cabinet colleagues.[25]

As expected Austro-German forces attacked Serbia in early October, and four days later the Bulgarians joined in. The Dardanelles Committee met almost daily as the Balkan crisis developed. Meanwhile the Anglo-French offensive on the Western Front at Loos-Champagne had ground to a halt, and it became clear that there would be no future operations on that front for at least the next three months. Only when certain that the offensive in France had stalled, Asquith told the cabinet it was time to make some decision about the east. He made it absolutely clear to his colleagues that in his opinion the Western Front was "decisive." Nonetheless, he believed that in the interim "it seemed best an attack on Gallipoli should be renewed" in agreement with Kitchener, Churchill, Curzon, and others. The alternative was to initiate a front at Salonika, an idea supported by Lloyd George, Law, and Carson. Asquith believed that they simply could not throw a large body of troops into

Salonika, especially when it might mean the abandonment of Gallipoli, which Kitchener told the cabinet would be "the most disastrous event in the history of the Empire." Ultimately on October 11 the cabinet followed Asquith's proposal that an "adequate and substantial" force be moved to Egypt without any commitment to its ultimate destination and that either Kitchener or Haig be sent to the east to report on the situation and make recommendations.[26]

When Kitchener arrived at Mudros, he carried out extensive conferences with naval and military authorities and even personally inspected the peninsula. He concluded that, with Serbia's defeat and Bulgaria's alliance with the Central Powers, the Germans could now supply the Turks directly. This made the Allied position in the Dardanelles untenable and evacuation likely inevitable. He recommended an immediate evacuation of Suvla and Anzac but retaining the position at Cape Helles for the time being.[27]

In the end it was Salonika that brought an end the Dardanelles campaign. Asquith, with Kitchener's support, decided it was time to conclude the Salonika adventure. He and the Field Marshall headed to Calais for a conference with the French. Kitchener effectively argued that the retention of 150,000 men at Salonika was inviting a military disaster. It was simply too late to save Serbia. Asquith supported Kitchener with a prepared statement arguing that military considerations dictated an immediate withdrawal. Despite objections by French Prime Minister Aristide Briand, Asquith remained firm, and the French reluctantly agreed to a withdrawal.[28] When Briand returned to Paris, however, he faced a revolt over the decision to withdraw by the socialists who threatened to withdraw from the government. The French asked that the decision to withdraw be reversed. They were joined in this request by the Serbian, Italian, and Russian military representatives meeting at an Allied military conference at Chantilly. Asquith complained to his friend Sylvia Henley that "'Le belle Alliance' has its drawbacks," and it was "clear that the Briand Gov't wd not survive an announcement that they had agreed with us. . . . But que faire? Our joint 150,000 are in real peril, which is impossible to make the Frogs realize or appreciate."[29]

Asquith was cornered. Under the circumstances, the need to keep the Briand government afloat and the maintenance of harmony among the Allies trumped withdrawal from Salonika. The result would be the abandonment of Gallipoli. On December 7 the cabinet agreed to Kitchener's original recommendation for the evacuation of Suvla and Anzac while retaining a force at Helles.[30]

The Dardanelles Campaign was one of the great Allied disasters of the war, and Asquith as leader of the government bears his share of the responsibility. From the very first, the plan had his enthusiastic support, and it continued to have his support until the very end. It is also true that the attack, which was to be a purely naval operation, had the unanimous support not only of the naval hierarchy but also of Lord Kitchener. Even Lord Fisher's objections were based upon his championing a totally different operation, and he voiced no objection to the Dardanelles plan for naval reasons. The fact is that the operation had the strong support of almost everyone involved in the decision-making process, both political and military. The predictions of success may have been overly optimistic, but no information was available to Asquith or other leaders that could have warranted a creditable objection to the scheme.

As the campaign began to unravel, Asquith at every critical point of military decision ultimately supported the recommendations of the naval and military authorities. When Kitchener objected to sending the 29th Division until the Western Front was secure, Asquith backed him. When Admiral De Robeck recommended calling off the naval attack, Asquith refused to overrule the decision. Finally Asquith went along with the withdrawal of forces only after Kitchener and all other military advisors supported such a move. In all these largely military decisions, should he or could he have done otherwise? In some cases it might well be argued that he should have intervened, challenged military authority, and altered the course that was taken. Churchill for example criticized Asquith after the war for not overruling Admiral De Robeck and ordering the renewal of the initial naval attack. This of course assumes that a renewed attack would have been successful—in and of itself a questionable, if not doubtful, proposition. Even if a more favorable outcome might have resulted, the larger question is whether or not, under the circumstances, Asquith could reasonably have acted contrary to naval and military advice. To do so would have presented enormous, even insurmountable, difficulties. Asquith never considered himself a military expert, but he was a consummate politician. Asquith had always to keep in mind the political ramifications of any failed military action taken against the unanimous recommendation of the services. The negative political fallout would have been so great as to be almost impossible to calculate. And so Asquith throughout the Dardanelles campaign—and indeed throughout the war—for good or ill, tended almost always to defer to the final recommendations of the naval and military authorities. To be fair to Asquith, political and military circumstances left him little room to do otherwise.

After the failure of General Hamilton's offensive operation in the Dardanelles in mid-August, attention once again shifted to the Western Front. Kitchener met with General Joffre and reported to Asquith that the French were now making preparations for yet another large-scale attack on the Western Front and expected full British support. The rationale was the same. If there were no attack in the west, the Russians might soon be knocked out of the war. This time the French were dead set in their intention to attack. In fact, Joffre told Kitchener that British reluctance to support the French might mean their withdrawal from the war. Kitchener reluctantly agreed to the offensive only because, as Asquith informed the King, he was "strongly of the opinion that we cannot, without serious & perhaps fatal injury to the alliance refuse the cooperation General Joffre invites and expects." Asquith and others in the cabinet meeting on August 20 pointed out the many drawbacks of the plan, and sadly Kitchener readily admitted little chance of any tangible results. In the end, however, the cabinet reluctantly accepted Kitchener's recommendation.[31] What was the alternative? The collapse of the Russians was not just idle speculation. No doubt an attack in the West would relieve some pressure on the Russians. Then, too, the French appeared to be serious in their threat to seek a separate peace. Reporting on the cabinet meeting, Asquith wrote, "The French are determined upon a big offensive—both on military & still more on political grounds: to satisfy their own army & people, & to placate the Russians, who are inclined to be angry and suspicious."[32] With no other politically viable alternative, the cabinet concluded "That it was not possible to send out the large divisional units [to the Dardanelles] asked for, since a joint operation was contemplated in France."[33]

By the autumn of 1915 it had become plain to everyone that the Dardanelles Committee was not effectively managing the war. On September 22 Asquith suggested to the cabinet that it should be replaced with two committees, one to deal with the actual conduct of the war and the other to concern itself with the financial outlook.[34] A month passed and inexplicably Asquith took no action on his suggestion. Rather at the cabinet meeting on October 21, when Crewe was chairing the meeting in Asquith's absence because of illness, the frustrated ministers themselves raised the subject. According to Crewe, "without any prearranged scheme," most of the Ministers expressed the view that a change was needed. Crewe was asked to convey to the Prime Minster "the unanimous conviction of the Cabinet that a drastic change is imperatively necessary."[35]

A consensus had developed in the cabinet that the new War Committee should be composed of between three to five men "to deal executively with the conduct of the war."[36] Originally, Asquith thought it should be made up of himself, the Minister of War, and the First Lord of the Admiralty. This would mean that Lloyd George would be excluded. The Welshman, of course, would have none of it, writing to Asquith on October 31 and threatening to resign if Kitchener remained in the government.[37] The War Committee, as it was finally constituted on in early November, consisted of Asquith, Law, Balfour, Lloyd George, and McKenna with a place reserved for Kitchener when he returned from the Middle East. The new committee structure was doomed to failure. The membership could not be kept small, and before long it grew to more than eight. Even more of a cause for its failure was Asquith's firm resolve to follow what he saw as the constitutional imperative to leave final responsibility for all important decisions with the full cabinet.[38]

In the autumn of 1915, the real problem for Asquith was not so much the reorganization of strategic management of the war but Lord Kitchener. No doubt Kitchener had proved invaluable; his reputation gave an instant credibility to the government's war policies and strategy. Over time, however, it had become readily apparent that Kitchener, thrust into the political world from the military, was no politician. The list of complaints about him had grown longer and longer over time. The Field Marshall was secretive. He contradicted himself even in the same meeting. He often ascribed opinions to his Generals that they did not hold.[39] The list went on and on. If Kitchener was not a politician, Asquith certainly was. The Prime Minister realized that his War Minister remained highly popular with the public and his dismissal would have a tremendous negative impact on morale. As Eric Drummond, Asquith's former private secretary, put it at the time, Kitchener "may be a wooden idol but he is still worshiped."[40] There was the further difficulty of finding a suitable replacement. Lloyd George was a natural choice, but Asquith hesitated to give the man who was fast becoming his rival additional responsibilities.

The Kitchener issue came to a head at the end of October. At the close of the October 21 cabinet meeting, the one where the cabinet sent word to Asquith that a small War Committee needed to be appointed, all of the cabinet members except Kitchener stayed behind for a conversation. They all agreed that Kitchener had to go. The cabinet wasn't telling Asquith something he didn't already know. He had actually come to the same conclusion several weeks earlier.[41] Lloyd George and Law went so far as to let Asquith know that they could no longer remain in a cabinet with Kitchener. Understanding that if Kitchener left of his own free will, the negative publicity would be minimized, the Prime Minister took the step of offering him an appointment to the Near East as Commander-in-Chief of all British Forces outside of France. Kitchener did not take the bait. He understood his own importance to the war effort: his personal popularity was part of the glue holding the national effort together. Kitchener was genuinely interested in what was best for the country. The two men discussed other options, and a compromise was reached with the help of Balfour, incorporating each of their positions. Kitchener would retain his position as Secretary of State for War but would leave immediately on a fact-finding mission to Egypt and Gallipoli.[42]

As Asquith explained to Lloyd George on November 3, the government was avoiding "the immediate suppression of K. as War Minister, while attaining the same result."[43] The wisdom of Prime Minister's reticence about actually removing Kitchener was confirmed when the *Globe* inaccurately announced that the Field Marshall had resigned because of disagreements with his colleagues in the cabinet. The public response was immediate. Such was the outcry that Asquith had to assure the House of Commons that Kitchener would be continuing as Secretary of State for War.[44]

With Kitchener at least temporarily out of the way, Asquith moved quickly to make some important changes in the War Office. Most important, to keep Lloyd George happy, he moved the Ordinance Board and Inventions Branch from the War Office to the Ministry of Munitions, a step Lloyd George had been advocating for some time. He next removed Sir John French as Commander-in-Chief of the British forces in France. As Asquith explained, he had for some time had "growing doubts" as to French's "capacity to stand the strain of the task with ever increasing and unforeseeable responsibilities." On the one hand, he had already had a number of conversations with Kitchener on the subject, but the Field Marshall was reluctant to make the change.[45] On the other hand, the Prime Minister did not even consult the cabinet on the issue. Most knew that the sixty-three-year-old French was in failing health and needed to be removed, and Asquith was particularly convinced of this after reviewing an investigation of the conduct of the Battle of Loos. French was placed in charge of the Home Forces. Initially, French's response to what amounted to a demotion was gracious, thanking "most warmly" the Prime Minister in a letter "for all your personal kindnesses to me since I was called upon to command the Army in France."[46] For his replacement French recommended General Sir William Robertson, but Asquith had other ideas. Instead Sir Douglas Haig was placed in command of the British forces in France, and Robertson was appointed head of the CIGS. This was all part of the Prime Minister's larger plan. When Kitchener returned, Asquith wanted the CIGS to be the sole advisor to the government on all matters of strategy. If this was going to work, whoever headed up the CIGS would have to be able to stand up to Kitchener, and Robertson proved to be an excellent choice in this regard.[47]

But the Prime Minister had not quite threaded the needle. Kitchener returned at the end of November, and when he learned that he had lost the Ordinance Board and Inventions Branch to Lloyd George, he told Asquith he intended to resign. The Prime Minister, however, knew how best to get to the Field Marshall—he appealed to his sense of duty. While he did admit to Kitchener that the cabinet had lost confidence in his judgment, nevertheless, the Prime Minister told him he was a symbol of the nation's will to fight and that to resign now would be a betrayal of the army, the public, and the King.[48] It worked—at least for the moment. Kitchener agreed to meet with Robinson to work out the ground rules for their future relationship.

Robertson drafted a memorandum setting forth the new arrangement. The War Committee should have supreme authority on matters directly dealing with military strategy, and be advised only by the CIGS. Operational orders should be issued not by the Secretary for War, but by the CIGS under authority of the War Committee. In short, the Secretary of War's duties were to be more or less limited to raising and equipping the army.[49] This was not exactly what the Prime Minister had in mind, and it certainly was not what Kitchener desired. According to Hankey's diary, Asquith was not about to let the new War Committee usurp the cabinet's ultimate authority. He wanted a process that would keep the cabinet ultimately in charge, bring Robertson into power, and keep Kitchener in a place of public prominence.[50] When Kitchener met with Asquith, he somewhat surprisingly agreed with Robertson's recommendations but said he would prefer a position as a roving generalissimo of the British Army rather than remain as Secretary of War. Asquith "was attracted to the idea" but wanted to think it over. "This wd. solve a lot of difficulties if we cd. precisely define & circumscribe the functions of the G. (with a very big G')."[51] In the end, Kitchener and Robertson agreed that Robertson alone should be responsible for presenting military advice to the cabinet, which retained ultimate military authority. Kitchener would remain responsible for recruiting and supplying the army. Both Robertson and Kitchener at Kitchener's insistence would sign military orders. All of this was formalized in a Royal Order in Council in January 1916.

Asquith might have weakened his own position by pushing Kitchener to the side, since the Field Marshall, despite his obvious drawbacks, had served Asquith and his government well. Most important in the early stages of the war, Kitchener had been a unifying force in the nation's war effort. But the political sands had shifted. Important members of the government, particularly Lloyd George and Law, could no longer stomach Kitchener and more important were willing to bring down the government if he remained. Kitchener had unwillingly and unwittingly become a source of division. The public did not see Kitchener in this light, and Asquith knew it. Applying his consummate negotiating skills, the Prime Minister was able successfully to move Kitchener to the one side so as to satisfy his critics, yet avoid a disastrous public break-up of the government which could only have seriously hampered the war effort.

With the failure of the Dardanelles campaign and the continued stalemate in the west, it was becoming more and more apparent that the war was turning into an inhuman and numbing issue of attrition, particularly on the Western Front. A war of attrition meant, of course, an almost insatiable demand for more and more men to throw into battle. In the opening year or so of the war the Army had more than enough volunteers to meet its manpower needs, but by late 1915 many believed the war could not be won with an all-volunteer force. All the other combatants had depended on conscription since the beginning of the war, and conscription now had to be seriously considered by Britain. It became perhaps the most contentious issue to face Asquith's coalition. The cabinet was fairly evenly split on the issue. Most of the Conservatives supported the idea, some more energetically than others. The Liberals except for Churchill and later Lloyd George were dead set against it. Traditionally Asquith has been seen as supporting conscription only reluctantly, after being forced to give in to Tory pressure and to quiet Lloyd George or face a collapse of his government. R. J. Q. Adams has convincingly shown that the whole episode was neither a victory of clever conscriptionists, who slowly beat down the resistance of the Prime Minister, nor merely another example of Asquith's famous "wait-and-see" attitude. Rather, says Adams, compulsory military service in Britain came about only after Asquith himself had successfully maneuvered events and outwitted both Tory conscriptionists and anti-conscription Liberals to pave the way for its acceptance. He rather than others controlled the timetable.[52] It was one of his greatest tightrope acts.

What had caught almost everyone by surprise was the fact that by 1915 the war demanded more men and material than had ever been expected. When the war began, Britain had twenty-six divisions, consisting of six regular and fourteen territorial divisions, together with regular garrisons overseas. These forces had increased dramatically as the war progressed, so that by 1915 the Army totaled seventy-one divisions, which included forty-two regular, twenty-eight territorial, and one naval divisions.[53] This had been accomplished through voluntary recruitment, and yet it was not enough.

Some, such as Churchill, believed from the outset that compulsory military service would be required. In the very first month of the war, he made a pitch to the cabinet that traditional voluntary recruitment should be abandoned in favor of conscription, which was already employed in France, Germany, and Russia. He got nowhere with his Liberal colleagues. In Asquith's mind, there was no need for such a move, as long as there were sufficient volunteers, and to attempt such a drastic move would "divide the country from one end to the other."[54] Even more important it would seriously split the Liberal Party.

Asquith was correct in his analysis of the politics of conscription in the early stage of the war. The trade unions were adamantly opposed to any talk of military conscription, for they feared that if the nation accepted military conscription, then industrial conscription, with its loss of union bargaining power, would not be far behind.[55] Further, most in the Liberal Party saw military conscription as the ultimate intrusion of government into the lives of citizens. Authoritarian powers such as Germany or Russia might conscript, but not Britain.

Kitchener was the key. He did not want conscription, and his personal appeal had brought millions of volunteers to the colors. His formula was simple: "When I do want it [conscription], I will ask for it."[56] Kitchener was no fan of conscripts because of his traditional belief that a volunteer was "worth ten pressed men" and his experience with Egyptian conscripts.[57] As long as Kitchener could recruit more troops than existing resources could train and equip, neither Asquith nor his cabinet had any reason to consider conscription.

At about the same time Asquith formed the First Coalition in May 1915, however, the situation began to change. Enlistments were dropping. The June 1915 figure had dropped 15 percent from May, and in July recruitment dropped another 17 percent.[58] In addition as Asquith explained in his memoirs, there was also the problem of "the coordination of the claims of military service with those of other departments of work equally necessary to the successful prosecution of the War." To add to all this, as Asquith noted, there was the troublesome "distinction as regards priority of liability between the married and the unmarried men."[59]

Only a month after the formation of the First Coalition, Asquith agreed to what he knew was an initial step toward conscription, determining just exactly what manpower was available. In late June the government proposed a National Registration bill, and it passed by an overwhelming majority in July. Sunday, August 15, 1915, was proclaimed "Registration Day"; under the act all adult males up to the age of sixty-five had to complete a form stating their name, date of birth, skills, employer, and other important information.[60] As the summer progressed, events began to point to a greater and greater need for conscription. In July Kitchener met with Allied commanders at Calais and pledged Britain to a seventy-division army, almost twice the size of the armies then fielded. There was also a growing number of losses. In August the failure of the offensive in the Dardanelles brought with it large numbers of casualties, and in September and October the British suffered 50,000 casualties in the Battle of Loos.[61]

On August 12 Asquith appointed a new "War Policy Cabinet Committee," chaired by Lord Crewe and composed of Churchill, Curzon, Austen Chamberlain, Selborne, and Arthur Henderson, the leader of the Labour Party. Crewe circulated a minute by Churchill setting out the committee's assignment "to assemble the broad facts connected with men, munitions, and money, which are necessary to enable the Cabinet to discuss the following question, viz: how large should be the Army which we should endeavour to keep in the field during the year 1916?" Further, "If the main facts can be established upon an agreed basis, the Cabinet as a whole will be able to discuss the questions of policy which will then arise."[62] Asquith was carefully taking the second step toward conscription by appointing this committee composed of a clear majority of experienced and capable ministers who supported conscription. Although not stated directly, this committee was being asked gather the evidence necessary to make the case for compulsory service.

The War Policy Committee met twelve times between August 15 and 25 taking testimony from among others Lloyd George and Walter Long, who strongly supported conscription as well as Runciman and McKenna, who opposed the idea. Kitchener also testified but was able to straddle the issue, supported by some of his generals.[63] When the committee finished its work, one of the official reports called for a freeze on the current size of the Army and to continue volunteerism to fill the ranks as the need arose. There were, however, two other reports issued, one of which, endorsed by a majority of the committee members, suggested the immediate implementation of a compulsory service system for both military and civilian needs.[64]

The third report, however, caught Asquith's attention. Signed by only Arthur Henderson, it stressed the importance of getting the people behind conscription before it was forced upon them. "The unity of the nation is in danger," Henderson declared, and the aim should be "to handle the situation so that compulsion, if it comes, comes by the action of the people themselves." The public would choose conscription only if faced with either conscription or defeat. Yet "they cannot be brought to that alternative suddenly, or apart from the conviction that it is a military necessity." In short, "They must have time."[65]

Asquith hardly needed Henderson to tell him that the working class largely opposed conscription. A meeting of the Trade Union Congress, representing three million members, in Bristol in September passed a resolution stating that the "reactionary Press" was attempting to foist conscription on the country, a system "which always proves a burden to the workers and will divide the nation at a time when absolute unanimity is essential." No reliable evidence had yet been presented to demonstrate that the voluntary system of recruitment had failed and that all the men necessary "can and will be obtained through a voluntary system." It was a resounding "no" to conscription.[66] All in all, the Prime Minister reported to Parliament, he had received in the last three months over four hundred petitions from labor organizations voicing their opposition to conscription.[67]

For Asquith, the committee solved nothing for the short term and in fact placed him in even more of a dilemma. As Hankey accurately observed in his memoirs, "This had put Asquith in a fix, as at that time any attempt on his part to force though compulsory service would have involved resignations, and the unity of the Coalition Cabinet would have been lost."[68] Asquith was above all a masterful politician with a keen eye to public opinion and saw immediately the truth in Henderson's memorandum calling for public opinion to coalesce behind conscription. He desperately needed time for this to take place, but it was unclear how long he could hold up against the mounting political pressure to begin compulsory military service.

At this point Asquith turned to his old friend A. J. Balfour for help. Balfour was the one true volunteerist among the opposition, and Asquith needed his assistance in righting the balance at the moment between the conscriptionists and the volunteerists in the cabinet. Writing to Balfour on September 15, he confessed that "It has become quite clear that the question of 'compulsion' cannot & will not be discussed, in Parliament and the country, merely or perhaps mainly, on its merits." Labour was dead set against conscription, and as for the Liberals, he wrote, "I sincerely believe that, great as my personal authority (I can say so without undue vanity) if I were to announce myself tomorrow a reluctant but whole-hearted convert to compulsion, I should still have to face the hostility of some of the best, and in the country some of the most powerful, elements in the Liberal Party." Asquith still firmly believed in the voluntary system that had "stood the ordeal of fiery experiment with marvellous success." If it had any weaknesses, they would best be handled "in better-considered and better-administered organization." He concluded, "I have come to think that it is only by our joint efforts that a bridge can be constructed over a yawning & perilous chasm."[69]

Balfour immediately prepared a memorandum attacking conscription. Despite Balfour's entry into the debate, the key supporters of conscription in the cabinet—Landsdowne, Curzon, F. E. Smith, Chamberlain, and Churchill—believed they had so positioned the prime Minister that within a week he would have to consent to compulsory service.[70] Asquith, however, had one more trick up his sleeve, and a remarkable trick it proved to be. In late September he and Kitchener arranged for Edward George Villiers Stanley, the 17th Earl of Derby, a Tory and a strong supporter of conscription, to serve as Director General of Recruiting at the War Office. Even before the war, Derby had served as President of the National Service League, the most prominent compulsory service pressure group. This new appointment would mean further delay in a final decision on conscription, since Derby would need a chance to analyze the situation and present his own plan of action.

As Derby worked at his new assignment, there was, however, one anxious moment for Asquith in early October when Kitchener submitted a cabinet paper titled "Recruiting the Army," suggesting a form of conscription in districts where voluntary enlistments were insufficient. This caused all sorts of rumors that Kitchener and others in the cabinet might resign if the plan were not adopted. It all blew over, in part because Asquith scrambled and wrote frankly to the Field Marshall on October 17, "So long as you & I stand together, we carry the whole country with us otherwise, the Deluge!"[71] He requested, "Cannot you say that, while you aim at & wd like to obtain 70 Divisions, the thing should be done gradually & with general consent, & that if you can get under the voluntary system (say) 750,000 men by March 31 . . .

you would be satisfied ... I ... am certain in the interests of the country & the effective prosecution of the war that it is essential that you and I should stand together, & that the intrigue which has as its main object both to divide & discredit us both, shd be frustrated." The following day, Asquith delayed the cabinet meeting so that he could talk personally with Kitchener, and although we have no record of the meeting, the men left the meeting united. Asquith's problem was the politicians. That afternoon when the cabinet did meet, Asquith was unwell. After the discussion of a number of disasters, including the Dardanelles, and the possibility of new problems in either Egypt or India, he passed a note to Lord Landsdowne and left the room. Landsdowne explained to his colleagues that the Prime Minister was not feeling well and had been obliged to leave the meeting.[72] Some have intimated that Asquith may have been feigning illness in order slow down the pace of the conscriptionist forces. Even Margot thought that he was not so much physically ill as "stale and morally disgusted."[73] Yet he had never used the excuse of illness, either before or after this incident, for political advantage, and to do so at this critical juncture would seem totally out of character for Asquith. He was in fact confined to bed for a week and carried out no official duties for two weeks. One cannot deny the advantage to Asquith of his real or faked illness. As Lord Crewe reported to the King, "nothing in the nature of a crisis can well occur in connection with this [conscription debate], for some time to come if at all. ... For one thing it is not likely to be discussed in detail during the unfortunate absence of the Prime Minister. ...."[74]

Lord Derby announced on October 19 a somewhat bizarre plan, apparently of his own creation, that required all males between the ages of nineteen and forty-one officially to "attest" that they would serve in the army if called on. If there were insufficient numbers willing to attest, then conscription would almost certainly have to be imposed.

Although Asquith found Derby "unfortunately ... short of brains," there is no evidence that Asquith himself meant for the Derby scheme to fail.[75] Either success or failure of the plan would have helped the Prime Minister. If it succeeded, conscription would be in place. If it failed, at least it would give Asquith and Kitchener the time they needed to create public support. He did, however, indicate to the cabinet his willingness, as he had already promised Derby, for the Derby scheme to be the final test for voluntary service.[76]

While the Derby scheme gave Asquith some breathing room, it did not halt the friction in the cabinet over conscription. Far from it. Some members of the opposition wanted Asquith to pass a conscription bill that would have a plan for compulsory service ready and in place should the Derby scheme fail. Asquith thought this a great mistake. As he told Stamfordham, the King's secretary, "To introduce in Parliament such a Bill would be to strangle Lord

Derby's scheme in the cradle." Asquith's concern was, as it had always been, national unity. Such a bill introduced at this time "would arouse all the animosity of the anti-conscriptionists, every clause would be debated and even it might be finally rejected—meanwhile the necessary number may have been secured: if so all the turmoil and bitterness engendered in passing or discussing the Bill would have been unnecessary."[77]

Asquith was conducting the most delicate of balancing acts and at least so far had been successful in holding his cabinet together. At about this same time, even Lloyd George's mistress, Frances Stevenson, by no means a fan of the Prime Minister, felt compelled to admit in her journal,

> One thing I cannot help marvelling at, is the way in which the old P.M. has kept his Cabinet together during all this difficult time. He has done it by pure craft and cunning, propitiating here, or pretending to propitiate, making concessions there, or pretending to make them; giving promises which he never intended to keep, but which were just sufficient to keep the person concerned dangling until something could "turn up" to alter his frame of mind. Always wait & see! And the extraordinary thing is that this policy seems to work so extraordinarily well, even in war time, from the P. M.'s point of view; though I am afraid the policy of Britain in this war has suffered sadly by it . . . [78]

The cabinet did not receive Derby's final report until mid-December, and the results were of little surprise. More than half a million single men had neither attested nor were employed in work essential to the war effort.[79] With the failure of the Derby scheme, the only question now was how to bring about conscription with the least division in the government and in the nation. The cabinet was already beginning to split along party lines. Asquith's first step was to announce on December 21 a bill to increase the size of the army by a million men, necessary if Britain was to meet the seventy-division standard. Such a request would give him leverage when he finally introduced a conscription bill. Asquith recorded the next day, "we seem to be on the brink of a precipice. The practical question is—Shall I be able during the next ten days to devise and build a bridge?"[80] By the day after Christmas, the situation had little improved. On that day, Asquith confessed to Sylvia Henley, "I find it very difficult to imagine how a split can be avoided, and whatever course I resolve to take, I am pretty sure to be called either a promise breaker, or a procrastinator, or a renegade (according to the camp in which the particular critic is enlisted)."[81]

When the cabinet met the next afternoon, Asquith had his hands full. That morning Lloyd George threatened to resign if the government failed to honor its pledge to call up single men first.[82] Again, it was a battle of time for Asquith. The first item he brought up for discussion was the question of whether to endorse the War Committee's new recommendation to evacuate Cape Helles, the final Allied holdout of the Dardanelles campaign. The Prime Minister afforded each minister the opportunity to have his word on the subject, not just once but twice, which meant that it was 5 o'clock by the time the subject had been fully discussed. Noting the late hour, Asquith observed that there was not enough time left to take up the issue of conscription. Curzon angrily accused the Prime Minister of deliberately stalling to avoid a decision about conscription, but to no avail, the meeting was adjourned.[83] When the cabinet met again the next day, as Asquith reported to the King, "Much divergence of opinion was manifested" about conscription. Asquith set forth a compromise proposal. Unattested single men would be conscripted unless within a prescribed time they could successfully argue good grounds for exemption before a local military tribunal. This seemed to do the trick. The conscriptionists accepted it and, with Asquith's urging, so did the Liberals with the exception of McKenna and Runciman, who said they needed some time to consider their position.[84] After lunch, Asquith must have been surprised when Runciman and McKenna appeared to tender their resignations not because of their objections to Asquith's compromise plan but because they believed that, by implication, the cabinet had decided to give the Army all the men they would ask for. Asquith assured them this was not the case. They still said they had reservations and would have to consider their position.[85]

At this critical juncture the Liberals who opposed conscription began a last ditch attempt to change the course in which the government was clearly headed. Runciman and McKenna once again informed the Prime Minister that they intended to resign if the proposed compromise was accepted as the basis for a conscription bill. Their problem was not with the plan itself but with the military's insistence on a seventy-division Army. They believed the country simply could not meet its industrial requirements and also field that large a force. The Prime Minister was a bit miffed to say the least. He pointed out that both men had said nothing when he made his pledge to the Commons regarding conscripting single men first. He also noted that the exact number of divisions had yet to be decided, and he could not see any relationship between conscription and the particular size of the Army. Despite his efforts, Asquith failed to convince the two to back down, and the meeting had a frosty ending.[86] Later that afternoon the Prime Minister received Simon's letter of resignation. It now appeared that the government really was about to break up over the issue of compulsory service.

That evening, after asking other Liberal loyalists to use their influence to keep their Liberal colleagues in line, Asquith wrote a personal letter to each of the three dissidents. He began by recalling the years they had been together. "We have fought side by side in all the great domestic controversies of the last ten years, & not one of you has ever failed me in loyal and unselfish devotion, or in the highest requirements of administration & policy." This could not help but remind the three not only of their loyalty to their leader but of their leader's loyalty to them over the years. He then appealed to their patriotism and their sense of duty. Their resignations "must surely invalidate the authority of the Gov't with the country, & especially with our own party. . . . Your simultaneous departure would be a shattering blow to the Gov't, & I honestly believe to the National Cause."[87]

Just when the skies could not have been any darker, Asquith received a hard and unexpected blow from one of his oldest and most loyal friends, Grey. Writing to the Prime Minister on December 29, Grey announced that the main point upon which McKenna and Runciman was resigning "is one on which I am in full agreement." The resignation of these two men, with whom Grey felt very close, "makes me feel I must ask you to accept my own resignation." He also said that he should have resigned a year ago because of his eyesight. "I shrink from adding to your difficulties," he summarized, "but with at least three members of the Cabinet resigning with whose views on the financial and economic needs I am in full accord, I have no confidence or expectation that this view will prevail in the Cabinet and it will in the long run be easier for you that I should go with them now rather than that I should resign separately at a later and probably more inconvenient moment."[88]

Asquith would have been less than human not to be shocked by Grey's move. His best friend seemed to be letting him down when he most needed his support. He replied immediately, "I have just read your letter which fills me with despair. If I am to be deserted in this time of stress by all my oldest and best friends, it is clear that I must reconsider my own position." Did he mean he himself might have to resign? Or was he signaling that he might have to reconsider his own position on conscription? He then hit Grey hard. "I have not as yet received any definite resignation from any colleague. Yours would, of course, be universally interpreted as a German triumph."[89]

Putting his concern about Grey to the side for a moment, Asquith scrambled to convince Runciman and McKenna to stay. Simon's more definite resignation had convinced the Prime Minister that he was a lost cause. Asquith might still, however, hold Runciman and McKenna in line. Meeting with both of them that afternoon for two hours, he told them that if their real concern was the size of the Army, they were free to raise that issue and that they could count on Balfour's and his own support. Despite these Herculean efforts, it did not appear that the Prime Minister had won the day with either man. As Asquith admitted to Sylvia Henley that evening, he was still in "deep water."[90]

Grey on the other hand seemed to be coming around. He wrote to Asquith the next day, December 30, "I was much touched by your letter, and the situation is very critical and distressing." He had heard that the cabinet the next day was "to deal with the question of numbers of the army with reference to finance and trade." He went on, "In my view this is the main and critical point, and I have urged McKenna and Runciman to come to the Cabinet and take part in the discussion. . . ." This statement reveals that the three men were in contact with each other over their threatened resignations. Grey believed "that if there is to be a division in the Cabinet it should be on the big point on which I believe we [Grey, Runciman, and McKenna] are in agreement." The relief for Asquith came when he stated, "In any case I am ready to come to the Cabinet to discuss the main issue."[91] Asquith knew he had one more shot.

When the cabinet met, all were there except John Simon, which was expected. At first there appeared to be no consensus. As Asquith wrote, at one point he "thought the situation quite desperate and disruption already in sight." Fortunately, at this key moment Balfour suggested the formation of yet another cabinet committee before any fateful decision was to be made. Whether he made the suggestion with Asquith's prior knowledge is unknown. This new committee was to look at the fiscal and manpower implications of the decision to implement compulsory service and would be composed of Chamberlain (a conscriptionist), McKenna (a volunteerist), and Asquith as chair. They were to spend the next few days meeting with the officials of the Treasury and the General staff "to endeavour to discern the basis of a concordat." "Everyone jumped at this," Asquith reported for "no one really desires a smash."[92]

Asquith introduced the Military Service Bill in the House of Commons on January 5, 1916. In his speech asking leave to introduce the bill, Asquith stated, "I am of the opinion that, in view of the results of Lord Derby's campaign, no case has been made out for general compulsion." The nuance here was "general" compulsion. The bill was confined to a specific purpose, that is, in order to meet his pledge to the Commons on November 2 that married men should not be compelled to go to war before unmarried men.

Labor groups initially opposed the bill, and at one point Arthur Henderson, the Labour Party leader, even offered his resignation from the government. Asquith during the committee stage was successfully able to convince the Labour leadership, however, that married men would not be called up and that there was no intention whatsoever for the bill to be used as the first step toward industrial conscription. With these assurances, Henderson withdrew his resignation, and a Labour Party's special conference defeated a motion to oppose the bill.[93] With opposition crumbling, the Military Service bill quickly moved through both Houses by overwhelming majorities and received royal assent on January 27.

The breakup of the government had been narrowly averted, but the question of conscription, as it turned out, had not been finally answered. Those who supported general conscription began to agitate almost immediately for a broader compulsory service scheme. The Cabinet Committee on the Co-ordination of the Military and Financial Effort, established to keep Grey, McKenna, and Runciman in the government, recommended in early February placing sixty-two divisions in the field by the end of June. According to the report, "men can be found in sufficient numbers and sufficiently quickly to accrue this result without industrial disaster," but warned it could not be done "without grave dislocation of industry, and even some risk."[94] By mid-March Robertson, supported now by Kitchener, together with Lloyd George and the Conservatives, was recommending that all men of military age, both married and single, not needed for industry be made subject to conscription. As Robinson put it, the military personnel requirements could only be met "by putting the same strain upon the social and business life of the community as has long been borne in France."[95] By mid-April, Kitchener was convinced that Asquith would give way on the issue; yet, as it turned out, the Prime Minister was not quite there.[96]

In the previous January, as the conscription crisis was reaching its peak, American President Woodrow Wilson sent his intimate friend and trusted counselor, Colonel Edward House, on a peace mission to Europe. The idea was to see if the warring powers might be convinced to end the war and restore the *status quo ante* with perhaps some territorial compensation given outside Europe to the Germans in return for returning to its pre-war borders. Asquith was sceptical from the outset about the mission. He agreed with Hankey, who recorded in his diary, "No doubt Wilson wants to get kudos for the Presidential elections next November by posing as peacemaker."[97] Asquith "appears to regard the whole thing as humbug, and a mere manoeuvre of American politics."[98] The timing was not right. There might indeed someday come a time when British financial resources were exhausted or some other disaster happened, and the British would welcome a bailout arranged by the Americans, but not now. The British were still confident that they could win the war and dictate the peace.[99]

Remembering his stance during House's peace mission in 1915, this time Asquith, despite his skepticism, played an active role in the discussions. An American peace feeler might prove advantageous to the British so long as they controlled its timing and its terms. Informal discussions between Asquith, other British leaders, and House later became formalized in what became known as the House-Grey Memorandum, initialled on February 22, which stated that "on hearing from France and England that the moment was opportune, to propose that a Conference should be summoned to put an end to the war" and should "the Allies accept and Germany refuse, the United States would probably enter the war against Germany." The offer would be made on the basis of returning Alsace-Lorraine to France, the restoration of Belgium and Serbia, an outlet to the sea for Russia, and Germany being compensated with territories outside Europe.[100]

After Colonel House wired Grey on March 8 that President Wilson had confirmed their Memorandum with a minor amendment, the War Committee discussed the proposal one last time on March 21. It decided not to go forward at this time. There was still a chance of Allied victory, and as long as that possibility existed there was no need for American intervention in the form of peace negotiations. It might prove necessary one day, but that day had not yet come.[101]

A few days after the War Committee disposed of the House-Grey Memorandum, Asquith set out for Rome. He had been invited there by the King of Italy, whom Asquith had met years before when he was Chancellor of the Exchequer. Joining the Prime Minister on his trip were his private secretary, Bonham-Carter, Colonel Hankey, and Hugh O'Beirne of the Foreign Office. Arriving first in Paris on the afternoon of March 26, the following day they attended an Inter-Allied Conference. Asquith described the meeting to his wife. "The Conference was much what one might have expected—30 people of six or seven nationalities, sitting around a table and emitting a good deal of gas."[102] Although he may have been frustrated, Asquith was very good at this type of meeting, and the conference turned out to be a success, not because of any specific actions taken, but because of the goodwill engendered.[103] In Asquith's words, "no harm was done, and we all parted good friends."[104] Leaving the conference, the Prime Minister's party took a detour to see the Marne battlefield where the Germans had been at last stopped in 1914. "The long lines of graves with little flags are very pathetic," Asquith reported. "Very few people realize that the Germans were as near Paris as Slough, or even Hounslow, is to London. . . ."[105]

The next leg of the trip south to Rome was taken in style. The President of France had loaned the Prime Minister his special train equipped with all the modern conveniences. "I have never travelled in such luxury," he wrote Margot from the train, "large saloons, eating car, wonderfully appointed bedrooms, etc.; no stoppages except now and then to take in water."[106] It was a relaxed trip. Asquith played bridge, wrote letters, and read only one English newspaper on the entire trip with the result, he confessed to Margot, that he had "a very scanty idea of what is going on."[107] When he arrived in Rome, he drove with Prime Minister Antonio Salandra through cheering crowds to the British Embassy, where he was the guest of Ambassador Sir Rennell Rodd and Lady Rodd. Asquith and Rodd hit it off. Rodd was a historian and a classical scholar and, as Hankey observed, "was a worthy companion to the P.M. whose vast store of knowledge on all classical and historical matters fills me with amazement and envy."[108]

Asquith was then treated to what he had predicted would be "rather a trying programme of fêtes and ceremonies," including meetings with the Queen of Italy, the Duke of Genoa, who was acting as Regent while the King was at the front, and the Queen Mother, together with laying a wreath at the tomb of King Victor Emmanuel in the Pantheon. As with the earlier experience in France, Asquith received good marks for his sojourn to Italy. Hankey recorded in his diary that the trip to Italy was on the whole a "gigantic success" and that when they were at the train station about to leave Rome, "a number of people went out of their way to say what a good impression the Prime Minister had made." The "Prime Minister in all his speeches had touched the right note."[109] Ambassador Rodd wrote to Grey that Asquith's message to the Italian Senate had been received with "enthusiasm," and that Senate leaders spoke "in warmest terms of the good effect produced by the visit," referring to the Germans as the enemy for the first time. The Ambassador summarized that a "marked change in the political atmosphere" had occurred.[110]

As Asquith made his way back to England, he stopped again in Paris, where the news was not good. The French were fiercely resisting the German attack at Verdun, but they were about to exhaust themselves. Briand and the French Finance Minister, Alexandre Ribot, frankly told the Prime Minister that France might not be able to go on without an immediate £60 million loan and a British attack in concert with a French offensive to relieve the pressure on Verdun. Asquith did not hesitate to reassure the French officials that Britain would do all it could to help them in their hour of need.[111] When he finally returned home, he told the cabinet that if France did not get the requested aid, "she must put up the shutters."[112] It was a sombre ending to his otherwise successful trip to the continent.

The conscription problem was far from ended by the First Military Service Act passed in January. An Army Council report now demanded for full-scale conscription.[113] In a seven-page letter sent on April 17, Bonar Law let Asquith know of his support for the Army Council report and made his belief quite clear that there must be universal conscription. The Conservative leader convincingly argued that he remained loyal to the government, but the time had come to support full conscription. As for the politics of the situation, he wrote, "there is hardly a single Unionist Member who does not believe that the needs of the war now demand general compulsion." Frankly, he wrote, "I think it is easier for you to carry your supporters in favour of compulsion that it is for us to obtain the support of our Party against it." He concluded, "In these circumstances, I feel that the attempt to carry our Party in favour of your proposals would fail, and it would be impossible for me to acquiesce in those proposals."[114]

While Asquith did not suspect Law of using conscription as wedge to topple the government, at least at this point, the same could be said about

Lloyd George, who had been telling people that he would quit the government if universal conscription was not adopted. The Prime Minister suspected that Lloyd George had leaked the disagreements in the cabinet and was orchestrating a crisis to break up the coalition.[115] While Lloyd George might have shown bravado to others, he told his mistress on April 18 that he was anxious to avoid a break and that Asquith was the only man who could get a conscription measure through the House.[116]

It all came to a head on April 19. "Things look as black as Erebus this morning," Asquith later wrote describing the events of the day, "and I was preparing to order my frock-coat to visit the Sovereign. . . ."[117] He appeared before the House of Commons and frankly told the assembled MPs, "There are still, I regret to say, material points of disagreement in the Cabinet, and if these points cannot be settled by agreement, the result must be the break-up of the Government." He further admitted, "The Cabinet is united in believing that such an event would be a national disaster of the most formidable kind . . ."[118] This caused a bit of a panic in the Liberal ranks, and shortly afterward the Liberal MPs gathered and unanimously passed a resolution: "We desire to express to the Prime Minister our conviction that his continuance as head of the Government is a national necessity."[119]

The government was hanging by a tread. As evidence of how bad the situation was, when the cabinet met that afternoon, the following dialogue reportedly occurred:

Asquith: "What am I to say to the House of Commons at 3:45 this afternoon?"

Balfour: "That the British Constitution is bankrupt, that we have broken down and are unfit to conduct the War, and that we tell the Allies to make the best peace they can as soon as they can?"

Asquith: "Am I to say that?"

Unionist Minister: "The Unionist and the Liberal parties ought to be told the situation and asked their views."

Asquith: "That would be the abdication of all government."[120]

After Henderson reported that the executive committee of the Labour Party would not support a broadening of conscription based on the evidence so far, he met directly with General Robertson. The result was a compromise formula: another opportunity would be given to unattested married men to come forward, and if 50,000 did not do so by May 27 and 15,000 the week thereafter, general conscription would be introduced. All were finally in agreement—a bill would be introduced after the Easter holiday, and Asquith was free to go to The Wharf for a well-earned holiday. The King wrote to him that very day, it was with "the greatest satisfaction" that he had learned of "the happy agreement arrived at by the Cabinet to-day" and expressed his "complete confidence" in his Prime Minister. "During the last six years you and I have passed through some strenuous and critical times and once again, thank God, we have 'weathered the storm'!"[121] The same day the crisis passed, Asquith confided to Sylvia Henley, "Things have now straightened out, as they generally do, if you give them time, & don't strike before the hour. (This, I suppose, is the philosophy of 'wait & see'—that much abused formula.) At any rate the Crisis (with the biggest of 'C's) is over. Ll. G. at heel, and the rest acquiescent, & even a little more. It has been a hellish experience, and I am too old a hand to think that trouble is over. But we have taken the big fence."[122] He was proud of his accomplishment, as well he should be, but he also understood that especially in politics glory is fleeting.

Asquith was right to be cautious. Parliament met in secret session on April 25 and 26. The legislation reflecting the cabinet's compromise formula almost immediately began to founder under the vicious attack of those who called for *immediate* full conscription. It soon became evident that the bill had no chance of passing, and the Prime Minister withdrew it. Three days later on April 29 Asquith told the cabinet that there was no alternative but to introduce legislation for full conscription. Henderson warned the cabinet of the possibility of "serious labour trouble" particularly in south Wales, and Runciman was apprehensive of the attitude of railroad employees. Lloyd George countered that these "fears & forebodings" were "exaggerated," and finally the cabinet unanimously approved and Asquith introduced the Second Military Service bill on May 3.[123] This measure extended conscription to all men ages eighteen to forty-one, regardless of marital status, and allowed the War Office to retain for the duration of the war the services of those whose enlistment time expired. The bill sailed through both Houses and received royal assent on May 25.

The conscription crisis was one of Asquith's greatest challenges of the war, if not of his entire Parliamentary career. Some have argued that he should not have delayed but faced up to the inevitable and boldly asked the country in 1915 to accept full conscription on the basis of an appeal to patriotism. He might then have avoided disunity within the Liberal Party and an erosion of the public's confidence in him as a courageous leader.[124] This may well be true, but at what risk? Asquith understood that some form of mandatory service was necessary as soon as the war of attrition began. The challenge was how politically to get to a point that such service would find general public acceptance. He did not need Arthur Henderson to tell him how unpopular conscription was with the working class, and he knew that conscription was the one issue that might well split the Liberal Party. Like the good lawyer he was, he refused to be sidetracked but kept his focus throughout on the central issue: any large-scale, public division in Britain—whether over conscription, class conflict, or party partisanship—would only benefit Britain's enemies. Unity must be preserved at all costs. It is difficult to argue with Asquith's logic in this regard. It took all of his many Parliamentary skills and acute sense of timing to bring the majority of the politicians and the public to agree on conscription, or at least to a point of not harming the nation's war effort. In the end he succeeded. It was a remarkable *tour de force* of insight, understanding, and leadership. At numerous points along the way, it appeared the government might split over the issue, only to be saved from the brink at the last moment by Asquith's maneuverings. It might well be true that his own political future or the future of the Liberal Party could have been enhanced by taking bolder, more accelerated steps, but such moves would have run the high risk of the calamity of demonstrating to the world the disunity of British government and people and, since the issue dealt with the willingness of citizens to serve, perhaps even lead to questioning the resolve of the nation to pay the great sacrifices necessary to win the war. As a patriot, this was simply a risk Asquith to his credit was not willing to take.

As the government was grappling with conscription, the War Committee on April 7 took up the French request for a major coordinated offensive to relieve Verdun. Haig had written that Joffre expected British assistance and that Haig himself recognized the necessity of the joint offensive. Robertson also endorsed the idea and argued that Haig should be given full authority to determine the nature of the attack, assuring the committee that Haig would employ his forces prudently. Robertson did not tell Asquith or the committee that he and Haig had already agreed with Joffre that the nature of the attack would be a full-scale offensive. Asquith's understanding, based upon what Kitchener had said, was that the British effort would be limited to a series of minor attacks along the line. At any rate, Asquith and the committee gave Haig full authority to determine the scale of the offensive.[125]

Of the many war crises, decisions, and flash points the government faced in April 1916, one that was not expected was Ireland. With the outbreak of the war, leaders both for and against Home Rule had agreed to put the issue to the side for the duration of the conflict. Then, on April 20, the Germans attempted to land arms in Ireland using a disguised merchant ship attended by a German submarine. The plot was foiled, and the ship was sunk. One of the prisoners taken was Sir Roger Casement, who had been in Germany recruiting Irish prisoners of war to fight for Germany. This was a relatively minor incident, and even when the Chief Secretary for Ireland, Augustine Birrell, received reports of a possible outbreak of Sinn Féin activity, he ignored them. Then on April 24, Easter Sunday morning, a group of Sinn Féiners in Dublin occupied Stephen's Green, seized the General Post Office, and proclaimed an Irish Republic. The government's response was swift. Ireland was placed under martial law, and troops were rushed to Dublin from Belfast and from England under the command of Sir John Marshall. The British had no problem suppressing the rebellion, which had little support from the Irish people, but only after four days of fierce and bloody fighting with loss of life on both sides and a great deal of destruction to the city.

Although Asquith urged leniency whenever possible and the cabinet instructed that the "period of execution" should be ended as soon as possible, the military authorities over the next nine days executed thirteen of the rebels. Augustine Birrell, who had been forced to resign, wisely observed before leaving Dublin, "It is not an Irish rebellion, and it would be a pity if ex post facto it became one."[126] Yet this was exactly what was happening. The executions appeared to be random. Some of the leading rebels were spared, while others of less importance were executed. All were becoming martyrs.

With Birrell gone and the situation deteriorating rapidly, Asquith with no concern for his own personal safety decided to go to Ireland himself to survey the situation and come up with recommendations on how best to proceed. He departed on Thursday, May 11, and arrived first in Dublin, where he toured the devastated areas of the city. His main concern was that the treatment of the Irish not transform a disturbance into a rebellion. On Sunday he visited Richmond Barracks, where 300 to 400 alleged Sinn Féin members were imprisoned. As a result of his long legal career, Asquith certainly understood how to interview witnesses. After talking with some of the men, even though he realized many were lying, he nevertheless became convinced that many had not participated in the rebellion. He wrote to Herbert Samuel that day, "The Police have been drag-netting the countryside, and I have little doubt that a number of the men ought not to have been arrested." As a result, Asquith directed the military authorities to begin at once "combing them out" with the hope that comparatively few would be sent to England for trial.[127]

The Prime Minister was also encouraged by his public reception in Dublin which he hoped was a sign that the explosive situation could be defused. "There were quite large crowds about," he wrote his wife, "who cheered and were most civil; not a sign of any kind of glumness." He concluded, "They are extraordinary people."[128] On Tuesday he was driven three and a half hours to Belfast. There he had lunch with what he described as "eight or ten of the most hard-bitten Carsonite leaders to be found in the place." He talked to them freely on disarmament, political settlement, and the relation of Ulster to the rest of Ireland. For the most part he found them highly intelligent. Asquith had a hard time understanding their "genuine and inextinguishable hatred of and contempt for the Catholics of the South." He realized that they saw absolutely no difference between Sinn Féiners and Redmonites. Even so, he parted from the meeting on what he believed to be the best of terms and to his great surprise was enthusiastically cheered by the Belfast crowds. He summed it all up, "You never get to the bottom of this most perplexing and damnable country."[129]

Asquith returned to England on May, as his daughter-in-law wrote, "looking rubicund and pleased with his joyriding," but he was also more convinced than ever that something had to be done as quickly as possible to prevent the Irish from slipping into the hands of the Sinn Féin.[130] He decided to show that the British Parliament was not about to back down on Home Rule. Toward this end, his first step was to convince the Unionist members of the cabinet at least to allow the government to discuss with leaders of the Irish parties bringing the Home Rule Act into operation as soon as possible. This he was able to do, and he assigned Lloyd George the task of meeting with Carson and Redmond to see what could be done. Without too much trouble, the three men agreed on a compromise. The Home Rule Act of 1914 should go into immediate effect with an amending act excluding the six Ulster counties for the duration of the war and a short specified interval following the end of hostilities. The ultimate disposition of the Ulster counties would be dealt with after the war, when an imperial conference which would take up the subject.[131]

In the cabinet meeting on June 27, the Unionist cabinet ministers were not happy. Lord Landsdowne and Walter Long saw the compromise plan as giving in to the rebels and questioned the sincerity of the Redmondites. Others did not believe such a plan would have a chance in the House of Lords. Balfour, however, stood behind the compromise, stressing the importance of not alienating American opinion. As was often his practice, Asquith held his own response until after all had expressed their opinions. He was convinced the compromise was the right thing to do, and he appealed to his colleagues' patriotism. "At this critical conjuncture in the war," he said, "a series of resignations & a consequent possible dissolution of the Govt. wd be not only a national calamity but a national crime" and urged his colleagues to avert such a catastrophe. To avoid the plan being aborted, he proposed, and the cabinet agreed, that another committee should be formed, composed of himself, Lloyd George, Lord Cecil, and Attorney General F. E. Smith, to see what additions to the plan were necessary and to report back to the cabinet.[132]

This committee returned to the cabinet on July 5 with the suggestion that the government go forward with the three-point compromise plan, but with the Irish Home Rule Bill amended so as to specifically safeguard the Imperial control of the military and naval situation in Ireland. Lord Landsdowne and Long reluctantly agreed, and as Asquith reported to the King, "The P. M.

acknowledged the patriotism & public spirit displayed by his two colleagues, wh had averted a most undesirable & dangerous situation. . . ."¹³³

Asquith's optimism was premature. Six days later on July 11, when Lord Landsdowne explained the proposed settlement to the House of Lords, he did so in terms that infuriated Redmond. He talked about the plan "making a structural alteration in the Act of 1914 and would therefore be 'permanent and enduring in its character.'" He also listed measures the government intended to make "to undo the mischief which has arisen in the last few years" such as maintaining a "sufficient garrison to prevent a recurrence of disorder."¹³⁴ The performance was a disaster and wrecked the settlement. "Landsdowne's speech has given the greatest offence to the Irish," Asquith wrote Lord Crewe the following day, noting that it was the speech's "tone and temper which especially irritates them."¹³⁵

Yet it was not just Lord Landsdowne's speech that derailed the plan. It never really had a chance. Soon after the speech, the Unionist cabinet members refused to consent to the retention of the Irish members in full numbers in the House of Commons after the Irish Parliament had been set up. Asquith had to watch sadly as another chance to grasp the moment and avoid an Irish disaster slipped away. The plan was dropped, and Irish governance remained with a Lord Lieutenant and Chief Secretary at Dublin Castle. Asquith wrote to a friend at the end of the month, "'The time is out of joint,' and sometimes—indeed often—I am tempted to say with Hamlet, 'O cursed spite, that ever I was born to set it right.' Perhaps I wasn't."¹³⁶

On the afternoon of June 5, the British cruiser *H.M.S Hampshire* steamed out of Scapa Flow bound for Archangel carrying Lord Kitchener. The Secretary of State for War had been invited by the Tsar himself to visit Russia and inspect the front. There were not only to be discussions about the requests by the Russians for additional supplies but also for further extensions of credit. Asquith had been considering sending a high-ranking official to Russia for some time, and the Tsar's invitation coincided with Kitchener's own desire to go to Russia.¹³⁷ That evening, as the ship passed west of the Orkneys in stormy seas, it struck a mine and sank within minutes beneath the icy waters of the North Sea. Although Asquith had been recently forced by political considerations to shift power away from Lord Kitchener, news of his death was a blow. When he came into the room to tell Margot the news the next morning, his face was so grim that she thought Raymond or Oc had been killed in battle, and the Asquiths hugged each other in tears.¹³⁸

The position of Secretary of State for War was second only to the Prime Minister, and Asquith's choice for a replacement would be of the utmost significance not only for the nation but for the survival of his government. As with all important decisions, Asquith bided his time; however, those who sought the position, namely Lloyd George and Law, were hard at work advancing their cases. "All this canvassing & wire-pulling about the succession, while poor K.'s body is still tossing about in the North Sea," Asquith wrote at the time, "seems to me to be in the highest degree indecent."[139]

The most obvious choice was Lloyd George. No other civilian member of the cabinet had been more closely associated with the conduct of the war than the Minister of Munitions. The downsides were both practical and political. On the practical side, Lloyd George had long been critical of the military's prevailing strategy, the CIGS, and much of the military establishment, including Robertson, who was loath to serve under him.[140] What is more, Lloyd George was demanding that if he were selected he wanted total control of the War Office, including powers granted to Robertson as CIGS. On the political side, Lloyd George had become the Prime Minister's greatest rival, and Asquith was reluctant to promote him to such an important position. Law, as leader of the Conservative Party, was also an obvious choice, although he had not nearly the experience of Lloyd George. There were other possibilities. Robertson suggested Austin Chamberlain, whom Asquith saw as a worthy candidate; he would not be seen as a rival and could be counted on not to make waves.[141]

Some even suggested that Asquith himself take over the duties of the War Office, as he had done following the Curragh incident in 1914 and when Kitchener traveled to the Near East. Someone like Derby could serve as his second-in-command. Rather an impressive group supported the idea, including Sir John French, the Army Council, key figures in the right wing of the Conservative Party, and even the King himself. Despite the allure of the position, Asquith was smart enough to understand that his duties and responsibilities made it impossible in time of war to serve as both Prime Minister and Secretary of State for War.[142]

Law and Lloyd George met secretly at the home of Max Aitken at Leatherhead on Sunday, June 11. Law had no love for Lloyd George, and his general sympathy at the time was with Asquith. The meeting did not begin well. Bonar Law cataloged his complaints against Lloyd George, in effect repeating those that Asquith had about his Minister of Munitions. Despite the slow start, ultimately the two men came to an agreement. Lloyd George was the obvious man to succeed Kitchener, and the only alternative would be a weak "satellite" of Asquith or a man agreeable to the military. Both men agreed either way a weak Secretary of State for War would be harmful, if not fatal, to the conduct of the war.[143]

The following day Law traveled to The Wharf to meet with Asquith. When the Prime Minister was told of the agreement between Law and Lloyd George that Lloyd George should be appointed Secretary of State for War, Asquith offered the position then and there to Law, who rejected it. The leader of the Conservatives told Asquith that had he been pressed the previous week to take the position, he might have considered it, but now he believed Lloyd George was the best man for the job.[144] Under an ultimatum from two of the most powerful men in his cabinet, Asquith had no alternative but to acquiesce.

The question remained, however, as to the terms under which Lloyd George would accept the appointment. The Minister of Munitions had been telling his friends repeatedly that he would not accept the position under the terms of the previous Kitchener-Robertson agreement. He told C. P. Scott that he would become the War Minister "only if he were given full powers and that he had intimated as much to the Prime Minister."[145] Although Asquith knew there was no alternative to Lloyd George, he also undoubtedly knew that Lloyd George was on weak ground in demanding the end of the Kitchener-Robertson agreement. If anything, the Minister of Munitions was a politician who cared greatly about his own political future. If he were to resign over a refusal by the Prime Minister to give him greatly increased powers as Secretary of War, it would almost certainly be seen by the public as shirking duty in time of war—in short, political suicide. Lloyd George had no political leverage; all Asquith had to do was wait and see. Finally on June 24, Lloyd George accepted the position of Secretary of War without altering the Kitchener-Robertson arrangement.[146] Duff Cooper, who was staying with the Asquiths at The Wharf, the following day reported in his diary, "They say the Prime minister is worried about having made Lloyd George Secretary of State for War. He thinks it is the mistake of his life."[147] Margot too was worried. She wrote perceptively in her own diary that day, "We are out, it is only a question of time when we shall have to leave Downing Street."[148]

Early in the morning of July 1 a 40,000-pound mine beneath the German lines at Hawthorne Ridge Redoubt exploded. Within minutes, thirteen British divisions began to advance north of the Somme River, supported by the advance of eleven French divisions south of the river. The Battle of the Somme, one of the greatest battles of the war, had begun. By the end of the day, the British had suffered 57,000 casualties with more than 19,000 dead, representing 20 percent of the entire British fighting force. Haig's original strategic objective was a breakthrough of the German lines, but it became apparent by the end of the month that this was not going to happen. The CIGS, General Robertson, informed Haig that "'The Powers that be' are beginning to get a little uneasy in regard to the situation." Haig replied on August 1 but mentioned meeting only lesser objectives such as the relief of Verdun, keeping German troops away from the Russian front, and "inflicting very heavy losses on the enemy." He still insisted that "The maintenance of a steady offensive pressure will result eventually in his complete overthrow."[149] The Somme confirmed Asquith's aversion to frontal assaults that promised a breakthrough but in fact produced only minor advances with major casualties. Over time, the Prime Minister had been more and more impressed that it was campaigns that set as an objective attrition that could make significant inroads into German resources. Nevertheless, even when the limited extent of the gains of the Somme offensive became more and more apparent, the optimist in Asquith seemed to prevail, and he told the War Committee that Briand had informed him that the British drive had "saved" Verdun and improved the morale of the French government.[150]

There were other reasons for the Prime Minister's optimism. The Italians were making their first gains of the war along the Isonzo front, and the Russians had won a victory over the Austrians, reportedly destroying half the entire Austrian army and advancing deep into Austrian territory. To add to all this, Romania finally joined the Allied cause toward the end of August.

The Battle of the Somme dragged on throughout the late summer and early autumn, and Asquith did not question General Haig's strategy or show disappointment in the progress of the campaign. He wrote Sylvia Henley at the end of August, "Haig is I think doing very well: sticking to his original plan and not allowing himself to be hustled."[151] Nor did his view change when he traveled to France in the first week of September to view the front first hand.

One of the highlights of the trip for Asquith was the opportunity to see his son Raymond. Asquith wrote to Margot that he found his son "very well and in good spirits." He further described their visit together. "Our guns were firing all around and just as we were walking to the top of the little hill to visit the wonderful dug-out, a German shell came whizzing over our heads and fell a little way beyond."[152] Raymond reported to his wife, "The P.M. was not discomposed by this, but the G.H.Q. chauffeur to whom I had handed over my horse to hold, flung the reins into the air and himself flat on his belly in the mud."[153] Even though Asquith spent hours writing his friends, he never once wrote his son during his more than ten months at the front, a circumstance difficult to understand. Raymond airily dismissed this apparent lack of interest, writing to his wife that "He [his father] has plenty of other things to do; and so have I. . . ."[154] About the only explanation came from Asquith's son Beb when his father "did not address one word of inquiry to him" after he returned from the front in 1918: that Asquith "had at times an excessive belief in the powers of the unspoken word."[155]

Asquith had a long talk with Haig after dinner at the advanced headquarters. According to Haig's diary, not always the most reliable source, Asquith and the government were "well pleased with the way the operations have been conducted here, and he is anxious to help me in every way possible. . . ."[156] Asquith's support for the actions on the Western Front was confirmed when he returned to London. Lloyd George was again promoting the Balkan campaign, and Robertson told the War Committee that if it adopted a Balkan plan the General Staff deemed unsound, he would not accept responsibility for its execution. He did not have to convince the Prime Minister, who said that under no circumstances would he allow a Balkan diversion to jeopardize the renewal of Haig's offensive planned to begin on September 15.[157]

On the morning of the attack, the Grenadier Guards regiment was set to advance to the right of one of the most heavily fortified fortresses on the entire German line. This meant that they would be subjected to withering fire on their flank as well as on their front. With the signal to advance, Raymond Asquith led his troops out of the trenches and was almost immediately hit in the chest as his company ran into a hail of machine gun fire. Knowing that his wound was fatal but not wanting to alarm his men, he casually lit a cigarette as he was taken by stretcher bearers to the rear dressing station. His aide Needham later wrote to Raymond's wife, Katherine, "such coolness under shell fire as Mr. Asquith displayed would be difficult to equal."[158] Raymond died a short time later—the "breakthrough" of the German lines as elusive as ever.

Two days later while the Asquiths were enjoying a weekend party at The Wharf, Margot was called to the telephone at 9:30 in the evening. On the line was David Davies, recently appointed the Prime Minister's second secretary. "Terrible terrible news, Margot," he reported, "Raymond was shot dead on the 15th." Margot, choking back tears, composed herself and had the butler fetch the Prime Minister. When Asquith saw his wife's face at the end of the hallway, he guessed what she was about to tell him. Margot, his daughter Elizabeth, and son Puffin gathered round for a while in an attempt to comfort him, and then they left him alone with his thoughts. Well after midnight Margot found him sitting in the same chair, "his poor face set with tears, but quite a simple and natural—a wonderful exhibition of emotion, self-mastery, and un-self-consciousness." She continued in her diary, "I was never more struck by the size and depth of his nature, the absence of bitterness and rebuke, the nobility and largeness of his heart and purpose than I was that night."[159] This was the same man who, only a few years before when his son achieved a classics award at Oxford, had written with pride in large letters in his diary "Raymond got the Ireland!" He confessed to Sylvia Henley a few days later, "I can honestly say that in my own life he was the thing of which I was truly proud, and in him & his future I had invested my stock and hope. That is all gone, and for the moment I feel bankrupt."[160] As Raymond was being carried away on a stretcher he gave his flask to one of the orderlies and asked that it be sent to his father. Asquith always kept it on his bedside table.[161] After the war, Raymond was reinterred at the Guillemont Road Cemetery near where he fell. Asquith helped choose the inscription on his grave marker from Act 5, scene 2 of Shakespeare's *Henry V*,

> Small time, but in that small,
> Most greatly lived
> This star of England.

For the next few weeks, Asquith was—understandably—for the most part indisposed. About this time he began to correspond with Hilda Harrison, wife of Asquith's old friend Major Roland Harrison. She was living in a farm house at Easton Grey with her baby daughter while her husband was at the front.[162] Raymond's death has "been a great blow to me and I am much shaken by it," he wrote. "There ought to be every kind of consolation" from all the many condolence letters from all sorts of people, "But I don't know that it all helps one much."[163] Even with such a great calamity in his life, Asquith was ever the stoic. It was a terrific blow, but he knew his duty. He missed a number of cabinet meetings, and it was not until October 11 that he attended his first session of Parliament since Raymond's death. It was a trying affair for him, but he told Harrison, "I got on rather better than I expected as everyone was very kind and sympathetic."[164]

During his absence the difficult problems facing the Prime Minister had not disappeared. Lloyd George, in collusion with the French, was still lobbying for his old hobby horse, a major campaign in the Balkans. He then enlisted the French to call for a conference to further discuss the idea, and a meeting was held at Boulogne of October 20. Prime Minister Briand was confident of a successful breakthrough to aid the Romanians, and he was even willing to commit two French divisions to the effort. Asquith was unimpressed. He explained that the British General Staff believed that it would take at least ten to fifteen additional divisions, together with supporting artillery and ammunition, to defeat the Bulgarians. Even if such a force were available, it could not make it to the battle area in time to make any significant contribution to saving the Romanians. Even though Lloyd George backed the French, Asquith with the full support of the British military, avoided any commitment except that the British would consider Briand's request that the British commit another division to the Balkans.[165]

The War Committee met on October 24 to discuss the Boulogne Conference and the extent to which the British should support the Balkan offensive. It was a difficult decision. General Robertson told the committee that on purely military grounds additional support at Salonika would have no effect and "might make things worse." His opponents argued that reinforcements would help Romanian and Russian morale. Robertson responded that if the committee thought this outweighed the disadvantages, then he could come up with the reinforcements. In the end Asquith and his cabinet agreed to send reinforcements. Unlike many of his fellow cabinet members, Asquith could change his mind when confronted by convincing evidence and argument. In this case, he told his colleagues that he had entered the discussion with a predilection not to reinforce, but he was now convinced that "a point blank refusal at this stage would have a worse effect on Romania and Russia."[166]

At this time an old ghost came back to haunt the Prime Minister. Back in August a Dardanelles Commission had been formally constituted to look into and evaluate the conduct of the campaign. Law, acting in place of Asquith in June, had promised the House of Commons to lay all the pertinent documents before the country. Upon reflection and listening to Hankey, Asquith later decided public revelation of the documents would cause untold military and diplomatic damage. When he announced this change of course, there was such a row in the House of Commons that he had to agree to set up a Dardanelles (as well as Mesopotamian) Commission to hear evidence for the most part in secret and to present a detailed report. Asquith wrote at the time, "It is infinitely better to have a couple of secret inquiries, which will do no harm & may even do some good, than the publication of papers which, however edited, would have been in the last degree mischievous."[167] Asquith himself testified before the Commission on October 31 and made a good impression. "He was simply splendid," Hankey recorded, "Answered all the questions with extraordinary promptitude—like a racket's ball coming back of the back wall—and with great dignity and confidence, and perfect urbanity and good nature . . . P. M. was very pleased with himself as we walked home."[168]

The next important item on the Prime Minister's agenda was the upcoming conference with the French leaders to be held in Paris on November 15. In preparation, Asquith, assisted by Hankey, drafted a speech setting forth his view of the war at this stage. Lloyd George sent the Prime Minister his own draft harshly criticizing the policy of attrition, but Asquith largely ignored it because he believed it would outrage Robertson and to no effect.[169] As the conference was about to open, Asquith and Lloyd George held a private meeting at the Quai d'Orsay with Briand and his Minister of Marine, Admiral Lucien Lacaze. At this meeting Asquith read his speech in French. Asquith drew a depressing picture. After two years of conflict, there were no real victories, and in fact the Allies seemed to be losing in southeastern Europe. The Germans had ample reserves, which the British General Staff estimated to be between three and four million men, with one million coming into service each year. How long could the Allies bear the strain? His not so subtle point was that the Allies needed a new strategy to avoid defeat.[170] Briand was distracted by internal political struggles but did ask for a copy of Asquith's remarks. In Lloyd George's words, "Mr. Asquith and I drove off to the Hotel

Crillon, feeling like men whose proposals, to which weeks of thought and debate had been given, had been received with civil torpidity."[171]

When the conference, which included delegates from Italy and Russia, convened that afternoon the discussion centered on whether the politicians or the military should be responsible for war policy. The minutes of the meeting record that "The British Prime Minister was of the opinion that it was not the military authorities but rather the Governments which ought to undertake responsibility for the political and strategical conduct of the War. . . ."[172] Although Asquith would defer to the expert opinion of his generals on military matters, he firmly believed in his and other governments' ultimate authority and responsibility. The political leaders agreed that they ultimately should be in control of policy. Their resolve did not last twenty-four hours. When the generals were brought in the next day, they presented a report almost identical to one presented at the last conference held in Chantilly almost a year before. Their conclusion: France should remain the principal theater of the war, and not surprisingly, another major offensive should be planned for no later than mid-February 1917. The politicians, including Asquith, folded. Briand took the lead in endorsing the military's conclusions, and all the rest went along.[173] Asquith and the other political leaders were caught in a bind. Although he desperately wanted to avoid another frontal assault with massive casualties like the Somme, he realized that to challenge directly the almost unanimous advice of the military authorities would invite political disaster. Any alternative suggested by the politicians without the support of the military would never get off the ground.

By December 1916, Asquith and his government were facing the full pressure of a total war. There was a growing anxiety. The demand for fresh troops seemed to have no end. The casualties at the Somme were beyond anything the British had yet seen, and the French were fast reaching their limit. Asquith had to admit at the end of November that only compulsion could provide the men needed to win the war. The War Committee, going beyond even the Army Council's demand, unanimously agreed in principle on November 30 to introduce compulsory national service for all adult males up to the age of sixty.[174] Money was running out too. At a cost of £5 million a day, the war was draining Britain's supply of gold and convertible securities. It might soon become necessary to seek war loans from the United States, where the New York Reserve Bank had already made clear that it might refuse further loans to Britain's allies. In these trying times Lord Landsdowne was the first leader to question whether outright victory was worth the price. In a memorandum to his cabinet colleagues dated November 13, Landsdowne doubted whether another year of war would produce a more advantageous position and urged that the government examine the possibility of a negotiated peace.[175]

Although Asquith disagreed with Landsdowne's pessimistic assessment, he thought Landsdowne had acted with courage and honesty in frankly presenting an unpopular position. To Asquith's mind, the situation was not nearly as dire as Landsdowne thought, and even if it was, the Germans would never offer any terms acceptable to the British.[176] Asquith desperately wanted an end to the war but not at any cost. As he told an audience at the Guildhall on November 9, "Peace, yes; but on one condition only—that the war, with its waste and sacrifices, its untold sufferings, and undying examples of courage and unselfishness, shall not have been in vain." There would be no separate peace, and the struggle was far from over. "I will not disguise from you for a moment," he told the crowd, "my convictions that the struggle will tax all our resources and our whole stock of patience and resolve—the peace when it comes must be such as will build upon a sure and stable foundation the security of the weak, the liberties of Europe, and a free future of the world."[177] Asquith knew there would be no shortcut. It would be either total victory or total defeat.

There were unmistakable and growing signs of discontent not just with the war itself, but more particularly with Asquith's coalition government's handling of the war effort. Grumblings had been going on for some time. Back in April during the conscription crisis, when the House revolted against the government's plan, Lord Robert Cecil had asked Asquith for the government's resignation. "I can only regard the proceedings yesterday in the House of Commons," Cecil stated, "as proof that the Government no longer in any real sense commands the confidence of that assembly." His suggestion was that a truly national government, rather than a coalition, be formed with Asquith as its leader.[178] Nothing ever happened to the suggestion, but at the same time Lloyd George's mistress reported, "He [Lloyd George] has been very quiet lately, but he says he will not stand it much longer. The country is sick to death of Asquith, & would welcome change." Foreshadowing events to come, she observed that Lloyd George "bides his time, but when he does hit, he hits hard."[179] Nor did Lloyd George save his comments about Asquith only for his mistress. He told Lord Riddell a few days later that he would have to resign from the government soon because Asquith "has no plan, no initiative, no grip, no driving force."[180] After the disastrous results of the Battle of the Somme and little progress in the war as summer turned to autumn, Asquith found himself the subject of criticism from all sides. Some were growing war weary and faulted Asquith and the Liberal leaders for getting Britain into the conflict in the first place. Others were more bellicose and believed Asquith was not doing enough to win the war.[181]

Then on the evening of November 8 the House of Commons took up a rather noncontroversial measure to offer for sale captured German assets in Nigeria to the highest non-German bidder. Colonial Secretary Law was presenting the measure when he suddenly came under attack from Edward Carson. Carson, who had resigned from the cabinet in October, was the chairman and hero of the Unionist War Committee, the informal yet powerful back-bench "ginger group" formed the previous January. The measure was attacked on the grounds that bids on the property should be limited to those of British citizens, but everyone knew this was not the issue. Carson and his cohort were challenging the coalition's management of the war. Law had always maintained that he would leave the coalition if he ever lost Conservative support, and if a majority of the Conservatives failed to support him now on this minor measure, he might be forced to resign. The challenge ultimately failed, and the bill passed with a slim majority of Conservatives in support. The first shot had been fired. Only a week later, Cynthia Asquith recorded in her diary, "London appears to be seething with intrigue and politicians behaving like 'politicians.' Lloyd George is hand in glove with Carson and Winston, and they are doing their best to unseat the P. M. and throw out the Government."[182] Intrigue was nothing new, but no one expected that within a month Asquith would be out of office.

The German asset bill debate was a warning to Law that Conservative support for the coalition was fast slipping away. Law had no love for Asquith, but he was smart enough to realize that the Prime Minister not only had the absolute loyalty of a large majority of the Liberal MPs but was also popular in the country as a whole.[183] Nevertheless he was dissatisfied with the large War Committee and sought some arrangement that would narrow the responsibility for the day-to-day running of the war. Soon after the Nigeria debate, he met with Asquith and warned that a "radical change in government must be made, and made at once." According to Law's account of their meeting, Asquith was not impressed, and the Conservative leader said that he would return when he had some definite plan.[184] Law next met with Carson, Ulster leader and *de facto* leader of the Opposition, and expressed his view of the importance of Asquith. "[U]nder a Constitution such as ours," he explained to Carson, "the control of the political machine, even from the point of view of the conduct of the war, was essential as the preparation of big armies; and . . . that in the present House of Commons no one I thought could control that machine so well as Mr. Asquith," to which Carson said he did not "altogether disagree."[185]

Max Aitken, the wealthy newspaper publisher and Conservative MP, joined the intrigue on November 14 when he urged Law to abandon Asquith and join with Lloyd George and Carson, who were working closely together to restructure the control of war policy. What they were proposing was the creation of a small committee of three or four to manage the war in the place of the role traditionally played by the cabinet. Law was unenthusiastic, but he did agree to meet with Carson and Lloyd George to discuss the matter further. Before he did so, however, Law met with Asquith the next day at 10 Downing Street and revealed to the Prime Minister what was up. Asquith showed no surprise, and while he disliked the plan he raised no objections to its being informally discussed.

By this time Lloyd George thought that the Prime Minister was hopelessly unable to make up his mind about anything. He thought that if Carson could join the cabinet, then Carson, Law, and he could arrange to run the War Committee, leaving Asquith to run "his show," that is, the cabinet.[186] A series of meetings then transpired from November 20 to 25 involving Aitken, Carson, Lloyd George, and Law. These consultations produced a plan similar to the one Lloyd George had outlined earlier. The group generated a hurried, handwritten announcement for Asquith to make:

> I have decided therefore to create what I regard as a Civilian General Staff. That staff will consist of myself as President & of three members of the Cabinet who will have no portfolios & who will devote their whole time to the problems which arise in connexion with the prosecution of the War. The three members who have undertaken to fulfil [l] these duties are _____ & I have invited Mr Lloyd George & he has consented to act as Chairman & to preside at any meeting which owing to the pressure of other duties I find it impossible to attend.[187]

Law took the proposed announcement that very afternoon to Asquith and told him that, if he acted quickly, there could be a reorganization of the government without any loss of dignity to himself. Otherwise a smooth transition would be "impossible to carry out." Asquith only glanced at the document and merely repeated to Law that he doubted this was the last of Lloyd George's demands and that he was not keen on Carson coming back into the government. He was not attracted to the proposal, but he did tell Law that he would consider it over the weekend while at The Wharf and give him an answer on Monday.[188]

True to his word, Asquith delivered his response in a letter to Bonar Law on Monday. His reply was frank and lawyer-like in putting forth his objections. He began by stating that he had a "less disparaging view" of the War Committee and believed it was doing valuable work in "thrashing out difficult problems." He did say that he was open to suggestions for a new arrangement, but he believed any committee in charge of war policy must contain the heads of the War Office and the Admiralty. As to the suggestion that Carson be included in the proposed four-man War Committee, Asquith noted that this would mean passing over men like Balfour, Curzon, and McKenna, "all of whom have the advantage of intimate knowledge of the secret history of the last twelve months." He told Law that such a move "would be deeply resented, not only by them and by my political friends, but by almost all your Unionist colleagues." The Prime Minister was most frank in his discussion of Lloyd George. "He has many qualities that would fit him for the first place," Asquith pointed out, "but he lacks the one thing needful—he does not inspire trust." The proposed arrangement the Prime Minster believed "has been engineered by him [Lloyd George] with the purpose, not perhaps at the moment, but as soon as a fitting pretext could be found, of his displacing me." The letter concluded, "In short, the plan could not, in my opinion, be carried out without fatally impairing the confidence of loyal and valued colleagues, and undermining my own authority."[189] When Law received the response, he immediately told the Prime Minister that "he and Lloyd George should work together with close co-operation" and suggested the two Liberal leaders meet together "to have a frank talk together and see to what extent they could come to an agreement."[190]

Some have argued that at this moment Asquith might have saved his government.[191] The conspirators at this time were somewhat divided, and more important Law could see that his Conservative colleagues might not favor a plan that would advance Lloyd George's ambitions. In short, if Asquith had been willing to compromise, he might well have detached Law from Carson and Lloyd George. Of course, this is all speculation. The fact is that Asquith believed he still had considerable political power and was not about to be dictated to with regard to the composition of the government.

The private phase of the negotiations was fast coming to an end. The *Morning Post* on November 23 published a leader urging that Lloyd George was the only man capable of leading the nation to victory. This came as a surprise to everyone, because the editor of the *Morning Post*, H. A. Gwynne, known to be a mouthpiece for Carson, had in the past been a harsh critic of Lloyd George. The handwriting was on the wall for all to see: Carson and Lloyd George were working together.[192] In addition Lord Robert Cecil, all on his own, on November 27 circulated a cabinet memorandum, similar to a proposal Asquith had put forward earlier, calling for a reorganization that was to establish two executive committees—one for war and one for domestic affairs.[193]

When the cabinet met on Wednesday, November 29, the question of the organization for war was at the top of the agenda. The general view, to which Asquith readily agreed, was that some change was necessary. The cabinet discussed Cecil's proposal, and it was favored by many, including not only Asquith but also some of the Conservative ministers. The Prime Minister said that too often orders from above had been ignored, and the new plan would ensure that this would not continue. Interestingly there is no report of either Law or Lloyd George making a comment on the proposal. Finally, as

Asquith reported to the King, "It was, after discussion, considered desirable to set up, side by side with the War Committee, another Cabinet Committee to deal with domestic questions of National Organization for the purposes of the War."[194] Asquith apparently believed the crisis had passed, for he wrote confidently to Sylvia Henley that night voicing no alarm and telling her, "I am setting up, as a counterpart to the War Committee, a Civil Committee of the Cabinet to deal with such things as food, coal, and general national organization." He added, "At the same time I think we shall have to cut down the numbers of the War Committee."[195]

Law now found himself in an awkward position. He had been conspiring with Lloyd George and Carson, and it seemed the cabinet was headed in a different direction from the one the conspirators had anticipated. His Conservative colleagues would soon find out that he had been working behind their backs. The next afternoon he met with the Conservative Ministers in his room in the House to reveal to them the plan he, Carson, and Lloyd George had concocted. The proposal immediately received a negative reaction. Long, Chamberlain, and Landsdowne were hostile, and Cecil went so far as to say the Conservative leader was "ruining the Conservative Party by dragging it at the coat-tails of Lloyd George."[196] In the face of such strong criticism, Law nevertheless made it clear he would not go on under the present system. The general direction of the war must be taken from Asquith and given to Lloyd George; otherwise he would resign. The Conservative leader was shocked at the hostility to his plan and began to feel isolated.[197] On the following day, he wrote to Landsdowne, "I recommended both Asquith and George to have it out with each other, and I consider therefore that for the moment the matter is out of my hands."[198]

As Law suggested, Lloyd George did in fact meet with Asquith on Friday morning, December 1. He presented the Prime Minister with a memorandum setting forth yet another plan for reorganization. Under this plan Asquith would be excluded from a three-member War Committee's deliberations, but he would be able at his discretion to refer any matter to the full cabinet for ratification. Another one of the Prime Minister's objections to the earlier plan was also addressed by making two of the three members the Secretary of State for War and the First Lord of the Admiralty.[199] Hankey recorded that the Minister of Munitions was "practically threatening to resign" if Asquith did not accept this plan.[200]

Asquith responded that very afternoon in a letter to Lloyd George. He wrote that he was "in complete agreement that we have reached a critical situation in the war, and that our methods of procedure, with the experience that we have gained during the last three months, call for reconsideration and revision." Yet Asquith simply was not about to be made a titular Prime

Minster. He was confident enough of his control of the situation that he left Saturday morning for a weekend at Walmer Castle.

On Saturday and Sunday the press broke the news of a possible cabinet crisis. Primed by Aitken and undoubtedly with the blessing of Lloyd George, it began with the *Daily Chronicle* and the *Daily Express* on Saturday morning running a series of stories about infighting in the cabinet. That afternoon Northcliffe's *Evening News*'s headline screamed "LLOYD GEORGE PACKING UP." On Sunday, *Reynold's News* carried the most sensational and detailed story of all under the headline "GRAVE CABINET CRISIS: LLOYD GEORGE TO RESIGN." Lloyd George had met with the editor of *Reynold's News*, an old friend, the previous afternoon, and the article revealed with accurate detail that Lloyd George intended to resign if his terms were not met and implied Law would join him.[201]

Having learned of the impending crisis, Asquith hurried back on Sunday morning from Walmer Castle. Law arrived after lunch, coming from a meeting where the Conservative leadership had passed a resolution urging Asquith to tender the resignation of the government. Strangely Law did not show the actual resolution to Asquith. The Unionist leader later said he "forgot," and no one seems to know why the resolution was never presented to the Prime Minister. Almost certainly Law revealed the essential points of the resolution. Historians disagree as to how Asquith took this ultimatum. Some claim that he saw it as a massive desertion of Conservative support for his government. This seems doubtful. Although Asquith himself never specifically commented on his reaction, he did quote with approval in his memoirs Lord Crewe's account, which he more than likely received from Asquith: "it was implied that the demand was not made in Mr. Lloyd George's interests, but in order that the Government might be reconstructed."[202] Following the meeting Law went back to his Conservative colleagues and, according to the Earl of Crawford who was present, reported that Asquith "positively refused to serve with Ll. G. unless his own position of control was assured." Further "he would not dream of being Chancellor of the Exchequer or Lord Chancellor" and that "no government could stand which did not contain both himself and Lloyd George." Indeed, "He almost indicated that he would fight, call a meeting of his party for a vote of confidence—and let Ll.G. do his best or worst in isolation."[203] From all of this evidence, whatever his reaction to the Conservatives' resolution, Asquith's position seems not to have changed. One thing, however, was clear to the Prime Minister, as he told Law—a reconstructed government would be impossible without Lloyd George's participation. So Asquith called for Lloyd George.

The two men met late that afternoon. Lloyd George had quickly returned from his retreat at Walton-Heath in Surrey but stopped by the War Office on his way over to 10 Downing Street to practice his arguments before Aitken, who updated him on the latest developments. He then met with Asquith face to face. Despite the bad blood between the two Liberal leaders, considering that both men wanted to reach a compromise, it is not that surprising that one was tentatively reached in a relatively short time. At least that is what both men *thought*. Historian J. M. McEwen has convincingly shown that more than likely a *mis*understanding was reached.[204] Both men agreed that nothing was settled as to the personnel for the committee, and Asquith believed that he had said nothing that could be construed as a surrender of his decision-making power. As he described their agreement in a letter to Lloyd George on December 4, "The Prime Minister to have supreme and effective control of War Policy. The Agenda of the War Committee will be submitted to him daily: he can direct it to consider particular topics or proposals; and all its conclusions will be subject to his approval or veto. He can, of course, at his own discretion attend meetings of the Committee." Later Asquith gave a similar description to newspaper editor Robert Donald, whose notes stated, "There was practically no difference of opinion as to the general scheme. The Prime Minister, of course, was to be a member of the Council and to attend as often as he could. As a matter of course he could not attend all the meetings, because the idea was that the Council should meet daily; in his absence Mr. Lloyd George was to be chairman."[205] Apparently Lloyd George in his desire to avoid a total break with his leader heard more of a willingness to stand aside than the Prime Minister ever expressed.

As further evidence that Asquith at least in his mind had not capitulated on the point of his ultimate authority as Prime Minister, Lord Crewe, who saw Asquith that very evening, reported that the meetings with Law and Lloyd George that day "seemed to have confirmed Mr. Asquith in the belief that an accommodation with Mr. Lloyd George would ultimately be achieved, without sacrifice of his own position as chief of the War Committee."[206]

Asquith's long day was not quite over. Sometime that evening apparently the three Conservative leaders—Curzon, Robert Cecil, and Chamberlain ("the three C.s")—met with the Prime Minister and may well have discussed the two-committee structure that had been before the cabinet earlier and explained to him that their resolution asking him to resign, far from being antagonistic, was actually meant to strengthen his hand in a reorganization of the government.[207] Their intention, they told him, was not to remove him from power, but to call Lloyd George's bluff. They were only calling for Asquith's resignation and the resignation of his entire government so as to force Lloyd George to have to attempt to form a government, which they believed was impossible.[208] Finally, just before midnight, Asquith authorized the following statement to be issued to the press: "The Prime Minister, with a view to the most effective prosecution of the war, has decided to advise His Majesty the King to consent to a reconstruction of the Government."[209] This was not an announcement of his resignation or that of his entire government, but rather of his intent to reorganize the government from within as he had always planned.

The next morning Asquith opened *The Times* to a lead article on the controversy. The tenor of the article depicted Lloyd George holding a gun to Asquith's head. Asquith immediately wrote to Lloyd George about the article and reasserted the terms of their agreement the day before.[210] Lloyd George replied that he hoped the Prime Minister would "not attach undue importance to these effusions [*The Times* article]" and claiming it was Northcliffe who "would like to make this & any other arrangement under your Premiership impossible." Most importantly he stated, "I fully accept in letter & in spirit your summary of the suggested arrangement—subject of course to personnel."[211]

The Prime Minister's own announcement that came out in the press Monday morning shocked many of Asquith's friends. He had taken few into his confidence since the crisis had begun. Grey, McKenna, Harcourt, and Runciman met with the Prime Minister early that morning. When told of the compromise Asquith thought he had reached with Lloyd George, basically for a small War Committee, they were surprised and dismayed. McKenna urged Asquith to stand firm and fight; to accept the plan was a humiliation that no statesman could endure. They were willing to stand by him, and Asquith now realized he was not in quite the dangerous position as he thought only the evening before.[212]

Just after noon on the same day, Asquith traveled to Buckingham Palace to inform the King that he intended to form a new government, and the King gave his permission. He then proceeded after lunch to the House of Commons, where he moved its adjournment to Thursday, December 7, so that he might reconstruct the government. Law was still nervous as to exactly what the Prime Minister intended to do. Did the compromise Lloyd George thought he had reached with Asquith the day before still stand? His suspicions were well-founded. Asquith now told Law that Lloyd George seemed to have broken faith by intriguing with the press. He also stated the more honest reason for what he was about to do—hostility to the deal from both Liberals and many Conservatives. The conversation between the two men was cut short when the Prime Minister was called back to the House to answer questions. Asquith went directly from there to 10 Downing Street, where he and Law had another brief conversation. Law again left no doubt that he would resign if Asquith failed to accept the compromise Lloyd George understood they had reached the day before. The Prime Minister did not respond.[213]

How much support did the Prime Minister actually have? Had he been, as Beaverbrook later said, "like a night-walker who has been frightened by the shape of a tree in the dark looming like some great monster—then goes and looks at it by daylight"?[214] To some extent this was the case. A clearer vision came to Asquith only after he met with leading Liberal ministers that afternoon. When asked whether they thought his acceptance of Lloyd George's terms would be inconsistent with his constitutional responsibilities as Prime Minister, they all agreed that it would. Their recommendation was that Asquith resign and force Lloyd George and Law to form a government. Their failure would prove that Asquith was the only person who could be Prime Minister. All well and good, if it worked. But what if it didn't? asked the Prime Minister. A government led by Lloyd George and supported by Law and Carson might drive Labour away and give strength to the pacifist movement. At any rate, Asquith was not yet ready to make a final decision.[215]

In a letter he wrote Lloyd George early that evening, Asquith at last stated his conclusion about the new War Committee. "I have come decidedly to the conclusion that it is not possible that such a Committee could be made workable and effective without the Prime Minister as its Chairman." He did recognize that other calls on the Prime Minister's time would mean that he would have "to delegate from time to time the Chairmanship to another Minister as his representative and locum tenens." Nevertheless, "(if he is to retain the authority which corresponds to his responsibility as Prime Minister) he must continue to be, as he always has been, its permanent President." As to the personnel changes they had discussed, he wrote that he would not remove Balfour as First Lord of the Admiralty and that Carson was not "the man best qualified among my colleagues, present and past, to be a member of the War Committee."[216] In short, except for shrinking the War Committee, Asquith was firmly rejecting Lloyd George's entire plan.

When Asquith sent this letter, he knew that he had strong support within the Liberal Party, strong enough to withstand any challenge from Lloyd George. He had also been led to believe that he had sufficient support within the Conservative Party leadership, even without Law, to reconstitute a national government. The rapid events of the next day would prove that second assumption false.

When Lloyd George received Asquith's rejection letter the next morning, Tuesday, December 5, he immediately contacted Law, whose support he knew to be critical. From the very beginning of the crisis Law had hoped to keep both Asquith and Lloyd George in harness together. Asquith's letter made it clear this was now impossible, and thus Law believed he had no option but "to back Lloyd George in his further action."[217]

With the support of Law assured, Lloyd George resigned. He expressed surprise that the Prime Minister was now rejecting the plan he believed they had both apparently agreed to over the weekend. He was not going to go quietly. He wrote, "it is my duty to leave the Government in order to inform the people of the real condition of affairs and to give them an opportunity before it is too late to save their native land from a disaster which is inevitable if the present methods are longer persisted in."[218]

Lloyd George's resignation was expected. Balfour's was not. Ill and bedridden, Balfour had gotten wind of the dispute between Asquith and Lloyd George over his remaining as First Lord of the Admiralty.[219] In his letter to the Prime Minister, he endorsed Lloyd George's plan and recognized the fact that it "would work more satisfactorily if the Admiralty were not represented by me. In these circumstances I cannot consent to retain my office, and must ask you to accept my resignation." Asquith responded immediately, asking him to reconsider and sending him a copy of his earlier letter to Lloyd George in which he had insisted on Balfour remaining as head of the Admiralty.

Crewe, whom Asquith trusted more than anyone, was summoned to 10 Downing Street after a meeting of the Privy Council in which the King had told him that he hoped there would not need to be a complete change of government. Asquith showed Crewe Lloyd George's letter of resignation. Crewe accurately surmised that the key now was the extent to which the Conservatives were going to support Lloyd George. As Crewe explained to the Prime Minister, if the Conservatives "refused reconstruction and insisted on Mr. Asquith's resignation, whether in order to substitute Lloyd George or not, the Government could not continue in any form." Later that afternoon Asquith met with the Liberal leadership, and they too agreed with this view.[220] The path was now clear. After the meeting with the leadership ended, the Prime Minister wrote to Lloyd George accepting his resignation.[221] It was to be a showdown now between Asquith and Lloyd George with the Conservative leadership making the decision. Who would have imagined only a few months before that the Conservatives would be deciding the fate of the Liberals' leaders?

At 3:00 p.m. Asquith sent for Curzon, Chamberlain, and Cecil to sound out their position. To his dismay they informed him that Law's throwing his lot with Lloyd George had changed everything. They told the Prime Minister that they would not serve in any government without Law and Lloyd George. As a practical matter, they believed no government could last with Law, Lloyd George, and Carson in opposition. When Asquith asked them if they would serve under Lloyd George, they replied that their only object was a stable administration capable of winning the war. They would serve under anyone, including Lloyd George, if they thought this objective could be met.

They urged Asquith to accept an office in a Lloyd George ministry, which he rejected out of hand.[222] Asquith's last hope was dashed when Balfour refused Asquith's appeal to reconsider his resignation. Balfour was not to be moved, and he insisted that his resignation should be accepted and Lloyd George should be given a fair chance.[223]

Lacking Conservative support, Asquith could no longer remain in office. He met again with the Liberal leadership late that afternoon, and told them of his meeting with Curzon, Chamberlain, and Cecil. He also read to them his correspondence with Balfour. The group agreed that it would be impossible to carry on, "and [they] ought not to give the appearance of wishing to do so."[224] As the meeting broke up, Curzon arrived with a letter from Law. The letter began, "Lord Curzon, Lord Robert Cecil and Mr. A. Chamberlain have reported to a meeting of all the Unionist members of the Cabinet, except Mr. Balfour who is unable to be present, the substance of their conversation with you." This letter continued, "After full consideration we are of the opinion that the course which we urged upon you on Sunday is a necessity and that it is imperative that this course should be taken today." Finally it concluded, "We hope that you have arrived at the same conclusion, but if this is not so, we feel that we have no choice but to ask you to act upon our resignations."[225] Asquith told Curzon that the decision to resign had already been made. With that the Prime Minister got into his waiting car and headed to Buckingham Palace, where at seven o'clock that evening, December 5, he submitted his resignation to the King. Always calm in the midst of a storm, he returned to 10 Downing Street for dinner, where his daughter-in-law found him "serene and dignified" and "puffing on a guinea cigar, . . . and talking of going to Honolulu."[226]

The events of the following two days were largely anticlimactic. The King sent for Bonar Law to form a government. By prearrangement with Lloyd George, Law would try to talk Asquith into serving in the new government. If he did not succeed, then Lloyd George would attempt to form a government. After meeting with the King, Law proceeded directly to 10 Downing Street where he asked Asquith to serve in either a government led by Law, or somewhat surprisingly, Balfour. Asquith declined. The King then arranged for a conference of party leaders at Buckingham Palace at 3:00 p.m. In attendance were Asquith, Balfour, Lloyd George, Law, and Henderson. A number of suggestions were discussed. Lloyd George said that Asquith should attempt to form a government among his Liberal supporters. Balfour pleaded with Asquith, on patriotic grounds, to serve under Law. The meeting reached no conclusion and ended with Asquith stating that he needed to consult his supporters.[227]

Asquith then met with the Liberal leadership minus, of course, Lloyd George. Henderson also attended to the meeting. The group quickly dismissed Lloyd George's suggestion that the Liberals attempt to form a government. A government that did not include Law and Lloyd George could not survive. The only remaining question was whether Asquith should serve in the new government. Except for perhaps Henderson and Montagu, all agreed that he should not. Asquith assented. The meeting brought out several good reasons for this decision. As a subordinate member of the government, Asquith would have to submit to the will of the new War Committee, there being no assurance he would even be a member. A disagreement was inevitable, and it would be dangerous for the nation to endure yet another splitting up of the government. If a new system were to be tried, "it had best be entrusted to colleagues of the same school of thought as the new Prime Minister." Second, Asquith's influence, which at present was still "powerful and pervading," would melt away if he joined in a new government. The best course forward was the creation of "a sober and responsible Opposition . . . steadily supporting the Government in the conduct of the War, criticizing when necessary, and in the last resort offering an alternative administration."[228]

Asquith gave his reply to Law at six o'clock that evening, and Law immediately went to Buckingham Palace to inform the King that he would have to decline the royal commission to form a government; whereupon the King sent for Lloyd George, who agreed to try. A discreet canvassing of the Liberal MPs on Wednesday revealed forty-nine would support Lloyd George for certain, while another 126 could be counted on once he became Prime Minister.[229] That evening Law, along with the Conservative Chief Whip, met with Balfour to offer him the position of Foreign Secretary. When he was asked, Balfour, according to Bonar Law, rose from his seat without any hesitation and said, "That is indeed putting a pistol at my head, but I at once say, 'yes.'"[230] The next day Lloyd George fit in the last piece of the puzzle. Speaking to Labour's National Executive, he made all sorts of promises to gain its support for the new government. Ramsay McDonald described the presentation as "exceedingly amiable, but excessively indefinite. He was like a bit of mercury." It worked, and they responded favorably.[231] That evening on December 6, 1916, at 7:30 Lloyd George reported to the King that he was in a position to form a ministry, and kissed hands on his appointment as Asquith's successor.

If Asquith's letter to his friend Sylvia Henley on the evening of November 29 is any indication of Asquith's frame of mind during this trying time, there is no indication of any concern about the survival of his government. Yet only six days later, he found himself at Buckingham Palace submitting his resignation to the King. How did this happen? There is every indication that he did not see the crisis coming, unusual for Asquith, who, if anything, was an experienced and seasoned politician with his ear constantly to the ground when it came to political maneuverings. He rarely, if ever, was caught with his guard down. In his defense, there was plenty of evidence that his position was secure. He had the strong and loyal support of the vast majority of the Liberal Party. Even when the crisis broke, this group remained by his side until the end. He knew that only two men had the political clout to form a government—himself and Lloyd George. As a result, Asquith with his strong Liberal support knew that it was impossible for Lloyd George to take his place without strong Conservative support. With the Conservatives' intense dislike of Lloyd George, this seemed a very remote possibility. However, over time Asquith relied in his reading of the situation more and more on one specific element of the Conservative leadership (Landsdowne, Curzon, Long, and Cecil) and failed to see that others were becoming more and more estranged.[232]

Asquith failed to understand the depth of growing disappointment among Conservative members of his government in his leadership. Law had finally become convinced that Lloyd George was right—Asquith must be removed from the real decision making about the war. Neither man sought to have Asquith totally removed from the government and in fact had no problem with his remaining as titular Prime Minister or, if he preferred, assuming some position such as Lord Chancellor. Once these two powerful men reached this conclusion and were willing to stick by their guns, the pressure was on the Conservative members of the government to get behind the idea or remain loyal to Asquith. In the end, they chose to swallow the bitter pill and stand with Lloyd George. Balfour was critically important in this regard. Asquith required his support and yet badly miscalculated the extent of his loyalty. Without the Conservative Ministers' support, one of the key elements to the foundation of Asquith's power had now disappeared. There was nothing else to do but resign. While Asquith and his Liberal supporters might well have believed that a new Lloyd George government would be unstable and not last long, leading to Asquith's return to power, they knew that governing without Lloyd George was impossible.[233]

Should Asquith have graciously accepted the invitation of Law and Lloyd George to remain in the government, either as titular Prime Minister or in some other position? From a human standpoint, this would be asking a great deal of a man to join forces with those who had plotted against him and successfully deposed him from power. Asquith did have his pride. Even so, he was also a patriot, and if he had believed it was in the nation's interest to remain in the government, he would have done so with little hesitation. His decision not to go along was based primarily on the belief that to do so would only be delaying an inevitable break. He did not believe that Lloyd George's government would last. The day after his resignation Asquith met with Robert Donald, editor of the Liberal *Daily Chronicle*. Asquith "spoke with great bitterness with regard to the calumnious and unscrupulous campaign which had been directed against him and his colleagues," although he "seemed more concerned for his colleagues than for himself." Donald also got the impression that Asquith was "quite convinced that Mr. Lloyd George could not form a stable government" and doubted it would last long.[234] Even more so, Asquith deeply distrusted Lloyd George and feared that joining in his government would limit his hand in criticizing the unwise decisions Asquith must have believed the new Prime Minister was sure to make before long.

In a last act before leaving 10 Downing Street, Asquith met with Liberals of both Houses at the Reform Club. After he described the events of the past few days, he concluded by appealing to the patriotism of all present to support the new government. After sustained applause, a motion passed unanimously thanking him for his service to the nation and expressing confidence in his leadership.[235] After winning three consecutive general elections and holding office for more than a decade, although they did not know it at the time, the members of the old Liberal Party would never assemble together again at a single Liberal gathering.[236] Asquith's most honest thoughts at the time were revealed to Sylvia Henley in a letter the night before. "This is a bit of a cataclysm isn't it?" He confessed, however, "to feeling a certain sense of relief," continuing, "Nothing can be conceived as more hellish than the experience I have gone through during the last month. Almost for the first time I have felt that I was growing old."[237]

NOTES

1. Riddell, *War Diary*, 94.
2. Lord Hankey, *The Supreme Command 1914–1918*, vol. 1 (London: George Allen and Unwin, 1961), 319.
3. HHA to MA, 1 June 1915, Spender and Asquith, *Life of Asquith,* 2:173.
4. Douglas Haig, *The Private Papers of Douglas Haig 1914–1918,* ed. Robert Blake (London: Eyre & Spottiswoode, 1952), 39.
5. Hankey, Aide Memoire to HHA, 29 May 1915, MS. Asquith 27, ff. 247–50.
6. Cassar, *Asquith As War Leader*, 113.
7. Ibid., 113–14.
8. HHA to Sir John French, 3 June 1915, Spender and Asquith, *Life of Asquith*, 2:174.
9. HHA handwritten notes prepared following meeting with Sir J. French, BL, MS. Asquith 27, f. 266.
10. Ibid., 337.
11. Members were Landsdowne, Curzon, Kitchner, Balfour, Law, Grey, Crewe, Lloyd George, Churchill, Selbourne, and McKenna.

12. Hankey, *Supreme Command*, 1:336.
13. HHA to Geroge V (copy), 3 July 1915, BL, MS. Asquith 8, ff. 6364; Cassar, *Asquith As War Leader*, 116; HHA to Sylvia Henley, 2 July 1915, BL, MS. Eng. Lett., c. 542/1, f. 192.
14. Spender and Asquith, *Life of Asquith,* 2:182.
15. HHA to Sylvia Henley, 6 July 1915, Earl of Oxford and Asquith, *Memories*, 127.
16. Cassar, *Asquith As War Leader*, 117.
17. HHA to Sylvia Henley, July 1915, Earl of Oxford and Asquith, *Memories*, 128–29.
18. Ibid., 118.
19. Ibid., 119.
20. Spender and Asquith, *Life of Asquith,* 2:181.
21. HHA to George V (copy), 2 Oct. 1915, BL, MS. Asquith 8, f. 99.
22. Cassar, *Asquith as War Leader*, 125–26.
23. "Appreciation of the Situation in the Balkans by the General Staff, War Office," 24 Sept. 1915, NA, CAB 42/3/29.
24. HHA to George V (copy), 2 Oct. 1915, BL, MS. Asquith 8, f. 99.
25. Cassar, *Asquith As War Leader*, 126.
26. "Secretary's Notes of a Meeting of the Dardanelles Committee held at 10, Downing Street, October 11, 1915," NA, CAB 42/4/6.
27. Hankey, *Supreme Command*, 2:459.
28. "Anglo–French Conference at Calais," 5 Dec. 1915, NA, CAB 28/1/18-20; D. J. Dutton, "The Calais Conference of 1915," *Historical Journal* 21 (1978): 149–50.
29. HHA to Sylvia Henley, 7 Dec. 1915, BL, MS. Eng. let. C. 542/2, ff. 452–53.
30. HHA to George V (copy), 8 Dec. 1915, BL, MS. Asquith 8, f. 121.
31. HHA to George V (copy), 20 Aug. 1915, BL, MS. Asquith 8, ff. 82–83.
32. HHA to Sylvia Henley, 20 August 1915, BL, MS. Eng. Let. c. 542/2, f. 372.
33. Minutes of the Dardanelles Committee, 20 August 1915, NA, CAB 42/3/16, p. 6.
34. HHA to George V (copy), 23 Sept. 1915, BL, MS. Asquith 8, f. 97.
35. Lord Crewe to George V (copy), 22 Oct. 1915, BL, MS. Asquith 8, f. 112.
36. HHA to Sylvia Henley, 28 Oct. 1915, BL, Ms, Eng. Let. c. 542/2, f. 398; HHA, "Conduct of the War," 28 Oct. 1915, CAB 37/136/36.
37. Cassar, *Asquith As War Leader*, 132.
38. J. M. McEwen, "The Struggle for Mastery in Britain: Lloyd George versus Asquith, December 1916," *Journal of British Studies* 18 (1978): 136.
39. Gilbert, *Churchill: Challenge of War*, 557.
40. Eric Drummond to MA, ibid., 560.
41. Cassar, *Asquith As War Leader*, 132.
42. Gilbert, *Churchill: The Challenge of War*, 562.
43. HHA to Lloyd George, 3 Nov. 1915, ibid.
44. *Hansard*, 5, 75, 1401–3, 11 Nov. 1915. In addition, the government suspended publication of the *Globe,* and it was only allowed to reopen two weeks later on condition that a retraction be printed.

45. Earl of Oxford and Asquith, *Memories*, 2:136.
46. Ibid., 2:137. After Sir John French and Asquith later fell out with each other, Asquith even published a full facsimile of this letter in his memoirs.
47. Cassar, *Asquith As War Leader*, 135–36.
48. Ibid., 137.
49. Ibid.
50. Ibid.,138.
51. HHA to Sylvia Henley, 7 Dec. 1915, BL, MS. Eng. Let. c. 542/2, ff. 453–54.
52. R. J. Q. Adams, "Asquith's Choice: The May Coalition and the Coming of Conscription, 1915–1916," *Journal of British Studies* 25, no. 3 (July 1986): 243–63. Much of this section is taken from Adams's work.
53. Earl of Oxford and Asquith, *Memories*, 2:146.
54. Cassar, *Asquith as War Leader*, 148.
55. Dennis Hayes, *Conscription Conflict: The Conflict of Ideas in the Struggle for and Against Military Conscription in Britain Between 1901 and 1939* (New York: Garland, 1973), 228–52; G. D. H. Cole, *Labour in War Time* (London: G. Bell and Sons, 1915), 207–13.
56. Grey, *Twenty-five Years*, 2:72.
57. Adams, "Asquith's Choice," 247.
58. *Statistics of the Military Effort of the British Empire During the Great War, 1914–1920* (London: His Majesty's Stationary Office, 1922), 364.
59. Asquith, *Memories*, 2:147.
60. R. J. Q. Adams, *Arms and the Wizard: Lloyd George and the Ministry of Munitions, 1915–1916* (College Station: Texas A & M University Press, 1978), 101.
61. Adams, "Asquith's Choice," 248–49.
62. "Winston S. Churchill: minute," Gilbert, *Churchill, Companion Volume III*, 1132.
63. Adams, "Asquith's Choice," 251.
64. Ibid.
65. Arthur Henderson, untitled memorandum, 7 Sept. 1915, NA, CAB 37/135/5.
66. *The Annual Register: A Review of Public Events at Home and Abroad for the Year 1915* (London: Longmans, Green, 1916), 154.
67. *Hansard*, 5, 74, 833, 29 Sept. 1915.
68. Hankey, *Supreme Command*, 1:427.
69. HHA to Balfour (copy), 18 Sept. 1915, BL, MS. Asquith 28, ff. 162–66.
70. Diary entry, Lord Derby, 28 Aug. 1921, Randolph S. Churchill, *Lord Derby "King of Lancashire": The Official Life of Edward, Seventeenth Earl of Derby, 1865–1948* (London: Heinemann, 1959), 192.
71. Adams, "Asquith's Choice," 255.
72. Diary entry for 19 Oct. 1915, Taylor, ed., *Lloyd George: A Diary by Frances Stevenson*, 70.
73. MA to Lord Murray of Elibank, 20 Oct. 1915, Cassar, *Asquith As War Leader*, 157.
74. Lord Crewe to George V (copy), 19 Oct. 1915, BL, MS. Asquith 8, ff. 105–6.
75. Adams, "Asquith's Choice," 253.

76. Ibid., 254.
77. Cassar, *Asquith As War Leader*, 155.
78. Diary entry 16 Nov. 1915, Taylor, ed., *Lloyd George: A Diary by Frances Stevenson*, 75.
79. Derby, "Memorandum," 20 Dec. 1915, NA, CAB 37/139/41.
80. Earl of Oxford and Asquith, *Memories*, 2:135.
81. HHA to Sylvia Henley, 26 Dec. 1915, MS. Eng. let. c. 542/2, f. 498.
82. Taylor, ed., *Lloyd George: A Diary by Frances Stevenson*, 89.
83. Ibid.
84. HHA to George V, 28 Dec. 1915, NA, CAB 37/139/58.
85. HHA to Sylvia Henley, 28 Dec. 1915, BL, MS. Eng. Let. c. 542/2, ff. 508–9.
86. Ibid.; Cassar, *Asquith As War Leader*, 161.
87. HHA to Simon, McKenna, and Runciman, 28 Dec. 1915, Cassar, *Asquith As War Leader*, 161.
88. Grey to HHA, 29 Dec. 1915, Trevelyan, *Grey of Fallodon*, 370.
89. HHA to Grey, 29 Dec. 1915, ibid., 370–71.
90. Cassar, *Asquith As War Leader*, 162.
91. Grey to HHA, 30 Dec. 1915, Trevelyan, *Grey of Fallodon*, 371.
92. HHA to George V (copy), 1 Jan. 1916, BL, MS. Asquith 8, f. 128; HHA to Sylvia Henley, 1 Jan. 1916, BL, MS. Eng. Litt., c. 542/3, ff. 517–18.
93. Cassar, *Asquith As War Leader*, 164.
94. "Cabinet Committee on the Co–ordination of the Military and Financial Effort," 4 Feb. 1916, NA, CAB 37/142/11.
95. "Memorandum by the Chief of the Imperial General Staff Regarding the Supply of Personnel," 21 Mar. 1916, NA, CAB 42/11/8.
96. Esher, *Journals and Letters*, 4:17.
97. Hankey, *Supreme Command*, 478.
98. Hankey Diary entry, 16 Mar. 1916, David French, *British Strategy & War Aims 1914–1916* (London: Allen & Unwin, 1986), 192.
99. Cassar, *Asquith As War Leader*, 174.
100. Edward Grey Memorandum, 22 Feb. 1916, Grey, *Twenty-five Years*, 2:127–28.
101. Cassar, *Asquith As War Leader*, 176
102. HHA to MA, 29 Mar. 1916, Spender and Asquith, *Life of Asquith*, 2:175
103. Ridell, *War Diary*, 168.
104. HHA to MA, 29 Mar. 1916, Spender and Asquith, *Life of Asquith*, 2:175.
105. HHA to MA, 29 Mar. 1916, ibid., 2:176.
106. HHA to MA, 31 Mar. 1916 ibid., 2:176.
107. Ibid.
108. Cassar, *Asquith As War Leader*, 181.
109. Hankey Diary, 1 Apr. 1916, Hankey, *Supreme Command*, 2:483; Sir James Rennell Rodd, *Social and Diplomatic Memories (Third Series) 1902–1919* (London: Edward Arnold, 1925), 290.
110. Rennell Rodd to Sir Edward Grey, 8 Apr. 1916, BL, MS. Asquith 30, ff. 2–3; Cassar, *Asquith As War Leader*, 182.
111. Cassar, *Asquith As War Leader*, 182.

112. Minutes of the Eightieth Meeting of the War Committee held at 10 Downing Street, Friday, April 7, 1916, at 11:30 a.m., NA, CAB 42/12/5.

113. Cassar, *Asquith As War Leader*, 165.

114. Bonar Law to HHA, 17 Apr. 1916, BL, MS. Asquith 16, f. 153.

115. Cassar, *Asquith As War Leader*, 166–67.

116. Diary entry 19 Apr. 1916, Taylor, ed., *Lloyd George: A Diary by Frances Stevenson*.

117. Asquith, *Memories*, 2:148.

118. *Hansard*, 5, 81, 2351, 19 Apr. 1916.

119. Copy of resolution by Liberal M.P.s, 19 Apr. 1916, BL, MS. Asquith 30, f. 50.

120. Spender and Asquith, *Life of Asquith*, 2:209.

121. George V to HHA, 20 Apr. 1916, Earl of Oxford and Asquith, *Memories*, 150–51.

122. HHA to Sylvia Henley, 20 Apr. 1916, BL, MS. Eng. Litt. c. 542/3, ff. 834–35.

123. HHA to George V (copy), 29 Apr. 1916, BL, MS. Asquith 8, ff. 159–60; Cassar, *Asquith As War Leader*, 168.

124. Cassar, *Asquith As War Leader*, 169.

125. Ibid., 182; W. R. Robertson, "Future Military Operations," NA, CAB 42/12/5.

126. Spender and Asquith, *Life of Lord Asquith*, 2:215.

127. HHA to Herbert Samuel, 14 May 1916, Spender and Asquith, *Life of Lord Asquith*, 217.

128. HHA to MA, 14 May 1916, ibid., 216.

129. HHA to MA, 16 May 1916, ibid., 216–17.

130. Diary entry 19 May 1916, Horsley, ed., *Cynthia Asquith Diaries*, 166.

131. Spender and Asquith, *Life of Lord Asquith*, 218.

132. HHA to George V (copy), 27 June 1916, BL, MS. Asquith 8, ff. 177–78.

133. HHA to George V (copy), 5 July 1916, BL, MS. Asquith 8, f. 180.

134. *Hansard*, 5, 22, 645–52, 11 July 1916.

135. HHA to Lord Landsdowne, 12 July 1916, Spender and Asquith, *Life of Lord Asquith*, 222.

136. HHA to Hilda Harrison, 25 July 1916, MacCarthy, ed., *H.H.A.: Letters of the Earl of Oxford and Asquith to a Friend First Series*, 8.

137. Ibid., 2:506.

138. Bonham-Carter, *Winston Churchill*, 378; Margot Asquith Diary, BL, M.S. Eng. d. 3214, f. 449.

139. HHA to Stamfordham, 8 June 1916, Cassar, *Asquith As War Leader*, 186.

140. David R. Woodward, *Lloyd George and the Generals* (Newark, NJ: University of Delaware Press, 1983), 98.

141. Cassar, *Asquith As War Leader*, 186–87.

142. Ibid., 188.

143. Beaverbrook, *Politicians and the War*, 207–8.

144. Ibid., 209.

145. Trevor Wilson, ed., *The Political Diaries of C. P. Scott 1911–1928* (Ithaca: Cornell University Press, 1970), 218.

146. Cassar, *Asquith As War Leader*, 187.
147. Cooper, *Old Men Forget*, 54.
148. Spender and Asquith, *Life of Lord Asquith*, 2:228.
149. Haig, *Private Papers*, 157.
150. "Minutes of the One Hundred and Fifth Meeting of the War Committee held at 10 Downing Street, S.W., Saturday, August 5th, 1916, at 11:30 a.m.," NA, CAB 42/17/3.
151. HHA to Sylvia Henley, 26 Aug. 1916, BL, MS. Eng. Litt. c. 542/4, ff. 730–31.
152. HHA to MA, 7 Sept. 1916, BL, MS. Eng. c. 6691, ff. 230–35.
153. Raymond Asquith to Katharine Asquith, 7 Sept. 1916, John Jolliffe, *Raymond Asquith, Life and Letters* (Collins, 1980), 294.
154. Raymond Asquith to Katharine Asquith, 22 Aug. 1916, Jolliffe, *Raymond Asquith, Life and Letters*, 287.
155. Horsley, ed., *Cynthia Asquith Diaries*, xviii.
156. Haig diary, 6 Sept. 1916, Cassar, *Asquith As War Leader*, 195.
157. Ibid., 196.
158. Jolliffe, *Raymond Asquith, Life and Letters*, 296.
159. 17 Sept. 1916, Brock, *Margot Asquith's Great War Diary*, 289.
160. HHA to Sylvia Henley, 20 Sept. 1916, BL, MS. Eng. Litt. c. 542/4, ff. 748–49. A month later he sent her a picture of Raymond's grave. BL, MS. Eng. Litt. c. 452/4, f. 771.
161. Clifford, *Asquiths*, 367.
162. Major Roland Harrison was killed in action in 1917. Asquith left a bequest in his will for the education of the Harrison children.
163. HHA to Hilda Harrison, 11 Oct. 1916, MacCarthy, ed., *H. H. A.: Letters of the Earl of Oxford and Asquith to a First Series*, 10.
164. Ibid.
165. "Conference of Allied Ministers at Boulogne, held on October 20, 1916," NA, CAB 28/1/76–81.
166. "Minutes of the One Hundred and Twenty-Fourth Meeting of the War Committee held at 10 Downing Street, Tuesday, October 24th, 1916, at 11:30 a.m.," NA, CAB 42/22/5.
167. HHA to Sylvia Henley, 20 July 1916, MS. Eng. Litt. c. 542/3, ff. 692–93.
168. Hankey diary, 31 Oct. 1916, Cassar, *Asquith As War Leader*, 201–2.
169. Ibid., 204.
170. "Copy of a Statement Read by the Prime Minister as a Conference Attended Only by Himself, Mr Lloyd George, M. Briand and Admiral Lacaze on the Morning of Wednesday, 15 November 1916," (in French), CAB 28/1/85–86.
171. George, *War Memories*, 2:344.
172. Ibid., 2:350.
173. "Note by the Secretary of War Committee of the Results of the Paris Conference, 15 and 16 November 1916," CAB 28/1/95–96 ; Hankey, *The Supreme Command*, 2:561–62.
174. "Minutes of the One Hundred and Forty-Third Meeting of the War Committee held at 10 Downing Street, S. W., Thursday, November 30th, 1916, at 11:30 a.m.," NA, CAB 42/26/4.

175. Landsdowne, untitled memorandum, 13 Nov. 1916, NA, CAB 37/159/32.
176. Spender and Asquith, *Life of Lord Asquith,* 2:240.
177. Ibid., 2:242.
178. Memorandum from Lord Robert Cecil (copy), 28 Apr. 1916, BL, MS. Asquith 30, ff. 78–81.
179. Diary entry 27 Mar. 1916, Taylor, ed., *Lloyd George: A Diary by Frances Stevenson,* 105.
180. Diary entry 1 Apr. 1916, Ridell, *War Diary,* 168.
181. R. J. Scally, *The Origins of the Lloyd George Coalition* (Princeton: Princeton University Press, 1975), 296.
182. Diary entry 15 Nov. 1916, Horsley, ed., *Cynthia Asquith Diaries,* 234.
183. R. J. Q. Adams, "Andrew Bonar Law and the Fall of the Asquith Coalition: The December 1916 Cabinet Crisis," *Canadian Journal of History/Annales Canadiennes d'histoire* 32 (August 1997): 189.
184. Ibid., 189.
185. Ibid.
186. Diary entry 22 Nov. 1916, Taylor, ed., *Lloyd George: A Diary by Frances Stevenson,* 127.
187. BL, MS. Asquith 31, f. 1.
188. Beaverbrook, *Politicians and the War,* 351; Cassar, *Asquith As War Leader,* 212–13.
189. HHA to Bonar Law, 25 Nov. 1916, Spender and Asquith, *Life of Lord Asquith,* 2:250.
190. Bonar Law confidential memorandum dictated on 30 Dec. 1916, House of Lords Record Office, Bonar Law Papers 85/A/1.
191. Cassar, *Asquith As War Leader,* 214.
192. J. M. McEwen, "The Press and the Fall of Asquith," *Historical Journal* 21 (1978): 869–70.
193. R. J. Q. Adams, "Bonar Law," 194.
194. HHA to George V (copy), BL, MS. Asquith 8, f. 215; Cassar, *Asquith As War Leader,* 213.
195. HHA to Sylvia Henley, 29 Nov. 1916, BL, MS. Eng. Litt. c. 542/4, ff. 795–96.
196. Beaverbrook, *Politicians and the War,* 366.
197. Ibid., 362–77.
198. Bonar Law to Lord Landsdowne, 1 Dec. 1916, ibid., 372.
199. BL, MS. Asquith 31, n.d., f. 2.
200. Hankey diary, 1 Dec. 1916, Hankey, *Supreme Command,* 2:565.
201. McEwen, "Struggle for Mastery," 142.
202. Marquis of Crewe, "The Break-up of the First Coalition," 20 Dec. 1916, Earl of Oxford and Asquith, *Memories,* 2: 156; McEwen, "Struggle for Mastery," 144.
203. Vincent, ed., *Crawford Papers,* 371.
204. McEwen, "Struggle for Mastery."
205. H. A. Taylor, *Robert Donald* (London: Stanley Paul, 1934), 119.
206. Earl of Oxford and Asquith, *Memories,* 2:157.

207. There is some discrepancy as to whether this meeting took place that evening or the following day.
208. Cassar, *Asquith As War Leader*, 223.
209. McEwen, "Struggle for Mastery," 149–53.
210. HHA to Lloyd George (copy), 4 Dec. 1916, BL, MS. Asquith 31, f. 19.
211. Lloyd George to HHA, 4 Dec. 1916, BL, MS Asquith 31, ff. 21–22.
212. Beaverbrook, *Politicians and the War*, 339–40.
213. Bonar Law confidential memorandum dictated on 30 Dec. 1916, House of Lords Record Office, Bonar Law Papers 85/A/1.
214. Beaverbrook, *Politicians at War*, 449.
215. Cassar, *Asquith As War Leader*, 224.
216. HHA to Lloyd George (copy), 4 Dec. 1916, BL, MS. Asquith 31, ff. 28–30.
217. Cassar, *Asquith As War Leader*, 225.
218. Lloyd George to HHA, 5 Dec. 1916, BL, MS. Asquith 31, ff. 34–37. HHA wrote in the margin, "I replied pointing out that I could not accept his version of what took place between us, and that in particular he has omitted to quote the first & most important part of my letter of Monday." HHA 5 Dec. 16.
219. Adams, *Balfour*, 318.
220. Crewe, "The Break-up of the First Coalition," 20 Dec. 1916, Earl of Oxford and Asquith, *Memories*, 2:159.
221. Cassar, *Asquith As War Leader*, 226.
222. Ibid., 227.
223. A. J. Balfour to HHA, 5 Dec. 1916, MS. Asquith 31, ff. 52–53.
224. Cassar, *Asquith As War Leader*, 227.
225. Bonar Law to HHA, 5 Dec. 1916, BL, MS. Asquith 31, ff. 43–44.
226. Diary entry 5 Dec. 1916, Horsley, ed., *Cynthia Asquith Diaries*, 241.
227. Cassar, *Asquith As War Leader*, 229.
228. Crewe, "The Break-up of the First Coalition," 20 Dec. 1916, Earl of Oxford and Asquith, *Memories*, 2:162–63.
229. Grigg, *From Peace to War*, 476.
230. Ibid., 476.
231. Ibid., 479.
232. Scally, *Origins of the Lloyd George Coalition*, 260.
233. Wilson, *Downfall of the Liberal Party*, 102–3.
234. Taylor, *Robert Donald*, 123.
235. Cassar, *Asquith As War Leader*, 232.
236. Wilson, *Downfall of the Liberal Party*, 101.
237. HHA to Sylvia Henley, 6 Dec. 1916, BL, MS. Eng. Litt. c. 542/4, ff. 798–99.

Chapter Ten

Last of the Romans (December 1916–October 1927)

Exhausted after the resignation crisis, Asquith retreated with his daughter Violet and her husband, Maurice Bonham-Carter, to Walmer Castle, where as Prime Minister he had spent many happy weekends. After months of pressure and strain, he enjoyed four days in bed. "I think I was really tired," he wrote to Sylvia Henley, "for a couple of days I was completely indifferent to the outside world, and not only didn't read a newspaper I was quite incurious as to what it might contain."[1] To another friend he confided, "You cannot imagine what a relief it is not to have the daily stream of boxes and telegrams: not to mention Cabinets and Committees and colleagues, etc."[2]

He had not left office under a cloud, and as the crisis of his departure demonstrated, many wished that he had either retained some office in the new government or would soon return on his own terms. Hankey wrote in his diary, "I felt very much affected at parting, . . . seeing the desperate times we have lived through together. In many respects he was the greatest man I have ever met, or ever hope to meet . . ."[3] He wrote his former chief of his admiration for him and added that he believed their official separation to be "temporary."[4] King George V offered Asquith the Garter, which he declined, signaling he was not quite ready to be put out to pasture.[5] Many other friends and colleagues wrote to tell Asquith of their support. Conservative editor, politician, and friend Henry Crust wrote of his "full contempt at the utterly ridiculous result" and his "great sense of loss, but a greater sense of pride," referring to himself as only part of "a choir 'temporarily invisible but immense.'"[6] "Lloyd George has many qualities," Robert Cecil wrote, "but he will never equal his predecessor in patience, in courtesy or in that largeness of mind which despises the lesser arts by which political success is attained."[7] As to Asquith's own thoughts about his departure, the day after Christmas he sent Sylvia Henley an article by G. K. Chesterton of which he obviously approved. The article began, "Mr. Asquith has acted generously and courageously by all the standards of that generation of Englishmen which was content, in Mr. Newbolt's poem, to play the game," and Chesterton believed he had "most emphatically and heroically" done so. Unfortunately, "the politicians of the cruder type, who have tripped up Mr. Asquith with the help of the Yellow Press, have no better record as realists: they have dealt even more in fiction. They also play the game—and cheat at it."[8]

As the New Year dawned, Asquith was far from retired from politics. It was an odd arrangement with in effect two Liberal groups in Parliament. One, led by Lloyd George, participated in and supported the new coalition government. The other was the official Liberal Party, still led by Asquith, in opposition to the government. This resulted in the anomaly of two sets of Liberal whips, those serving Lloyd George and occupying the government whips' office (together with the Conservative whips) and those loyal to Asquith now located in the opposition whips' office. Yet this perhaps overstates the Liberal division at the beginning of 1917. Both groups of Liberal whips canvassed all Liberals, not just those associated with their particular group. Asquith and most of his supporters in public denied they were in conflict with the government.[9] *Liberal Magazine*, semi-official publication of the Liberal Party, wrote that the Asquithian Liberals "have nothing but the sincerest good wishes for the new Administration" and quoted Asquith himself as saying he was not an opposition leader and would offer the government "support, organized support."[10]

Asquith was true to his word throughout his first year out of power. In March the government, against the advice of the Liberal Ministers in the coalition, introduced a form of tariff protection for the Indian cotton industry. Many of Asquith's supporters urged him to take up the gauntlet and defend the Liberal principle of free trade. Asquith merely put forward a compromise resolution, almost certainly pre-arranged with the government, stating that the matter would be reviewed after the war. In other instances Asquith, although reluctantly, supported the government in the interest of national unity. He said nothing when the government banned the overseas circulation of *The Nation*, and even though he spoke against a bill providing state bounties for agriculture, he could not bring himself to vote against it. The most difficult vote came when Lloyd George apparently under pressure from the Conservative rank and file decided to extend conscription to Ireland. This provoked such an uproar among many Liberal MPs that the government did not attempt to implement the statute. Asquith, however, almost certainly influenced by the now desperate military situation on the Western Front, said he would do nothing to oppose the government.[11]

Despite his public support for the government, Asquith was not about to be coaxed into joining Lloyd George's cabinet. In May 1917 during Whitsun weekend, Lord Murray of Elibank and Lord Reading, the Lord Chief Justice, came to The Wharf and brought up the subject with the former Prime Minister. The discussion began on Saturday with talk about possible changes in the war cabinet. Asquith told the two men that the war cabinet was a hopeless and unworkable experiment, and that "Self-respecting statesmen cd. not be expected to take part in such a crazy adventure." Asquith wrote a memorandum summarizing the discussions and recorded that Reading on Monday made a more "frontal attack," telling Asquith that he and many others regarded Asquith's participation in the government as "essential" and hinting that "this was the view of the Prime Minister." Asquith replied that, while he was "quite ready to go on giving the Govt full support, so long as they carried on the war in the proper spirit, & to use my influence with my party, & in the country, in the same sense," they should "understand clearly" that under no conditions would he serve in a government headed by Lloyd George. Asquith had "learned by long & close association to mistrust him profoundly" and "knew him to be incapable of loyalty or lasting gratitude." Lloyd George had "many brilliant & useful faculties, but needed to have someone over him." "In my judgement," Asquith frankly told them, "he had incurable defects, both of intellect and character, wh. totally unfitted him to be at the head."[12] Understandably, Lloyd George made no offer. As Asquith explained to Sylvia Henley in late June, "I have had no communication of any sort or kind, direct or indirect with Ll. G: and I imagine that he knows better than to make offers that are sure to be refused."[13]

What disturbed Asquith most was the new Prime Minister's intervention in military affairs, for Lloyd George failed to see the bright line that Asquith drew between the political and the military. As will be seen, the two times Asquith came closest to attacking the government publicly were in November 1917 when Lloyd George made a speech in Paris attacking Allied strategy and in February 1918 following the resignation of General Sir William Robertson as CIGS. Not only did Asquith see these moves by Lloyd George as an unscrupulous attempt to overthrow the nation's military leaders, but he must also have viewed these attacks, basically on Haig's and Robertson's strategy, as a condemnation of his own running of the war.[14]

Asquith and his Liberal supporters did, however, readily criticized those who took the bait and joined the government. In June 1917 Asquith rebuffed Edwin Montagu, his protégé who had married Venetia Stanley, for joining a government committee of reconstruction, and when Montagu actually crossed over to the coalition side the next month, Asquith and his followers treated him as an apostate.[15] When he learned that Montagu, even after changing affiliations, would not be given a cabinet position, Asquith gleefully quipped that his former close associate "has swallowed the ginger-bread ungilded."[16]

In the summer of 1917 the Mesopotamian Commission investigating the Mesopotamian campaign delivered its report to be debated in the House of Commons. Since the report touched upon the conduct of the government while Asquith was Prime Minister, it was only natural that he would respond, which he did on the second day of the debate. The central point of Asquith's remarks on this occasion, however, was a defense of his government's decision to attempt to take Baghdad. His argument is important in many ways because it reveals Asquith's philosophy of the respective roles of government and the military, the political and the strategic, in time of war. There were excellent political reasons to take Baghdad at the time, and the military experts told the government that there was more than a reasonable chance that it could be done. "I cannot recall any step taken in this War," he told the House, "which was more completely warranted by every relevant consideration of policy and strategy, and which was more strongly fortified in advance by an absolute concurrence of expert authority." Yet he made clear his belief that there would always be political considerations. The final decision must be that of the government. He rhetorically asked: "We who bear the responsibility of State, we who are accountable to this House and to our Sovereign, are we to avoid all responsibility, and hand over everything to our expert advisers?" For Asquith the answer was clear: "That is the part of cowardice, not statesmanship."[17] So many criticized the idea of a judicial tribunal to mete out punishment that the government ultimately abandoned the idea. Military and naval authorities were left, if they saw fit, to deal in their own way with the officers censured in the Report.

In the autumn of 1917, Lloyd George decided to press for the establishment of a Supreme Inter-Allied War Council and a permanent general staff at Paris. The disastrous breach of the Italian line at Caporetto in late October confirmed in his mind the need for such a council, and with the blessing of the French government and the British War Cabinet the council was put in place on the first week in November. Lloyd George knew General Robertson and the Army Council opposed the move, and they would find much support for their position in Parliament, in the press, and especially with Asquith. To land the first punch, the Prime Minister decided to give a speech in Paris ostensibly devoted to explaining the necessity of the new council but in fact to give a negative critique of the military strategies of the past.[18] For years, he said, the Allies had been "hammering with all our might at the impenetrable barrier in the west." The Allies' strength had been wasted in the profitless battles of 1915 and "the bloody assaults of the Somme" in 1916. Opportunities such as saving Serbia and aiding Romania had been thrown away.[19] The response to the speech in Britain from the pro-military elements was predictable. "HANDS OFF THE ARMY" ran the typical headline, and a debate on the formation of the council was set for November 19 in the House of Commons.

Asquith, who had been patient with the Lloyd George government for the entire year, was disgusted with the Prime Minister's remarks and decided to enter the debate. After stating that he was certain the government was not about to set up any command body that "would in any way derogate from either the authority or the ultimate responsibility of each of the Allied governments over its own forces and its own people," he nevertheless took exception to the Prime Minister's remarks in Paris. These remarks, Asquith told the House, "amount to a severe indictment of the general strategy of the Allies on the ground that it has been, in several capital instances, dilatory or misdirected, and that the valour and devotion of our soldiers . . . was used at the wrong time or in the wrong place." He then launched into a full-scale defense of the major policy decisions of the war to that point. He particularly focused on Lloyd George's criticism of the Somme offensive. His son Raymond had been killed during the battle, and Asquith was not about to stand by and let his nemesis dismiss the battle, a battle which he himself had authorized, as a waste. He asked the House to remember that "this was a most critical moment of the War—the most critical moment certainly in the fortunes of the Western campaign." If Verdun had fallen, "the results were simply incalculable." Asquith agreed that "there is not too much to show for it in acreage . . . ," but "it is not too much to say that these bloody assaults saved the whole situation, and did as least as much as—I am not sure I should not be right in saying they did more than—anything in the whole War to damage the prestige of the German command and the morale of the German army." He concluded by saying that he was not making these points "in any spirit of wanton controversy" but because it was "all-important that our soldiers . . . should not get the impression that, through carelessness, or indifference, or obstinacy on the part of their Chiefs, whether military or political, their lives are being wasted, their sufferings needlessly prolonged, and their heroism spent in vain."[20]

Five days before Christmas, his son Oc was seriously wounded. Asquith described the event in a letter to Sylvia Henley a week after he was hit. "[I]t was due to a sudden lifting of the curtain of mist, which enabled a German sniper to take 3 shots at him with a rifle: happily the third, after he had fallen to the ground, missed & only kicked up the sand."[21] Another person reported, "It hurt like hell, poor boy, and the morphia took ages to work and the frost made the stretcher bearers slip and the ambulance jolt over the frozen ruts."[22] His father had always shown great pride in his son's military accomplishments. In June that year, when his son Beb's wife was visiting at 20 Cavendish Square, she observed that "the dear Old Boy [Asquith] was delighted with Oc's great success as colonel of the Hood Battalion—he had just been awarded a clasp to his D.S.O. and his father handed the King's letter of congratulation all around the table with proud sniffs."[23] The last time Asquith had seen his son was in September when Asquith had crossed the Channel to France to meet with General Haig. One day Asquith and Haig lunched with General Sir Henry Horne and had the added treat of seeing Oc, who had been given leave to join them. Afterward they toured Vimy Ridge together and watched as the German and British batteries dueled with each other. Asquith reported to Margot that he found Oc "very well and in capital form" but complained about "a most infernal & complicated apparatus which has been developed as a safeguard against gas." Oc confirmed that his father's "Gas-Box respirator drill leaves a good deal to be desired."[24]

The Lloyd George coalition had been in power a little over a year, and so far Asquith, despite his disgust with many of the government's actions, had been able to avoid a complete public break with those now running the war. What seems now to have been inevitable, however, finally happened in May 1918 in what came to be known as the "Maurice debate." The disagreements and disputes over military strategy that played such a large part in Asquith's fall from power did not end with Lloyd George becoming Prime Minister. Far from it. The war cabinet continued to be in conflict with General Haig, the Commander-in-Chief of British forces in France, demonstrated by the Prime Minister's remarks in Paris the previous November. At the heart of the conflict was Haig's desire to continue the Passchendaele offensive during the autumn of 1917. Apart from any ground that might be gained on the front, he believed that the continuation of the battle was imperative because by keeping a large number of German forces engaged, it would aid and perhaps even save from disaster the French and the Italians. The Prime Minister and his colleagues were more than skeptical. Was merely keeping the Germans engaged worth the mounting casualties? Despite the war cabinet's misgivings, there was no other choice but to support Haig. Failure to do so would probably mean his resignation with unknown and more than likely dangerous political consequences. The war cabinet decided that once the Passchendaele campaign came to a close, however, there would be no further offensive action in the west until the United States, which had entered the war on the side of the Allies months earlier, fielded a force in France. In the meantime, only such troops that would allow a defensive position would be supplied by Britain.[25]

With the fall of the Imperial Russian government to the Bolsheviks in November 1917, it was apparent that as soon as a formal peace could be signed the Germans would be moving a large number of troops from the east to the Western Front to carry out what they had hoped would be a final blow to end the war. General Haig urgently warned of such an attack and requested reinforcements, but the cabinet thought him unduly alarmist and refused to supply the men requested. To make matters worse, Haig was required to extend his front by fourteen miles, further thinning his line. All seemed well enough, until March 21, 1918, when the Germans launched a massive *Kaiserschlacht* offensive. By the end of the first day, the British had lost 20,000 dead and 35,000 wounded. Soon the Germans had broken through several points on the front with the British 5th Army, and after only two days, the British were in full retreat. One hundred and seventy thousand men were immediately to be rushed to France from Britain. Two divisions and artillery support had to be hurriedly brought from Palestine to help hold the line. Not until early April was the front finally reestablished with large loss of territory to the Germans. The government had a great deal to explain.

Many asked whether or not such reverses could have been avoided if sufficient reserve troops had been sent to France before the German offensive began, as Haig had requested.

On May 7 the *Times* published a letter by Major General Sir Frederick Maurice, who had recently been removed as Director of Military Operations. The letter, which also appeared in the *Morning Post*, the *Daily Chronicle*, and the *Daily News*, openly challenged recent statements to Parliament by the Prime Minister and Bonar Law regarding the extension of the British front and the strength of the army in France at the time the Germans began their advance. The Prime Minister, according to the letter, had declared, "Notwithstanding the heavy casualties in 1917, the army in France was considerably stronger on 1st January, 1918, than on 1st January 1917." "That statement," General Maurice declared, "implies that Sir Douglas Haig's fighting strength on 1 January 1918, on the eve of the great battle which began on 21 March, had not been diminished. That is not correct."[26]

General Robertson, who had himself recently resigned as CIGS over manpower deployment, was the person instrumental in getting Maurice to go public with his accusations. Naturally, some thought Asquith might well have been behind the plan to embarrass the government or at least had seen the letter before its publication. This was not the case. In fact, Maurice wrote to Asquith on the day the letter was sent to the press that while he had thought about showing it to Asquith, "on second thoughts I came to the conclusion that, if I consulted you, it would be tantamount to asking you to take responsibility for the letter, and that I alone must take responsibility."[27] In any case, on the day the letter was published Asquith rose in the House to ask Bonar Law what steps the government proposed to take to enable the House to examine the allegations. Law replied that, "inasmuch as these allegations affect the honour of Ministers," the government proposed to invite two of His

Majesty's judges to act as a court of honor and inquire into the charges of misstatements. He also agreed that the House would be given the opportunity to discuss the matter of the inquiry further.[28] The next day a commentator in the *Manchester Guardian* remarked that Asquith "has never before taken so positive a step in opposition."[29]

For the next two days Asquith was flooded with requests from both soldiers and politicians to insist that General Maurice's statements be investigated fully. Margot gleefully thought this might well be the end of Lloyd George's government and "went up and down Bond Street," as Mary Herbert described to Cynthia Asquith, "like the Ancient Mariner clutching at mannequins, commissionaires, friends, taxi-drivers, policemen, and whispering to them the good news of their return to Downing Street."[30]

Asquith moved in the House of Commons on May 9 that a Select Committee inquire into the Maurice accusations. Asquith began by stating that "either in intention or effect" his motion should not be considered in any way a "Vote of Censure upon the Government." He noted that he had done everything he could to assist the current government in the prosecution of the war. "If I did feel it my duty . . . to ask the House to censure the Government, I hope I should have the courage and the candour to do so in a direct and an unequivocal form." His motion was "confined to the examination of two or three very simple issues of fact, and from which the Government, as I am sure they would . . . emerge not with diminished, but with enhanced authority and prestige." To the disappointment of many of his supporters, Asquith's long and tedious speech entirely avoided the substance of the Maurice accusations. The performance was lackluster. As the *Times* commented the next day, Asquith's speech "was not one of his best efforts" and "never recovered from a bad start."[31]

The Prime Minister's response must have come as a shock to Asquith and his supporters, although they should have known better. Lloyd George, if anything, was a fighter and a good one at that. Totally ignoring the issue of procedure, Lloyd George went right to the substance of the charges and cleverly turned the debate into just what Asquith had said it was not—a vote of censure. Lloyd George argued that his statements to the House had been based upon information supplied by the Department of Military Operations headed by none other than General Maurice. This simple and clever maneuver avoided any real discussion of the accuracy of the statements. It was a remarkable performance. By the time he took his seat, Lloyd George had taken full command of the situation. Asquith was well-armed with the facts, and since Lloyd George had opened the door, he could now shift into a full-blown debate on the merits. Yet, much of the information to be discussed was of a sensitive nature, and the floor of the House, not sitting in secret session, was not the place to have such a debate. Asquith could be tough in debate and held back few punches, but he could not bring himself to reveal information that might well harm the war effort. He could withdraw the motion on the grounds that any public discussion was impossible at that moment. This would be a sort of tactical retreat. And so he found himself in no man's land. He had come too far to retreat, and yet he could go no further. This left only one viable alternative, not a good one, and that was to proceed with the motion without getting to the real merits, almost certainly knowing that Lloyd George would win the day. The result was a disaster for Asquith. There was no clear guidance given to Liberal members, prearranged speakers did not rise, and a division was taken before the Liberal front bench even had a chance to reply to the Prime Minister. In the end only 106 followed Asquith into the Lobby in support of his motion, 98 Liberals voting for it and 71 against.[32]

The next morning the *Times* called the vote "the début of an organized Opposition."[33] The *Manchester Guardian* was not so sure what it all meant and found Asquith's behavior "most difficult to comprehend." Grave charges against the government had been couched in what appeared to be technical matters of procedure. "People do not understand," the paper declared, "this formalistic attitude to affairs of life and death."[34] As only Margot could put it, "The Press were drunk with pleasure & gave themselves over like Dancing Dervishes to an orgy—Praise of their great P.M. & abuse of Henry."[35]

Asquith's motivations for his actions in the Maurice debate are difficult to discern. He knew Lloyd George had misled the public and in the process had weakened the credibility of some of the commanders in the field. While he objected to the government, he probably realized that toppling it at this point was impossible. Then too, a full frontal attack might trigger Lloyd George to call for a general election, which Asquith knew was not in the best interest of the country. Asquith wanted to return to power but not at the cost of destroying the government while the country faced a military crisis of the first order. This, at least, is what Hankey thought was behind Asquith's hesitancy.[36] Six months later during the heat of the "Coupon" election, he described as "blackguardly" a passage in which Lloyd George painted the Maurice incident as a conspiracy to overthrow the government and prevent the unity of command.[37] Asquith appears to have been attempting to wound the government and at least begin the process of loosening Lloyd George's grip on Parliament.[38] He must have harbored at least some hope of doing this, for it seems a rather worthless effort without at least some possibility of success. Asquith's mistake was a tactical one. He underestimated Lloyd George's reaction to his attack and the quickness and cleverness of the counterattack. In short, Asquith was playing with fire, and he was badly burned.

Despite Lloyd George's devastating response to Asquith in the Maurice debate, it was still to the Prime Minister's advantage to have Asquith inside the government tent rather than on the outside. In September another attempt was made to include Asquith. Lord Murray of Elibank again approached him on behalf of the Prime Minister in September 1918 with an offer of the Lord Chancellorship. Asquith would not be moved. Aside from the unacceptable conditions that Lloyd George had attached, he told Murray that he would "in no circumstances whatever" serve under the Prime Minister. Murray recorded, "The inwardness of Mr. A's attitude is that he does not really trust either Lloyd George or Balfour, and could not therefore serve in the Government with them. He spoke strongly on these lines."[39]

And so the Liberals stood divided as the war was fast drawing to a close in the autumn of 1918, each Liberal group suspiciously eyeing the other, neither faction wanting to split the party, yet neither side willing to submit. As early as July 1918, Lloyd George decided to call an election as soon as the war was over and to campaign in coalition with the Conservatives. A committee of prominent Liberals in the government was appointed to review the situation and recommended on July 13, in addition to coming up with an agreed program with the Conservatives, "That a form of agreement with the Conservatives as to candidates should be prepared and signed without delay."[40] By the end of October, F. E. Guest, Lloyd George's whip, was able to report to the Prime Minister, "I have come to an agreement with Mr. Bonar Law that we should receive their support, where necessary, for 150 Lloyd George candidates, 100 of whom are our old Guard."[41] Lloyd George had cut his deal.

Ignorant of Lloyd George's arrangement with the Conservatives and knowing that an election would have to be held at some point, a deputation from the National Liberal Federation, the Scottish Liberal Federation, and the Manchester Liberal Federation met with the Prime Minister to plead for a rapprochement between Lloyd George's Liberal followers and the official Liberals under Asquith. Considering that he had already cut his deal with the Conservatives to run on a coalition ticket, he naturally was unable to give them a satisfactory answer.[42] Soon after this meeting, Asquith met one on one with Lloyd George. No one else was present, but immediately after the meeting, Asquith saw Vivian Phillipps, the Prime Minister's Private Secretary. According to Phillipps, Asquith said that Lloyd George had asked him once again to join the government, but Asquith told him that would be impossible under the circumstances. He also told the Prime Minister "that he would be willing to 'lend a hand'—that was his phrase—as one of the British delegates to the Peace Conference," to which Lloyd George made no response.[43]

The Great War finally came to an end on November 11. Asquith was pleased to receive a telegram from the King. "I look back with gratitude," the message read, "to your wise counsel and calm resolve in the days when great issues had to be decided resulting in our entry into the war." In the same vein

Queen Alexandria sent a telegram to Margot reading, "In the great rejoicings which we share with you and people all over our Empire, we do not forget your husband today."[44] The day after the Armistice went into effect, Lloyd George announced his plan to call an election to a meeting of some 150 to 200 Liberals he had specifically invited to 10 Downing Street. He told them that he had done nothing since he became Prime Minister to make him ashamed to meet his fellow Liberals and declared, "Please God, I am determined I never shall."[45] He did not, however, let on about his deal with the Conservatives, and so the speech was well received. Asquith welcomed the Prime Minister's remarks, saying they would in no way impair the unity of the Liberal Party that he and his followers desired to maintain.[46]

Four days later Lloyd George began to show his real hand. In a speech on November 16, he urged electors to investigate "ruthlessly" the credentials of those in the Liberal Party who claimed to be his supporters.[47] Indeed, he was more than willing to help in this regard. The deal he cut with the Conservatives had identified 150 "Lloyd George candidates," and these now needed to be identified to the public. Selected candidates received a letter signed by both Lloyd George and Bonar Law recognizing them as government candidates. Using the rationing language of the day, Asquith famously dubbed this letter a political "coupon."

The primary consideration for Lloyd George in granting a coupon was to safeguard those Liberals willing to support the government in what would be Lloyd George's assault on the Asquithian Liberals during the campaign. The chief constraint, of course, was that Lloyd George only had 150 coupons to distribute. All Liberal candidates beyond that number, whether they had supported the government or not, would not receive a coupon.[48] No Liberal who had voted for Asquith's motion in the Maurice debate received a coupon, and they were forced to face either a Liberal with a coupon or more often a Conservative.[49]

The campaign was a nasty one. Asquith told Sylvia Henley that it was a "wicked fraud, and would settle nothing."[50] The Prime Minister declared on November 23 that those who had supported the Maurice debate constituted "a Parliamentary conspiracy" to overthrow a government "in the midst of a crisis while wrestling for victory."[51] Asquith quickly responded a few days later at Huddersfield. He readily accepted responsibility for the motion to investigate General Maurice's allegations, declaring that there was no act in his thirty years in Parliament "for which I am less repentant and ashamed." He reminded his listeners that the government itself had first called for some kind of inquiry; his only concern was how that inquiry should proceed. The government "most absurdly" treated his motion as a "vote of want of confidence and censure, and now we are told that unless you get a pledge-bound majority in the next House of Commons the same thing may occur." Asquith would have none of it. Coupon candidates had given up their independence. "I would never sit in the House of Commons again—much as I prize it," he declared. "I would rather not sit there under conditions so humiliating."[52] As to other major issues in the campaign, Liberal candidates like Asquith, who had the courage to point out to voters the impossibility of Germany's paying unreasonably high reparations as urged by Lloyd George, were pilloried for wanting to let Germany off.[53]

The polling took place before Christmas, but owing to the necessity of collecting soldiers' votes, the results were not declared until December 28. On that day Asquith, Lloyd George, and other dignitaries attended a luncheon held by the Lord Mayor at the Mansion House for visiting President Wilson, who was to receive the Freedom of the City of London. Asquith had a long talk with the American President and was impressed. He told a friend that the President "had good intelligence and (what is more important) real personality." Most of all he found him "a great & refreshing change . . . from the gas-bag Americans of the Roosevelt type."[54] J. A. Spender was there, and during the lunch he was slipped a paper from the reporters' table informing him that Asquith had been defeated at East Fife.[55] Could it be true? East Fife had loyally supported Asquith since his first election to Parliament over thirty years ago in 1886.

Asquith was out. When Margot told her husband the news, she burst into tears. He held her, and she recorded his saying, "Don't cry darling. It's a great relief! I assure you I am too glad. I don't mind at all." She added that his face showed "signs of emotion as he pressed my shaking body into his arms & patted my head against his breast."[56] His daughter Violet summed it up in a speech she gave a little over a year later and which Asquith himself quoted in his own *Memories and Reflections*. "He saw himself deserted by men who owed him their political existence, by men whom he had never failed, by men whom he had led from victory to victory. He saw—and this was the hardest thing of all for him to bear—he saw those who stood by him go under."[57]

There was no hiding it. Asquith's defeat at East Fife shocked almost everyone. Asquith himself had never thought it possible that his old constituency would turn him out. As a result, he had spent much of the campaign supporting Liberal candidates in other districts. Asquith faced his loss stoically. He blamed his defeat and that of many others on the newly enfranchised women "who appear to have voted in droves."[58] Whether he was being truthful or not, he wrote to Sylvia Henley, "I am much more glad than sorry that I am out. . . ."[59] He reflected on his life thus far in a letter to Margot, who had gone to Italy for her health. "I see no reason why we should not be happy," he told her. "I am in my 67th year, and looking back (while

I think worse both of men's brains, & their hearts & characters than I once did) I have not many grievances against fortune." He concluded, "Few men have had a life more crowded with interests, both big and small: and none that I know has been so nearly blessed in his home."[60]

In his mid-sixties and for the first time in more than thirty years no longer serving in Parliament, Asquith used the early months of 1919 traveling and resting. Beginning in February, he spent a month at Biarritz. It was pleasurable, with plenty of time for playing golf and visiting with good friends. This was followed by a two-week tour of Spain. In addition to seeing the sights in Toledo, Seville, Granada, and Cordoba, he had lunch with the King and Queen of Spain and dinner with the Prime Minister. His other travels that year included a visit to the British Army of Occupation in July and a journey to Venice for a fortnight in September.[61]

The year was not all rest and relaxation. He was appointed to chair the new Oxford and Cambridge Commission. Asquith had always had a great interest in Britain's major universities, and so he excitedly took to his task. Practical as always, Asquith was perhaps seen by some more radical university reformers as too conservative. Harold Laski commented that when it came to Oxford, Asquith was "living on his memories of the Jowett days which he finds satisfactory merely because he was himself successful."[62] The commission published its report in March 1922 and came up with useful proposals to modernize the universities, especially in the area of research. An important suggestion was that Oxford and Cambridge should receive an outright annual grant of £110,000 and be charged with making sure that full scholarships be given only to those showing actual financial need.[63]

While Asquith enjoyed his travels and his work with the Oxford and Cambridge Commission, he must have been discouraged about his political future, if indeed he even imagined one. For the entire first six months of 1919, not a single Liberal Association invited him to speak.[64] It was obvious that if Asquith was ever going to re-enter the political arena, he must regain a seat in Parliament—a remote possibility in the current political climate. Then in early 1920, Sir John McCullum, a Liberal who represented Paisley, a constituency just outside Glasgow, died, thus setting up a by-election and the possibility of Asquith's being returned to Parliament. Prospects for his election did not look good. Unlike East Fife's large area of scattered communities, Paisley was a compact, industrial center of about 90,000. And while Paisley was a traditionally Liberal district, in the Coupon election of 1918 McCullum, an Asquith supporter, had been returned with a majority of only 106. Furthermore, the local Liberal Association was still split into Asquith and Lloyd George factions. The thought of taking a seat in a House of Commons that was the offspring of the "Coupon" election had little attraction for

Asquith; nevertheless, when invited by the local Paisley Liberal Association to be its candidate, an invitation passed by a vote of 92 to 75, he thought it his duty to accept.[65] Violet Asquith wrote to Gilbert Murray on January 29, as she was about to head to Paisley to campaign with her father, "I am full of doubt as to the issue—but I feel it must be made a magnificent fight—whatever the outcome."[66]

Asquith surprised almost everyone with his enthusiasm for the campaign. His personal secretary, Vivian Phillipps, recorded that "for a fortnight, he [Asquith] carried through a campaign of meetings—often as many as five in a single day—which would have taxed the physique of many a much younger man, but from start to finish, he showed no trace of fatigue or staleness."[67] Asquith took up a different topic each night, and by the end of the campaign, the voters had a clear picture of his view of what the Liberal attitude should be on the main domestic and international problems of the day.[68] These speeches were later published in a small book, *The Paisley Policy*.[69] The crowds were large and for the most part receptive. Violet, who campaigned hard for her father, noted in her diary, "the Paisley people were wonderful material to work upon—an extraordinary combination of cool heads and warm hearts." According to her, "They wld. listen for hours to slabs of solid facts & figures from Father," she wrote, "admirably handled & presented of course, but quite undiluted by gas, fluff or claptrap of any kind—appraising it all clearly—coolly—critically."[70]

In his speeches, Asquith criticized the Versailles Treaty as being too harsh and courageously called for moderation when it came to German reparation payments. "This is a bad and doubtful debt," he told his audience, "and a prudent man of business will not let it enter into the account at all." His coalition opponent said the statement was proof that Asquith was "a pro-German," and Paisley was soon plastered with signs reading "Asquith is going to let Germany off."[71] He also warned voters that the new states established in central Europe would quickly surround themselves with tariff walls unless actions were taken to establish customs unions. As for Ireland, he declared that he himself was "quite prepared to run such risks as there are in giving the new Irish Parliament control over their customs and excise, in other words to put them on the same footing in that respect as all our great self-governing Dominions."[72]

Although the Conservative candidate in the race had been endorsed by Bonar Law on behalf of the coalition government, Asquith's real competition came from the Labour Party candidate, J. M. Biggar, who had come close to victory in the Coupon election just a little over a year before.

By polling day, all the signs pointed to an Asquith victory. A week before the polling, Asquith himself had written "certainly there is a growth of outward signs of enthusiasm."[73] Sure enough, Asquith was returned with a majority of 2,834 with the Conservative candidate losing his deposit. The interest in the campaign had been immense. The total poll had increased from 22,179 to 30,433 over the Coupon election only fifteen months earlier. "Perhaps the most satisfactory feature of the whole business," Asquith wrote a friend, "was the sorry figure cut by the wretched Coalitionist McKean [who had called Asquith 'pro-German']: he fought dirtily and deserves the penalty he has to suffer of losing his deposit."[74]

Almost 5,000 people saw the Asquiths off at a Paisley farewell meeting, and after taking the night train to Glasgow he was, as he described it, "nearly done to death by the demonstrative attentions of the University students." When he finally arrived at London, there was another noisy demonstration at Euston station, and greeting him at his house were "more letters and telegrams than it is possible to count."[75] Friends overwhelmed him with congratulations. Future Poet Laureate John Masefield wrote, "our delight is centred on your own personal success, and on the thought that the nation is turning back to what is sane and fine in it, after the fever—the trickery of the last years." Lord Bryce told him that he had "given the best proof since the G.O.M. [Gladstone] took up Home Rule in 1886 that courage has not vanished from political life."[76]

Despite the adulation the hard, cold fact remained that he was now back in Parliament, sitting in a House of Commons elected in the "Coupon" election and dominated by a hostile coalition. He was far from the center of power. Violet watched him when he took his seat once again in the House of Commons, a place where she had seen him "lead great armies to great triumphs." But this time, although she was ultimately optimistic about the prospects of her father and his supporters, "when I saw that little gallant handful of men which is all his following now, and heard their thin cheer raised," she asked herself for a moment, "Is this all, are these all he has behind him?"[77]

When Asquith returned to the House of Commons, he focused first on Ireland. He had made it one of the central issues in his campaign in Paisley, arguing effectively for Dominion Home Rule. Asquith had watched with dismay as the coalition government continued to refuse to introduce the Self-Government bill it had promised when the Compulsory Service bill including Ireland had passed in 1918. With each passing month, the radical Sinn Féin pulled more and more support from the Constitutional Party, and in the Coupon election of December 1918 Sinn Féin was triumphant. After Asquith returned to Parliament, the coalition government put forward a bill that in Asquith's words "was passed for the purpose of giving a section of Ulster a Parliament which it did not want, and to the remaining three-quarters of Ireland a Parliament which it would not have."[78] As a result of Parliament's fickleness and Ireland's impatience, Ireland deteriorated into a murderous series of atrocities between Sinn Féin and the infamous "Black and Tans," representing the government.

In a letter to *The Times* on October 4, 1920, Asquith blasted the government for putting "forward a paltering compromise, which is repudiated by every section of Irish opinion, though it may for the moment be favoured with the contemptuous and cynical patronage of Sir Edward Carson, who thinks he sees in what is proposed the prospect of an insurmountable block to the attainment of Irish unity." Asquith argued that there were two conditions to any workable solution. First the Irish people must be made to believe that Great Britain was acting in good faith. Second "after making all necessary allowance for the provisional abstention, not of an artificial, but of a genuine local minority, it should meet and satisfy Irish aspiration." This could only be done by giving Ireland Dominion status. To those who thought such a move humiliating and hazardous, he asked "What is your alternative?"[79]

Lloyd George was quick to respond. Five days later in a speech at Carnarvon, he denounced Dominion Home Rule as "lunacy." Under such a plan, the Prime Minister rather hysterically argued Ireland could become the home of a hostile fleet with submarines sowing the seas with mines. Asquith was not to be deterred. Several days later in a speech at Ayr, he called for Great Britain to "face the facts." The government was engaged in civil war, "war in its worst and most hideous guise." The vast majority of actions taken by the government against the Irish were not acts of self-defence but rather "acts of blind and indiscriminate vengeance."[80] Soon after the speech Asquith wrote with some satisfaction, "Now that Ll. G. calls me a lunatic and Carson calls me a traitor I began to feel sure that I must be right on all lines."[81]

As for opposing the government's harsh policy in the use of the Black and Tans, Asquith had plenty of support. In a vote of censure against the Black and Tans in November 1920 Asquith was supported by all his Independent Liberals as well as Labour. Dominion status was another matter. Few were willing to go as far as Asquith, which was very frustrating for him. "Life is very difficult just now," he wrote. "We are under a Government of reckless gamblers, and we drift from one folly and wickedness to another." "If one tries to strike a bold true note, half one's friends shiver and cower, and implore one not 'to get in front of the band': in other words, to renounce both the duties and risks of leadership."[82] Although he did not know it, time was on Asquith's side. By the summer of 1921 the government realized that it had a choice—either seek peace by negotiation or subdue Ireland by a force that would take an estimated 100,000 men. The government chose negotiation. In July the talks began, lasting until December, when a treaty established the Irish Free State with the constitutional status of a Dominion.

Northern Ireland remained under British rule. Asquith must have smiled with satisfaction at the government's defeat but rued the blundering that had cost many innocent lives.

Asquith's energetic leadership on the Irish question contrasted with what some Liberals saw as his remoteness and non-participation on other issues. *The Times* reported that in a heated Liberal meeting in June 1921 "the young Independents made it clear that they are dissatisfied with the want of leadership of a rather forlorn, if gallant, band of thirty strong."[83] A year later A. C. Murray wrote Lord Reading that Asquith was only "turning up in the House once in a blue moon" and "leaving all the hard work as Leader of the Opposition to Donald Maclean."[84] At about the same time Donald Maclean, an Asquith supporter, told Harold Laski that Asquith was "devoted to bridge and small talk, doing no real work, and leaving the party leaderless." Laski gathered they all wanted him to go but "see no means of explaining to him how much he stands in the way."[85]

By October 1922, the Conservatives had had enough of Lloyd George and withdrew from the coalition after criticism of the Prime Minister over the Chanak crisis concerning Britain's foreign policy in Turkey. The new Prime Minister, Bonar Law, immediately called for a general election, and Parliament was dissolved toward the end of October. The old Liberal Party faced the election divided. Asquith led the "Independent Liberals," who had refused to follow Lloyd George into the coalition and had lost decisively at the hands of Lloyd George in the Coupon election. Lloyd George headed what were known as the "National Liberals," who since mid-1920 had been setting up their own Liberal organization. Coalition Liberal councils, each serving one or more counties, were established to parallel the Liberal Party's regional federations. Although Lloyd George had plenty of money to carry out the setting up of these new organizations, there was not a great deal of interest, and little effort was made to set up organizations in individual constituencies.[86]

The question became whether Independent Liberals would stand in individual constituencies against National Liberal candidates, which in many cases would almost assuredly mean the defeat of both by a Conservative or a Labour candidate. The Independent Liberals left the decision to the local Liberal associations, which allowed Liberal candidates to oppose each other in a number of constituencies.[87] The National Liberals were obsessed with attempting to buy Conservative support in some constituencies and were prepared to promise, as did Lloyd George, "general support" for the Conservatives.[88] All of this was a recipe for disaster for the Liberal cause.

For Asquith and the Independent Liberals, already suffering from declining support, a winning strategy for the campaign did not exist. Asquith believed the "suicide of the Coalition before the election took much of the punch out of the fight" and left the country divided between "Tranquillity and Socialism."[89] Lloyd George had still not given up the idea of a centrist party and went about the country defending the coalition and stating that he was ready to act with "men of moderate opinion" in any party. The Labour Party was growing rapidly and remained hostile to the Liberals. The Conservatives were free at least to distance themselves from the failures of the coalition government that were so identified in peoples' minds with Lloyd George.

Asquith again had the fight of his life on his hands in Paisley. Violet Asquith knew things were going to be different the minute she arrived to help. "I felt a very different atmosphere," she wrote in her diary. "There were 5,000 unemployed in the streets & great distress."[90] It was a very close call. On the night of the counting, Violet waited downstairs. She saw on the face of supporters that something had perhaps happened, and for a moment she thought they had lost, until someone murmured about a majority of "three hundred." When she rushed in to find her father in the counting room, he "looked almost for the first time in his life I thought rather shaken" and told her, "the tightest fit you ever saw."[91] Even though he polled more votes than he did in the previous election, he explained that the drop in his majority was "entirely due to the enormous addition to the Labour vote, owing to the 5,000 unemployed in Paisley (of whom there were none in 1920) and the sullen anti-bourgeois feeling which is swelling like a tidal wave over the whole of the West of Scotland."[92]

The overall results were to some extent better than expected. The Independent Liberals doubled the number of seats they had won in 1918. Most of their advances were made in rural areas like the Scottish Highlands, Yorkshire, and a few seats in southern England. But the handwriting was on the wall. When facing a Conservative or a National Liberal one on one, the Independent Liberals fared well. In the thirty-one constituencies where this was the case, Independent Liberals increased their vote total by more than 10 percent. Yet when a Labour candidate was in the race, their chances faded. In the fifty-one constituencies where all three parties contended, the Independent Liberals increased their total vote by just over 4 percent.[93] Labour was fast making inroads into Liberal support.

When the new Parliament met at the end of November, Asquith led a small but talented group of Independent Liberals. What it lacked in numbers, it more than made up for in talent and debating power. Joining Asquith on the opposition front bench was an array of first-class parliamentarians, including Sir John Simon, Wedgwood Benn, Godfrey Collins, Charles Roberts, and George Lambert in addition to a strong group of backbenchers. Vivian Phillipps, Asquith's private secretary, commented at the time, "Few Parties in the House can ever have worked together with a more unselfish team spirit, or in an atmosphere of happier personal relations."[94] All was overshadowed to some extent by the continuing enmity between Asquith and Lloyd George. Attempts to reconcile the two came to Asquith's attention. "There was a kind of 'fraternity' gathering last night," he wrote on November 28, "in one of the Committee rooms between the rank and file of our lot and the ex-Coalie Liberals. The latter seem to be prepared to 'reunite' on almost any terms. . . . It looks as if it would soon come to that." Yet Asquith concluded, "I am against forcing the peace and surrendering any ground."[95]

As it turned out, the peace did become forced, not by the Liberals themselves but by events outside the Liberal Party. At the end of May 1923, Bonar Law, dying of cancer, resigned as Prime Minister, and the Conservatives replaced him with the genial Stanley Baldwin. This in and of itself did not signal any major change of policy. On October 22, however, Baldwin dropped a bombshell by announcing in a speech in Plymouth that he favored protectionism as the only remedy for unemployment. This contradicted Bonar Law's pledge during the last general election that the Conservative government would impose protection only in limited experiments in "safeguarding." With Baldwin now taking a different view, there was no other option but to call an election, and so on November 13 Prime Minister Stanley Baldwin informed the House that it would be dissolved in three days. He would not attempt to lead the country through the winter of 1924–1925 without the use of the "instrument" of protectionism.[96]

Would the Liberals be able to unite once again under the old banner of free trade that had swept them to victory in 1906? Asquith and Lloyd George held a conference which was described as "very easy and cordial."[97] They issued a joint manifesto rallying the country to free trade, with Lloyd George putting his name beneath that of Asquith. Even more important Lloyd George agreed to contribute £90,000 to the campaign coffers. All incumbent Liberals would receive joint support, and in constituencies without an incumbent, the National and Independent Liberals would join together to select a candidate.[98]

Asquith hit the campaign trail with a passion for the next three weeks. He and Lloyd George even shared a platform at the Clark Town Hall in Paisley on November 24. At one point he reported, "We had a first-rate meeting, at which for the first time my utterances were 'broadcast' by the agency of the microphone." Asquith was clearly enjoying himself, describing his opponents to a friend as "the familiar and three times defeated Biggar, an imported Communist solicitor called Cormack, who, if he persists, as I hope, in his candidature, will draw off from Biggar the Wild Men's votes, and a delightful old lunatic Brown, who is over 70 and drives a cab in Paisley with a white horse, which he declares to be of Arab pedigree."[99] Asquith was once again returned by Paisley and increased his majority from 316 in the last election to over

1,700, due largely to the presence of an independent socialist who split the Labour vote. The national vote was not so clear cut. The Conservatives were reduced from 347 to 255, yet with 191 Labour members and 158 Liberals, no party had a majority. Furthermore, though Asquith now led a united Liberal Party, Lloyd George was still present, issuing his own policy statements, maintaining a separate headquarters, and most important of all controlling a large campaign fund.[100]

Several options seemed open to Asquith, but in reality there was only one. The first option was to join with the Conservatives to prevent the first socialist government under the Labour Party. This could be done either by supporting Baldwin as Prime Minister or by taking the position himself with Conservative support. "You would be amused," he wrote three days after Christmas, "if you saw the contents of my daily post-bag; appeals, threats, prayers from all parts, and from all sorts and conditions of men, women, and lunatics, to step in and save the country from the horrors of Socialism and Confiscation." He went on, "If I were to agree at this moment to enter into a compact with the Tories, I have little doubt that I could count on a majority in the House of Commons of more than two to one."[101] Even so, he could never have seriously considered such a decision. How could he now join forces with the protectionists as if the election had never happened and he had never championed free trade? How would it look to the nation if the two "middle-class" parties united to deprive Labour of an opportunity to govern, when both the Liberals and the Conservatives would have claimed it their right in similar circumstances?[102] In the end, there was only one option: to throw Liberal support behind Labour. As he told a gathering of all the Liberal members of the new House meeting at the National Liberal Club on December 18, "Well, this may reassure some trembling minds outside: If a Labour Government is ever to be tried in this country, as it will sooner or later, it could hardly be tried under safer conditions."[103]

Asquith knew that the new Labour government would not last long, but he genuinely wanted to give them a chance to govern. There is no indication and Sir John Simon specifically denied that Asquith ever calculated that once Labour stumbled the Liberals would be in a position to claim office for themselves.[104] In fact, on February 15 Asquith wrote, "I suppose we could, if we liked, force a political crisis—the last thing I want to do, as far the best policy both for us and the country is to give the Labour Government a free and full rope."[105] It is not clear from his letter whether he hoped the rope might be used by Labour to hang itself.

Cooperation between Labour and the Liberals ended with the government's handling of the proposed treaty with the Soviet Union and the prosecution of J. R. Campbell, editor of the *Workers Weekly*, for incitement to mutiny. The government had promised that a proposed Russian treaty would contain no provision for a guaranteed loan, only to reverse itself when pressured by a group of Labour members. Along the same lines, after proceedings were begun against Campbell, they were suddenly dropped after similar pressure was applied. Conservatives and Liberals alike were in an uproar at the government's obeisance to unknown Labour forces. Asquith struggled to hold his party in line and did all that he could to keep the government in power. He wrote a "letter to a correspondent" that held the door open to modifications in the treaty and even sought to save the situation by suggesting the appointment of a select committee to look into the Campbell case. All to no avail. "The Labour Government stumbled on," Asquith wrote, and it finally came to an end after the "squalid crises" of the Russian treaty and the Campbell case, "each of which could have been avoided, or at least prevented, if they had played their cards with a modicum of either luck or skill."[106] The Conservatives proposed a censure motion in the House, and the Liberals offered an amendment. Labour announced that both votes would be considered votes of confidence. When the Liberals' amendment passed, the King granted MacDonald's request for a dissolution of Parliament the following day.

Fear of an election had motivated Asquith to try to keep Labour in power. As it turned out, his fear was well founded. Asquith's Independent Liberals decided to attempt to run a sufficient number of candidates (450 to 500) to convince the country that they were making a serious bid for power. Lloyd George thought this foolish, and the delays while decisions were being made on this issue held up overall plans for the campaign. In the end, a lack of funds reduced the number of Liberal candidates to only 343.[107]

At age seventy-two Asquith faced his fourth election in Paisley in less than five years. With her usual exaggeration, Margot wrote to Violet that "It will be our last Gen. Election & the greatest moment of our lives."[108] The good news was that the Conservative headquarters in Scotland decided not to oppose him and persuaded his prospective Conservative opponent to stand elsewhere. Still, getting the Conservatives in Paisley to vote for him was another matter and was critical to Asquith's election. He courted them assiduously. He even went so far as to declare, "Both the old political parties in this election have found themselves, as they believe, confronted with a common danger, which without any loss of identity or compromise of principle on one side or upon the other, they are making reciprocal sacrifices to avert."[109] The statement drew criticism from Liberal circles. The *Glasgow Herald* charged, "in order to save his own seat in Paisley Mr. Asquith has entered into a compact with the Tories to facilitate a Tory majority in this election."[110]

Although Asquith's Paisley organization had three battles already under its belt and had achieved what Violet called "an almost Prussian perfection," the campaign was the first in which Asquith had to face a Labour candidate one on one. Labour put forward a new candidate, Edward Rosslyn Mitchell.[111] On the evening of the polling Violet, as she always did, waited for her father as they counted the votes. When the doors opened and she saw the looks on their supporters faces, the "icy fear in my heart was confirmed. We were beaten." She approached her father, who was "absolutely controlled" and merely said, "'I'm out by 2,000.'" In his motion of thanks, his opponent kindly conceded that "the result gives me no personal satisfaction," telling Violet, "'I'm so sorry—so terribly sorry this has happened.'" Asquith, as was the custom, immediately went to the Liberal Club to thank supporters. Violet captured her father completely in her remarkable diary entry of the event. "Father spoke to them with perfect fortitude and serenity. He has the courage of real philosophy & greatness—no teeth-set, tight-lipped Stoicism—something much bigger & more natural—a sort of power of seeing events immediately in scale & eliminating his own personal position completely from his perspective."[112] Even in defeat, Asquith remained the stoic Roman.

In the context of the Liberals' nationwide showing in the 1924 general election, Asquith's defeat at Paisley is not surprising. The Liberal gains of a year before were wiped out. In 1923 they had won 158 seats; this time they secured only 43. The Conservative Party captured 415 seats as against 258 in 1923.[113] It was the last hurrah for Asquith and the old Liberal Party.

Within a week of his defeat, Asquith received a letter from King George V expressing his regret. The King wrote that after Asquith's eminent career he "should not be subject to further political contests, with all their attendant turmoil and unpleasantness, nor the exacting, wearing life of the House of Commons . . ." "For these reasons," the King continued, "it would be a matter of the greatest satisfaction to me to confer upon you a Peerage."[114] Asquith wrote to Hilda Harrison that it was "very tactful and kind of him to write in the interregnum between two governments: so that it would be entirely his own proposal."[115] Asquith responded to the King that he wished some time to consider the kind proposal.

With his final political campaign over, Asquith gladly took Oc's suggestion to accompany him on a tour of Egypt and the Sudan. In Cairo he was a guest at the residence of Lord and Lady Allenby. Unfortunately, while he was staying there, Sir Oliver Stack, Sirdar of the Egyptian army and Governor of the Sudan, was assassinated in one of the principal streets of Cairo. Asquith's party then journeyed on to Palestine. He was not impressed. After touring the Dead Sea, Jericho, the Garden of Gethsemane, the Church of the Nativity, and other sights, he wrote in late November, "If it were not for these historic [biblical] associations no one, who could go anywhere else, would visit Palestine. It is just what I expected to find—an arid, hummocky, treeless expanse, with ranges of hills here and there rising to no great height." As for the political situation in Palestine, while he believed the Jews who had come to the area were undoubtedly better off than they had been in Europe, "the talk of making Palestine into a Jewish 'National Home' seems to me as fantastic as it always has done."[116] He returned to Cairo via Beirut, which he found "an odious and garish seaport" but beautifully situated at the foot of the Lebanese mountains, and departed from Port Said for Marseilles at the beginning of the new year.[117]

While on his travels to the Middle East, Asquith decided to accept the King's offer of a peerage. He wrote to the King on January 20 informing him that any reservations he might have had "were completely overcome by my deep and abiding sense of obligation and affection to the King, whom it was my privilege to serve for so many successive years as his Chief Minister." He concluded, "If it should be your Majesty's pleasure, in accordance with precedent, to confer upon me the dignity of an Earl, I should propose to take the title of Oxford, which has fine traditions in our history, and which was given by Queen Anne to her Prime Minister Robert Harley."[118] The King responded that he could "quite realize and appreciate the various difficulties which required careful consideration before a decision could be arrived at." He knew full well how much Asquith was a child of the Commons and what a great "wrench" it must be to leave. Nevertheless he told Asquith, "It is a gain to the public of England and the Empire that the House of Lords should have as its leaders on either side some of the foremost Statesmen of the time."[119] There were some minor complaints from those who claimed they had patent rights to the dormant title of Oxford, and some objected saying there was no precedent when he proposed to perpetuate his own name by adding "and Asquith" to the title. Nevertheless, Herbert Henry Asquith took his seat in the House of Lords as the Earl of Oxford and Asquith on February 17 with his old friends Lord Balfour and Lord Curzon as his supporters.[120]

Other honors and awards followed. He accepted the King's offer of the Order of the Garter, which he had previously declined in December 1918. He was also appointed a member of the Judicial Committee of the Privy Council. The City of London conveyed the Freedom of the City, and speaking at the ceremony, Prime Minster Baldwin said that all recognized "the stability of his character, the serenity of his temper, his freedom from jealousies and enmities, the magnitude of his mind and the plenitude of his utterance."[121] The one honor he desired but was denied was Chancellor of the University of Oxford in 1925. He had allowed his name to go forward with the reasonable expectation that, as almost certainly the most distinguished living Oxonian, he would be unopposed. Conservative graduates were not about to let this happen. It took some time for opponents to find a candidate, but they were finally able to persuade Lord Cave, the new Lord Chancellor in the Conservative government, to stand. When he was defeated, Asquith wrote to a friend, "Zadok, the priest, and Abiathar, the priest, with their followers in rural parsonages, were too much for us."[122]

Once elevated to the House of Lords, Asquith should have relinquished his leadership of the Liberal Party. Unfortunately he did not. The problem of course was that Lloyd George continued to maintain his own campaign fund and act independently. Leading up to and during the 1924 election, Asquith's Liberals had become so desperate for funds that on several occasion Asquith himself was forced to plead with Lloyd George to supply them.[123] Asquith was very much of the old school when it came to campaign finances. For him the leader of the party should in no way be associated with its financial dealings. It would place the leader in the controlling position of paymaster to his Parliamentary supporters, and a leader's involvement in the party's finances would inevitably lead to accusations that contributors were controlling policy.[124] Being forced to plead with Lloyd George for money must have been especially galling. Following the disastrous results of the 1924 election, the Liberal Party reorganized itself and in January 1925 launched an appeal for a million pounds. By the end of the year the campaign had failed, and Asquith recorded that he himself was driven "to the humiliating task of making a personal appeal to the better-to-do among our followers to come to the rescue, and provide us with a wholly independent fund of adequate amount." By 1926, Asquith revealed, "the fact remains that at this moment our Central Office is faced in the near future with the certainty of serious and perhaps fatal financial stress, in relief of which it is idle, in the present condition of the Party, to expect that a repetition of last year's appeal or any other expedient, would meet with a substantial response."[125]

The event that ultimately led to Asquith's downfall as leader of the Liberal Party was the General Strike which broke out on May 3, 1926. The Liberal shadow cabinet meeting that very day condemned the strike and agreed to support the government in suppressing it. Asquith, Lord Grey, and Sir John Simon dutifully presented the Liberal position in Parliament and in the *British Gazette*, published by the government since newspaper workers were on strike. Lloyd George, predictably struck out on a different path. His speeches in the House of Commons condemned the government much more than the strikers. The Liberal Chief Whip announced another meeting of the shadow cabinet on May 10. Lloyd George responded that he would not attend because he dissented from the line taken by "the leader of the party and others wielding great authority in the party." Moreover he thought the action of the government "precipitate, unwarrantable and mischievous."[126] Asquith was fed up. He wrote to a friend the next day that Lloyd George "was in the sulks, and had cast in his lot for the moment with the clericals—Archbishops and Deans and the whole company of the various Churches (a hopeless lot)—in the hope of getting a foot-hold for himself in the Labour camp." He went on, "He is already, being a creature of certain temperament, suffering from cold feet."[127] The General Strike fell apart the day after Lloyd George sent his letter, but Asquith was not about to let the matter end there. On May 20 he responded to Lloyd George, telling him that he regretted the course Lloyd George had pursued "in the greatest domestic crisis the country has had to confront in your time or mine." He recounted in detail the events and the position he and other leaders of the Liberal Party had taken throughout the crisis. Lloyd George's refusal to meet with the shadow cabinet at the height of the crisis Asquith considered a "very grave matter." "It was, in my judgment," he explained, "the primary duty of all who were responsible for Liberal policy, and certainly not least the Chairman of the Parliamentary Party in the House of Commons, at such time to meet together for free and full discussion, and to contribute their counsels to the common stock." In the end he wrote, "Your refusal to do so I find impossible to reconcile with my conception of the obligations of political comradeship."[128]

After sending his letter to Lloyd George, Asquith left to visit his friend Geoffrey Howard at Castle Howard in Yorkshire. Word was getting out of yet another dispute between the two Liberal leaders, and unfortunately Asquith authorized the publication of his letter. Lloyd George, apprised of Asquith's intention, sent his response. Both letters were published simultaneously on May 26. Having the distinct advantage of the last word, Lloyd George portrayed himself as the offended party. He wrote that he said nothing publicly that clashed with the decision of the Liberal shadow cabinet to oppose the government. All he had done was to urge conciliation and support the appeal of the Archbishop of Canterbury for a resumption of negotiations.

Asquith knew that his leadership was being challenged. Harold Laski wrote at the time, "Asquith has made a profound mistake by trying to set up standards of party orthodoxy to which no man can possibly be asked to conform" and concluded with the thought, almost certainly shared by many Liberals, that Asquith had proved "utterly incapable of adjusting himself to the demands of a new age."[129] On June 1 Asquith addressed a letter to the Liberal Chief Whip, Sir Godfrey Collins, again recounting the events of the last weeks, stating, "Mr. Lloyd George, in the exercise of his own judgment and for reasons of which I am the last to question the gravity, chose to separate himself, in the most formal manner, from our deliberations in a moment of great emergency. He was not driven out, he refused to come in." Then he threw down the gauntlet. "I have honestly striven, during the last two years," he told the Chief Whip, "to recreate and to revive the broken fabric of the Liberal unity." "It has been a burdensome, and in some of its aspects, a thankless task. I will not continue to hold the leadership for a day unless I am satisfied that I retain the full measure of the confidence of the party."[130] The Liberals could choose—it was to be either Asquith or Lloyd George.

Lloyd George was not about to be driven from the party. In spirited speeches and articles he characterized the battle as between himself representing progressive Liberals and the "official gang." Liberals found themselves in an awkward position. Asquith had always had the support of the party outside Parliament, but this time the rank and file hesitated. The rebuff came when Asquith failed to persuade either the National Liberal Federation's annual meeting or the Candidates' Association to condemn Lloyd George. The latter resolved on June 11 to send a delegation to Asquith asking him to restore unity in the party under Asquith's leadership.[131]

At this critical juncture, Asquith's consistently strong health finally began to fail him. On the day after the Candidates Association passed its resolution, he suffered the first of several debilitating strokes, and by late September Asquith had made up his mind to resign the leadership position. It is grimly fitting that the last battle with his old nemesis Lloyd George would be the beginning of the end for Asquith. At the end of June, he had a last meeting with his old colleagues at Lord Grey's house. He wrote to Violet with the news of his decision on October 4. "If I was to remain," he told her, "I should be forced to do one of two things: either (1) to lead a faction fight against Ll. G., who is equipped with all the sinews of war or (2) to take part once more, under the most humiliating conditions, in the hollow farce of 'reconciliation' and 'Restoring Unity.' Nothing will induce me to do either the one or the other, and I have of course abundant justification for going in age, health, &c." He sent a "confidential and secret" memorandum to his closest friends: under the present conditions, "to talk of Liberal unity as a thing which either has been, or has any fair prospect of being, achieved, seems to me to be an abuse of language. If there are those who take a more sanguine view, I can only express a sincere hope that they may prove to be right." He also mentioned that his health had given him a "serious warning." For all these reasons, he informed his friends he was resigning as leader of the party he had served so loyally for over forty years.

NOTES

1. HHA to Sylvia Henley, 15 Dec. 1916, MS. Eng. Litt. c. 542/4, ff. 804–5.
2. HHA to Hilda Harrison, 10 Dec. 1916, MacCarthy, *H. H. A.: Letters of the Earl of Oxford and Asquith to a Friend, First Series*, 13.

3. Diary entry 10 Dec. 1916, Stephen Roskill, *Hankey: Man of Secrets, Volume 1 1877–1918* (London: Cassell, 1971), 329.
4. Hankey to HHA, 7 Dec. 1916, BL, MSS Asquith 17, ff. 198–99.
5. HHA to Hilda Harrison, 10 Dec. 1916, MacCarthy, ed., *H. H. A.: Letters of the Earl of Oxford and Asquith to a Friend, First Series*, 13.
6. Harry Cust to HHA, 9 Dec. 1916, BL, MS. Asquith 17, ff. 209–10.
7. Robert Cecil to HHA, 8 Dec. 1916, BL, MS. Asquith 17, ff. 202–3.
8. Enclosure in HHA to Sylvia Henley, 26 Dec. 1916, BL, MS. Eng. Litt. c. 542/4, ff. 813–15. The reference in the article is to Sir Henry Newbolt's poem, *Vitaï Lampada,* a verse of which reads:

> The sand of the desert is sodden red,—
> Red with the wreck of a square that broke;—
> The Gatling's jammed and the colonel dead,
> And the regiment blind with dust and smoke.
> The river of death has brimmed his banks,
> And England's far, and Honour a name,
> But the voice of schoolboy rallies the ranks,
> "Play up! play up! and play the game!"

9. Wilson, *Downfall of the Liberal Party*, 105–6.
10. Ibid., 106.
11. Ibid., 107.
12. Ibid., 123.
13. HHA to Sylvia Henley, 30 June 1917, BL, MS. Eng. Litt. c. 542/5, ff. 907–8.
14. Wilson, *Downfall of the Liberal Party,* 109.
15. Ibid., 106.
16. HHA to Sylvia Henley, 30 June 1917, BL, MS. Eng. Litt. c. 542/5, ff. 907–8.
17. *Hansard*, 5, 95, 2358–2367, 13 July 1917.
18. Peter Rowland, *David Lloyd George: A Biography* (New York: Macmillan, 1975), 421.
19. Spender and Asquith, *Life of Asquith,* 2:291.
20. *Hansard*, 5, 99, 883–93, 19 Nov. 1917.
21. HHA to Sylvia Henley, 28 Dec. 1917, BL, MS. Eng. Litt. c. 542/5, ff. 990–91.
22. Shaw-Stewart to Diana Manners, 20 Dec. 1917, Clifford, *Asquiths*, 430.
23. Diary entry 12 June 1917, Horsley, ed., *Cynthia Asquith Diaries*, 311.
24. HHA to MA, 15 Sept. 1917, BL, MA. Eng. c. 6692, ff. 7–8; HHA to MA, 17 Sept. 1915, BL, MS. Eng. c. 6692, ff. 9–10; Arthur "Oc" Asquith to MA, 12 Oct. 1917, BL, MS. Eng. d. 3289, ff. 27–29.
25. Spender and Asquith, *Life of Asquith,* 2:300.
26. Ibid., 2:303.
27. Major-General Sir Frederick Maurice to HHA, 6 May 1918, Spender and Asquith, *Life of Asquith,* 2:303.
28. *Hansard*, 5, 105, 1981–1983, 7 May 1918.
29. *Manchester Guardian*, 8 May 1918, Trevor Wilson, *Downfall of the Liberal Party*, 109.

30. Horsley, ed., *Cynthia Asquith Diaries*, 438.
31. *The Times,* 10 May 1918, 7.
32. Spender and Asquith, *Life of Asquith,* 2:308.
33. *The Times*, 10 May 1918, 7.
34. *Manchester Guardian*, 10 May 1918, Wilson, *Downfall of the Liberal Party*, 110.
35. Margot Asquith diary, 9 May 1918, BL, MS, Eng. 3216, f. 156.
36. Roskill, *Hankey: Man of Secrets*, 548–49.
37. HHA to Helen Harrison, 25 Nov. 1918, MacCarthy, ed., *H. H. A.: Letters of the Earl of Oxford and Asquith to a Friend, First Series*, 85.
38. Wilson, *Downfall of the Liberal Party*, 110–11.
39. Ibid., 124.
40. F. E. Guest to Lloyd George, 13 July 1918, ibid., 142.
41. F. E. Guest to Lloyd George, 29 Oct. 1918, ibid., 143.
42. Spender and Asquith, *Life of Lord Asquith,* 2:312.
43. Phillipps's recollection is contained in an article in *The Times*, 9 Mar. 1929.
44. Spender and Asquith, *Life of Asquith,* 2:310.
45. Wilson, *Downfall of the Liberal Party*, 136.
46. *Manchester Guardian*, 14 and 18 Nov. 1918, Wilson, *Downfall of the Liberal Party*, 138.
47. Ibid., 139.
48. Ibid., 149.
49. Spender and Asquith. *Life of Asquith,* 2:316.
50. HHA to Sylvia Henley, 25 Nov. 1918, BL, MS. Eng. Litt. c. 542/5, ff. 1067–68.
51. Spender and Asquith, *Life of Asquith,* 2:316–17.
52. Ibid., 2:318.
53. Simon, *Retrospect*, 187.
54. HHA to Sylvia Henley, 31 Dec. 1918, BL, MS. Eng. Litt. c. 542/5, ff. 1070–71.
55. Spender, *Life, Journalism and Politics*, 2:79.
56. Margot Asquith diary, 28 Dec. 1918, BL, MS. Eng. d. 3217, f. 70.
57. Earl of Oxford and Asquith, *Memories*, 2:217.
58. HHA to Sylvia Henley, 31 Dec. 1918, MS. Eng. litt. c. 542/5, ff. 1070–71.
59. Ibid.
60. HHA to MA, 31 Jan. 1919, MS. Eng. c. 6692, ff. 17–18.
61. Spender and Asquith, *Life of Asquith*, 2:322.
62. Harold J. Laski to Oliver Wendell Holmes, 29 October 1921, Howe, ed., *Holmes-Laski Letters*, 1:380.
63. Spender and Asquith, *Life of Asquith,* 2:323.
64. Ibid., 2:328.
65. Earl of Oxford and Asquith, *Memories* 2: 212–13; Spender and Asquith, *Life of Asquith,* 2:328.
66. Violet Asquith to Gilbert Murray, 24 Jan. 1920, Mark Pottle, ed., *Champion Redoubtable: The Diaries and Letters of Violet Bonham Carter 1914–1945* (London: Weidenfeld & Nicolson, 1998), 108.
67. Spender and Asquith, *Life of Asquith,* 2:329.
68. Ibid.

69. H. H. Asquith, *The Paisley Policy* (London: Cassell and Company, 1920).
70. Violet Asquith diary, n.d., Pottle, ed., *Champion Redoubtable: The Diaries and Letters of Violet Bonham Carter*, 109.
71. MacCarthy, ed., *H. H. A.: Letters of the Earl of Oxford and Asquith to a Friend, First Series*, 125.
72. Asquith, *Paisley Policy*, 64.
73. HHA to Hilda Harrison, 5 Feb. 1920, MacCarthy, ed., *H. H. A.: Letters of the Earl of Oxford and Asquith to a Friend, First Series*, 127.
74. HHA to Hilda Harrison, 26 Feb. 1920, ibid., 129–30.
75. HHA to Hilda Harrison, 26 Feb. 1920, ibid., 130.
76. Earl of Oxford and Asquith, *Memories*, 2:218–19.
77. Ibid., 2:217.
78. Ibid., 2:226.
79. *The Times*, 5 Oct. 1920, 11.
80. Spender and Asquith, *Life of Asquith*, 2:335–36.
81. Earl of Oxford and Asquith, *Memories*, 2:229.
82. Ibid.
83. *The Times*, 29 June 1921.
84. A.C. Murray to Reading, 2 Aug. 1922, Wilson, *Downfall of the Liberal Party*, 213.
85. Harold J. Laski to Oliver Wendell Holmes, 13 Sept. 1922, Howe, ed., *Holmes-Laski Letters*, 449–50.
86. Wilson, *Downfall of the Liberal Party*, 200–201.
87. Spender and Asquith, *Life of Asquith*, 2:339.
88. Wilson, *Downfall of the Liberal Party*, 228.
89. HHA to Hilda Harrison, 17 Nov. 1922, Desmond MacCarthy, ed., *H. H. A.: Letters of the Earl of Oxford and Asquith to a Friend, Second Series 1922–1927* (London: Geoffrey Bles, 1934), 36.
90. Violet Asquith Diary, 23 Oct. 1922–Nov. 1922, Pottle, ed., *Champion Redoubtable: The Diaries and Letters of Violet Bonham-Carter*, 137.
91. Ibid., 138.
92. HHA to Hilda Harrison, 17 Nov. 1922, MacCarthy, ed., *H. H. A.: Letters of the Earl of Oxford and Asquith to a Friend, Second Series*, 36.
93. Wilson, *Downfall of the Liberal Party*, 238.
94. Spender and Asquith, *Life of Asquith* 2:346.
95. Asquith, *Memories*, 2:244.
96. *Hansard*, 5, 168, 39, 13 Nov. 1923.
97. Wilson, *Downfall of the Liberal Party*, 250.
98. Ibid., 250–51.
99. HHA to Hilda Harrison, 6 Nov. 1923, 21 Nov. 1923, MacCarthy, ed., *H. H. A.: Letters of the Earl of Oxford and Asquith to a Friend, Second Series*, 80, 82.
100. Ibid., 252.
101. Earl of Oxford and Asquith, *Memories*, 2:248.
102. Spender and Asquith, *Life of Asquith*, 2:343.
103. Earl of Oxford and Asquith, *Memories*, 2:249.

104. Simon, *Retrospect*, 130.
105. 15 February 1924, Earl of Oxford and Asquith, *Memories*, 2:251.
106. Ibid., 2:254.
107. Spender and Asquith, *Life of Asquith*, 2:347, 358–59.
108. MA to Violet Asquith, 4 Oct. 1924, Pottle, ed., *Champion Redoubtable: The Diaries and Letters of Violet Bonham Carter*, 162.
109. Wilson, *Downfall of the Liberal Party*, 303.
110. Ibid., 304.
111. Violet Asquith Diary, October 1924, Pottle, ed., *Champion Redoubtable: The Diaries and Letters of Violet Bonham Carter*, 163.
112. Ibid., 164.
113. Wilson, *Downfall of the Liberal Party*, 305.
114. George V to HHA, 4 Nov. 1924, Spender and Asquith, *Life of Asquith*, 351.
115. HHA to Hilda Harrison, 5 Nov. 1924, MacCarthy, ed., *H. H. A.: Letters of the Earl of Oxford and Asquith to a Friend, Second Series*, 108.
116. Earl of Oxford and Asquith, *Memories*, 2:260.
117. Ibid., 2:263.
118. Ibid., 2:265.
119. George V to HHA, 23 Jan. 1925, Earl of Oxford and Asquith, *Memories*, 2:266.
120. Spender and Asquith, *Life of Asquith*, 2:355, 357.
121. Ibid., 2:357.
122. Ibid., 2:356.
123. Wilson, *Downfall of the Liberal Party*, 294–96.
124. Spender and Asquith, *Life of Asquith*, 2:359.
125. HHA Memorandum, 6 Oct. 1926, Wilson, *Downfall of the Liberal Party*, 318.
126. Spender and Asquith, *Life of Asquith*, 2:361.
127. HHA to Hilda Harrison, 11 May 1926, MacCarthy, ed., *H. H. A.: Letters of the Earl of Oxford and Asquith to a Friend, Second Series*, 171.
128. HHA to Lloyd George, 20 May 1926, Spender and Asquith, *Life of Asquith*, 2:362–64.
129. Harold J. Laski to O. W. Holmes, 30 May 1926, Howe, ed., *Holmes-Laski Letters*, 2:843.
130. Spender and Asquith, *Life of Lord Asquith*, 2:366.
131. Wilson, *Downfall of the Liberal Party*, 331–33.

Conclusion

Violet commented to her husband when she got the news of her father's resignation as leader of the Liberal Party that "the Party did bulk very big in his life." She knew that "He wasn't . . . bored by addressing meetings up & down the country—& really enjoyed the devotion of the rank & file. I think he will miss it all terribly—& miss being able to poke an oar into national policy at crucial moments—tho' this I suppose he can still do."[1] This turned out to be wishful thinking. His health recovered enough that he was able on October 15 to give a farewell speech at Greennock. There was still a bit of the old fight in him and certainly some of the optimism. "Let none of you, and especially let none of the younger of you," he admonished his audience, "be content to think that the mission of Liberalism is exhausted." He ended, "Keep the faith; carry on the torch which we, who have done our best to keep it alight, hand over to your custody."[2]

In early 1927 he suffered another stroke, this one more serious than the first. For periods during the spring and summer he was incapacitated, and by the end of 1927 he was unable to move without difficulty. Most tragically to his close friends and family, his famous mind had begun to slip. Violet wrote Gilbert Murray in January, "To watch Father's glorious mind breaking up & sinking—like a great ship—is a pain beyond all my imagining." There were moments when he was his "old self," but "these alas! Seem to me to became rarer & more fleeting." On Christmas eve he struggled to write a last letter to Margot:

> Till one by one,
> Some with lives came to nothing,
> Some with deeds as well undone,
> Death steps tacitly, & took them.

Where men never see the sun.
I shall see thee, once more, O Soul of my Soul.
And with God the Rest[3]

After lingering for another month, Asquith died on Wednesday, February 15, 1928, surrounded by his family. The King immediately sent a message offering his condolences, calling Asquith "an old and dear friend and . . . a faithful and wise counsellor."[4] With the full concurrence of the government, the Dean of Westminster offered Lady Oxford and Asquith to bury her husband in the Abbey. This was not, however, what Asquith had wished. The family decided to follow his specific instructions that there be "nothing in the nature of a public funeral" and that his burial should be carried out "with the utmost of simplicity." The funeral would be at All Saints, the parish church in Sutton Courtenay, on Monday with only family and a few close friends in attendance.

The day after the burial at Sutton Courtenay, a memorial service was held at Westminster Abbey. The congregation began to form an hour before the service, and the Abbey was filled with men who had participated in the political life of the nation with Asquith for a generation—Grey, Haldane, Churchill, Baldwin, and even Lloyd George, who predictably took a seat close to the lectern. Despite it being a winter day, the sun was shining and light poured through the great rose window in the transept. The final hymn was one of Asquith's favorites, Isaac Watts's "O God, Our Help in Ages Past." As tradition dictated, there was no eulogy.

Hundreds of condolence messages arrived from around the world. Both Houses of Parliament moved to adjourn in tribute to their colleague. Friends and foes alike spoke to his greatness. His two oldest companions, Grey and Haldane, rose in the House of Lords to praise their friend. Grey spoke of the three men's "political cooperation which became terms of the most intimate unbroken friendship." Haldane graciously said that the tie that bound them was so close that "the all-severing wave of time . . . never impaired it." To Haldane, Asquith was "essentially a man of character," who never made a decision because it might be popular or bring him fame. "He simply went on the lines of the conclusion to which he had come. And that was his character right through the course of his public life."[5] Prime Minister Baldwin recognized him as "possibly the greatest Parliamentarian of the last century," a man who "never harboured a mean thought" and who was "ever ready to resign credit and to take blame."[6]

His colleagues knew their man. They accurately observed a consistency in Asquith's character throughout his long and distinguished career. There was a stability and calmness that never left him. He could be the fiercest and most brilliant of opponents, and yet he could always be trusted by both friend and foe alike. His word was his bond. While he never suffered fools well, he presented the picture of a man who seemed to be above it all—never jealous and on occasion showing great magnanimity. He lived his stoic ideal.

Asquith can be viewed as the "last of the Romans" because in the eyes of many of his contemporaries and now in the eyes of history he represents the end of an era. As Edward Grey, one of his closest friends and his Foreign Secretary, observed, we "acquired our sense of values and formed our first opinions in the latter part of the Victorian Age." He and Asquith in his own words "belonged to one epoch and . . . lived on into another."[7] This was true in so many ways. On a simple level, Asquith was old fashioned, until his death always using a quill pen and detesting the telephone and central heat.[8] In a much more important respect, like so many Victorians, he had the utmost confidence in progress. For Asquith, the greatest gift of humankind lay in the unique capacity to do good and improve itself. He once wrote of the human situation, "Somewhere and somehow, he has been endowed with something which is to be found nowhere else in the realm of nature; the power of initiative and self-determination, of conceiving and pursuing ideals; the capacity to build up and organize communal life, which is not merely cynical or stereotyped (like that of the ants and the bees and the wolves), but contains within itself the potentiality and the seeds of progress—material, intellectual, spiritual."[9]

He easily translated this progressive view of life into his politics. He opened his mind to progress, as can be seen in the many social reforms passed by his government. To him, a political career was just one of the many avenues open to individuals to improve their situations. In this regard, as historian Joseph Grimond has astutely noted, Asquith was carrying on the old Gladstonian tradition of politics "as an heroic and endless engagement in trying to translate moral attitude into practice and raise the standards of aesthetic and intellectual as well as economic life."[10]

Asquith brought his peculiar combination of pagan stoic philosophy and a Christian belief in progress to some of the most difficult problems and challenges since the Napoleonic Wars: the constitutional crisis over the power of the House of Lords, Home Rule for Ireland, women's suffrage, social reforms, and the challenges of the Great War. Through all of these crises, Asquith anchored his actions in his belief in the "power of initiative and self-determination"—his steadfast belief that the human condition could be improved. The obvious exception was his opposition to women's suffrage, where he remained locked in the Victorian culture in which he was raised. Otherwise, while often criticized for his supposed "wait and see" attitude, he played a major role in reforming Parliament, moving toward Home Rule for Ireland, legislating progressive social reforms, and bringing Britain through the most difficult years of World War I.

Through it all, Asquith never gave up on his belief in progress or his adherence to his Liberal heritage, even after the First World War, when many abandoned notions of progress as naïve and old fashioned. All had changed from his early days at Oxford, even politics itself. Universal suffrage and the popular press dramatically shifted the focus of the political world. By the time of his death in 1928, Asquith did indeed appear to be of a different era—the last of the Romans. "In the beginning of the twentieth century," the *Irish Times*'s obituary accurately observed, Asquith "found himself the ruler of a political society which in a hundred ways was alien from his tastes as a scholar, and from his instincts as a gentleman." Sadly, the former Prime Minister, who was the "soul of honour," had become "the sport of intrigue, the victim of ingratitude and misrepresentation," remaining "always loyal, always proudly serene, most patient when provocation was bitterest and least deserved." The obituary concluded, "The keynote of Lord Oxford's character was magnanimity, and with his death a high and subtle quality has gone out of English politics."[11]

There is, for modern readers, nostalgia in Asquith's story. We can never return to the "heroic age" Asquith represents, if indeed such an age ever existed. Like our own period, his age had its demagogues and its heroes. What I hope, however, is that in some small way, by looking with a new perspective at the life of Asquith, this book will recapture that "high and subtle quality" in politics he represented, with the hope that it may one day return to our political life.

Perhaps we should leave Asquith with his own lines, uttered when still a schoolboy at the City of London School in 1870. It was the annual prize-giving, and it was his job as Captain of the School to give the declamation in praise of the school's founder, John Carpenter. "In acknowledging our obligations to the heroes of the past," the young Asquith had noted, "it is always a relief to be able to desert the common-places of eulogy and to point to the fabric built upon their self-denying efforts as the best memorial at once to their greatness and of our gratitude."[12]

NOTES

1. Violet Asquith to Mark Bonham Carter, 5 Oct. 1926, Pottle, ed., *Champion Redoubtable: The Diaries and Letters of Violet Bonham Carter*, 170.
2. Spender and Asquith, *Life of Asquith*, 2:373.
3. HHA to MA, 24 Dec. 1927, BL, MS. Eng. c. 6692, f. 142.
4. *The Times,* 16 Feb. 1928, 14.
5. *Hansard*, 5 (Lords), 70, 163, 16 Feb. 1928.

6. *The Times,* 17 Feb. 1928, 8, 14.
7. Grey, *Twenty-five Years,* 1:xxi.
8. Terence Freely, *Number 10: The Private Lives of Six Prime Ministers* (London: Didgwick & Jackson, 1982), 129.
9. H. H. Asquith, *Some Aspects of the Victorian Age* (Oxford: Clarendon Press, 1918), 27.
10. Grimond, "H. H. Asquith," 198.
11. Earl of Oxford and Asquith, *Memories and Reflections 1852–1927,* 1:xii–xiii.
12. *The Times,* 20 Feb. 1928, 8.

Bibliography

Papers

Acland Family Papers, Bodleian Library, Oxford
H. H. Asquith Papers, Bodleian Library, Oxford
A. J. Balfour Papers, British Library, London
Bonham Carter Papers, Bodleian Library, Oxford
Viscount Bryce Papers, Bodleian Library, Oxford
Cabinet Papers, National Archives, Kew
Henry Campbell-Bannerman Papers, British Library, London
W. E. Gladstone Papers, British Library, London
H. V. Harcourt Papers, Bodleian Library, Oxford
Sylvia Henley Papers, Bodleian Library, Oxford
F. W. Hurst Papers, Bodleian Library, Oxford
Home Office Papers, National Achieves, Kew
Alfred Milner Papers, Bodleian Library, Oxford
Ripon Papers, British Library, London

Statutes

46 and 47 Vic. C. 51 (1883)
51 and 52 Vic. C. 25 (1888)

Cases

Carlil v. The Carbolic Smoke Ball Company, 2 O.B. 484 (1892)
Powell v. Kempton Park Race Course Co., A. C. 143 (1889)
The Taff Vale Railway Company v. The Amalgamated Society of Railway Servants,
    (1901) UKHL1, (1901) AC 246

Books

Abel, Richard L. *The Legal Profession in England and Wales.* Oxford: Blackwell, 1988.

Adams, R. J. Q. "Andrew Bonar Law and the Fall of the Asquith Coalition: The December 1916 Cabinet Crisis," *Canadian Journal of History/Annales Canadiennes d'histoire* 32 (August 1997): 185–200.

———. *Arms and the Wizard: Lloyd George and the Ministry of Munitions, 1915–1916.* College Station: Texas A & M University Press, 1978.

———. "Asquith's Choice: The May Coalition and the Coming of Conscription, 1915–1916," *Journal of British Studies* 25, no. 3 (July 1986): 243–63.

———. *Balfour: The Last Grandee.* London: John Murray, 2007.

Alderman, Geoffrey. *The Railway Interest.* Leicester, Leicester University Press, 1973.

Alderson, J. P. *Mr. Asquith.* London: Methuen, 1905.

Amery, Julian. *Joseph Chamberlain and the Tariff Reform Campaign: The Life of Joseph Chamberlain, vol. 6, 1903–1968.* New York: Macmillan, 1969.

Anderson, Adelaide Mary. *Women in the Factory: An Administrative Adventure.* London: John Murray, 1922.

The Annual Register: A Review of Public Events at Home and Abroad for the Year 1900. New York: Longmans, Green and Co., 1901.

The Annual Register: A Review of Public Events at Home and Abroad for the Year 1915. London: Longmans, Green, and Co., 1916.

Askwith, George Ranken. *Lord James Herford.* London: Ernest Benn, 1930.

Asquith, H. H. *An Election Guide: Rules for the Conduct and Management of Elections in England and Wales under the Corrupt Practices Act, 1883.* London: National Press Agency, 1884.

———. *The Genesis of the War.* New York: George H. Doran, 1923.

———. *Moments of Memory.* London: Hutchison, 1937.

———. *The Paisley Policy.* London: Cassell and Company, 1920.

———. *Some Aspects of the Victorian Age.* Oxford: Clarendon Press, 1918.

———. *Speeches 1892–1908.* London, 1908.

Asquith, Margot. *The Autobiography of Margot Asquith.* 2 vols. London: Penguin Books, 1936.

———. *The Autobiography of Margot Asquith.* Edited by Mark Bonham-Carter. Boston: Haughton Mifflin Company, 1963.

Bahlman, W. R. Dudley, ed. *The Diary of Sir Edward Walter Hamilton 1885–1906.* Hull: University of Hull Press, 1993.

Ball, Walter W. R. *A Student's Guide to the Bar,* 2nd ed. London: Macmillan, 1879.

Beaverbrook, Lord. *Politicians and the War 1914–1916.* London: Collins, 1928 and 1932.

Bennet, Daphne. *Margot: A Life of the Countess of Oxford & Asquith.* New York: Franklin Watts, 1985.

Binfield, Clyde. *So Down to Prayers: Studies in English Nonconformity 1780–1920.* London: J. M. Dent & Sons, 1977.

Biron, Sir Charles. *Without Prejudice: Impressions of Life and Law by Sir Charles Biron.* London: Faber and Faber, 1936.
Birrell, Augustine. *Sir Frank Lockwood: A Biographical Sketch*, 2nd ed. London: Smith, Elder and Co., 1898.
———. *Things Past Redress.* London: Faber and Faber, n.d.
Blake, Robert. *The Unknown Prime Minister: the Life and Times of Andrew Bonar Law.* London: Eyre & Spottiswoode, 1955.
Bonham-Carter, Violet. *Winston Churchill: An Intimate Portrait.* New York: Harcourt, Brace & World, 1965.
Bowen-Rowlands, Ernest. *In the Light of the Law.* London: G. Richards, Fronto, 1931.
Bowra, C. M. *Memories 1898–1939.* Cambridge: Harvard University Press, 1967.
Boyle, T. "The Foundation of Campbell-Bannerman's Government in December 1905: A Memorandum by J.A. Spender." *Bulletin of the Inst. of Hist. Research.* XLV (1972): 283–302.
Briggs, Asa. "The Political Scene" in Simon Newell-Smith. *Edwardian England 1901–1914.* London: Oxford University Press, 1964.
Brock, M. G. and M. C. Curthoys, eds. *The Nineteenth Century*, vol. 7, part 2 of *The History of the University of Oxford.* Oxford: Clarendon Press, 2000.
Brock, Michael and Eleanor. *H. H. Asquith: Letters to Venetia Stanley.* Oxford: Oxford University Press, 1982.
Brogan, D. W. "Last of the Romans," *The New York Times Book Review*, June 27, 1965, 1.
Cassar, George H. *Asquith As War Leader.* London: Hambledon Press, 1994.
Cecil, Algernon. "Lord Oxford and Asquith." *Quarterly Review* 260 (January 1933): 1–26.
Chilston, Eric Alexander Akers-Douglas, 3rd Viscount Chilston. *Chief Whip: The Political Life and Times of Aretas Akers-Douglas, 1st Viscount Chilston.* London: Routledge & Kegan Paul, 1961).
Churchill, Randolph S. *Lord Derby "King of Lancashire": The Official Life of Edward, Seventeenth Earl of Derby, 1865–1948.* London: Heinemann, 1959.
———. *Winston S. Churchill: Volume II 1901–1914 Young Statesman.* Boston: Houghton Mifflin Company, 1967.
Churchill, Winston S. *Great Contemporaries.* rev. edn. London: Thornton Butterworth, 1938.
———. *The World Crisis.* New York: Charles Scribner's Sons, 1923.
Clifford, Colin. *The Asquiths.* London: John Murray, 2002.
Cocks, Raymond. "Dignity and Emoluments: Thomas Blofeld's Life as a Victorian Barrister." *Kingston Law Review* 8 (1978): 41–42.
Cole, G. D. H. Cole. *Labour in War Time.* London: G. Bell and Sons, 1915.
Colvin, Ian. *Carson the Statesman.* New York: Macmillan, 1935.
Cooper, Duff. *Old Men Forget.* London: Rupert Hart-Davis, 1953.
Cox, Edward W. *The Advocate, His Training, Practice, Rights and Duties.* London: John Crockford, 1852.

Cregier, Don M. *Bounder from Wales: Lloyd George's Career Before the First World War*. Columbia: University of Missouri Press, 1976.
Dale, Iain, ed. *Liberal Party General Election Manifestos 1900–1997*. London: Routledge, 2000.
David, Edward, ed. *Inside Asquith's Cabinet: From the Diaries of Charles Hobhouse*. London: John Murray, 1977.
Douglas-Smith, A. E. *The City of London School*. Oxford: Basil Blackwell, 1965.
Duman, Daniel. *The English and Colonial Bars in the Nineteenth Century*. London: Croom Helm, 1983.
Dutton, D. J. "The Calais Conference of 1915," *Historical Journal* 21 (1978): 143–156.
Egremont, Max. *Balfour: A Life of Arthur James Balfour*. London: Collins, 1980.
Elias, Frank. *The Right Hon. H.H. Asquith, MP: A Biography and Appreciation*. London: James Clarke, 1909.
Emy, H. V. *Liberals, Radicals and Social Politics, 1892–1914*. Cambridge: Cambridge University Press, 1973.
Ensor, R. C. K. *England 1870–1914*. Oxford: Clarendon Press, 1936.
Esher, Reginald Viscount. *Journals and Letters of Reginald Viscount Esher*. Edited by Maurice V. Brett. 4 vols. London: Ivor Nicolson & Watson, 1934–938.
Faber, Sir Geoffrey. *Jowett: A Portrait with a Background*. London: Farber & Farber, 1957.
Fitzroy, Sir Almeric. *Memoirs*. 2 vols. New York: George H. Doran, 1925.
Freeden, Michael. *The New Liberalism: An Ideology of Social Reform*. Oxford: Clarendon Press, 1978.
Freely, Terence. *Number 10: The Private Lives of Six Prime Ministers*. London: Didgwick & Jackson, 1982.
French, David. *British Strategy & War Aims 1914–1916*. London: Allen & Unwin, 1986.
Gardiner, A. G. *The Life of Sir William Harcourt*. 2 vols. New York: George H. Doran, 1923.
Garvin, J. L. and Julian Amery. *Joseph Chamberlain and the Tariff Reform Campaign—The Life of Joseph Chamberlain Volume 5—1901–1903*. London: Macmillan, 1969.
George, David Lloyd. *War Memories of David Lloyd George 1914–1915*. Boston: Little Brown, 1935.
George, Richard Lloyd. *My Father Lloyd George*. New York: Crown Publishers, 1960.
George, William. *My Brother and I*. London: Eyre & Spottiswoode, 1958.
Gilbert, Bentley Brinkerhoff. *David Lloyd George: A Political Life, vol. 1 The Architect of Change*. Columbus: Ohio State University Press, 1987.
Gilbert, Martin. *Churchill: A Life*. New York: Henry Holt, 1991.
———. *Winston S. Churchill, Companion Volume III, Part 2 May 1915–December 1916*. Boston: Houghton Mifflin, 1973.
———. *Winston S. Churchill, vol. III 1914–1916, The Challenge of War*. Boston: Houghton Mifflin, 1971.

Grey of Fallodon, Viscount. *Twenty-five Years 1892–1916*. 2 vols. London: Hodder and Stroughton, 1925.

Griffith-Boscawen, A. S. T. *Fourteen Years in Parliament*. London: John Murray, 1907.

Grigg, John. *Lloyd George: From Peace to War 1912–1916*. London: Methuen, 1985.

———. *Lloyd George: The People's Champion 1902–1911*. Berkeley: University of California Press, 1978.

———. *Young Lloyd George*. Berkeley: University of California Press, 1973.

Grimond, Joseph. "H. H. Asquith" in Herbert Van Thal. *The Prime Ministers*. 2 vols. London: George Allen & Unwin, 1975.

Gwynn, Denis. *The Life of Lord Redmond*. London: George C. Harp, 1932.

Haig, Douglas. *The Private Papers of Douglas Haig 1914–1918*. Edited by Robert Blake. London: Eyre & Spottiswoode, 1952.

Haldane, R. B. *Before the War*. London: Cassell, 1920.

Haldane, Richard Burdon. *Richard Burdon Haldane: An Autobiography*. London: Hodder and Stoughton, 1929.

Halévy, Elie. *A History of the English People in the Nineteenth Century*. Vol. 5, *Imperialism and the Rise of Labour*. London: Ernest Benn, 1926.

———. *The Rule of Democracy 1905–1914 (Book I)*. London: Ernest Benn, 1952.

Hankey, Lord. *The Supreme Command 1914–1918*. 2 vols. London: George Allen and Unwin, 1961.

Havighurst, Alfred F. *Britain in Transition*. Chicago: University of Chicago Press, 1985.

Hayes, Dennis. *Conscription Conflict: The Conflict of Ideas in the Struggle for and Against Military Conscription in Britain Between 1901 and 1939*. New York: Garland, 1973.

Headlam, Cecil, ed. *The Milner Papers South Africa 1877–1899*. London: Cassell, 1931.

Hendrick, Burton J. *The Life and Letters of Walter H. Page*. Garden City: Doubleday, Page, 1922.

Hirst, Francis W. *In the Golden Days*. London: Frederick Muller, 1947.

Holroyd, Michael. *Lytton Strachey: A Critical Biography, vol. 2 The Years of Achievement (1910–1932)*. New York: Holt, Rinehart and Winston, 1968.

Horsley, E. M. ed. *Lady Cynthia Asquith Diaries 1915–1918*. New York: Alfred A. Knopf, 1969).

Howe, Mark DeWolfe, ed., *Holmes-Laski Letters: The Correspondence of Mr. Justice Holmes and Harold J. Laski 1916–1935*, 2 vols. Cambridge, MA: Harvard University Press, 1953.

Hutchinson, Horace G. ed. *Private Diaries of The Rt. Hon. Sir Algernon West, G.C.B.* London: John Murray, 1922.

Jackson, Patrick. *Harcourt and Son: A Political Biography of Sir William Harcourt, 1827–1904*. Madison: Fairleigh Dickinson University Press, 2004.

Jackson, T. A. *Ireland Her Own: An Outline of the Irish Struggle for National Freedom and Independence*. New York: International Publishers, 1947.

James, Robert Rhodes. *Rosebery*. New York: Macmillan, 1963.

Jenkins, Roy. *Asquith*. London: Collins, 1964.

Jolliffe, John. *Raymond Asquith, Life and Letters*. Collins, 1980.
Jones, Clyve and David Lewis Jones, eds. *Peers, Politics and Power: The House of Lords, 1603–1911*. London: Hambledon, 1986.
Jones, John. *Balliol College: A History, 1263–1939*. Oxford: Oxford University Press, 1988.
Jones, L. E. *An Edwardian Youth*. London: Macmillan, 1956.
Keynes, John Maynard. *Essays in Biography*. New York: W. W. Norton, 1951.
Koss, Stephen. *Asquith*. New York: St. Martin's Press, 1976.
———. *Lord Haldane: Scapegoat for Liberalism*. New York: Columbia, 1969.
Lysaght, Charles. *Brendan Bracken*. London: Allen Lane, 1979.
Lester, V. Markham. "The Employers' Liability/Workmen's Compensation Debate of the 1890s Revisited." *The Historical Journal* 44, no. 2 (2001): 471–95.
Levine, Naomi B. *Politics, Religion and Love: the Story of H. H. Asquith, Venetia Stanley and Edwin Montagu, Based on the Life and Letters of Edwin Samuel Montagu*. New York: New York University Press, 1991.
Lewis, J. R. *The Victorian Bar*. London: Robert Hale, 1982.
Lucy, Henry W. *A Diary of the Unionist Parliament 1895–1900*. Bristol: J. W. Arrowsmith, 1901.
Lucy, H. W. *The Balfourian Parliament 1900–1905*. London: Hodder & Stoughton, 1906.
Lysaght, Charles. *Brenden Bracken*. London: Allen Lane, 1979.
MacCarthy, Desmond ed., *H. H. A.: Letters of the Earl of Oxford and Asquith to a Friend, First Series 1915–1922*. London: Geoffrey Bles, 1933.
———. *H. H. A.: Letters of the Earl of Oxford and Asquith to a Friend, Second Series 1922–1927*. London: Geoffrey Bles, 1934.
Mackay, Ruddock F. *Fisher of Kilverstone*. Oxford: Clarendon Press, 1973.
Mallet, Sir Charles Edward. "Lord Oxford's 'Life.'" *Contemporary Review* CXLIII (1933): 34–41.
Mallock, W. H. *Memoirs of Life and Literature*. London: Chapman and Hall, 1920.
Marder, Arthur J. *Fear God and Dreadnaught: The Correspondence of Admiral of the Fleet Lord Fisher of Kilverstone, vol. 3 Restoration, Abdication, and Last Years, 1914–1920*. London: Jonathan Cape, 1959.
Marsh, Peter T. *Joseph Chamberlain: Entrepreneur in Politics*. New Haven: Yale University Press, 1994).
Masterman, Lucy. *C.F.G. Masterman: A Biography*. New York: Augustus M. Kelley, 1969.
Matthew, H. G. C. "Asquith, Herbert Henry, First Earl of Oxford and Asquith," *Oxford Dictionary of National Biography*. Oxford: Oxford University Press, 2004.
———. "H. H. Asquith's Political Journalism." *Bulletin of the Institute of Historical Research* 49 (1976): 146–51.
———. *The Liberal Imperialists: The Ideas and Politics of Post-Gladstonian Elite*. Oxford: Oxford University Press, 1973.
Maurice, Major General Sir Frederick. *Haldane 1856–1915: The Life of Viscount Haldane of Cloan*. Westport, CT: Greenwood Press, 1937.

McCallum, R. B. *Asquith*. London: Duckworth, 1936.
McEwen, J. M., "The Press and the Fall of Asquith," *Historical Journal* 21 (1978): 863–83.
———. "The Struggle for Mastery in Britain: Lloyd George versus Asquith, December 1916." *Journal of British Studies* 18 (1978): 131–56.
Milner, The Vicountess. *My Picture Gallery 1886–1901*. London: John Murray, 1951.
Mommsen, W. J., ed. *The Emergence of the Welfare State in Britain and Germany 1850–1950*. London: Croom Helm, 1981.
Morgan, Kenneth O. *Wales in British Politics 1868–1922*, rev. ed. Cardiff: University of Wales Press, 1970.
Morley, John. *On Compromise*. London: Chapman and Hall, 1874.
———. *Recollections*. 2 vols. London: Macmillan, 1917.
Morris, Homer Lawrence. "Parliamentary Franchise Reform in England from 1885 to 1918." *Studies in History, Economics and Public Law* 91, no. 2 (1921).
Mosley, Sir Oswald. *My Life*. London: Nelson, 1968.
Murray, Arthur C. *Master and Brother: Murrays of Elibank*. London: John Murray, 1945.
Murray, Bruce K. *The People's Budget 1909/10: Lloyd George and Liberal Politics*. Oxford: Clarendon Press, 1980.
Nicholson, Harold. *King George V: His Life and Reign*. London: Constable & Co. Ltd., 1952.
Notestein, Wallace. "The Career of Mr. Asquith." *Political Science Quarterly* 31 (September 1916): 336–79.
Nowell-Smith, Simon. *Edwardian England 1901–1914*. London: Oxford University Press, 1964.
Oxford and Asquith, Earl of. *Fifty Years of British Parliament*. 2 vols. Boston: Little, Brown, 1926.
———. *Speeches by the Earl of Oxford and Asquith, K.G*. London, 1927.
———. *Memories and Reflections 1852–1927*. 2 vols. Boston: Little Brown, 1928.
Page, Christopher. *Command in the Royal Naval Division: A Military Biography of Brigadier General A. M. Asquith DSO*. Staplehurst: Spellmount, 1999.
Parliamentary Papers 1893–94.
Parliamentary Papers 1895.
Plutrach, John Dryden, and Arthur Hugh Clough. *Plutarch's Lives*. London: Samson Low, 1859.
Pottle, Mark, ed. *Champion Redoubtable: The Diaries and Letters of Violet Bonham Carter 1914–1945*. London: Weidenfeld & Nicolson, 1998.
Pugh, Martin D. "Asquith, Bonar Law and the First Coalition." *The Historical Journal* 17 (1974): 813–36.
Quinault, Roland. "Asquith's Liberalism." *History* 77 (Feb. 1992): 33–49.
Report from the Select Committee on Income Tax. London: H. M. Stationary Office, 1906.
Ricter, Melvin. *The Politics of Conscience: T.H. Green and His Age*. Cambridge, MA: Harvard University Press, 1964.

Riddell, Lord. *Lord Riddell's War Diary, 1914–1918*. London: Ivor Nicholson & Watson, 1933.

———. *More Pages from My Diary*. London, Country Life, 1934.

Robbins, Keith. *Sir Edward Grey: A Biography of Lord Grey of Fallodon*. London: Cassell, 1971.

Robertson, Field-Marshall Sir William. *Soldiers and Statesmen 1914–1918*. London: Cassell, 1926.

Rodd, Sir James Rennell. *Social and Diplomatic Memories (Third Series) 1902–1919*. London: Edward Arnold, 1925.

Roskill, Stephen. *Hankey: Man of Secrets, Volume I 1877–1918*. London: Cassell, 1971.

Rowland, Peter. *David Lloyd George: A Biography*. New York: Macmillan, 1975.

———. *The Last Liberal Governments: The Promised Land, 1905–1910*. London: Barrie & Rockcliff, 1968.

Scally, R. J. *The Origins of the Lloyd George Coalition*. Princeton: Princeton University Press, 1975.

Scott, James Brown, ed. *Diplomatic Documents Relating to the Outbreak of the European War, Part II*. New York: Oxford University Press, 1916.

Searle, G. R. *The Liberal Party: Triumph and Disintegration, 1886–1929*. New York: Palgrave, 2001.

Seymour, Charles. *The Intimate Papers of Colonel House*. Boston: Houghton Mifflin Company, 1926.

Simon, John Viscount. *Retrospect: Memoirs of the Rt. Hon. Viscount Simon*. London: Hutchinson, 1952.

Smith, William. *Rambles About Morley with Descriptive and Historic Sketches*. London: John Russell Smith, 1886.

Spender, J. A. *Life Journalism and Politics*. vol. 2. New York: Frederick A. Stokes, n.d. [1927].

Spender, J. A. and Cyril Asquith. *Life of Herbert Henry Asquith, Lord Oxford and Asquith*. 2 vols. London: Hutchinson, 1932.

Stansky, Peter. *Ambitions and Strategies: The Struggle for Leadership of the Liberal Party in the 1890s*. Oxford: Clarendon Press, 1964.

Statistics of the Military Effort of the British Empire During the Great War, 1914–1920. London: His Majesty's Stationary Office, 1922.

Stodart Walker, Archibald. *The Oxford Book of English Verse 1340–1913*. London: Eveleigh Nash, 1914.

Sullivan, Arthur and W. S. Gilbert. *H. M. S. Pinafore; or The Lass that Loved a Sailor*. 1878.

Taylor, A. J. P. *Beaverbrook*. New York: Simon and Schuster, 1972.

———, ed., *Lloyd George: A Diary by Frances Stevenson*. New York: Harper & Row, 1971.

Taylor, H. A. *Robert Donald*. London: Stanley Paul & Co., 1934.

A Templar. *A Guide to the Bar, with an appendix containing the consolidated regulations of the inns of court, by a Templar*. London: Stevens and Sons, 1871.

Trevelyan, George Macaulay. *Grey of Fallodon: The Life and Letters of Sir Edward Grey, afterwards Viscount Grey of Fallodon.* Boston: Houghton Mifflin, 1937.

Van Thal, Herbert. *The Prime Ministers*, 2 vols. London: George Allen & Unwin, 1975.

Vincent, John, ed. *The Crawford Papers: The Journals of David Lindsay Twenty-Seventh Earl of Crawford and Tenth Earl of Balcarres 1871–1940 during the Years 1892 to 1940.* Manchester: Manchester University Press, 1984.

Warren, Samuel. *A Practical and Popular Introduction to Law Studies.* 2nd ed. London: Maxwell, 1845.

Webb, Beatrice. *The Diary of Beatrice Webb*, ed. Norman MacKenzie and Jeanne MacKenzie. 4 vols. Cambridge, MA: Belknap Press, 1982–1985.

Wilson, John. *C. B.: A Life of Sir Henry Campbell-Bannerman.* London: Constable, 1973.

Wilson, Trevor. *The Downfall of the Liberal Party 1914–1935.* Ithaca: Cornell University Press, 1966.

———, ed. *The Political Diaries of C.P. Scott 1911–1928.* Ithaca: Cornell University Press, 1970.

Woodward, David R. *Lloyd George and the Generals.* Newark, NJ: University of Delaware Press, 1983.

Wrigley, Chris. *Winston Churchill: A Biographical Companion.* Santa Barbara: ABC-CLIO, 2002.

Index

Abbott, Dr. Edwin, 16, 19, 25
Abd al-Hafid, Sultan, 200
Aberdee, 7th Earl of (John Campbell Hamilton Gordon), 191
Aberdeen, Lady, 192
Acland, Sir Arthur H. D., 42, 44, 55, 69, 70, 73, 125
Adams, R. J. Q., 158, 265
Aitken, W. M. *See* Beaverbrook
Albert I, King of Belgium, 213, 222
Alexandria, Queen of England, 321
Allenby, Field Marshall Edmund, 1st Viscount Allenby, 332
Anderson, Adelaide, 68
Anglo-French naval agreement (1913), 204–5
Argyll, 8th Duke of (George Campbell), 60
Armenians, 88, 93
Askwith, William, 11
Asquith, Anthony ("Puffin"), 92, 286
Asquith, Arthur ("Oc"), 34, 49, 92, 130–32, 282, 315, 332
Asquith, Cynthia (née Charteris), 192, 291, 318
Asquith, Cyril ("Cys"), 3, 4, 132, 193, 197
Asquith, Clark and Co., 11

Asquith, Elizabeth, 92, 286
Asquith, Emily (mother, née Willans), 12, 13, 15
Asquith, Emily Evelyn (sister), 13, 14
Asquith, Helen (first wife, née Melland), 33, 40, 46, 51, 63–65, 90–92, 147
Asquith, Helen (daughter of Raymond), 192
Asquith, Herbert ("Beb"), 34–35, 46, 91, 146, 192
Asquith, Herbert Henry, 1st Earl of Oxford and Asquith, 1, 3–6, 9, 30, 37, 128, 191, 221, 237, 274, 311, 331; Budget (1907), 2, 129, 132–33, 149, 182; Budget (1909 "Peoples' Budget"), 154–56; formation of first cabinet, 148–49; formation of Campbell–Bannerman government, 117, 123–26; City of London School, 16–19; character traits, 142–47; constitutional crisis, 156–70, 182; "Coupon" election (1919), 321–22; "Curragh incident," 177–79; Irish dynamiters, 59–59; Easter rebellion, 280–82; Education Act (1902), 83–86; employer's liability, 86–87; death of Campbell-Bannerman, 137–38; formation

357

of coalition government, 241–48; factory Workshops Act (1891), 66–68; family, 131–32; Featherstone incident, 68–69; foreign affairs before First World War, 197–201, 204–7; end of government, 292–303; Home Rule Bill (1893), 59–63; Home Rule Bill (1912), 170–80; appointment as Home Secretary, 52–54; last illness, 341–42; trip to Italy, 275–76; leadership style, 238, 253–54, 289, 343–44; early legal career, 30–33, 37–39; Liberal Imperialists, 92–93; Licensing Bill (1908), 136–37; opposition to Lloyd George government, 312–15; Marconi scandal, 173–74; correspondence with Margot before Helen's death, 64–66; marriage to Margot, 71; relationship with Margot, 193–94; Maurice debate, 317–19, 321; marriage to Helen Melland, 33–34, 46–47; naval estimates, 151–54, 202–06; Old Age Pension Bill, 149–51; student at Oxford University, 19–26; munitions, 235; Paisley elections, (1920) 323–25, (1922) 328–30, (1924) 331–32; first election to and early friends in Parliament, 40–44; Parnell Commission case, 44–46; accepts Peerage, 333; appointed Queen's Council, 46; "Relugas compact," 117–21, 123, 125; service in Rosebery cabinet, 72–77; South African War and aftermath, 94–105; relationship with Venetia Stanley, 147–48, 194–96, 239–40; stoicism, 25, 145–46, 332; tariff reform, 106–112; Trade Disputes Bill (1906), 133–35; Trafalgar Square incident, 55–57; decision to enter the war, 208–14; management of the war, 197–98, 219, 222, 224–26, 228–35, 255–64, 274, 283–88, 290, 314; Welsh church disestablishment, 73–77; early youth, 13–15

Asquith, John, 192
Asquith, Joseph, 11
Asquith, Joseph Dixon (father), 12, 13, 14
Asquith, Joshua, 11
Asquith, Katherine, 192, 286
Asquith, Margot, Countess of Oxford and Asquith (Emma Alice Margaret Tennant), 4, 9, 55, 64, 90, 130–32, 141, 164–65, 189, 190, 321–22, 331, 341–42; effect on and relationship with Asquith, 91, 111, 147, 193–96; Asquith's letters to, quoted, 56, 63, 65, 66, 70, 72, 82, 83, 88, 96, 98, 127, 153, 193, 205, 269, 284–85; comments on formation of Campbell-Bannerman government, 120–21, 123; courtship and marriage, 10, 66, 70–72, 89; health, 147; death of Raymond, 286; relationship with Violet, 191–92
Asquith, Perdita, 192
Asquith, Raymond, 34–35, 91, 131, 141, 192, 282, 285; death of, 286–87
Asquith, Samuel, 11
Asquith, Thomas, 11
Asquith, Violet. *See* Bonham Carter
Asquith, William Willans (brother), 13, 15, 21

Bains, Edward, 12, 15
Baldwin, Stanley, 1st Earl Baldwin of Bewdley, 329–30, 342
Balfour, Arthur James, 1st Earl of Balfour, 71, 83, 90, 150, 199, 220, 230, 234, 236, 261, 277, 292, 383; fall of Asquith government, 299–302; view of Asquith, 75, 143; conscription, 268; constitutional crisis, 165–66, 170; appointment as First Lord of the Admiralty, 246–47; Old Age Pensions, 150–51; resignation as Prime Minister, 122;

member of "The Souls," 64; tariff
  reform, 107, 109
Balfour of Buleigh, Lord (A. H. Bruce),
  109
Ballin, Albert, 203
Balliol College, 19–21, 24, 30, 36–37
Battenberg, Prince Louis of, 209
Battersea, Lord (Cyril Flowers), 63
Beaverbrook, Lord (Sir W. M. Aitken),
  4, 146, 175, 291, 295–96, 298
Beconsfield, 1st Earl of (Benjamin
  Disraeli), 17, 36, 182
Benn, Wedgewood, 328
Beresford, Dorothy, 194
Berlin, Treaty of (1878), 198–99
Bethman-Hollweg, Theobald von, 202–3
Biggar, J. M., 324
Birkenhead, 1st Earl of (Sir F. E.
  Smith), 135, 170, 268, 281
Biron, Sir Charles, 32
Birrell, Augustine, 126, 136, 143, 165,
  177, 279–80
Blofeld, Thomas, 32
Boer War, *See* South African War
Bonham Carter, Mark, 72
Bonham Carter, Sir Maurice, 241–2,
  275, 311
Bonham Carter, Lady Violet (Violet
  Asquith), 4, 10, 46, 130, 141, 159,
  241, 311, 322, 336, 341; relationship
  with Margot, 92, 191–92; Paisley
  elections, 324, 328, 331–32
Bosnian Crisis, First, 198
Botha, Lewis, 97, 99
Bowen, Charles, Baron Bowen, 30–32,
  69
Bracken, Brendan, 195
Bradlaugh, Charles, 39
Briand, Aristide, 259, 285, 287–89
Bright, John, 111
Briggs, Asa, 2
Broadbentt, Henry, 21
Brock, Michael and Eleanor, 147
Broqueville, Baron Charles de, 223
Bryce, James, 58–59 106, 325

Buckmaster, Sir Stanley, 246
Budget League, 155
Buller, General Sir Redvers, 97–98
Burns, John, 39, 155, 211
Burke, Thomas Henry, 44
Buxton, Charles and Noel, 228
Buxton, Sidney, 42

Callan, Thomas, 58
Cambon, Paul, 197, 203, 205, 212
Cambridge, University of, 19, 30–31
Campbell, J. R., 330–31
Campbell-Bannerman, Sir Henry, 69,
  76–77, 85, 88, 96, 103–4, 110,
  118–19, 122, 134, 141–42, 160,
  171; Anglo-French naval agreement,
  197–98; view of Asquith, 112, 138;
  formation of cabinet, 117, 121,
  123–26; last illness and death, 137,
  149; leadership of Liberal Party,
  104–06; resigns as Prime Minister, 2,
  9; "Relugas compact," 118–20; South
  African War, 96–97, 99, 100–2
Campbell-Bannerman, Lady, Charlotte,
  124
Cape Colony, 94–96, 99
*Carlill v. The Carbolic Smoke Ball
  Company*, 38
Carden, Vice Admiral Sir Sackville
  Hamilton, 228, 231
Carol, King of Romania, 228
Carson, Sir Edward, 258, 298, 326; end
  of Asquith government, 291–94;
  appointment as Attorney General,
  247; Home Rule, 174, 176, 210
Casement, Sir Rodger, 279
Cassar, George H., 5
Cassell, Sir Ernest J., 202
Cave, Sir George, Viscount Cave, 334
Cavendish, Lord Frederick, 44
Cawdor, 3rd Earl of (Frederick
  Campbell), 165
Cecil, Algernon, 71
Cecil, Lord Hugh, Lord Quickswood,
  170

Cecil, Lord Robert, Viscount Cecil of Chelwood, 281, 290, 293, 296, 299–300, 311
Chamberlain, Sir Austen, 165–66, 266, 268, 273, 296, 299–300
Chamberlain, Joseph, 1, 37, 61–62, 94, 96, 98; tariff reform, 107–12
Charteris, Cynthia. *See* Asquith
Children Act, 180
Churchill, Clementine, 194
Churchill, Winston, 126, 149, 153, 158, 194–95, 200–2, 204–5, 209, 212, 214, 225–26, 236–37, 246, 266, 342; offer to go to Antwerp, 222–23; view of Asquith, 3, 4, 142–43; support of conscription, 268; Dardanelles campaign, 227–28, 230–34, 258, 260; resignation of Fisher, 240–244; "naval holiday" proposal, 205–6
Church of England, 89, 147
City Liberal Reform Club, 103
City of London School, 1, 6, 10, 15–19, 21, 24 145, 344; Asquith's years at, 15–19
Clarke, Edward, 46
Clifford, Colin, 131, 190
Cluer, A. R., 21
Coal Mines Regulation Act, 180
Cobden, Richard, 12, 111
Cockburn, Sir Alexander (Lord Chief Justice), 18
Coleridge, Samuel Taylor, 3–4
Collins, Sir Godfrey, 228, 335
Coloured Cloth Hall (Leeds), 11
Commons, House of, 2, 9–10, 42, 59, 62, 82, 124
Congregationalists, 11–13
conscription, 253, 265–74, 276–79
Constantine I, King of Greece, 258
Cooper, Duff, 146, 284
Corrupt Practices Act (1883), 39
Courtney, Leonard, 99
Cox, Edward, 29–30
Craig, Captain James, 1st Viscount Craigavon, 179

Crawford, 27th Earl of (D. A. E. Lindsey), 190, 295
Crewe, Earl (later Marq.) of (Robert Q. A. Crewe-Milnes), 212, 226, 233, 243, 261, 266, 269, 296; constitutional crisis, 160, 165–66; fall of Asquith government, 299; appointment as Secretary of State for the Colonies, 149
Croft House (Morley), 12
Crowther, Isaac, 12
Crust, Henry, 311
Cunynghame, Henry, 31
"Curragh incident," 177–79, 220, 283
Curzon of Kedleston, Marq. (George N. Curzon), 64, 258, 266, 268, 271, 292; fall of Asquith government, 296, 299

Daniel, David, 154
Dardanelles campaign, 3, 227–31, 238, 253, 257–60, 264, 271, 288
Davies, David, 286
De Robeck, Admiral Sir John, 232, 238, 260
Desborough, Baroness (Ettie Grenfell), 64
Derby, 17th Earl of (E. G. V. Stanley), 268–70, 273
Devonshire, 8th Duke of (S. C. Cavendish, Marq. of Hartington), 60
Dilke, Sir Charles, 2, 129, 161
Dillon, John, 179–80
Disraeli, Benjamin. *See* Beconsfield
Dixon, Esther, 12
Dockers' Union, 56
Donald, Sir Robert, 237, 296, 303
Donop, Sir Stanley von, 233
Douglas-Smith, A. E., 19
Dreadnaught, H. M. S., 151–52
Drummond, Sir Eric, 211
Du Cane, General Sir John, 254

East Fife, 1, 3, 40, 63, 98, 127, 322–23
East Fife Liberal Association, 40–41, 98, 106

Education Act (1902), 83–86, 127, 136
Education bill (1906), 136
Edward VII, King of England, 9, 118–19, 123–24, 141, 149, 163–64, 199; constitutional crisis, 156–57, 161
Egan, James Francis, 58
Elcho, Lord (Hugo Charteris, 11th Earl of Wemyss), 192
Elcho, Lady Mary (Countess Wemyss), 192
Eldridge, W. H., 56
elections, general, (1892) 51–52, (1895) 83, (1900) 98–99, (1906) 127, (1910 1st) 158–59, (1910 2nd) 169, (1919 "Coupon" election) 3, 319, 321–22, 323, 325, 327, (1920) 3, (1922) 328–30, (1924), 331–32
Elibank, Master of. *See* Murray
Ellis, Arthur, 42
Ellis, Mrs., 14
Ellis, T. E. (Tom), 74–75, 77
Employer's Liability Act (1880), 86
employer's liability, 76, 86–87
Erroll, 21st Earl of (V. A. S. Hay), 190
Esher, 1st Viscount (R. B. Brett), 122, 141, 204
Ewart, Sir John Spencer, 177–79

Faber, Sir Geoffrey, 23
Fabian socialism, 44
Factories and Workshops Act (1895), 1, 66–68
Farnley Wood plot (1663), 11
Featherstone incident, 68–69
Ferguson, Ronald, 42
Fez, Treaty of (1912), 201
First World War, 1914–1918, 2–4, 180, 182, 207, 343–44
Fisher of Kilverstone, 1st Baron (Admiral Sir John Fisher), 152, 204, 226, 228, 230; resigns as First Sea Lord, 240–42, 244, 246
Fitzmaurice, 1st Baron (Edmund Fitzmaurice), 197
Fitzroy, Almeric, 167

Foch, Marshall Ferdinand, 255
Fowler, Henry H., Viscount Wolverhampton, 77, 89, 105, 117
Free Food League, 109
French, Sir John, 1st Earl of Ypres, 235, 254, 255–56, 263, 283; "Curragh incident," 177–79; retreat from Mons, 221–22

Gallipoli. *See* Dardanelles campaign
Gardiner, J. A., 144
George V, King of England, 132, 172, 174, 211, 213, 223, 301, 316; first audience with Asquith, 165; offers Asquith the Garter, 311; offers Asquith a Peerage, 332–33; Asquith's reports to, 204, 223, 246, 257–58, 261, 271; view of Asquith, 320–21, 342; Asquith's view of, 165; conscription, 277–78; constitutional crisis, 167–70; Home Rule, 175, 179
Germany, 94, 107, 196; naval race with Britain, 2, 152–54, 202–4
Gillroyd Mill Company, 11
Gilmour, J. G., 51, 83
Gladstone, Catherine, 71
Gladstone, Herbert J., 1st Viscount Gladstone, 90, 117, 122–23, 126
Gladstone, William Ewart, 1, 17, 22, 39, 41, 43, 51, 57, 69–70, 74, 87–88, 90, 213; selects Asquith as Home Secretary, 10, 52–54, 81; view of Margot Asquith, 71; Home Rule, 59–62, 172
Gordon, Archibald "Archie," 159, 191, 194
Gore, Charles, 21
Gorst, Sir John, 164
Goshen, Sir Edward, 198
Gosse, Sir Edmund, 117
Gough, Brigadier-General Hubert, 178–79
Graham, R. B. Cunninghame, 39
Great Western Railway, 38
Green, T. H., 23–24

Grey, Sir George, 55
Grey of Fallodon, Viscount (Sir Edward Grey), 41, 43, 53, 55, 93, 96, 104, 111, 142, 152–53, 176, 181, 196–200, 203, 206, 219, 221–22, 226, 229, 236, 258, 274, 336, 342; Anglo-French naval agreement, 204–5; Asquith's confidence in, 196; view of Asquith, 2, 343; conscription, 272; House-Grey Memorandum, 275–76; lead-up to First World War, 207–14; formation of Campbell-Bannerman's cabinet, 123–26; "Relugas compact," 117–21, 137; South African War, 100–101, 105; threatens resignation, 243, 246–47
Grey, Dorothy, 54
Griffith-Boscawen, Sir Arthur, 104
Griggs, John, 160
Grimond, Joseph, 343
Guest, F. E. "Freddie," 224, 320
Gwynne, H. A., 293

Haig, General Sir Douglas, 1st Earl Haig, 254, 259, 263, 279, 284–85, 316–17
Haldane, James Alexander, 36
Haldane, Richard Burdon, Viscount Haldane of Cloan, 38, 43, 46–47, 54–55, 66, 69, 88–89, 91, 93, 103, 152, 177, 197, 201–2, 219, 226, 233, 342; early friendship with Asquith, 35–36, 42; formation of Campbell-Bannerman's cabinet, 124–26; Liberal League, 105; removal as Lord Chancellor, 244, 246–47; election to Parliament, 40; view of Margot Asquith, 90; mission to Germany, 203–4; "Relugas compact," 117–21, 137; South Africa, 96, 100–101; Trade Disputes bill, 133–34
Halévy, Elie, 135
Hamid, Sultan Abdul, 199
Hamilton, Sir Edward, 52, 90, 128–29

Hamilton, General Sir Ian S. M., 238, 257, 260
Hamilton, Lord George F., 109
Hampstead, 34–35, 41
Hankey, Sir Maurice, 1st Lord Hankey, 253–54, 264, 267, 288, 294; with Asquith in Italy, 275–76; Dardanelles campaign, 229–31, 238
Harcourt, Lewis, 153–54, 159, 226, 257, 296
Harcourt, Sir William, 42, 53, 61, 67, 69, 72–73, 75, 88, 95, 100, 108; view of Asquith, 46, 81; Trafalgar Square incident, 56–57
Hardinge of Penshurst, Charles, 1st Lord, 164
Harkins, Michael, 58
Harley, Robert, 333
Harrison, Hilda, 287, 332
Harrison, Major Roland, 287
Hartington, Lord. *See* Devonshire
Hawke v. Dunn, 82
Helmsley, Viscount (C. W. R. Duncombe), 144
Henderson, Arthur, 247, 266–67, 277–78, 300–1
Henley, Sylvia, Asquith's letters to, quoted, 239, 259, 270, 278, 285–86, 294, 301, 303, 312–13, 315, 321–22
Herbert, Mary, 318
Hicks-Beach, Sir Michael, 108
Hobhouse, Charles E. H., 238
Hobhouse, Emily, 99
Horner, Lady Francis (née Francis Graham), 33, 47, 52, 71, 131
Horner, Sir John, 131
Horner, Katherine, 131
Horton, Robert, 35
House, Colonel Edward, 206–7, 274–75
Howard, Geoffrey, 235
Huddersfield, 12, 14
Huddersfield Chamber of Commerce, 12
Huddersfield College, 14
Hudson, Robert, 77, 122
Hudson, Walter, 134

Incorporated Law Society, 33
Imperial Liberal Council, 105
Ireland, 93, 180, 279, 326–27; Easter rebellion, 280–82; Home Rule, 2, 51, 72, 81, 93, 107, 121–22, 142, 166, 173–80, 182, 207; Home Rule bill (1893), 55, 58–62; Home Rule bill, (1912), 170–73; Home Rule bill in war, 210
Irish Free State, 326
Isaacs, Rufus. *See* Reading
Isvolsky, Count Alexander, 199

James, Sir Henry, 1st Baron James of Hereford, 37, 39, 46, 58, 81, 108
Jameson, Sir Leander Star, 94
Jameson raid, 94, 97
Jenkins, Roy, 4, 103, 159, 173
Jekyll, Pamela. *See* McKenna
Jessel, Sir George, 33
Joffre, Marshall Joseph, 222, 255, 260–61, 279
Jones, H. A., 35
Jones, Sir Lawrence, 194
Jowett, Benjamin, 20–21, 23, 37, 72

Keats, John, 34,
Ketchen, Mr., 41
Keynes, John Maynard, Lord Keynes, 145
Kimberly, 96–97
Kimberly, Earl of (John Wodehouse), 77–78
Kinnear, John Boyd, 40–41
Kitchener, H. H., 1st Earl Kitchener of Khartoum, 222, 226, 245, 254–55, 261, 266, 274, 283–84; conflict with General Sir John French, 224–25; conscription, 266–69; Dardanelles campaign, 227–29, 231, 238, 258, 260; death of, 282; munitions, 232–36; discussion of removing from office, 262–66; appointment as Secretary of State for War, 219–20; South African War, 97, 99

Knollys, Francis, 1st Viscount, 119, 158, 163–64
Koss, Stephen, 4–5, 125
Kruger, Paul, 94–96, 98–99

Ladysmith, 97
Landsdowne, 5th Marq. of (H. C. K. Petty-Fitzmaurice), 179, 199, 211, 245, 269, 289, 294, 302; conscription, 268; constitutional crisis, 157, 165, 170; Home Rule, 281–82; appointment as Minister without portfolio, 247; memorandum questioning continuing war, 289–90
Langtry, Lillie, 82
Law, Andrew Bonar, 173, 190, 211, 253, 258, 261, 264, 283, 291, 317, 320, 327; fall of Asquith government, 292–302; "Coupon" election (1919), 320–21; asked to form government, 300; formation of coalition cabinet, 242–43, 245–47; appointment as Colonial Secretary, 247; conscription, 276 ; Home Rule, 174–76, 179, 210; offered Secretary of State for War, 283–84; resignation as Prime Minister, 329
Lasky, Harold, 24, 147, 323, 335
Lee, Robert E., 17
Leeds, 12, 14
Leeds Liberal Federation, 62
Leeds and Manchester Railway, 10
Leeds Juvenile Missionary Society, 12
Leopold, King of Belgium, 72
Liberal Central Association, 39
Liberal Central Office, 77
Liberal Federation, 57
Liberal Imperialists, 92–93, 100, 103–5, 111, 117
Liberal League, 105–6, 122
Liberal Party, 1, 12, 36–37, 51, 60, 74, 93, 102, 106, 135, 183, 248, 302, 312, 321, 327, 335; Asquith's leadership of, 6, 42, 90, 334; conscription, 278–79; constitutional

crisis, 158–59; Education bill (1902), 84, 86; leadership of, 69, 87; South African War, 97, 100, 111
Liberal Unionists 40, 83
Licensing bill, (1908), 136–37, 142, 180
Lichnowsky, Prince Karl Max (note Prince), 210–11
Lincoln's Inn, 30, 33, 35, 45
Liverpool, 2d Earl of, Robert Jenkinson, 10
Lloyd George, David, 3, 4, 6, 148–49, 181, 201, 206, 212, 226, 236–37, 240, 247, 253, 261–64, 283–84, 288, 290, 311, 313–16, 326, 328–30, 334–35, 342; view of Asquith, 89; fall of Asquith government, 291–303; reconstruction of Asquith's cabinet, 242–43, 245; Balkan (Salonika) campaign, 226, 229, 258–59, 286–87; conscription, 267, 274, 277–78; constitutional crisis, 155–60, 162, 165; Dardanelles campaign, 228, 230; "Coupon" election, 320–21; Home Rule, 176–77, 179, 281; Marconi scandal, 173–74; Maurice debate, 318; munitions, 232–36; leader of National Liberals, 312, 327; appointment as President of the Board of Trade, 126; naval estimates, 152–54; South African War, 97, 100–101; Welsh church disestablishment, 74–75
Loch, Lord, 99
Lockwood, Sir Frank, 46
London County Council, 55
London Reform Union, 68
Long, Walter, 1st Viscount Long of Wraxall, 247, 267, 281
Lords, House of, 2, 68, 75, 96, 117, 123, 126–27, 155, 171; Asquith's appellate trials before, 38, 82; constitutional crisis, 137, 157–62, 164, 166, 168–70; Home Rule bill (1892), 62–63; veto of Liberal program, 136–37

Loreburn, Earl of (Sir Robert T. Reid), 126
Lowe, Robert, Viscount Sherbrooke, 17
Lucas, 9th Baron (Auberon T. Herbert), 233
Lucy, Sir H. W., 81, 102
Lyttleton, Alfred, 64
Lyttelton, Spencer, 54
Lymington, Viscount, 26

MacDonald, J. Ramsay, 301, 331
Mafeking, 96–97
Mallet, Sir Charles, 5
Mallock, William Hurrell, 21
Manchester Liberal Federation, 320
Manchester Reform Club, 60
Manchester Royal Infirmary, 33
Manners, Molly, 130
Manners, Violet, 64
Marshall, Sir John, 280
Masefield, John, 325
Massingham, H. W., 236
Masterman, C. F. G., 160, 163, 170
Matthew, H. G. Colin, 5, 36, 92
Matthews, Sir Henry, 39, 55, 65, 67
Maurice, Major General Sir Frederick, 317–18, 321
McCallum, R. B., 23
McCullum, Sir John, 323
McDonald, Simon, 45
McEwen, J. M., 296
McKenna, Pamela (née Jekyll), 194
McKenna, Reginald, 152, 182, 201, 212, 226, 236–37, 245, 261, 274, 292; appointed Chancellor of the Exchequer, 247; opposes conscription, 267, 271–73; appointment as First Lord of the Admiralty, 148; munitions, 233
Melland, Dr. Frederick, 33–34, 46
Melland, Helen Kelsall. *See* Asquith
Melland, Josephine (Mrs. Armitage), 33–34, 46
Metropolitan Police, 57

Metropolitan Radical Federation, 55, 57
Metternich, Count, 201
Millerand, Alexandre, 255
Milner, Sir Alfred, Viscount Milner, 40, 95, 96
Milner, Lady, 97
Mirfield Moravian School, 14
Mitchell, Edward Rosslyn, 332
Montagu, Edwin S., 194, 196, 234, 236–37, 247, 301, 313
Morgan, J. Pierpont, 193
Morley (Yorkshire), 10, 13, 90
Morley, John, Viscount Morley of Blackburn, 42, 52, 70–71, 73, 77, 100, 122, 141; influence on young Liberals, 43; Home Rule, 59; *On Compromise* (1874), 43; appointment as Secretary of State for India, 126
Moroccan Crisis, First, 197–98
Moroccan Crisis, Second, 200–1
Munro-Ferguson, Ronald C., 1st Viscount Novar, 93, 105
Murray, Alec, 167, 327
Murray, General Archibald, 225
Murray of Elibank, Lord (Alexander Murray, Master of Elibank), 161–62, 173, 313, 320
Murray, Gilbert, 324, 341

Napier, Mark, 31
Nash, Vaughn, 158
National Committee of Organized Labour for Old Age Pensions (NCOL), 150
National Liberal Club, 330
National Liberal Federation, 336
National Reform Union, 100
National Secular Society, 39
National Service League, 268
Newcastle Programme, 51, 66, 74, 81
New College, 35, 92
new liberalism, 2, 19, 149
Nicolas II, Tsar of Russia, 199, 211, 282
Northcliffe, 1st Viscount, 297

Oates, Captain Thomas, 11
O'Beirne, Hugh, 275
O'Connor, T. P., 171
O'Donnell, Hugh, 44
Old Age Pension bill, (1908), 150–51
Orange Free State, 98–106
Oxford and Asquith, 1st Earl of. *See* Asquith
Oxford and Cambridge Commission, 323
Oxford Undergraduate Journal, 20, 22
Oxford Union, 21, 25, 91–92
Oxford, University of, 10, 29–30, 34; studying "Greats" at, 6, 22–23, 25, 91

Page, Ambassador Walter Hines, 206
Paget, General Sir Arthur, 178
Paisley, 3, 6, 323–25, 328–29, 331
Paisley Liberal Association, 324
Parliament Act (1911), 2, 175
Parnell, Charles Stewart, 44, 46
Paul, Herbert W., 21, 30
Paulton, Harry, 122
Pease, J. A., 155, 164, 190
"Peoples' Budget" (1909), 2, 133, 150, 154–56, 171, 180, 202
Perks, Sir Robert W., 100
Phillipps, Vivian, 320, 324
Pigott, Richard, 45
Plumer, General Sir Herbert, 254
Ponsonby, Arthur, 1st Baron Ponsonby of Shulbrede, 141
Powell v. Kempton Park Race Course, 82
Pringle, W. M. R., 244
Privy Council, 81; Judicial Committee of, 38
Pugh, Martin, 242

Railway and Canal Traffic Act (1888), 37
Raleigh, Sir Thomas, 21, 30
Raleigh, Lady, 143
Ramsden Street Chapel, 12
Reading, 1st Marq. of (Sir Rufus Isaacs), 173–74, 313

Redmond, John, 59, 247; constitutional crisis, 160, 163–64; Home Rule, 72, 171, 176–77, 179–80, 282; Home Rule bill (1893), 58
Reform Club, 102
Rehoboth Chapel, 13
Reid, Sir Robert T. *See* Loreburn
"Relugas compact," 117–21, 123, 125
Repington, Lieutenant-Colonel Charles, 240
Rhodes, Cecil, 94
Ribot, Alexandre, 276
Riddell, George, 1st Baron Riddell, 159, 230, 253, 290
Ripon, Marq. of (G. F. S. Robinson), 95, 117, 166, 197
Ritchie, Charles T., 1st Viscount Ritchie of Dundee, 107, 109
Roberts, Charles, 328
Roberts, Field Marshall Earl, 97–99
Robertson, Field Marshall Sir William, 5, 263–64, 274, 277, 279, 284, 287–88, 313–14
Rodd, Sir Rennell, 1st Baron Rennell, 275–76
Rosebery, 5th Earl of (A. P. Primrose), 64, 71, 73, 77, 85, 103–4, 106, 111; Home Rule, 72, 122; leadership of Liberal Party, 69–70, 89; Liberal Imperialists, 92; South African War, 88, 96, 105
Roskill, John, 37
Royal College of Nursing, 89
Ribblesdale, 4th Baron (Thomas Lister), 64
Runciman, Walter, 1st Viscount Runciman, 160, 223, 274; opposes conscription, 267, 271–73, 278; munitions, 233
Russell, Sir Charles, 1st Baronet Russell of Killowen, 37, 45, 82

Sack, Sir Oliver, 332
Salandra, Antonio, 275

Salisbury, 3rd Marq. of (R. A. T. Gascoyne-Cecil) 51, 53–54, 69, 77, 83, 96
Samfordham, 1st Baron (Arthur Bigge), 269
Samuel, Herbert L., 1st Viscount Samuel, 160, 173, 212, 280
Saunders, William, 55–56
Scott, C. P., 141, 284
Scottish Liberal Federation, 320
Seely, J. E. B., 1st Baron Mottistone, 177–78
Simon, Sir John A., 1st Viscount, 144, 271, 273, 328, 334
Sinn Féin, 279–81, 325–26
Slade, Admiral Sir Edmund, 152
Smiles, Samuel, 35
Smith, F. E. *See* Birkenhead
Smith, Goldwin, 141
Snowden, Philip, 131
Social Democratic Federation, 55–56
Society for the Liberation from Patronage and Control, 73
Soloman, Joseph, 21
South African War, 1, 88, 92, 94–98, 100–101, 105–6, 109, 111, 118, 141
The Spectator, Asquith's contributions to, 36
Spencer, 5th Earl of (J. P. Spencer), 59, 69–70, 117, 197
Spender, J. A., 3–4, 122, 142–43, 146, 179, 246, 257, 322
Spurgeon, C. H., 18
Stanley, Edward G. V. *See* Derby
Stanley, Edward Lyulph, 4th Baron Sheffield and Stanley of Alderley, 194
Stanley, Venetia (Mrs. Edwin Montagu), 247; Asquith's friendship with, 147–48, 194–96; Friendship with Asquith ends, 239–40; Asquith's letters to her quoted, 174, 190, 207, 221–22, 224, 234, 237–38
Stevenson, Francis, 270

Stodart-Walker, Archibald, 144
Strachey, John St. Loe, 150
Strachey, Lytton, 143
Sutton Courtenay, 6, 342
Swaythling, 2d Baron (Louis Samuel Montagu), 196

Taff Vale decision (1901), 127, 133–36
tariff reform, 107–12
Tariff Reform League, 109
Tennant, Charles, 63
Tennant, Sir Charles, 63–64, 90, 130
Tennant, Charlotte "Charty," 64
Tennant, John, 63
Tennant, Know & Co., 64
Tennant, Laura, 64
Tennant, Lillian, 194
Tennant, Margot. *See* Asquith
Tennyson, Alfred, Lord, 142
Thatcher, Margaret, 10
Trade Disputes Act (1906), 133–36, 142
Trades Union Congress, 66, 267
Trafalgar Square, 39, 55–57
Transvaal, 94–96, 98
Tree, Herbert Beerbohm, 194
Tree, Maude, 194
Tree, Viola, 194
Tweedmouth, 1st Baron (D. C. Majoribanks), 77
Tyrell, Sir William, 206, 211, 214

Uitlanders, 94, 96
Ulster Unionist Council, 74
Ulster Volunteer Force, 178
United States of America, 107, 316

Vaughn, C. E., 20
Venizelos, Eleftherios, 258
Vereeniging, Treaty of, 106
Victoria, Queen of England, 55, 69–70, 74, 95
Vizetelly, Henry, 38

Walton, Lawson, 134
Waterhouse, Alfred, 20
Warren, Sir Thomas Herbert, 21–22, 26
Webb, Beatrice, 44, 90, 101, 103, 126
Webb, Sydney, 103
Webster, Sir Richard, 44
Welsh Church Act (1914), 76
Welsh Church disestablishment, 51, 73–77, 81
Wemyss, 11th Earl and Countess of. *See* Lord and Lady Elcho
West, Sir Algernon Edward, 63, 69
Wilhelm II, Kaiser of Germany, 203, 206–7
Willans, Emily. *See* Asquith
Willans, John W. (Asquith's uncle), 15, 30
Willans, William (Asquith's grandfather), 12, 14–15, 111
Wilson, Admiral Sir Arthur, 226
Wilson, General Sir Henry, 225
Wilson, John, 121
Wilson, President Woodrow, 206–7, 274, 322
women's suffrage, 2, 127, 181, 343
Workmen's Compensation Act (1897), 87
Wright, Sir Robert Samuel, 37, 39
Wrigley, Elizabeth, 12
Wolfe-Murray, Lieutenant-General Sir James, 226
World War I. *See* First World War
Zola, Emile, 38

About the Author

V. Markham Lester is Atchison Professor of History and Law at Birmingham-Southern College in Birmingham, Alabama, and Fellow of the Royal Historical Society. He is author of *Victorian Insolvency: Bankruptcy, Imprisonment for Debt, and Company Winding-Up in Nineteenth-Century England* (Oxford University Press, 1995). He has published articles on Asquith and nineteenth- and twentieth-century British political history, including the entry for Asquith in the *Reader's Guide to British History*.

www.ingramcontent.com/pod-product-compliance
Lightning Source LLC
Chambersburg PA
CBHW052055300426
44117CB00013B/2138